940.54 Morrison, Wilbur H.
MOR
     Above and beyond

DATE	BORROWER'S NAME	
	Jeremy will	

History / Military / W.W. II

ABOVE AND BEYOND

1941-1945

Other books by Wilbur H. Morrison

Hellbirds: The Story of the B-29s in Combat
The Incredible 305th: The "Can Do" Bombers of World War II
Wings over the Seven Seas: U.S. Naval Aviation's Fight for Survival
Point of No Return: The Story of the Twentieth Air Force
Fortress Without a Roof: The Allied Bombing of the Third Reich

ABOVE AND BEYOND

1941-1945

WILBUR H. MORRISON

ST. MARTIN'S PRESS
NEW YORK

ABOVE AND BEYOND: 1941–1945. Copyright © 1983 by Wilbur H. Morrison. All rights reserved. Printed in the United States of America. No part of this book may be used or reproduced in any manner whatsoever without written permission except in the case of brief quotations embodied in critical articles or reviews. For information, address St. Martin's Press, 175 Fifth Avenue, New York, N.Y. 10010.

Library of Congress Cataloging in Publication Data

Morrison, Wilbur H., 1915–
  Above and beyond.

  Bibliography: p. 297
  Includes index.
    1. World War, 1939–1945—Pacific Ocean. 2. World
War, 1939–1945—Personal narratives, American.
I. Title.
D767.M59   1983   940.54'26   82-19124
ISBN 0-312-00185-1

First Edition

10 9 8 7 6 5 4 3 2 1

Dedicated
to
Adm. James S. Russell, U.S.N. (Ret.)

CONTENTS

Sections of photographs follow pages 50, 130, and 230.

ACKNOWLEDGMENTS

Above and Beyond is the final volume of a trilogy about the air war in World War II. Like *Point of No Return: The Story of the Twentieth Air Force,* and *Fortress Without a Roof,* which describes the air war in Europe, this book relies heavily on stories of the people involved, both in the air and on the ground.

The author has been privileged to know many of those who were there and through extensive interviews has tried to bring a personal touch to the history of World War II. Most of the material in this book and in those that preceded it in the series is new.

Records of early interviews, some dating back to 1960, were lost in a fire at the author's home in 1970, so it is impossible to credit many of those deserving of recognition.

The author would like to extend his special thanks to Adm. James S. Russell and to Rear Adms. William T. Rassieur, A. B. Metsger, and James D. Ramage—all now retired—who provided extensive recollections.

Among those who provided assistance, the author would like to acknowledge Edward H. Heinemann; Anna C. Urban, Assistant Head (Magazines and Books), Department of the Navy; D. C. Allard, Head, Operational Archives Branch, Naval Historical Center; Capt. R. C. Knott, Editor, *Naval Aviation News;* and Patrick J. Carney, Director, and Raul R. Fernandez, Jr., Assistant Library Director, Camp Pendleton, California.

The author would also like to express his deep gratitude to his agent, David Stewart Hull, and to his editor, Jared Kieling, for their efforts.

Wilbur H. Morrison
Fallbrook, California

ABOVE AND

AND

BEYOND

1941 - 1945

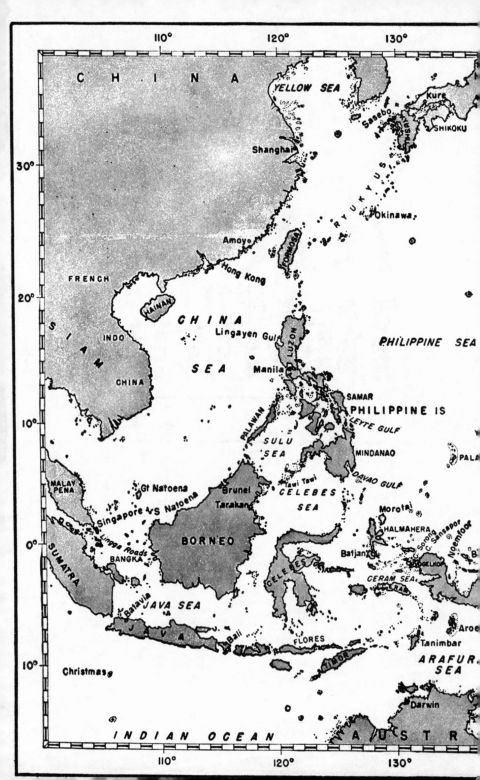

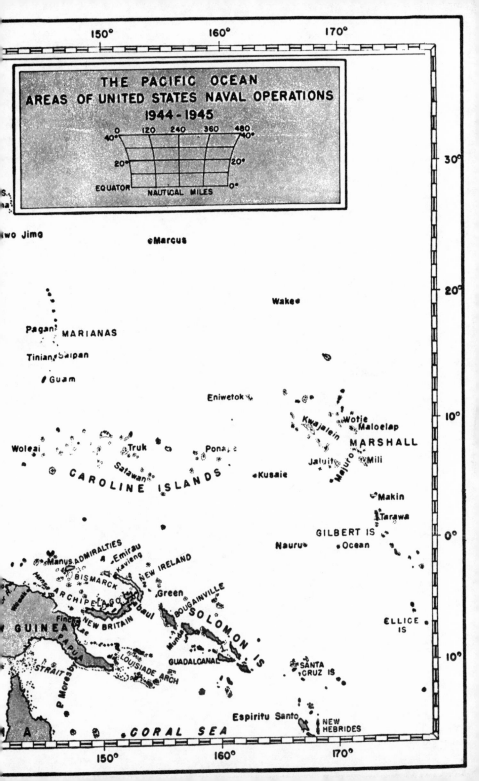

1

A TELLING BLOW

Six Japanese carriers turned gracefully into the wind 200 miles north of the Hawaiian Islands while most of America's armed forces at Pearl Harbor slept, never suspecting that they would soon be deluged by tons of bombs.

At 1:30 A.M. on December 7, 1941, Vice-Adm. Chuichi Nagumo turned to Lt. Comdr. Mitsuo Fuchida, who was about to lead an aerial attack on Pearl Harbor. He shook the thirty-nine-year-old aviator's hand and said solemnly, "I have confidence in you." He was expressing a sentiment that he did not feel; Nagumo predicted that at least half his carriers would be lost.

He and Fuchida watched as a circle of green light, framed by two parallel lines of soft blue, flashed on the *Akagi's* flight deck as Lt. Comdr. Shigeru Itaya led the first Zero fighters off the deck of the 36,500-ton heavy carrier. Itaya's plane, and those that followed, were so heavily loaded that they staggered off the deck.

The Japanese task force of thirty-one ships had penetrated the United States Navy's inner defense zone without detection, much to Nagumo's surprise. Tension had been mounting ever since the task force had left its anchorage in the Kurile Islands for the 1,000-mile journey into the heart of what had always been considered an American lake. Nagumo had opposed the attack ever since its recommendation by Adm. Isoroku Yamamoto, the commander in chief of Japan's Combined Fleet.

The heavyset, gray-haired Nagumo was a veteran seaman, but he was no airman. His experience had been primarily with battleships, and he considered aircraft carriers too vulnerable to use in an attack on Pearl Harbor. A torpedo expert, he was convinced that sea battles could only be won by battleships. He was not alone in his convictions; most American and British admirals agreed with him.

From his flagship, the *Akagi,* originally designed as a cruiser but converted to a carrier to meet the demands imposed by the Washington conference on naval disarmament in 1921–22, the aristocratic Nagumo commanded a fleet that included the heavy carriers *Kaga, Soryu, Hiryu, Zuikaku,* and *Shokaku.* Nagumo's task force also included two battleships and two heavy cruisers under Vice-Adm. Gunichi Mikawa and a scouting force under Rear Adm. Sentaro Omori with a light cruiser, nine destroyers, and supporting ships. In addition, three submarines prowled in advance and along the flanks.

Nagumo and Yamamoto had one thing in common. They had both opposed war with the United States. Yamamoto in particular had resisted efforts by the Japanese Army to prepare the nation for war not only with the United States but also with Great Britain and the Netherlands. After Yamamoto was invested with command of the Combined Fleet and the First Fleet at the Imperial Palace on August 30, 1939, he had again urged caution. Unlike Japan's army generals, who knew little about the Western world, Yamamoto had frequently visited the United States and Great Britain and knew their strength. Although the army generals ridiculed him, most navy officials privately agreed, as did many others in high positions.

Yamamoto's easygoing manner and gentleness were deceptive, concealing the inner toughness of this short, stoop-shouldered man who was 5 feet, 3 inches in height and weighed only 125 pounds. He knew war as few living Japanese did, having fought as a cadet in the Russo–Japanese War in 1905 and having lost the middle and index fingers of his left hand when a gun exploded on his ship. He had suffered other wounds as well, and the scars were still visible.

A brilliant naval strategist, Yamamoto had many other facets to his nature. Early in his career, he had learned that he could not tolerate alcohol in large quantities and through self-discipline had come to accept a regimen of temperance. He wrote poetry, yet he loved to gamble, and his strong sexual appetite was evident to several women, including his long-suffering wife, though not to the Japanese people, who revered him.

After he was given command of all Japanese naval units, Yamamoto sent a message to the fleet stating that he expected the tense situation developing in Europe to lead to world conflict and reminding it that during his command of the Imperial Navy Japan would face grave risks. Prophetically, he told intimates, "If it is necessary to fight, in the first six months to a year of war against the United States and England I will run wild. I will show you an uninterrupted succession of victories. But I must also tell you that if the war be prolonged for two or three years I have no confidence in our ultimate victory."

Yamamoto had become resigned to the inevitability of war after his country took a series of steps. First, Japan had signed a tripartite treaty with Germany and Italy in September 1940 in which the parties agreed to assist one another if attacked. The next year, an Imperial conference had agreed that war with the United States was inevitable, with only the timing to be determined. Finally, Japan's war party had triumphed when Gen. Hideki Tojo, long one of Adolf Hitler's ardent admirers, had been appointed prime minister in October 1941.

Yamamoto realized that the Imperial Fleet could achieve initial success only by delivering a crippling blow to the United States Pacific Fleet, based at Pearl Harbor in the Hawaiian Islands. When he revealed his plans in May 1940, he encountered objections from high navy and government officials, who considered an attack at such a great distance from the fleet's home bases tantamount to "putting one's head in the lion's mouth." Yamamoto, who had already insisted upon realistic mock battles at sea between a theoretical American fleet and his Combined Fleet, refused to be swayed by such arguments and sent his carriers to Kagoshima to prepare for the attack. The volcanic island of Sakurajima in Kagoshima's bay resembled Pearl Harbor and was used to train Japan's fliers.

One of Yamamoto's most brilliant airmen, Lt. Comdr. Mitsuo Fuchida, assigned to the staff of the Third Carrier Division, was brought back to his former position as flight commander of the *Akagi*. When Fuchida protested the apparent demotion, he was advised secretly by Chief of Staff Kusaka Ryunosuke that he had been selected by Yamamoto to head the attack group when the Imperial Fleet raided Pearl Harbor. Honored by Yamamoto's trust, Fuchida immediately started a rigorous and realistic training program not only for the *Akagi*'s pilots and crews but also for those of the First Air Fleet, which had recently been organized. The pilots were, however, opposed to the training because they believed that almost any pilot could attack ships at anchor and that such rehearsals were degrading to skilled aviators.

Some of Yamamoto's staff continued to voice opposition to an attack against Pearl Harbor on moral grounds, while others thought that the distance involved was too great. They preferred a more conservative plan that called for an attack on the Philippines, assuming that such an attack would bring out the United States Pacific Fleet to protect the nation's holdings and mandated areas. Once out of port, the American fleet could be attacked by carrier planes and submarines and reduced to a manageable size. The main Japanese fleet could then attempt to annihilate it. Yamamoto repeatedly countered his colleagues by reminding them that in an all-out war with the United States, Japan could only hope to survive at sea during the initial stages.

Special fleet exercises had begun on November 4 on orders from General Headquarters issued in the emperor's name. Navy Section Order No. 1 was released by Nagani Osami, chief of the naval general staff, to the commander in chief of the Combined Fleet. Yamamoto was informed that the empire would open hostilities with the United States, Britain, and the Netherlands during the first ten days of December. He immediately issued orders to assemble the main task force in Hittokappu Bay off Etorofu in the Kurile Islands.

In late November, Yamamoto had advised Admiral Nagumo, "Should the negotiations with the United States now in progress in Washington be successful, we shall order our forces to withdraw. If such an order is received, you are to turn about and come back to base, even if the attack force has already taken off from the carriers." Yamamoto, who would remain in Japan, was adamant about these last orders despite protests from Nagumo that it would be impossible to turn back once the operation was underway. Yamamoto could not be moved from his position, even though he agreed that such a cancellation would damage the morale of the Imperial Fleet. Up to the last moment, he hoped that the Washington negotiations would be successful and the Pearl Harbor attack canceled. It was a futile hope because Tojo's government had no intention of settling the disputes peacefully with the American government.

Nagumo's striking force left Hittokappu Bay on November 26, and his ships crossed the International Date Line on December 1. That same day, December 1, Yamamoto met with Emperor Hirohito, Tojo's cabinet, and top military officers at the Imperial Palace. While the emperor remained silent, Tojo told the group that the formal decision had been made to go to war with the United States.

Yamamoto wired Nagumo a coded message the following day: "Climb Mount Niitaka 1208." The message authorized the start of hostilities at midnight, Japanese time, December 8. Across the International Date Line it would still be December 7 in the Hawaiian Islands.

The Imperial Japanese Navy, although smaller than United States naval forces, had a distinct advantage because its ships were concentrated in the Pacific while the United States had responsibilities in the Atlantic as well. Of the United States Navy's 216 major ships, 114 remained on duty in the Atlantic. Japan was also able to use to the fullest extent the potent element of surprise, having prepared for war while technically remaining at peace. The 180-odd ships of her navy could therefore be poised for attack in overwhelming numbers in the area of the Pacific most advantageous to her strategic plans.

Six American carriers were in operational readiness when war came on December 7, and the newly commissioned *Hornet* was on her shakedown cruise. In the Atlantic were the flattops (aircraft carriers) *Wasp, Yorktown,* and *Ranger.* In the Pacific, the *Saratoga* was laid up for repairs at San Diego, and the *Enterprise,* with three cruisers and nine destroyers under Vice-Adm. William F. Halsey, was on its way back from Wake Island after delivering twelve marine fighter pilots and their Wildcats under Maj. Paul A. Putnam on December 4 to increase the strategic island's defenses.

A year and a half earlier, Vice-Admiral Halsey had been named commander, Aircraft Battle Force. This put him in charge of all carriers in the Pacific Fleet. One of the few aviators among senior officers in the prewar United States Navy, Halsey won his wings at Pensacola in May 1935, becoming a captain at the age of fifty-two. Like Adm. Ernest J. King, he was one of the senior naval officers selected for later high command in the navy's air arm. While most senior officers took an abbreviated course to gain a basic familiarity with aeronautical problems, Halsey insisted upon the entire program and became a fully trained naval aviator.

On November 27, Chief of Naval Operations Harold R. Stark sent his Pacific Fleet commander, Adm. Husband E. Kimmel, a war warning, and Halsey met that day with Kimmel to discuss it. Kimmel said he did not rule out an attack on Pearl Harbor but agreed with Washington officials that Japan would first strike to the south. Halsey later told his commanders that they had to use common sense during those tense times because there were only three American carriers in the Pacific against Japan's ten.

When Halsey sailed to Wake Island to deliver the marine fighter planes, he insisted that his ships be ready for action and prepared to fight at any moment. He warned his staff that Japanese submarines might be in the area and ordered planes to be armed with bombs and torpedoes. Intelligence sources had informed him that there were no American merchant ships or warships between Hawaii and Wake Island. Without equivocation, he said, "Sink anything you sight."

Comdr. William H. Buracker, Halsey's operations officer, had hurried to the bridge when he got his admiral's orders. He asked Halsey if he realized that his orders meant war.

"Yes!" Halsey barked.

"You can't start a private war of your own! Who's going to take the responsibility?"

"I'll take it. If anything gets in my way, we'll shoot first and argue afterward."

Halsey, of course, was privy to information denied to Buracker. He knew that war could break out at any moment, but he did not know where. At that time, the Japanese carrier force was already on its way to attack Pearl Harbor.

Wake Island, 2,100 miles southwest of Hawaii, had fewer than four hundred marine and navy personnel to defend it. Its coral atoll, roughly shaped in the form of a U, had a Pan American Airways station and a hotel on Peale Island. Civilians now crowded the island, hastily preparing military installations. To the few pilots there, this former bird sanctuary had been a quiet haven whose only menace was the interference of pirate and gooney birds with landings and takeoffs. Putnam's VMF–211 Squadron was the first military air unit to arrive on the island other than an occasional navy flying boat.

Meanwhile, the carrier *Lexington*, with three heavy cruisers and five destroyers under Rear Adm. John H. Newton, was bound for Midway to deliver Maj. C. J. Chappell, Jr.'s, VMSB–231 scout-bombing squadron, which also included eighteen SB2U Vindicators.

On the night prior to the attack, Nagumo and Fuchida had listened to the final words from Tokyo, which described the conditions at Pearl Harbor reported by Japanese spies in Honolulu. They learned that the *Utah* and a seaplane tender had entered the harbor at dusk on December 5. Among the American ships listed at anchor were nine battleships, three light cruisers, three seaplane tenders, and seventeen destroyers. These reports even noted, accurately, that four light cruisers and two destroyers were in dry docks and that all heavy cruisers and aircraft carriers were at sea. This final report had disappointed Yamamoto, who had hoped that at least some carriers, which were major elements of the Pacific Fleet, would be anchored at Pearl Harbor at the time of the attack.

As Nagumo positioned his task force north of the Hawaiian Islands, Yamamoto wired, "The fate of the empire rests on this enterprise."

Japan's Air Leader Fuchida banked his plane right at Kahukui, Oahu's northernmost point, and scanned the area tensely. Pearl Harbor lay ahead, and he could see ships belonging to the United States Pacific Fleet. The sight was a bomber commander's dream. He realized with astonishment that their approach had not been detected: There were no antiaircraft bursts, and not a single American fighter plane rose to challenge them. Through the opened canopy of his plane he fired a flare pistol, giving the signal to prepare for the attack.

Fuchida's eyes widened with surprise as he rode above the harbor, full of ships peacefully anchored. The morning was bright and clear, and they should have been spotted. He fired his flare pistol again to start the attack, noting as he did that Lt. Comdr. Shigeharu Murata's torpedo squadron was starting to descend to its attack position just off the water, while Lt. Comdr. Kakuichi Takahashi's dive-bombers began their climb to 13,000 feet.

Everything had proceeded according to plan, but to Fuchida's dismay things started to come apart.

The fighter pilots under Lt. Comdr. Shigeru Itaya, who were making a sweep around the other formations, had failed to see Fuchida's signal to attack. When Fuchida fired yet another flare, they read it as the signal to take up positions instead of to attack. Takahashi was confused by the third flare and assumed incorrectly that surprise had not been achieved and that his fifty or more dive-bombers should take the lead and try to destroy American aircraft and shore installations. He immediately gave the command to start diving. Murata also became confused and gave the order for his torpedo squadron to follow him immediately against the ships before the dive-bombers got in their way.

Fuchida turned to his radio operator and ordered him to transmit "To-renso," a repetition of the single syllable "To," over the radio. This was the agreed-upon signal for all to begin the attack. In the resulting confusion, the first bombs hit at 7:55 A.M., fifty-five minutes before the Japanese informed the United States government in Washington that a state of war existed between their two nations.

Murata's second in command, Lt. Inichi Goto, leveled off for a run at the battleships. Takahashi's Val dive-bombers flashed by Goto's column of Kate* torpedo planes, causing him momentary confusion. He had not seen Fuchida's second flare, which had

---

* The Americans gave code names to Japanese planes and these names are used throughout the book.

7

precipitated the dive-bombing attack, and as he headed for the *Arizona*, he felt momentary anger that the dive-bombers were trying to get all the glory. He dropped his torpedo close to the American battleship and pulled back on the stick, hitting hard right rudder to get away. He glanced back quickly to see the white wake of his torpedo, equipped with wooden fins to give it added buoyancy in the bay's shallow water. It struck the *Arizona*, and a huge geyser of flames and water shot up.

After gaining altitude, Goto shouted, "We hit her!" He circled the scene until he noted that American gunners were coming uncomfortably close and then pulled away and headed for his carrier.

Yamamoto, in a state of extreme anxiety aboard his flagship at the Hashirajima anchorage in Japan, waited impatiently for the first reports. When Nagumo wired, "Surprise attack successful," there was jubilation on board the flagship. Yamamoto did not share it because it was apparent to him that the first bombs had hit Pearl Harbor before Japan's ambassador in Washington had had a chance to inform the Americans of her declaration of war. This fact greatly disturbed Yamamoto, who believed that the world would condemn his fleet's action in making an unprovoked attack upon the United States. It would bother him for the rest of his life.

Nagumo's reports were considered inflated as he radioed, "Enemy warships torpedoed; outstanding results," and later, "Hickam Field attacked; outstanding results."

Meanwhile, Japanese pilots, who had been briefed thoroughly for what President Franklin D. Roosevelt later called "a day that will live in infamy," searched for their primary targets. "Destroy the carriers," they had been told. They had been informed that the carriers were normally berthed on the northwest side of Ford Island. Fortunately for the United States Pacific Fleet, the carriers were at sea. One Japanese air leader, however, thought that he had spotted the *Saratoga* and signaled to attack. He roared down, failing to realize that he was sighting on the old target ship *Utah*. It looked somewhat like a carrier, stripped down and timber-covered, but the "*Sara*" was 2,000 miles away.

The Japanese had used both high-level bombers and dive-bombers in their devastating attacks on military installations at the army base at Hickam Field while swarms of dive-bombers struck at the heavy navy ships in the harbor. High-level bombers now struck at the harbor, adding to the immense destruction.

Japanese commanders had planned well. Torpedo planes sought out the battleships because their torpedoes had been adapted specifically for shallow water, their short-run exploders made them deadly weapons.

The sun's first rays were just above the horizon on December 7 when Admiral Halsey's Air Group 6 planes from the carrier *Enterprise* roared off at 6:15 A.M. and headed for Ford Island 200 miles away, led by Comdr. Howard "Brig" Young. Radio monitors on the ship listened with detachment to the voices of the carrier's pilots, then jerked to abrupt attention when they heard, "Don't shoot! This is an American plane!" The room became a beehive of activity, and the lackadaisical air that had prevailed for hours evaporated in an instant.

"That's Ensign Manuel Gonzales," one of them said. "I'd know his voice anywhere."

The naval reservist's transmitter went dead, and the monitors looked at one another with astonishment. Miles away, Gonzales' Bombing–Six–Squadron SBD Dauntless had been shot down, and he had been killed.

It is incredible that Gonzales' cry did not alert Pearl Harbor's defenders, or at least put a doubt in their minds. Military officials in Washington, Pearl Harbor, and the Philippines had known since early December that a Japanese raid was a distinct possibility somewhere in the Pacific.

There was a lethargy throughout the Pacific Fleet at Pearl Harbor as early risers watched the sunrise and saw the sun's rays cast brilliant red streaks across the slopes of the mountains as they prepared for breakfast.

An army technician on Oahu practicing with a radarscope to improve his skill had detected a mysterious blip on the screen. After another and yet another showed up, he put in a hasty call to his lieutenant, who said, "Forget it."

Lt. William Tanner, pilot of a PBY–5, had radioed early that morning that he had dropped depth charges on a miniature submarine. His message was greeted with disbelief.

One observer later noticed sunlight flashing from the wings of airplanes circling lazily over Ford Island. He counted twenty-five of them. A navy man, who thought they looked different from the familiar American types, squinted into the bright morning sun. He had no binoculars so he could not be sure, but he was not concerned. He and several others watched as another squadron flew into the area from seaward.

They gaped in astonishment as a dive-bomber from the high

group shrieked earthward, heading directly for Ford Island Naval Air Station, home of Patrol Wing 2. Onlookers were so shocked as the first bombs hit that they stood petrified as the bombers continued to attack in screaming dives.

The *Enterprise*'s planes were caught by surprise when they arrived over Ford Island, and before they knew what was happening, many pilots and their gunners were shot down by American gunners on the ground and Japanese fighters in the air.

Aviation Chief Ordnanceman John W. Finn at Kaneohe, home of Patrol Wing 1, hurriedly assembled a machine gun on the exposed flight ramp and fired at the stream of Vals and Zekes that constantly roared down to attack the patrol bombers. As he resolutely stood his ground, Japanese pilots singled him out, and he stood bareheaded alone on the ramp with machine-gun bullets and cannon shells flashing around him from the diving planes. Time after time he was painfully wounded and only left his post when he was ordered to get medical treatment. As soon as his wounds were dressed, he returned to the flight line to supervise the ground defense of the airfield. Finn was the first member of a naval aviation unit to win the Medal of Honor for his incredible valor.

Morning colors were about to be piped on board the ships at Pearl Harbor, and sailors were getting up for another routine Sunday. Lt. Comdr. William T. Rassieur, who had qualified as a pilot aboard the *Langley* in 1927, was air officer on board the seaplane tender *Curtiss*. He was putting on his white uniform because, as duty officer, he had to go topside at 7:55 A.M. to supervise the colors ceremony. He paused while dressing when he heard the zoom of planes and a series of thumps. These were Japanese 500-pound bombs exploding, but he had never heard one go off and the sound was foreign to his ears. When bombs continued to explode, he rushed on deck to investigate, gazing in shock as Japanese planes dove against Battleship Row.

The *Curtiss* escaped the bombs and torpedoes for thirty-five minutes. Then, to the utter amazement of her crew, a miniature Japanese submarine appeared close aboard. Rassieur could hardly believe his eyes as his ship's gunners trained their 5-inchers on the Japanese submarine. He realized that it must have entered the harbor's channel while the gates were open to admit American ships. Now it was close, getting ready to launch a torpedo, as the *Curtiss* lay anchored in the channel a quarter of a mile from Battleship

Row. A destroyer's depth charges had evidently brought the submersible to the surface.

With acting captain George Owen in charge, the *Curtiss* opened fire on the submarine, which was so close that it was barely possible to depress the ship's guns. The Japanese submarine was hit and sank before she could launch her torpedoes.

Acting captain Owen had immediately called for ammunition to be brought from below at the start of the attack and, although it took only six minutes, it seemed like an eternity to him as his ship lay almost helpless in the channel.

Now a Japanese plane released a bomb made from a 12-inch shell, which slammed into the *Curtiss'* radio room, causing numerous deaths and injuries. Incredibly, a propeller from another Japanese plane also landed on the ship. It was later sent to Hamilton Standard for analysis.

The *Curtiss* suffered twenty-six casualties, who had to be taken that night to a hospital on shore. Rassieur led the small boats, singing out frequently to identify his group because gunners were trigger happy and firing at anything that moved.

Swarms of Japanese planes with large red discs on their wings continued to fly down the passes out of the north after crossing the Waianae and Koolau mountains. They unleashed a cascade of bombs on each target in turn while sirens started to wail and a few antiaircraft guns finally went into sporadic action. Soon the harbor air was filled with black smoke as burning ships exploded, leaving behind charred wreckage and blackened bodies.

The alarm was at last sounded at 7:58 A.M. "Air raid Pearl Harbor. This is no drill! To all units, planes headed for Pearl Harbor number unknown. All hands, Kaneohe being attacked by fifteen Japanese planes." Then came the hysterical cry, "Enemy planes coming over Pearl Harbor. Fire at will." The first of many wild rumors was spread by radio transmission. "Parachute troops landing at Barbers Point." This was untrue, but the report of the *California*'s being on fire was all too real as two fire tugs tried to save her.

Rear Adm. P. N. L. Bellinger, senior officer of the Naval Air Station at Pearl Harbor, had arrived while the attack was underway. Appalled by the bombed hangars and twisted wreckage of his airplanes, he ordered, "Get the planes in the air!" It was too late. After the first Japanese wave of bombers, only three aircraft were capable of flight.

An hour after the first assault, a second attack force under the command of Lt. Comdr. Shigakazu Shimazaki struck Pearl Harbor with another 170 planes and caused extensive damage. Taking advantage of their complete air superiority, the Japanese made second and third runs with their high-level bombers to assure perfect aim as they dropped their bombs on the battleships.

Despite the awesome destruction they caused, the Japanese had lost only twenty-nine aircraft by the time this raid was over.

At 9:45 A.M., after all attacks ceased, a heavy pall of smoke hung over the stricken area. The huge explosions that hurled smoke and flames into the sky seemed incongruous to those who had been familiar with the magical softness of the tropical air.

Air Leader Fuchida had remained over Oahu after the last strike, despite antiaircraft damage to his plane, until he had assessed the damage his planes had done. When Admiral Nagumo ordered his task force to return to Japan after the second wave struck Pearl Harbor, Fuchida tried to convince him that additional strikes should be made, reminding the admiral that he had personally been charged with the destruction of a large part of the American fleet. He stressed again Yamamoto's arguments that America's Pacific Fleet had to be immobilized for six months to permit Japan to move south to find new sources of oil.

Nagumo remained obstinately opposed to another attack, even though Fuchida claimed that arsenals, repair facilities, and oil tanks should be destroyed if the attack was to be considered successful. He explained that it would not be difficult to raise the sunken ships because they were resting in shallow water. Fuchida insisted that unless additional attacks were made, the United States would have its ships in action in a short time.

Nagumo believed, however, that he had won a great victory, and in a sense he had. At home, the Japanese people were delirious over the success of the attack on Pearl Harbor, and Yamamoto was hailed as a hero. The attack was a devastating blow to the Pacific Fleet, and it cost only twenty-nine Japanese aircraft and fifty-five men. Yamamoto and Nagumo had both fully expected to lose at least half their carriers, plus hundreds of men and airplanes.

Nagumo therefore ordered his fleet to turn north, to Fuchida's disgust. The air commander knew from personal observation that American bases in the Hawaiian Islands were virtually defenseless and that a great opportunity was being lost because of Nagumo's caution.

In Japan, Yamamoto reluctantly agreed with Nagumo's decision although he would have preferred follow-up attacks. He arbitrarily scaled down Nagumo's claims that two American battleships had been sunk, another four seriously damaged, and four cruisers also damaged, because he didn't believe them. The actual loss was much worse. Four American battleships had been sunk and three seriously damaged. It was a catastrophic defeat for the United States Navy, but the tragedy would have been worse if Nagumo had been more aggressive.

Yamamoto wired Nagumo to attack Midway and put it out of action. The cautious admiral ignored the order, saying bad weather prevented such an attack.

The main Japanese fleet had sortied from its Inland Sea anchorage at Hashirajima after dark on the night of the Pearl Harbor attack to protect Nagumo's task force en route home. With the flagship *Nagato*, the fleet of thirty ships included five battleships and the carrier *Hosho*. Escorted by destroyers through the Bungo Strait, it sailed south to rendezvous with Nagumo. When it became apparent that no escort would be needed, Yamamoto ordered the fleet to return home on the 13th.

There had been 301 navy planes of all types in the Oahu area before the attack, including 54 noncombat types. Of this number, 99 were still in storage as replacements. When the last Japanese plane headed back to its carrier, only 52 planes were able to take to the air, 16 of which were noncombat types. The air station at Kaneohe was a shambles, with all 34 planes out of commission, and the destruction at Ford Island Naval Air Station was just as complete.

Pacific Fleet Commander Admiral Kimmel sent out an emergency dispatch to all ships at sea. "Intercept and destroy enemy! Believed retreating on a course between Pearl and Jaluit. Intercept and destroy!" It was a futile gesture, though understandable at a time of great stress; the United States Navy in the Pacific had been dealt a crippling blow. Admiral Newton, whose small task force was heading for Midway with the carrier *Lexington*, turned around and raced back to Pearl Harbor.

It had taken only an hour and fifty minutes, but the 353 Japanese planes had left disaster. Over two thousand Americans were dead, and the Pacific Fleet had lost its backbone. If the Japanese had continued their attacks in the following days, not one battleship would have escaped a watery grave.

In one of the most remarkable salvage operations the world has known, many of the Pearl Harbor ships were saved to fight another day. The *Arizona*, horribly burned and blasted in two, was a total loss, and the *Oklahoma* was capsized, her twisted superstructure lying on the bottom. The old *Utah* would cruise no more. She was down, bottom up, a complete loss. But although the *West Virginia* had settled into shallow water, the *California* was sunk, and the *Nevada* had to be run aground to prevent sinking, these ships were salvaged. The other damaged battleships, the *Pennsylvania, Maryland*, and *Tennessee*, were eventually repaired. In the coming months, the Japanese were to find to their chagrin that ships that they thought were destroyed still had a deadly lease on life.

Publicly, the president admitted the loss of the battleship *Arizona* and the target ship *Utah*; the destroyers *Cassin, Downes,* and *Shaw*; and the mine-layer *Oglala*. The *Oklahoma*, which could have been repaired, was scrapped so that its materials and equipment could be diverted to other ships.

The navy had laid the keels for sixteen ships larger than a cruiser during 1941. Now top priority was given to new aircraft carriers. Orders were issued in Washington to start construction on some of the mightiest battleships the world had ever seen. Meanwhile, those sunk or damaged at Pearl Harbor were redesigned with new super-structures that made them better warships than they had been in the past.

The Japanese had struck a telling blow, and it was not to be the only one. A timetable, established years before, initiated strikes that day on such widely scattered points as Hong Kong, Singapore, Thailand, and Kota Bharu on the Thai–Malayan border. She struck Midway Island, 1,100 miles from Hawaii, and Wake Island, another thousand miles away. The attacks were simultaneous on a perimeter extending from Pearl Harbor to the Gulf of Siam. Task forces and scores of troop transports roamed the western Pacific. Tens of thousands of trained soldiers, many of them hardened veterans of the conquest of China, pushed Japan's frontiers even farther from her home islands, hoping eventually to encompass all of eastern and southern Asia.

Viscount Tani had said fifty years before, "Japan must with patience wait for the time of confusion in Europe to gain its objectives." Count Shigenobu Okuma, the Japanese premier in 1915, had inspired Japan's militarists for years with his ringing cry, "Japan will meet Europe on the plains of Asia in the twentieth century and wrest from her the mastery of the world." Japan was on the march after years of patiently waiting for the opportune moment.

The commander in chief, Pacific Fleet (CINCPAC) wired, "To all ships present: Hostilities with Japan commence with air raid on Pearl." Adm. William Halsey ordered his *Enterprise* group, only 150 miles from Pearl Harbor, to search to the north in an attempt to find the Japanese attackers. Studying conflicting dispatches and noting that communications were fouled up, he resigned himself to a futile search, and in fact neither his scout planes nor Nagumo's spotted the other.

The following day, Halsey's *Enterprise* task force headed home because fuel was short. Arriving at Pearl Harbor at dusk on December 8, Halsey was tight-lipped and his jaw stuck out pugnaciously as he surveyed the wreckage of key elements of the Pacific Fleet. He turned to his chief of staff. "Before we're through with 'em, the Japanese language will be spoken in hell!"

Ashore, Adm. Husband E. Kimmel's headquarters was in a state of chaos. When Halsey heard one staff officer there report that Japanese gliders and paratroopers had landed on Oahu's east coast, he laughed, and Kimmel, a longtime friend and classmate, turned on Halsey angrily.

Halsey could see that Kimmel was in a state of nervous collapse, so he explained his laughter. In ridiculing the report, he said, he simply meant that "the Japanese aren't going to waste their precious carrier decks on such nonsense."

The destruction caused by the Japanese was serious, but they missed the 4½-million-barrel tank farm, the destruction of which would have forced the Pacific Fleet to retire to bases on the west coast of the United States. Equally important, the Japanese had not bombed Pearl Harbor's repair facilities and its submarine bases.

The Pearl Harbor attack came as a complete surprise to all Americans on Oahu, but it should not have. Army Chief of Staff Gen. George C. Marshall had been alerted by the U.S. State Department, which had earlier broken the Japanese diplomatic code, that the Japanese were expected to reject the American peace plan. This determination was reached after evaluation of a decoded fourteen-part message that had been sent during the night from the Japanese foreign minister to his embassy officials in Washington.

In a final message to its embassy, the Japanese foreign office sent the following during the early morning hours of December 7: "Will the ambassador please submit to the United States government (if possible to the secretary of state) our reply to the U.S. at 1:00 P.M. on the 7th, your time."

This wire was decoded by 6 A.M. Washington time and Marshall's staff and members of navy intelligence quickly realized that war was imminent because they understood the significance of the 1 P.M. reference—dawn in the mid-Pacific—an ideal time for the Japanese to attack the U.S. somewhere in the Pacific.

Marshall was horseback riding and did not return to his office until 10:30 A.M. He was shown his staff's assessment of the situation and immediately ordered that a message be sent to Pacific commanders warning them that war was imminent. Navy officials offered to send it to their communications network, but Marshall rejected the offer. Instead it was passed to army communications with instructions to send a copy to Admiral Kimmel. The army circuit to Hawaii was out of commission and, not appreciating the urgency of the message, an army routing clerk passed it to Western Union for transmission by commercial wireless.

The delivery boy did not arrive at Fort Shafter army headquarters until three o'clock Sunday afternoon—hours after the attack.

Japanese naval codes were not deciphered by the Americans until the spring of 1942. The diplomatic code, which had been broken before the war, carried no mention of Japanese war plans. Therefore, Marshall's message contained just a general war warning and did not mention Hawaii as the target.

The success of the Japanese attack should have been foreseen. In 1938, Adm. H. E. Yarnell had simulated such an attack and, theoretically, all Pearl Harbor ships were destroyed. His pleas for countermeasures had nevertheless fallen on deaf ears.

As recently as the fall of 1940, Great Britain's Fleet Air Arm had sunk three of Italy's six battleships with torpedo bombers at their Taranto base. Aside from Great Britain's admirals, one of the few military men who took serious note of this successful attack was a naval aviator from Japan named Comdr. Minoru Genda. He had been stationed by his government in London to report on military matters.

American Secretary of Navy Frank Knox was also concerned about the vulnerability of warships in a harbor. Following the British attack on Taranto, he told Secretary of War Henry L. Stimson that precautionary measures should be taken immediately to protect ships at Pearl Harbor. In the event of a surprise attack, he said, the greatest danger would come from aircraft with aerial torpedoes. Stimson agreed. Admiral Kimmel was advised of their concern, but he took no action. He said that the placement of torpedo nets in the harbor would interfere with the movement of his warships. Furthermore, Japanese pilots and their planes were considered inferior, and such an attack was believed to be beyond their capabilities. When war came, this attitude proved fatal.

Later, excuses were plentiful. The diplomatic code breaking was used as an excuse for what amounted to gross incompetence in the Pacific. According to some, the possiblity of a Japanese raid was not passed through lower channels because the information might tip off the Japanese that their code had been broken. It was a tragedy of errors in judgment that resulted in dire consequences for the United States.

2

"WHEN WAR BREAKS OUT,
THEY LOOK FOR
THE SONS OF BITCHES."

The professionalism of the Japanese carrier force that bombed Pearl Harbor shocked American naval commanders. If officials of the United States Navy had given credence to reports about Japan's growing naval power in the Pacific and, particularly, the expertise of its larger carriers, the disaster might never have occurred. Rear Adm. John H. Towers, chief of the United States Navy's Bureau of Aeronautics and one of its finest aviators, had warned early in 1941 that "the aircraft carrier will spearhead the next war." Towers, a strong advocate of aviation since World War I, was disliked by most surface admirals, and his views were ignored.

Carrier aviation in Japan got its start in 1919 when the I.J.N. *Hosho*, a flush-deck carrier of 7,470 tons, was ordered. When it was completed in late December 1922, it carried twenty-six planes and was used much like the United States Navy's first carrier, the *Langley*.

Japan's naval aviation received a huge boost after the Washington naval disarmament treaties were signed in 1922. The incomplete hulls of the battle cruisers *Kaga* and *Akagi* were converted to carriers. The 38,200-ton *Kaga* was the largest carrier in the world, with the *Akagi* a close second at 36,500 tons. These ships were larger than the first *Lexington* and the *Saratoga,* American ships that were built later. This fact was concealed for years because the Japanese said that the tonnage of their carriers was only 26,900 each. Thus, they were able to "save" 21,000 tons under the terms of the treaties for another ship. The *Akagi* was completed in March 1927 and the *Kaga* a year later. Although they were larger, the Japanese ships could carry only sixty airplanes each, while the *Lexington* and *Saratoga* could carry ninety.

During the early 1930's, Admiral Yamamoto was in charge of the Japanese Imperial Navy's aeronautics department. Yamamoto, who had learned to fly late in his career, was an early advocate of attack aviation and believed that carrier support operations would prove to be decisive in naval battle.

Furthermore, he knew that the Japanese navy was at that time inferior in size to the United States Navy. In the event of war, the Imperial Fleet would have to use carrier aircraft and submarines to reduce the size of the United States Pacific Fleet before the two met in a major battle. Yamamoto therefore pressed the navy to produce its own military aircraft and at every opportunity stressed that Japan should concentrate on building aircraft carriers, not battleships.

Battleship adherents were, however, as strong in the Imperial Japanese Navy as they were in the United States Navy, and many of the same arguments were voiced in each. Like their United States counterparts, admirals of the Imperial Fleet fought a long delaying action against Yamamoto in support of their theory that battleships formed the backbone of a modern navy.

Technically, great strides in aeronautics were made under Yamamoto's leadership. The Zero fighters and the Type 1 land-based attack bomber were developed during his tenure. They were both ready for fleet trials in 1937, though the lack of self-sealing tanks or armor plating for the pilot were serious deficiencies in the early Zeros. (Japanese engineers and pilots had decided that the added weight would restrict their performance.) Yamamoto was a frequent visitor to Japanese aircraft plants and was instrumental in getting them established. He used his strong influence to break down bureaucratic red tape and get materials flowing to these vital factories.

Yamamoto was no stranger to the West. He attended the London naval conference on naval disarmament in 1930 as Japan's chief delegate. During two visits to the United States, he was impressed by the nation's industrial strength. He was convinced, he told intimates upon his return to Japan, that an unrestricted shipbuilding race with the United States would be foolhardy and would eventually lead to disaster for his country.

During the mid-1930's, delegates from Great Britain, the United States, and Japan tried to agree on a new formula for limiting the strength of their navies. The attempt failed, but Yamamoto told Emperor Hirohito after his return that although it had been impossible to reach an agreement, he was personally convinced that further efforts should be made.

There was strong opposition to Yamamoto's views among many officials in Japan, including top army generals who felt that Japan should abrogate the disarmament treaties. Yamamoto's appeal to the emperor was done deliberately in hopes of securing his support. He was aware that the emperor had little authority, but he did have a strong appeal to the Japanese people. Yamamoto was also aware that the emperor privately agreed that war with the West was unthinkable.

When the Japanese army invaded China in mid-1937, Yamamoto spoke out strongly against the invasion. Thereafter, the enmity with which Japanese army generals regarded him became so vicious that at one time they considered his assassination. Yamamoto feared that the army would get bogged down in a major land campaign in China, thus diluting efforts to build up the Imperial Fleet. His protestations against the occupation of China were not successful, however, and army generals gained increasing control of the Japanese government.

The Japanese people were unaware of this bitter behind-the-scenes rivalry because the controlled press did not discuss it.

By 1940, Yamamoto saw that Japan's rightist army generals were bent on escalating the war, not only in China but throughout the Far East. There were more demands for a tripartite pact with Germany and Italy, which Yamamoto said would result in war with the United States. Such a step, he warned, would be a major calamity for the world. For Japan, he told friends, it would end in disaster.

Most navy friends agreed with Yamamoto's views, but there were others who sided with the army. They freely expressed their belief that Japan should seize control of the Far East despite certain opposition from the United States.

When the Tripartite Pact was signed in the fall of 1940, Yamamoto considered resigning as commander in chief of the Imperial Fleet, but he knew that his resignation would have little effect on the militarists, and quite possibly he might be assassinated if he tried to precipitate a government crisis. He chose instead to accelerate steps to prepare the Japanese navy for war with the United States. He considered war inevitable and saw no way in which he could help stop it. Despite his objections to war with the West, his loyalty to his country came first.

After France fell to Nazi Germany's blitzkrieg tactics in May

1940, France was forced to agree to Japan's demands for the joint defense of Indochina. The helpless French were in no position to resist Japanese intrusions. A joint defense pact was signed at Vichy on July 29, and a year later Japan sent army and navy units into the southern part of the country.

Once Japan started setting up bases in Indochina the United States reacted quickly, freezing Japanese assets, and naming Douglas MacArthur as commander of United States forces in the Far East, now that the Philippines and Malaya appeared to be threatened. On August 1, 1941 a ban on practically all exports to Japan was approved, including scrap iron, steel, and oil products, although food and cotton were exempted. The ban was eventually extended to all nations outside the Western Hemisphere except Great Britain.

The oil cutoff was not immediatly crucial to Japan because she had stockpiled 5.5 million tons. It did, however, force her to move south to acquire new oil reserves for the future.

Relations between the United States and Japan worsened throughout the fall of 1941. Prince Konoye's cabinet fell on October 18, and Gen. Hideki Tojo became prime minister. He immediately replaced the men who had surrounded the vacillating Konoye with followers who believed in war with the West. The prince's father, Emperor Hirohito, was equally helpless to stem the war tide.

Meanwhile, Japanese Ambassador Kichisaburo Nomura had been trying to reach an agreement with the American government in Washington. He was acting in good faith, not fully appreciating that the military government in Japan under General Tojo was bent on war. He was joined in Washington on November 5 by Saburo Kurusu as special envoy. Despite their efforts, Secretary of State Cordell Hull stiffened the attitude of the United States toward Japan in late November. The Japanese diplomatic code had been broken, and Hull became aware of Japanese intentions.

Although ostensibly the Tripartite Pact posed the most serious problem between the two governments, Hull's knowledge of secret Japanese correspondence, which he could not reveal lest American code breaking become known to the Japanese, was the real stumbling block. He knew that Japan's emissaries were lying. In late November, Hull demanded complete Japanese withdrawal from China and French Indochina, nonrecognition of the puppet regime in China, and dissolution of the Tripartite Pact. Otherwise, he said, no agreement between the United States and Japan was possible.

Kurusu told Hull that war could be avoided only if President

Roosevelt sent a personal cable to Emperor Hirohito. Such a cable was actually sent, but it arrived in Tokyo nineteen minutes before the first Japanese planes struck Pearl Harbor.

Final instructions arrived at the Japanese embassy in Washington in fourteen separate sections on the night of December 6/7, but they took so long to decode that Kurusu was late in meeting with the American secretary of state to inform him that their nations were at war.

Nomura and Kurusu met with Hull at 2:30 P.M. Washington time, fifty-five minutes after the attack, and they presented him with a war memorandum. As Hull read it, he exclaimed in fury that in fifty years of public service he had never seen a document more crowded with infamous falsehoods and distortions. Nomura and Kurusu left quickly as the outraged Hull stormed out of his department for a conference with the president.

Ernest J. King, the man who would eventually do more than anyone else in the Unites States Navy to thwart Yamamoto's plans in the Pacific, became interested in naval aviation at the age of fifty after a long career as a surface officer and a submariner. King and Yamamoto had much in common. They were both caustic, austere men of exceptional capabilities. Each had a drinking problem, although Yamamoto recognized his vice early and abstained from drinking hard liquor. King did drink during the war, and his services were almost denied to the United States Navy during a crucial period in its history because of this failing. Both men were womanizers, though in this case their shared failing, if it can be called that, remained unknown to their respective wider publics. Nevertheless, their indulgences frequently caused concern among top officials in their countries.

Wives of other officers dreaded to be seated next to Admiral King at dinner parties. His unwanted attentions proved embarrassing to women, but one was more than a match for him. At one point during a dinner, this lovely lady found King's hand on her knee. She grabbed the offending hand and brought it up to the top of the table. "Admiral King, I will have you know this is a tablecloth, and not a bed sheet!"

King began his first important career advancement after Rear Adm. William A. Moffett, the United States Navy's first chief of its Bureau of Aeronautics, talked to him in April 1926. He told King that the United States Congress was expected to legislate that all aviation units should be commanded by naval aviators or observers. As a result, Moffett said, carriers and naval aviators would need senior-rated officers. Moffett assured King that, despite his age, if he learned to fly he would be given command of an aircraft carrier. Although King knew that the navy's future lay in aviation, his interest in changing careers at age fifty was not high. But he had applied earlier for the command of a light cruiser and had realized that there were too many senior captains ahead of him. After some consideration, he accepted Moffett's suggestion.

Moffett decided that King should first command the seaplane tender U.S.S. *Wright.* Her commander, Capt. John V. Babcock, was one of King's Annapolis classmates. Babcock explained that she was not part of fleet activities but acted primarily as a mobile support base for seaplanes. He admitted that she was rather loosely run. King assumed command of the *Wright* in June 1926, immediately establishing some long-needed discipline and refitting the ship.

King decided that his own pilots should teach him to fly, and his progress was so good that by fall he asked Moffett to classify him as a student aviator. Moffett then insisted that King take formal flight training at Pensacola, which he agreed to do in 1927.

King, a captain, was treated no differently from other student aviators. His relations with other students were at first strained because of his rank, but that changed after a few nightly poker sessions. King had gone on one of his periodic abstentions from alcohol for the start of training, but when he learned that everyone was drinking after hours he heartily joined in. Because of his previous flight training, he was able to solo shortly after he arrived. He readily agreed with his instructors that he would never be a natural pilot—his age was a factor—but he developed habits of safety and performed only those flights necessary to qualify as a pilot. He received his observer wings on May 27, 1927, after flying the minimum two hundred hours.

Upon graduation from flight school, King resumed command of the *Wright* but was called back to salvage the submarine *S–4*. He had spent considerable time in submarines, so his expertise was needed. The task stretched out, and it was another spring before he could return to his ship.

Soon after, Admiral Moffett recommended to the Bureau of Navigation that King should be given command of the U.S.S. *Lexington.* King was excited by the prospect of taking over this new carrier, which was considered the navy's best aviation command and which would increase his chances of rising higher on the admiral's list. His hopes for such a command were dashed when Moffett's request was denied.

Moffett, who had organized naval aviation and established its first bureau in 1921, wanted the dynamic King to serve in some capacity in naval aviation. He placed King in the bureau as his assistant, but clashes soon developed between these two combative individuals. When King requested a change of duty nine months later, Moffett was glad to oblige. He got King orders to command the Naval Air Station at Norfolk, Virginia.

King was finally on his way up. Moffett told him that he would give him command of the *Saratoga* in the summer of 1930. King was disappointed because he still wanted to get the *Lexington*. He considered the *"Lex"* the finest ship in the world. King continued to fight for command of the *Lexington*. This time he got what he wanted.

The *Lexington* and her sister ship the *Saratoga* had, like the Japanese *Akagi*, begun the 1920s as battle cruisers. When these ships were to be scrapped under the terms of the naval disarmament treaty, their hulls were converted to aircraft carriers. Both ships were commissioned in late 1927. Each had a 900-foot flight deck, a total tonnage of 33,000, were manned by 2,000 men with more than 100 officers, and could cruise at over 30 knots.

King took command of the *Lexington* in June 1930 and found another loose ship. He immediately set to work to tighten discipline. Through transfers and tight controls, he had established an efficient command by the time four squadrons of sixty-five planes altogether arrived in February of the following year. Pilots were furious when King insisted that they inspect their aircraft before and after each flight. It is surprising today that pilots of that period stubbornly resisted a rule for their own safety. King enforced it, and gradually it came to be accepted practice in air operations.

Admiral Moffett was killed in the crash of the dirigible *Akron* on April 4, 1933, and King openly lobbied for his job as chief of the Bureau of Aeronautics. Never one to ignore an opportunity to advance himself, King went all the way to Adm. William V. Pratt, chief of naval operations. Pratt was not receptive to the suggestion; he had placed King in fourth place on his private list of potential candidates. Nevertheless, Secretary of Navy Claude A. Swanson thought highly of King and recommended him to President Franklin D. Roosevelt. King got the job and with it the two stars of a rear admiral even though he was not one of the president's intimates, otherwise almost a prerequisite for promotion to flag rank.

Two years later, King sought the three-star billet as commander, Aircraft, Battle Force, which called for a vice-admiral in charge of the navy's four carriers and their squadrons. He had, however, acquired too many enemies with his abrasive personality and stern ways, and was named instead commander, Aircraft, Base Force, which was a rear admiral's job in charge of seaplane patrol squadrons. Although he was disappointed in not getting the top job in charge of the navy's carriers, his own education was vastly improved by his new position. He forced pilots to fly under all kinds of weather conditions, frequently joining them on hazardous flights. He was a tough taskmaster, openly cursing those he found to be weak and ineffectual. His brusque, often insulting manner shocked many in the staid navy of the 1930s, but he got results. By 1938, when his organization was renamed Aircraft, Scouting Force, King had proved that seaplanes could be the eyes and ears of the fleet.

He moved upward at a faster pace as he gained experience in handling naval airpower. In January 1938, he became commander, Aircraft, Battle Force, which included the carriers *Lexington*, *Saratoga*, and *Ranger* and later the newly commissioned *Yorktown* and *Enterprise* in the spring of 1939. Three of his carrier captains later distinguished themselves. King looked for the best he could find, and he got three topnotchers in Capts. John H. Towers, John H. Hoover, and John S. McCain.

Impatient to prove his capabilities, King also asked that a scout force, with light cruisers, destroyers, and patrol planes, be added to his carriers to form a more potent striking force. His proposal to the Bureau of Navigation raised eyebrows because he was suggesting that two vice-admiral commands be combined under him. He argued that such action would release the 33-knot carriers from duty with 21-knot battleships and provide a fast-moving, far-ranging strike force for independent operations.

The proposal was particularly upsetting to Adm. Adolphus Andrews, a longtime battleship advocate who headed the bureau. King's arguments were so sound that they could not be ignored, and Andrews was forced to reply. He said that carriers were too vulnerable to operate without battleships for protection—a comment that Andrews would live to regret—and he turned down King's request. Shortly thereafter, as King expected, Andrews himself was given command of Aircraft, Scouting Force as a vice-admiral.

King had been frustrated for years by such thinking. Yamamoto had faced similar attitudes in the Japanese navy. Both fought to change such conservative attitudes about sea power. Yamamoto was successful prior to World War II, and King was not.

King pursued his own ideas for the employment of aircraft carriers in the years before the war began. The tactics developed by him and his staff proved so efficient that, after the start of hostilities, they were adopted as standard practice. Therefore, these frustrating years were not all in vain.

King was never reticent in describing himself. He wrote a letter to accompany his fitness report, saying that he believed that his next assignment should be either as chief of naval operations or commander, United States Fleet. He pointed to his personnel file, filled with letters of recommendation, as proof of his capabilities during a long career in which he had served in all branches of the navy.

Chief of Naval Operations William D. Leahy notified President Roosevelt that he would retire in the summer of 1939. When King learned that his name was not on the list submitted to the president, he began to suspect that his career was about at an end. He was more sure of it when Rear Adm. Harold R. Stark was nominated in March. At the time, there were only three flag officers with aviation experience, including King and Rear Adms. William F. Halsey and Charles A. Blakely, out of a total of seventy-four officers of flag rank. King wasn't surprised that Stark was nominated because he had figured that the hierarchy would name one of its own kind from the ranks of the surface navy. King had never been a Roosevelt intimate, and the president was aware of his excessive drinking. These factors may well have played a part in King's failure to get the nomination.

In July 1939, at the age of sixty, King was convinced that his career was really over, particularly after he was made a member of the General Board. Discouraged about his future, King believed that his new job was the end of the road, where elderly admirals ended up while awaiting retirement.

Chief of Naval Operations Stark tried to get King an active command because he was convinced that King's talents were going to waste. In December of the following year, King was given command of the Atlantic Squadron even though the position called for only a rear admiral. He accepted the job with alacrity just to get to sea.

On January 6, 1941, his command was designated the Atlantic Fleet. It was one of three fleets, including the Pacific and Asiatic fleets. The changes abolished the title commander in chief, United States Fleet, which had called for a full admiral.

King, realizing that he would soon be replaced, wrote his superiors, saying that there was too much business as usual and that most ships needed to be made combat-ready. He strongly urged that steps be taken immediately to make them so. One man, Secretary of Navy Frank Knox, appreciated his tough words, but nothing really changed. King reached his sixty-third birthday on November 23, 1941. He was only a year short of the navy's mandatory retirement age.

The Japanese attack on Pearl Harbor forced drastic changes in the United States Navy. A desperate President Roosevelt looked over the list of admirals for one who could bring order out of chaos. He had decided that Adm. Kimmel should be relieved as commander in chief, Pacific Fleet and brought home for investigation of his conduct.

Kimmel later testified at his trial that he had not been warned of Japanese intentions in the Pacific prior to the war. However, Admiral Stark had sent him a war warning on November 27, 1941, telling him to expect an aggressive move by Japan within the next few days. Hawaii was not specifically mentioned in the warning, but the Philippines, Thailand, the Kra Isthmus, and Borneo were named as possible targets of Japanese attacks. Stark's warning had ordered him to prepare to "execute deployment preparatory to carrying out the existing war plan."

Despite such a direct warning, neither Kimmel nor Lt. Gen. Walter Short, commander of all army forces in Hawaii, felt that there was a Japanese threat to the Hawaiian Islands. Unbelievably, they did not pass on the warning to their respective air arms, and no air raid drill had been authorized since November 12. Short had ordered all army aircraft parked wing tip-to-wing tip for protection against sabotage, but of course such placement made them particularly vulnerable to air attacks.

The navy had sent flying boats on patrol, but these flights were largely for training purposes. There was no positive intent to set up a system around the islands to seek out unfriendly ships or submarines.

Secretary of the Navy Knox told Admiral King that he was Knox's personal choice to be commander in chief, United States

Fleet, the position President Roosevelt had abolished the previous January. Meanwhile, Roosevelt continued to look over the list of admirals for an officer who could take charge of the entire United States Fleet and bring it up to a war footing. He thought of King, an officer of vast knowledge and commanding presence with some personal failings. Here was a man, he reasoned, who had not only the ability but also the toughness to provide the necessary leadership. Although he did not know King well, he convinced himself that this cold, often ruthless man was ideal for the job.

After the disastrous losses suffered by the United States Pacific Fleet, Roosevelt knew that the navy had grown too hidebound, conservative, and protective. It needed men with new ideas, and he decided that King, the man who so frequently had been passed over, should be the one to take command of the United States Fleet.

When told of his appointment, King said, "When war breaks out, they look for the sons of bitches."

The years of frustration fell away as King took over. First, he insisted that the acronym for commander in chief, United States Fleet—CINCUS—should be changed immediately to COMINCH. He said that CINCUS sounded too much like "sink us."

3

THE *PRINCE OF WALES* AND *REPULSE* SUNK

Across the International Date Line it was 3:00 A.M. on December 8 when the Japanese attacked Pearl Harbor. Adm. Thomas C. Hart, commander in chief of the United States Asiatic Fleet, was awakened by the ringing of his bedside telephone. The marine duty officer, Lt. Col. William Clement, said that he was coming over immediately with a message. It did not take him long because Hart lived in a Manila hotel a block from the navy's communication center.

Clement handed Hart the message: "Air raid on Pearl Harbor. This is no drill." Clement explained it was not an official message, but that it had been picked up by his radio operator and he was convinced of its authenticity.

Hart immediately called a meeting of his staff. The small, wiry admiral told them soberly, "We can expect an attack immediately. The Japanese must have the Philippines if they wish to move southward. We're right in their path." He added that defense of the Philippines was the responsibility of Gen. Douglas MacArthur and that the small Asiatic Fleet would fight a delaying action until the Pacific Fleet arrived from the Hawaiian Islands. He concluded, "I'm not surprised Japan has decided to go to war. I've expected it since June. What does astonish me is that they struck first at Pearl Harbor."

He wrote a memorandum for distribution to all elements of his command.

"Priority. Japan started hostilities. Govern yourseles accordingly."

It was written in such haste that no one noticed he had misspelled "yourselves."

Hart's Asiatic Fleet had only two cruisers and a few old destroyers. Naval aviation, whose designation was undeserved, was composed mostly of twenty-eight PBYs—or so-called flying boats—under Capt. Frank D. Wagner's Patrol Wing 10. With utility planes of all types, the total air arm amounted to forty-one airplanes.

The division of responsibility for air operations between the United States Army and Navy had caused bitterness for years. In the Philippines, this unrealistic rivalry now had disastrous consequences. Army aviation lost most of its strength before noon when a heavy force of Japanese fighters, bombers, and dive-bombers swept across army airfields near Manila. Two thirds of the army's fighter strength and one half of its bomber strength were destroyed.

Without fighter protection, Patrol Wing 10's PBY Catalinas found patrols not only hazardous but almost suicidal. What was needed was a strong carrier force.

The next day, Admiral Hart called in Patwing's commander for a brief conference. He noticed Wagner's haggard face, and the normally irascible Hart was sympathetic toward the brave captain. Wagner's two squadrons, VP–102 under Lt. Comdr. E. T. Neale and VP–101 under Lt. Comdr. J. V. Peterson, had already performed miracles with their slow PBYs, even making attacks that the airplanes were never designed to do.

Wagner told his commander that Lt. A. C. Keller, flying 300 miles west of Manila over the South China Sea, had spotted two battleships, two cruisers, and four destroyers at 7:25 that morning. They didn't fire at Keller's PBY, and the pilot thought that they were British. But a precautionary call to base quickly confirmed that they were not, and he was told to take another look. Keller realized that they were Japanese when float planes were catapulted from the battleships and antiaircraft guns started to fire at his plane. He decided to head for the clouds for protection.

Keller was told by the base not to attack but to keep them under surveillance, which he did by sending continuous MOs, repeating the letters so that other planes and ships could home in on his signal to find the Japanese ships.

Five more PBYs under Lt. Comdr. Peterson took off to attack the fleet, aware that such an attack could very well be a one-way mission.

Keller and the Japanese float planes played hide-and-seek among the clouds while Peterson sought out the Japanese ships. He spotted them at 11:30 and ordered his patrol planes to attack the largest battleships. Despite heavy antiaircraft fire, hits were scored on the stern of the *Kongo*, which immediately spun into a circle and finally stopped dead as the PBYs turned quickly and fled back to base. Hart shook his head in disbelief when he learned that all PBYs had returned safely. (Later that afternoon, two of three PBYs dispatched to make another attack were shot down.) The bravery of these fliers, making bombing attacks in airplanes that were never designed for strikes against capital ships, is among the greatest shown by pilots during the war.

Hart told Wagner, "Disperse your planes at outlying bases. Attack only when necessary. It's only a matter of time until the Asiatic Fleet has to retire, and we'll need you to search and scout for us."

On December 12, Japanese bombers caught twelve PBYs on the water and destroyed them. Other losses quickly reduced Patwing 10's Catalinas to seventeen, of which only eleven could fly because the other six were riddled with bullet holes. Then another PBY was lost at Lake Lanao in an accident.

Admiral Hart was soon forced to move the seaplane tenders *Langley, Preston,* and *Heron* south to the Netherlands East Indies, and Wagner went along. Of the planes left at Manila, four were repaired for service.

Two disasters followed in quick succession. Cavite Naval Yard was almost destroyed in an air raid. Worse, Japanese assault forces landed on Luzon, largest and northernmost island of the Philippines, at three different points.

A British squadron known as Force *Z* sailed from Singapore on the evening of December 8 under the Eastern Fleet's new commander in chief, Adm. Sir Tom Phillips. Word had been received that the Japanese had transports en route to the north of the Malayan Peninsula, and Phillips planned to attack them off Kota Bharu. Under his command were the new battleship *Prince of Wales,* the old battle cruiser *Repulse,* and four destroyers. He had hoped to have the new carrier *Indomitable,* but it had recently gone aground. Not only was Phillips without airpower at sea, but he also learned after his departure that he would have no aerial reconnaissance or fighter cover because of the invasion of the northern Malayan airfields.

Japanese invasion plans were on a large scale, with simultaneous landings scheduled for Malaya and Thailand. The Japanese fleet was at full strength, with two battleships under Vice-Adm. Takeo Kurita to escort twenty-eight troop transports. In addition, the Japanese

Twenty-second Air Flotilla had ninety-nine bombers, thirty-nine fighters, and six reconnaissance planes at Saigon and Soktran bases in French Indochina. Phillips was ignorant not only of Japanese plans but also of their sea, air, and ground strength.

His fleet was sighted by three Japanese reconnaissance aircraft on the afternoon of December 9 and by the Japanese submarine *I-65*. With the element of surprise gone, Phillips decided to return to Singapore. Unknown to either admiral, Kurita's fleet had been only 15 miles to the north when Phillips turned back.

While the Japanese Twenty-second Air Flotilla was preparing to attack Singapore, word came from the *I-65* that Phillips' fleet was at sea. Torpedoes were substituted for bombs, and the planes took off at 6:00 P.M. to search for the British ships. Despite the earlier sightings by the Japanese submarine and reconnaissance aircraft, the bombers never found the British ships and returned to their bases.

En route back to Singapore, Phillips received word that the Japanese were landing at Kuantan, halfway down the Malayan coast, and decided to investigate. His fleet arrived there at dawn on the 10th but found that all was quiet; the report had been in error. A tug was reported to the north, so he ordered a new course at 10 A.M. to investigate this sighting.

Adm. Nobutake Kondo, the Japanese commander in chief of the invading forces, had been receiving continuous reports about the British ships, and he ordered all available naval aircraft to attack during the early morning hours while his battle fleet steamed south at maximum speed to intercept the British fleet.

The Japanese submarine *I-58* had sighted Force Z at 2:30 A.M. and immediately attacked it. All five of its torpedoes missed; they were not even seen by the British ships.

The Twenty-second Air Flotilla now sent out twelve reconnaissance aircraft at 5 A.M. from bases in French Indochina, and a strike force of Nell and Betty twin-engine bombers took off an hour later. Fifty-two Nells and Bettys were armed with torpedoes; thirty-four Nells carried bombs.

At first, Phillips was confident that his ships could withstand a Japanese aerial attack. He believed that the new *Prince of Wales* was unsinkable and that the battle cruiser *Repulse*, despite its thin armor, could protect itself.

Japanese pilots orbited a wide area in their search for the British ships, glancing anxiously at fuel gauges when they registered below the half-full mark. They had brought lunches of bean paste-coated rice cakes and coffee syrup in vacuum bottles.

Ensign Hoashi caught sight of the British ships at 11:00 A.M. He radioed, "Sighted two enemy battleships seventy nautical miles southeast Kuantan, course southeast." The other aircraft of the Twenty-second Air Flotilla heard the general call on the return leg of their search. The flotilla, a highly trained organization under Rear Adm. Sadaichi Matsunaga, had given up hope of finding the British fleet.

The approaching Japanese bombers were first spotted by observers on the *Repulse.* "Enemy aircraft in sight. Action stations!"

Capt. William Tennant watched nine twin-engine bombers coming toward his ship in line abreast. He marveled at the tightness of the formations. The ship's guns roared as the bombers flew toward the *Repulse,* never wavering despite the intense fire. With a tightness in his throat, Tennant watched bombs separate from the planes and fall toward his cruiser. He was relieved when only a single bomb hit amidships, exploding on the armored deck in the marines' mess. He glanced at the planes as they droned away, flak bursts surrounding them. Within minutes, fires started by the bomb were under control, but Tennant knew that their ordeal was just beginning.

At 11:30 A.M., radar picked up torpedo planes racing toward the *Prince of Wales.* Once they became visible to anxious eyes on the battleship, coming in at high rates of speed in steep glides, it was seen that they approached in two groups of sixteen torpedo bombers. They flew ahead of the *Prince of Wales,* disappearing momentarily in the clouds at 3,000 feet. Suddenly, at 11:42, they dove to the port side of the battleship in clusters of two and three planes.

Bugles blared, and the call came, "Stand by for barrage!"

Tennant watched anxiously from the bridge of the *Repulse* as machine-gun tracers sent white arcs of fire toward the torpedo bombers. Light puffs from the *Prince's* 2-pound shells exploded near them while gray balls of smoke from its heavier guns mushroomed. Incredibly, the Japanese torpedo bombers came through the withering fire unscathed, most dropping their torpedoes at the *Prince of Wales* as others turned away from the flagship to race toward the *Repulse.*

Tennant called to the navigating officer, "Turn forty-five degrees to starboard!"

The *Repulse's* captain was fascinated by the daring of the Japanese pilots, who ignored his ship's heavy fire and pressed their attacks. One Japanese plane was hit and exploded with a roar, lighting the sky with an orange-yellow light. Another pilot flew alongside the ship and challenged its gunners, a foolhardy stunt that cost him his life when his plane was ripped apart.

After the *Repulse* completed her turn, the stern offered a smaller target to the approaching torpedoes, whose wake passed harmlessly to either side. Japanese pilots, their torpedoes released, circled the ship while their gunners raked British gun crews. Scores of sailors lay crumpled beside their mounts.

Despite his own problems, Tennant kept an eye on the *Prince of Wales*. Only 2,000 yards away, the flagship had failed to avoid some of the Japanese torpedoes. With dismay, Tennant saw a column of smoke rise from the flagship's stern while black smoke bellied from her vitals. Soon, he saw the *Prince of Wales* list 13 degrees to port, and it was evident that she was rapidly losing headway. He realized that she must have been hit by two torpedoes, which had struck her rudder and propeller shafts. Tennant watched the magnificent ship try to turn but succeed only in heeling over as water poured into her hull. The "unsinkable" *Prince of Wales* had become almost defenseless, Tennant knew, when he saw her signalmen raise the red canvas-and-wire balls that signified "not under control."

The *Repulse*'s captain immediately radioed Singapore, believing that the flagship was unable to do so. His was the first word headquarters had of the attack, and five fighters were dispatched from Sembawang.

Now it was the *Repulse*'s turn again. Shortly before noon, twelve Japanese bombers came from the south in a coordinated attack. Bombs tumbled out of their bomb bays, and several near misses sent drenching seawater over gun crews.

Tennant ordered evasive action, and the *Repulse* turned north.

A new threat materialized as torpedo planes arrived from the north. Crews were warned through loudspeakers to switch targets once the new planes were in range. A Nell was bracketed by intense gunfire, and the gunners were cheered when it disintegrated. Within minutes, this attack was beaten off.

Captain Tennant allowed himself another quick glance at the *Prince of Wales*. He saw to his dismay that the battleship was wallowing and dead in the water. He ordered his *Repulse* to turn 180 degrees and head toward the *Prince of Wales* far to the south. He signaled the flagship, "Thanks to Providence have so far dodged nineteen torpedoes."

There was no reply.

Japanese planes approached the *Repulse* again from the south at 12:20 P.M. when the two large ships were 800 yards apart. A squadron of nine planes dove at them, three heading toward the *Repulse* while the remainder took on the crippled *Prince of Wales*. Tennant ordered his ship to face the attackers bow-on to give the torpedoes as small a target as possible. As three wakes headed toward his ship, he turned his eyes to the *Prince of Wales*. A Japanese plane seemed about to drop its torpedo directly onto the flagship but at the last moment, Tennant saw the plane's wing tips go nearly vertical as the bomber turned toward his ship. Two more Nells joined this plane, and Tennant watched them drop their torpedoes, which headed straight for his ship. He felt helpless, knowing that if he ordered his ship to swing away to avoid these torpedoes, he would present his beam to the three other torpedoes approaching from another direction. Judging that at least one would hit the *Repulse*, he called, "Stand by for torpedo!"

The *Repulse* shuddered with the impact as a torpedo exploded amidships. Although able to maintain her 25-knot speed, the *Repulse* started to list to port.

Ensign Hoashi, whose reconnaissance plane had first reported the position of the British ships, orbited the battle zone and relayed a minute-by-minute account of the battle to Matsunaga in Saigon. The flotilla's admiral still had Nells in reserve if they were needed to complete the destruction of the British capital ships. At 12:30, he decided they would not and canceled their flights.

There were three uncommitted squadrons on the scene whose pilots had watched the first strikes with growing excitement. Their leader, noting how successfully the *Repulse* had evaded most of the torpedoes, ordered that the final attacks should be split. When the last attacks began, the *Repulse*'s air defense officer ordered gunners to concentrate only on those Japanese aircraft preparing to release torpedoes and to ignore all others. This tactic quickly proved successful: A Betty disintegrated in a red ball of fire as its fuel tanks exploded.

At 12:25, Captain Tennant counted *eight* torpedo wakes heading toward his ship. Despite her damage, the *Repulse* still answered her helm as he gave orders to evade as many torpedoes as possible. The quartermaster swung the bow to port as a deadly line of white foam slid past the ship. Tennant knew that the end was near when a torpedo struck his ship on its port side near the gun room. Now the rudder was jammed. Three more torpedoes crashed into her, two on the port side, the other to starboard, slamming the huge ship first one way and then the other.

Tennant's voice was steady as he called over the loudspeakers,

"All hands on deck. Prepare to abandon ship. Clear away Carley floats." Everyone was ordered up from below decks as the *Repulse* settled hard to port, still making 15 knots.

Explosions tore at the interior of the ship as men came topside. Guns were silent as the ship's crew methodically evacuated by lifeboats while the sea poured into her hull.

Tennant's commanding presence on the bridge calmed the men on the forecastle as two hundred of them waited for word to leave the ship, now listing at 40 degrees. Only when the wounded had been evacuated did Tennant say through a megaphone, "You've put up a good show. Now look after yourselves, and God bless you."

With the ship now listing at 60 degrees, it was too late to launch more lifeboats. Men slid into the ocean and swam toward the Carley floats. Many men sustained injuries as they slid precipitately over the coating of seaweed that had accumulated on the ship's hull in the tropical waters. Others struck the ship's keel so violently that their ankles or spines were broken. Although the sea was calm, fuel oil gushed from the ship's ruptured bunkers and impregnated the men's clothing, weighing them down and rendering them practically helpless. Many who struggled to reach the floats choked to death in the oil-saturated waters.

Tennant moved to *B* gundeck to watch his men slide down the ship's side. As the ship slowly sank, he was pulled beneath the surface, convinced that death was near. Suddenly, his body was thrust upward and something hit him hard on the head. He was knocked almost unconscious and probably would have been killed but for the protection afforded by his helmet. He dimly heard someone call, "Here you are, sir." He was pulled aboard a Carley float, more dead than alive.

The *Repulse* was gone, but, incredibly, the *Prince of Wales* remained afloat despite having received mortal wounds from three more torpedoes on her starboard side. The flagship was down to 15 knots and unable to maneuver. Admiral Phillips had ordered two of his destroyers to pick up survivors from the *Repulse*, but he had no illusions about the fate of his flagship: Most of her guns were shot out. The *Prince of Wales* was rapidly filling with water, which almost righted her.

The short admiral watched, grief-stricken, as nine Japanese bombers moved toward his ship from the south. They crossed from port to starboard, ignoring the few flak bursts from six of the battleship's remaining guns.

Phillips and his staff officers stood on the *Prince of Wales*'s compass platform, watching as bombs separated from the aircraft. Capt. John C. Leach yelled, "Now!" They dropped to the deck just before the bombs hit. Phillips was appalled by the destruction they caused; the stretcher parties scrambled to treat the bloody survivors.

Captain Leach sent word to the destroyer *Express* to remove the wounded and he wired Singapore to send tugs to bring them home. But it was too late to save his ship. Those last three torpedoes had exploded almost simultaneously in its bowels. Apprised of the devastation below decks, Leach ordered the ship abandoned.

There was little time to evacuate the flagship, and men scrambled down ropes and nets to the destroyer on the starboard side. Officers maintained discipline with difficulty, but all those capable of leaving the ship were soon over the side.

The *Prince of Wales* rolled to port at 1:20 P.M. Then the keel began to rise. The flagship tilted toward the destroyer, whose decks were jammed with survivors, and threatened to capsize it. Lt. Comdr. F. J. Cartwright held his ship alongside until the last survivor was on board and then hastily ordered the *Express* to pull away. There was not a moment to lose; within seconds the *Prince of Wales* turned over and sank.

The five British fighters from Sembawang, ordered out when the *Repulse* gave Singapore headquarters the first indication of the impending disaster, arrived as the *Prince of Wales* went down. Forty-two officers and 754 men out of 1,309 aboard the *Repulse* were picked up, and 90 officers and 1,195 ratings out of a total complement of 1,612 on the *Prince of Wales* were saved. Admiral Phillips' body was never found. The body of Captain Leach was discovered later floating in the sea.

With the war only three days old, the Japanese had, in separate actions thousands of miles apart, almost destroyed the United States Pacific Fleet at Pearl Harbor and then sunk two of Great Britain's finest warships. For the Japanese naval air arm, these were brilliant victories. The British ships were sunk, it was noted with dismay in England, by Japanese aircraft operating over 400 miles from their bases.

For the Allies, it was quickly apparent that only three American carriers and a few cruisers, destroyers, and submarines were available to contest Japan's conquest of the rich chain of islands to the south. If these ships too were rendered impotent, the raw materials that Japan so desperately needed to pursue her expansionist plans in the Far East would fall easily to her armed forces. Allied garrisons, no longer able to be supplied or reinforced, would soon be forced to capitulate. Perhaps most shocking of all to Allied leaders was the realization that the *Prince of Wales* and *Repulse* were sunk with the confirmed loss of only three Japanese planes.

Admiral Sir Alfred Dudley Pound received word of the disaster in London and immediately awakened Prime Minister Winston Churchill. The first sea lord's voice shook with emotion, and Churchill at first had difficulty understanding him. "I have to report to you that the *Prince of Wales* and the *Repulse* have both been sunk by aircraft. Tom Phillips is drowned."

Churchill was devastated by the news and blamed himself. He had sent the capital ships to the Far East and had personally selected Phillips as their commander in chief. He wrote later that he was thankful to have been alone when he heard the news because in all the war he had never received such a direct shock. When he spoke later to his cabinet about the incident, he reminded them that "the British don't like having their ships sunk."

Admiral Phillips' decision to move into waters controlled by Japanese land-based airpower resulted from overconfidence in the defensive capabilities of his ships to withstand determined air attacks. It was a common failing at this stage of the war, one that both British and American naval commanders had to outgrow the hard way. Air strategists for years had been saying that the battleship was no longer supreme. Henceforth, they now reiterated, war at sea must be conducted under the umbrella of carrier aviation or risk disaster. Unfortunately, thousands of men would die before that lesson was to be learned.

4

STUNNED
BY THE DISASTER

Allied commanders in the Far East had planned a fighting retreat, but they were under a grave handicap. The situation grew more desperate each day, especially for American naval forces after Cavite was destroyed. Temporary accommodations were assigned along the Manila waterfront, but Admiral Hart knew that the Manila Bay area was too dangerous for surface ships. Enemy aircraft could bomb almost without opposition. The Japanese were in control of the air, and the navy's PBYs, although fighting valiantly on each patrol, had been ineffective.

Tragedy for the Americans was not restricted to Pearl Harbor and the Philippines. After years of patiently waiting for the opportune moment, Japan was on the march, striking first at Midway and Wake islands.

On the first night after the Pearl Harbor attack, a bright moon silhouetted Midway's military installations, new construction put up hastily that fall as Japan's peace envoys dickered in Washington. The marines had been waiting for the Japanese to arrive since the first announcement early that morning of the attack on Hawaii. They remained at battle stations, a small force completely inadequate to ward off an invasion. One marine, glancing anxiously at the full moon, whose light on the surf outlined the island, said grimly, "I'll bet the Japs can see us for miles."

Two Japanese warships, a destroyer, and a cruiser opened fire later that night, and Midway's shore batteries answered back. The Japanese had expected to catch the marines off guard, but when surprise failed they quickly concluded the engagement. They needed Midway badly for their expansion plans, but Nagumo, fearing that it would be too costly a venture, had already declined Yamamoto's request for an all-out assault on Hawaii and Midway and was headed home. Little did the Japanese realize that Midway's defenses were at their weakest in these first few days after Pearl Harbor.

It was December 8 on the other side of the International Date Line when Maj. James Devereux, commander of the Marine Corps' First Defense Battalion on Wake Island, received news of the attack on Pearl Harbor. Later that day, twenty-four Japanese bombers hit the island's airfield, flying in V formations. Their fragmentation bombs created havoc among the new installations. Of the twelve fighters of Marine Fighting Squadron 211 under Maj. Paul Putnam that had flown in from the *Enterprise* on December 4, only four survived undamaged. At times, Major Putnam's squadron had difficulty keeping even one fighter in the air.

Day after day Japanese bombers appeared and dropped their bombs almost unmolested except by an occasional fighter that had been patched up for duty.

Capt. Henry T. Elrod of Marine Fighting Squadron 211 was one of the few survivors of the initial attacks. He had not only shot down two of twenty-two attacking Japanese planes but had later sunk the destroyer *Kisaragi* with bombs after strafing it during low-level runs. When the Japanese stormed the atoll two days before Christmas, there were no aircraft in flyable condition. With the remnants of his squadron, Elrod personally helped to man ground batteries. When the Japanese charged his defense position, Elrod captured an automatic weapon and led his men in a counterattack until he was mortally wounded. His Medal of Honor citation, awarded posthumously, stated that his superb skill as a pilot and his daring leadership distinguished him among the many brave defenders.

The battle for Wake Island ended tragically for the United States on December 23 when Japan's land, sea, and air forces overwhelmed all resistance. Although a small American task force of ships that were badly needed elsewhere had been on its way to relieve the beleaguered garrison, further resistance was impossible.

Within a fortnight, the carrier *Saratoga* was torpedoed. While the naval command at Pearl Harbor wondered where the ships would be found to fight a delaying action, the *Saratoga* was sent to dry dock for extensive repairs.

Four hundred naval personnel and 155 marines were also sacrificed on Guam, a strategic island that the Japanese had bombed repeatedly. Resistance ended there on December 22.

Two weeks after the attack on Pearl Harbor, Prime Minister Winston Churchill and President Franklin Roosevelt met with their staffs in Washington for the Arcadia Conference. Both leaders reaffirmed earlier intentions of defeating Germany first while maintaining a holding action in the Pacific against Japan until limited offensives were possible.

One of the first items of business was to create a unified command of American, British, Dutch, and Australian forces for the southwest Pacific, which was considered essential. Admiral Ernest King supported Gen. George C. Marshall's suggestion that the British general Sir Archibald Wavell be named supreme commander. Both the army chief of staff and Admiral King considered Wavell an experienced commander, and he was available for the job. Yet during later discussions about unity of command, King became somewhat testy, saying unity of command was not a panacea for all problems.

Roosevelt meanwhile insisted that the United States Navy go on the offensive instead of merely reacting to each Japanese move. King tried to explain that improved air cover was needed before the Pacific Fleet could take the offensive, but Roosevelt did not fully comprehend how impotent American airpower in the Pacific had been rendered by the heavy losses of men and planes.

King insisted that the lines of communication between Hawaii and Samoa be kept open as the number one priority. "All other projects must give way to this," he said with emphasis.

Roosevelt continued to demand action, if only against small Japanese task groups. Privately, after Wavell was given command, he told King that he was concerned about who would give General Wavell his orders to go on the offensive. Adm. Sir Dudley Pound, Great Britian's sea lord, learned of the president's concern and suggested that a Chief of Staff Committee, including American and British service chiefs, be empowered to determine Allied strategy and give the orders to theater commanders after strategy was approved by the president and the prime minister.

King recommended instead that a Southwestern Pacific Council, including representatives from all Allied countries, including Austrlia and the Netherlands, be set up to operate separately from the Chief of Staff Committee. King did not insist and it is quite possible that the idea was not his own but one proposed by the president. When Marshall expressed a preference for the British idea, King readily agreed, and the matter was turned over to the prime minister and the president for final resolution. Roosevelt held out for a separate body, but Churchill continued to support Pound's suggestion.

At a luncheon between King and the president, the admiral said that he thought that the Americans and the British, who were paying for and doing most of the fighting, should determine strategy. Eventually he persuaded the president, and the Combined Chiefs of Staff was formed, with headquarters in Washington.

During subsequent meetings to determine basic policy, President Roosevelt frequently glanced at King when a suggestion was made by Churchill or other members of the British delegation. If King shook his head slightly, Roosevelt would emphatically turn down the suggestion, even if it came from Churchill.

The Combined Chiefs of Staff determined the course of the war from then on. It was successful largely because its members honestly tried to resolve differences. At first it included Admiral King, head of the United States Fleet; Adm. Harold R. Stark, chief of naval operations; Army Chief of Staff Marshall; and Gen. Henry H. "Hap" Arnold, commanding general of the United States Army Air Forces, who were all part of the United States Joint Chiefs of Staff. Their counterparts on the British side were Gen. Sir John G. Dill, chief of the Imperial General Staff; Adm. Sir Alfred Dudley Pound; and Air Marshal Sir Charles Portal of the Royal Air Force. Later, Field Marshal Alan Brooke replaced Dill, and Admiral Stark was dropped after he was replaced as chief of naval operations by Admiral King. Roosevelt's naval advisor, Adm. William D. Leahy, served as unofficial chairman of the United States Joint Chiefs.

Adm. Chester W. Nimitz, who had served before the war as chief of the Bureau of Navigation, was now in command of the Pacific Fleet. The fifty-six-year-old Nimitz was a wise choice, although he and King often disagreed about men under his command and the conduct of the war in the Pacific. Despite his age, Nimitz was a vigorous man with a pink complexion and blond hair that was now turning white. He was an ideal buffer between his own subordinates and the caustic King.

Nimitz soon established a rapport with his commanders, whose opinions on how to improve operations he valued. When a commander reported from the battlefronts, Nimitz always found time in his busy schedule to interview him. He would stand as the officer entered his office, greet him genuinely, take time to review the task before them, and answer questions.

If one of his commanders got out of line, Nimitz removed him. He had a waiting bench of flag officers and was willing to give a man a chance to prove himself. Those who did not measure up to his strict standards found themselves transferred to some unimportant job.

A calm, prudent man, Nimitz had a tremendous capacity for organization, but he was also an inspiring leader. His appointment soon restored an air of confidence throughout the Pacific Fleet.

Japanese invasion forces followed the island chains ever southward, but they were not confined to an island-hopping strategy. They also reached inland along the Asiatic coast, their mighty land, sea, and air forces often making wide end-runs to occupy territory that had seemed secure. It soon became obvious to even the most stalwart believers in eventual Allied victory that Japan had the initiative and would not relinquish it until faced by overwhelming opposition.

Nimitz returned to Pearl Harbor after top secret talks with King in Washington, convinced that they had reached agreement on the only possible strategy for the months ahead. Both admirals realized that there was no hope of stopping the Japanese for the time being, but a revitalized Pacific Fleet might at least slow down their eastward movement, which was imperiling the sea-lanes between the United States and Australia.

Vice Adm. William F. Halsey and Rear Adm. Frank J. Fletcher were placed in charge of two task forces comprising most of the effective ships in the Pacific. Halsey's flag was raised on the carrier *Enterprise*, and he had three cruisers and six destroyers assigned to him. The *Yorktown* flew Fletcher's flag; two cruisers and four destroyers made up his slim task force. Their first job was to protect loads of troops en route to threatened Samoa.

On January 9, 1942, Halsey studied his latest orders from Nimitz: "You are to raid the southern Marshall and northern Gilbert areas as soon as possible. The 'lifeline' must be kept open." Thus, at 3:00 A.M. on the morning of February 1, Halsey's task force appeared 36 miles off Wotje, an atoll of the Marshall Islands. His fliers had been thoroughly briefed before the first fingers of light appeared in the east.

The *"Big E"* then turned into the wind until its speed across her deck reached 22 knots. The churning of her wake and the soft whistle of the trade winds in her superstructure were drowned as airplane engines broke into a roar. As her bow knifed through the waters, fighter planes swarmed off her deck, followed by scout bombers and then torpedo planes. En route, torpedo bombers separated to make their attacks on Kwajalein Atoll, where a new base had been established by Japan to strike at the Australian–American lifeline. The others headed for Roi at the northern end of the lagoon.

As the *Enterprise* serenely rode the waves, still more fighter planes charged off her deck, each with a single 100-pound bomb, and headed for Taroa and Maloelap islands. One plane spun crazily near the end of the deck and plunged into the sea before the pilot could free himself. The other five winged their way to the target.

None of the pilots was sure what to expect because their target maps were only photographic enlargements of clippings from old charts. This was to have an unfortunate effect on the group headed for Roi. In the misty dawn they failed to spot the place, alerting the Japanese and giving them twelve minutes warning of the attack.

Cruisers and destroyers opened fire as American fighter planes strafed the runways at Kwajalein, riddling many planes before they could get off the ground. A few dive-bombers in tight formation approached above the scattered clouds and found the harbor filled with ships. Air group commander "Brig" Young immediately detached eighteen planes from Bombing Six headed for Roi and sent them to the opposite end of the long atoll.

Lt. Comdr. William B. Hollingsworth led them in. He checked his altimeter before signaling to nose over. He glanced at the formation. It looked good. Practiced eyes scanned the fuel gauge and checked the carburetor mixture. Without having to think about what he was doing, he made sure that the engine's mixture control was set properly. His years of training were paying off. A glance showed him that the flaps on the engine cowling were closed. Then, drawing his goggles over his eyes, he opened the telescopic aiming sight, pulled back the cockpit hood with a strong yank of his right arm, locked it into position, and made final tab adjustments to the rudder and stabilizer. In seconds, he checked to see if his diving flaps were open to reduce his diving speed and retarded the throttle so that the propeller turned at only 1,900 rpm.

Hollingsworth nosed over, picking out a large building far below, and jockeyed stick and rudder to align his SBD with the target. The wind roared about his head as the speed of the plane increased. He was conscious of flak but, plunging downward, man and plane became one smoothly working machine. He brought his eye to the telescope, taking a quick peep at the altimeter every chance he could. He knew that it was easy to become fascinated by the bombing problem and fly the airplane straight into the ground.

Hollingsworth stared intently into his telescope, watching the bubble level on the bottom and the concentric circles framing the Japanese hanger. The bubble was to the left. He was skidding. He corrected quickly. When a last quick look at the altimeter showed that he was near the release point, he noted with satisfaction that the bubble was centered. He hesitated a split second to note any side movement. The dive was good! He released his bomb and pulled out. He closed the diving flaps, pushed the throttle forward, and reset the rudder and horizontal stabilizer for level flight.

It was over in fewer than forty-five seconds. Once the excitement of attack was past he felt as if every organ in the midsection of his body had been pummeled savagely. A black and blue spot slowly grew on his right hand and as he looked at it for a second, he wondered when he had slammed his hand into something. There had been no feeling of pain.

Hollingsworth looked down. He saw the second division come in low and fast, and the third behind it. He swallowed nervously as a scout bomber was riddled with flak and plunged into the water. Then, a Japanese fighter exploded in the air. He saw the bombs drop and then the attackers wheel out to sea with Japanese fighters hot in pursuit. Two more bombers flamed brightly and plummeted down, but two Japanese planes went with them.

The barracks, gun emplacements, and hangars were on fire. Then Hollingsworth felt his Dauntless rock slightly in the air and, looking down, saw the source of the concussion—a huge smoke cloud rising into the air over the field.

"Ammo dump," he said to himself.

He smiled as one of the pilots yelled on the radio. "Yippee! Right on the button."

It appeared that every building on the base had been leveled. Billows of smoke rose from several sections of the island as a flight of Devastators skimmed the water to launch their torpedoes at warships and cargo vessels at Kwajalein, harbor island of the atoll.

Air Group Commander Young could see a dozen fires on the island at 8:07. Then a tremendous, awe-inspiring explosion thrust out a bulbous orange blast that billowed, mushroomlike, hundreds of feet in the air. He noted down that a gasoline storage tank must have exploded. He listened eagerly to the radio chatter. "Get out of my way, Joe, that big baby is mine!"

Kwajalein had a fifty-minute respite before the third wave from the *Enterprise* arrived.

Lt. Comdr. Lance E. Massey led nine torpedo bombers toward the harbor. The fire from the ground was intense but they held to their course, flying at only 700 feet.

"That CL is making a sneak. Go get him!" Massey called, referring to a Japanese cruiser he saw heading for the entrance to the harbor. Three planes took off after the wounded ship. The others dropped their torpedoes and climbed away in a hurry. The Japanese were so confused that their gunners fired into their own shore batteries and their ships riding at anchor.

Back on the *Enterprise*, Halsey listened with growing satisfaction as the TBS radio brought the words from his pilots over the targets. It was a jumble of conversation, but it afforded all of them immense gratification. They chuckled when they heard, "I got him! Oh Mama! What a sock!"

The victory had been limited because only one transport was sunk and nine others badly damaged, but shore installations had been hit heavily and the atoll commander killed. More important than the damage done, however, was the tremendous lift to morale as the United States, reeling back from defeat, attacked the enemy in a vulnerable position.

During this action Lt. James S. Gray led his five fighters to Taroa. This arrow-shaped island near Kwajalein was a base for Japan's long-range heavy bombers. When Gray led his flight over the island he was astonished to find two long runways with airplanes parked between them. He led the attack and raked facilities and planes. He was then joined by four scout observation planes from the heavy cruiser U.S.S. *Chester*.

Lacking incendiary bullets, their attack was not effective, but the *Chester* and her destroyers moved in close to put salvo after salvo into the island's defenses. The shelling was so heavy that even the men on the ships found themselves bracing against the concussion of their own firing. The blasts seemed to rob the air from their lungs while it pinned them against the superstructure.

After a quick cup of coffee upon his return from Kwajalein, Hollingsworth led a flight of SBDs in a second attack, coming out of the sun to strike at the Japanese base. This time they caught twenty-five planes on the ground. Seven of them, including several two-engine bombers, were set afire. Then fighters approached from the *Enterprise* and swept the field.

As Hollingsworth led his planes back to the *Enterprise*, he noticed nine more bombers headed for Taroa. He knew that they would find opposition because they had disturbed a mad hornet's nest. A bomber was lost in this dual action, but three Japanese planes were shot down.

Now it was Wotje's turn. It was the least fully developed island in the Japanese chain of defenses, with a deep water anchorage and large shore installations. This was a job for surface ships, and only six fighters strafed the harbor and base until salvos from the big ships went into action. Scout and torpedo bombers later returned to Wotje but there was nothing worthwhile to bomb. The cruisers and destroyers had done their job well.

In the whole operation, the *Enterprise* lost five airplanes, a bomber and four scouts, and the fighter that had careened out of control on takeoff. A total of thirty-three planes were damaged, and six officers and five enlisted men were killed.

Halsey, after studying combat reports, gathered his air staff around him. "Our planes are slower than the Japs' and less maneuverable," he said. "It is a tribute to your men that they shot down ten of the enemy and destroyed twenty-four planes on the ground."

Most of Halsey's officers revered him. One reason was that he confided in them. He would invite one of the ship's officers to have dinner with him alone and question him thoroughly about his duties and responsibilities. Many officers who attended expecting to be put on a hot seat found Halsey genuinely interested in understanding the man's job and his problems. His officers came to look forward to these dinners, knowing that they had a unique opportunity to present their problems and frustrations directly to their boss. They found these sessions pleasant. During an extended cruise, officers from all parts of the flagship had a chance to dine informally with Halsey.

The Japanese were out for revenge. They called in bombers from western bases and struck savagely at the *"Big E."* Fighter pilots, exhausted by the day's operations, had to take to the air again in defense of their ship.

After cruisers and destroyers rejoined the carrier, Halsey ordered the formation to turn homeward.

Fletcher's task force, which had been assigned the southernmost islands of the Marshall group and Makin in the adjacent Gilbert Islands, found little of military value to bomb. Bad weather was their greatest enemy. Lt. Comdr. W. O. Burch of the *Yorktown*'s Scouting Five led his squadron to Makin. He got a hit on a seaplane tender with planes on board and his bomb exploded with a tremendous yellow flame and set the ship on fire. Next, he led his squadron in an attack on four-engine bombers. Burch headed for one, spraying it with machine-gun fire until it exploded violently in front of him. Just then a second bomber blew up as his wingmen cut loose. After renewed strafing attacks on the seaplane tender, they headed back to the *Yorktown*.

The *Enterprise* returned to Pearl Harbor on February 5 and the *Yorktown* the following day. These successful raids on the Marshall and Gilbert islands raised morale to a height unknown since the war started. It could not have happened at a more opportune time; there was nothing but bad news everywhere else in the Pacific. United States forces were waging a desperate rearguard action in the Philippines, and the Allied Fleet in the Netherlands East Indies was close to destruction. It was refreshing for members of the Pacific Fleet to be on the offensive, even though this was no solace to the defenders of Manila Bay and the Java Sea.

The two carrier task forces had much of which to be proud. They had damaged an enemy naval base and an important bomber base. Halsey was the first to acknowledge that they had learned much of value for future operations. "If nothing else," he said, "these raids are a valuable exercise in developing task forces for a new kind of war at sea, task forces built around a floating airfield."

This was a start, a feeble one at best, but a start on the long road back toward victory. Ships and planes and men were tragically short. The planes, in particular, were wholly inadequate for the big job of destroying Japanese aviation and ships across the broad reaches of the Pacific. They needed self-sealing fuel tanks, more armor, and much more firepower. The years of economy prior to the war would now have to be paid for in blood.

After a few days of rest, Halsey was impatient to get to sea. He was therefore excited when he received orders on February 11 to attack the Japanese invaders at Wake. His *Enterprise* carrier group would go to Wake while Fletcher's *Yorktown* group headed for Eniwetok. At the last minute, the *Yorktown* assignment was cancelled in favor of a more important convoy assignment.

The men of the *Enterprise* remembered Wake with a vengeance because they had been only a day's cruise away with supplies and reinforcements when the island surrendered. Their raid was a success, causing tremendous destruction.

Halsey headed back to Pearl but en route received new orders from CINCPAC. Marcus Island, only a thousand miles from Tokyo, was to be attacked. The wedge-shaped island, only five miles in circumference, had an important airfield. Its weather-reporting station was also of great value to the Japanese fleets in computing weather conditions in advance for their strikes throughout the Pacific.

The audacity of the raid against Marcus outraged the Japanese. Although damage to installations was not extensive, it made them reconsider their strategic plans and, possibly, their decision to turn eastward in future attacks was based on their fear of what might happen if they did not strengthen their outer perimeter defenses.

As February 1942 drew to a close, it was obvious that the American–British–Dutch–Australian (ABDA) Supreme Command under British general Wavell had been badly beaten. Wavell turned the command of his remaining forces over to the Dutch and returned to India, from whence he had come a short while before. Those who remained had no illusions about stopping the Japanese.

Meanwhile, American fighter planes were on their way to Java. They had been placed aboard the tender *Langley*, and the thirty-two P–40s were ready to fight. The British *Seawitch* also had twenty-seven planes en route to the combat zone, but they were crated in her hold. Fifty-nine fighters could not do much at this stage, but it was four times as many as could be found in the islands.

Comdr. Robert McConnell of the *Langley* wanted to remain at sea until he could make a night entry into Tjilatjap, a port on the south coast of Java that served as a base for the ABDA fleet. He hoped thereby to escape detection by Japanese patrol planes. A glance at his orders changed his mind. "We've got to go in by day." He tapped the orders significantly. "The need is urgent."

Japanese airmen found them that morning. During the first two attacks the *Langley* evaded falling bombs. The third wave hit her severely and set her parked aircraft on fire.

"Push those planes over the side," the captain ordered.

It was too late. The fire gained such headway that the ship had to be abandoned. It was sunk later by the destroyer *Whipple*. It was a tragic end for the navy's first carrier. Originally a collier, she had been converted to a flattop and then, when she was too old for combat duty as a carrier, she ended up as a tender.

The *Seawitch* was more successful. She reached Tjilatjap on the 28th, and her crated planes were hastily put ashore. They were, however, of little use. Although he was an outstanding fighting sailor, Adm. Karel Doorman of the Royal Netherlands Navy could not stop the Japanese invasion. The precious P-40s were destroyed by the Dutch before the Japanese landed.

There had been countless displays of desperate energy and courage, but those two admirable qualities were not sufficient. What was needed was a large Allied surface fleet, backed up by fast carriers. At the moment, all the Allied forces could do was to retreat and rebuild their shattered commands.

Patrol planes had reported Japanese invasion fleets on their way to Java on the 25th of February. When the head of the ABDA strike force, Adm. C. E. L. Helfrich of the Royal Netherlands Navy, received orders to sink or scatter the enemy's convoys, he could only shrug helplessly and do his best. The Allied ships under Doorman were ordered to attack. They had been in the Java Sea for several days looking for an opportunity to engage the enemy. Doorman had only five of his original thirteen destroyers and no airplanes to protect his small fleet.

The Battle of the Java Sea was as violent as any surface battle ever waged. When it ended, only the American cruiser *Houston* and the Australian light cruiser *Perth* survived out of a fleet of eighteen warships. Shortly thereafter, after stopping to refuel, these ships were also destroyed, leaving not one survivor of the Battle of the Java Sea.

Allied commanders were stunned by the disaster. They immediately recalled all Allied warships to Australian waters, leaving only American submarines to harass the enemy.

Adm. Chuichi Nagumo.
*Official U.S. Navy
photograph*

Adm. Isoroku Yamamoto
in his 1943 portrait by Shu-
gaku Homma.
*Official U.S. Navy photo-
graph*

Warships succumb to fierce Japanese attack at Pearl Harbor.
Courtesy U.S. Navy

Fleet Adm. Ernest J. King.
Courtesy U.S. Navy

Fleet Adm. William F. Halsey, Jr.
Courtesy U.S. Navy

One of Doolittle's B–52s takes off for Japan from the carrier *Hornet*.
Courtesy U.S. Navy

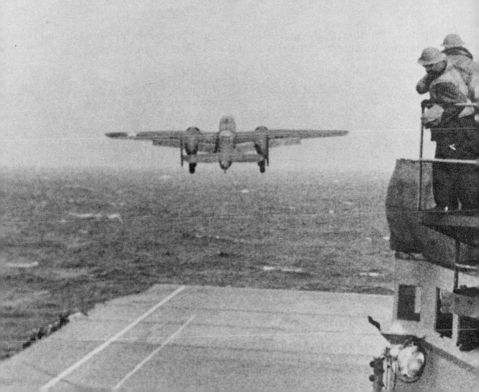

The *Lexington*'s fate is sealed during the Battle of the Coral Sea. Final explosion blasts aircraft from the deck. *Courtesy U.S. Navy*

Japanese bombers, attacking United States transports off Guadalcanal, run a gauntlet of antiaircraft fire. *Official U.S. Navy photograph*

Bomb and shell craters dot Guadalcanal's Henderson Field in August 1942.
Official U.S. Navy photograph

This Japanese-built Henderson Field structure became marine and navy air headquarters during 1942–43. *Official U.S. Navy photograph*

The *Enterprise* (foreground) and *Saratoga* in formation off Guadalcanal on December 19, 1942. Above them, an SBD dive-bomber.
Official U.S. Navy photograph

Comedian Joe E. Brown visits the Naval Air Station in Kodiak, Alaska, in early 1942. On right is Colonel Charles H. Corlett, who commanded the army garrison at the air station; Lt. Comdr. James S. Russell is at left.
Courtesy of Admiral James S. Russell

5

"HIT THE JAPS
AT EVERY OPPORTUNITY."

In Washington, at a meeting with the Combined Chiefs of Staff, Admiral King recommended that Great Britain assume responsibility for the further defense of Asia by forming a China–Burma–India Theater (CBI). He admitted that the American defense of the Philippines was coming to an end, and he recommended that the armed forces from Australia and New Zealand be assigned to Admiral Nimitz.

King met with President Roosevelt, presidential aide Harry Hopkins, and Gen. George C. Marshall on February 22. Following this conference, General MacArthur was ordered to withdraw from the Philippines and escape to Australia. King and Marshall painted a bleak picture of conditions in the Pacific, and both stressed the importance of maintaining a lifeline with Australia and New Zealand.

Out of this meeting came several important decisions. When King met with the Joint Chiefs on March 2 he read them a memorandum that he had prepared. "The general scheme or concept of operations is not only to protect the lines of communications with Australia but, in so doing, to set up 'strong points' from which a step-by-step general advance can be made through the New Hebrides, Solomons, and the Bismarck Archipelago."

The strategy that was to govern much of the later Pacific fighting began to emerge. King recommended that marines seize and occupy strong points in the southwest Pacific and advance in a northwesterly direction toward Japan through the New Hebrides, Solomons, and the Bismarck Archipelago. After each strong point was seized, he said, army troops should garrison it, thereby freeing marines for further conquests in an island-hopping campaign. Although a "Germany first" strategy had been approved by the Combined

Chiefs, King bluntly said that the Allies were getting licked in the Pacific, and he wanted to go on the offensive.

Marshall rebutted King's theories about priorities, saying that Germany was a far greater threat to the Allied powers than Japan and that a policy of containment in the Pacific should be followed. Once Germany was defeated, Marshall said, the United States could go all out to defeat Japan.

King insisted that the United States had no choice but to go on the offensive in the Pacific. He sought only two, possibly three, army divisions for garrison duty, but Marshall insisted adamantly that at this stage of the war they were not available and would not be for some time. The meeting of the Joint Chiefs ended with no decision about increasing the scale of Pacific operations.

Following the fall of Singapore, a depressed Prime Minister Churchill wrote President Roosevelt, "We have suffered the greatest disaster in our history." He made it clear that he expected even worse misfortunes to fall upon Great Britain's armed forces in Asia, saying, "It is not easy to assign limits to Japanese aggression." Roosevelt responded to the prime minister on March 9, admitting that the United States was in retreat in the Pacific and that the situation there was very grave.

News was bad throughout the Allied world. German armies were advancing victoriously on the Russian front and moving toward the Caucasus. Through crippling attacks on Alexandria harbor, German U-boats and Italian midget submarines had reduced the British Mediterranean fleet to a squadron of cruisers and destroyers. German submarines in the Atlantic Ocean and in the Caribbean were sinking merchant ships faster than they could be built. In the Middle East, Gen. Erwin Rommel had attacked the British army and almost destroyed it. And, in the Far East, the Japanese were closing in on the last American, British, and Dutch strongholds.

Relations between Admiral Stark as chief of naval operations and King as United States Fleet commander had deteriorated so badly that King talked to President Roosevelt about the frustrations caused by their overlapping responsibilities. He insisted that their relationship had to be clarified.

Roosevelt responded, "We'll take care of that."

The president was as good as his word and on March 12, King was named to both jobs. This was an astonishing development because it was the first time that the two jobs had been held by one man. Now King had total authority within the navy. As such, he and he alone reported directly to the president on all naval matters. Stark was sent to London as commander of United States Naval Forces in Europe and was removed from membership in the Joint Chiefs.

King now told Secretary of Navy Frank Knox that he had to have full authority to get the navy on the offensive. He reminded the secretary that he would ruthlessly eliminate those officers who did not measure up to demands of the times. He immediately selected a staff of brilliant men with whom he had previously worked and knew that he could depend upon. Next, he asked for command authority over the navy's bureaus, which had been independent for over a century. King lost this round because legislative action would have been required and Roosevelt refused to ask Congress for it. Roosevelt did promise to replace any bureau chief who caused King problems. No other chief of naval operations ever had the authority now vested in King, with supreme command of all operating units of the United States Navy. Most important, Roosevelt agreed that King would be directly responsible to him. Of course, as chief of naval operations, King would be under the nominal authority of Frank Knox as navy secretary. Once King had the president's ear, however, he never let anyone come between them.

Harry Hopkins wrote King a congratulatory note. "I can't tell you how pleased I was when the President told me of the action he was going to take about you. I think it is perfectly grand and I have a feeling it is going to be one of the most important things the President has done during the war. Great luck to you."

Roosevelt, more and more concerned about the disastrous events in the Pacific, turned for advice to King, who responded by pressing for an offensive in the Pacific, even though he acknowledged that such a move would preclude an invasion of Europe in 1942 and would reduce the American bomber offensive.

The president had been pressing for early action in Europe, but now he conceded that a 1942 invasion of the continent was not feasible—and certainly did not have Churchill's approval—so he found appealing King's plan to go on the offensive in the Far East. He gave his tacit approval, and the British voiced no opposition to turning over all operations in the Pacific to the Americans except for operations in India, Burma, and surrounding areas.

Now that MacArthur had safely returned to Australia, there was a great public outcry that he be appointed supreme commander in the Pacific. He also had General Marshall's strong backing, but King resisted such a move. He insisted that the United States Navy had been preparing to fight a Pacific war for twenty years and absolutely refused to subordinate the navy to an army commander. MacArthur did not understand sea power, he contended, and he would never agree to turn the Pacific Fleet over to him.

Actually, no top military commander in Washington wanted MacArthur as supreme commander. Roosevelt was privately opposed, but he was in a difficult position because MacArthur might end up as his strongest political adversary in the next general election. MacArthur, of course, believed that his background and experience entitled him to assume the role of supreme commander. He was also adamantly opposed to a subordinate role under Admiral Nimitz or any other navy officer. Some consideration was given to bringing MacArthur home as head of the defense department. Such a change at the top would require congressional approval, but because MacArthur had strong backers in Congress, receiving approval would not have been a problem. In the end, it was decided that MacArthur should stay in the Pacific and share command responsibilities with Nimitz.

General Marshall had supported MacArthur throughout the discussions, but he finally accepted King's plan for joint responsibilities and presented it to the Joint Chiefs on March 30. Agreement was reached that Nimitz and MacArthur would head independent commands and receive orders from their respective service chiefs. They would both report to the Joint Chiefs. Roosevelt approved the agreement the following day. Under terms of the compromise MacArthur would be responsible for the defense of Australia and its approaches through New Guinea and the Netherlands East Indies, and to the east, for defense of the territory between the Solomon Islands and New Hebrides. The navy under Nimitz would be responsible for all other operations. Later, the Philippines were added to MacArthur's sphere of influence. The plan had severe limitations because it did not provide for unity of command—one of General Marshall's treasured ideas. To his dismay, he had to accept a compromise that he knew would result in constant bickering.

King's persistence won, and now his plan became the basis for the entire Pacific strategy. MacArthur achieved more authority than he had before, but he was not happy about the divided command.

King wrote Roosevelt a memorandum about his plans for carrying the war to Japan, stressing again that the United States should not think only in defensive terms. He was concerned that the American people apparently did not comprehend the need for an offensive in the Pacific. He acknowledged that it was impossible to stop Japanese submarines from shelling coastal installations and cities or even of preventing their bombers from penetrating the western part of the nation. He reminded the president that it was the primary duty of the nation's armed forces to fight the Japanese in the Pacific and not build up unnecessary defense forces at home to ward off attacks that might never materialize. (Only one such attack did occur when a Japanese submarine shelled a refinery near Santa Barbara.) He concluded the memorandum by urging the president to use his best efforts to bring such fundamental premises about war strategy to the attention of the press and the American people.

This was what President Roosevelt wanted to hear. The memorandum fell on receptive ears.

In early January 1942, Adm. Chester W. Nimitz was named to command all navy, marine, and army ground and air units as commander in chief, Pacific Ocean Areas, while he retained his former position as commander in chief, Pacific Fleet. This latter job placed him in command of all naval forces in the Pacific Ocean Areas and in the years ahead, he never delegated any of this responsibility except for temporary assignment of some submarines and amphibious vehicles to MacArthur's command.

King gave Nimitz specific orders to prepare for major amphibious assaults in the Solomons, New Guinea, and the Bismarck Archipelago while maintaining the thin lifeline with the United States' allies down under. The words from King were clear and precise, "Hit the Japs at every opportunity."

Since March, Japanese naval aircraft had occupied bases at Lae and Salamaua on the northeast coast of New Guinea. By flying over the Owen Stanley Mountains, they were able to attack Allied bases. The Imperial government of Japan hoped that such attacks would force the Australian government to sue for peace. Buna was later added to the bases and destructive attacks were also made upon Port Moresby on the southern coast of New Guinea, which had a vital Allied base. Although these attacks caused serious destruction to port and airfield facilities, the garrisons stood firm.

If Port Moresby had fallen, Australia would have been wide open to Japanese assault. Cape York, the northernmost tip of the continent, is only 100 miles from the coast of New Guinea.

Aerial assaults failed to force surrender so the Japanese tried a land attack against Port Moresby although it is surrounded by some of the world's worst terrain. The Japanese again failed to dent Allied defenses.

An exasperated Prime Minister Tojo warned Australia on March 11 that it was virtually defenseless against Japan's invincible forces because of her sparse population. He cited Australia's vastness and her geographical position, which placed her at such a great distance from both the United States and Great Britain.

He followed up this warning the next day by speaking to the Japanese parliament in a special session. "Australia and New Zealand are now threatened directly by the might of the Imperial forces, and both of them should know that any resistance is futile. If the Australian government does not modify her present attitude, their continent will suffer the same fate as the Dutch East Indies."

The latter reference was particularly apt because it had just fallen to the victorious Japanese Army.

The Australian Prime Minister John Curtin warned the United States on March 13, "Australia is the last Allied bastion between the west coast of the United States and Japan. If she succumbs, the entire American continent will be wide open to invasion." He further emphasized that saving Australia would be like saving the west coast of the United States. If invaded, he said, Australians would adopt a scorched-earth policy and would fight to the last man.

The United States Joint Chiefs had no illusions about the danger to Australia. For the first time in her history, the very existence of Australia as a free nation was threatened because the Japanese had gained so many footholds on the islands of the South Pacific. Two months earlier, the Joint Chiefs had adopted a basic assumption that Australia was indispensable and that a line between the Aleutian Islands and New Caledonia had to be held at all costs. Limited numbers of men, planes, and ships had already been rushed to the South Pacific, but the two-front war posed problems of supply at this early stage and it would be some time before adequate men and equipment became available.

After General MacArthur reached Australia on March 17, a slow buildup began from his headquarters at Brisbane.

Admiral Nimitz at Pearl Harbor was finally able to organize a task force around the carrier *Lexington* with Vice-Adm. Wilson Brown in charge. While Halsey was raiding the Marshall and Gilbert islands, Brown's small force headed for the South Pacific.

The Joint Chiefs carefully reviewed available information and agreed that the Japanese would probably congregate their forces in the New Guinea–New Britain area. There they would have excellent harbors from which to launch operations south- and eastward.

Admiral King, in particular, was concerned that they might even move toward the Canal Zone. He did not rule out another strike at Pearl Harbor. "The Japanese might bypass Australia," he warned the Joint Chiefs. "If communications are cut between this country and the United States, Australia would quickly become impotent in the Pacific War."

After Brown's force arrived in the South Pacific, it was assigned to Vice-Adm. Herbert F. Leary, Australian and New Zealand (ANZAC) forces commander. The army, meanwhile, gathered whatever aviation squadrons were available and put them under a unified command.

Brown received permission to attack Rabaul as the first step of his offensive. This magnificent harbor on the northeastern tip of New Britain, the largest island in the Bismarck Archipelago, was an important Japanese assembly base. Brown knew that the risks in the operation were great because his task force would face opposition from Japanese warships in waters that were poorly charted. He had no illusions about halting the Japanese with his slim force, but he hoped that its actions would force the Japanese to change their plans, and whatever ships they could sink would subtract from Japan's total strength.

A joint operation, the plan called for the *Lexington*'s planes to strike Rabaul from the sea while heavy United States Army Air Force bombers under the Australian command approached from the south. Brown hoped that, if the attack was successful, he could order his surface ships to move in and bombard the Japanese anchorage.

The task force headed north into the Solomons and then passed Bougainville, the largest island. Watching intently for signs of Japanese air patrols or lurking submarines, the carrier, four cruisers, and ten destroyers proceeded cautiously through the narrow strait between New Britain and New Ireland.

Brown peered anxiously each day into the sun where Japanese bombers often hid, waiting for the right moment to catch them by surprise in a devastating attack.

The Japanese were spotted on February 20. The fighter patrol attacked a four-engine bomber and it was shot down. A second bomber flamed and plummeted into the sea, but the third headed away under full power.

Brown watched the fleeing bomber with dismay. He knew that this meant trouble because the Japanese would be alerted. Peering off in the direction of Rabaul, he saw tiny specks high above the horizon. The fighter patrol went into action, splashing eight out of nine Japanese twin-engine bombers.

Exultation aboard the ships was short-lived because another wave of nine bombers came down out of the sun. Admiral Brown's eyes searched the sky in vain for the combat patrol. Then a lone navy fighter tore into the formation. Lt. Edward H. "Butch" O'Hare, section leader of Squadron Three, had found himself separated from his teammates when he spotted the Japanese bombers. All alone he swept into the formation with guns blazing, closing at point-blank range until with incredible marksmanship he shot down five bombers with short bursts from his guns. A sixth escaped, but only barely, as it was riddled with O'Hare's gunfire. Brown watched the lone fighter with amazement, realizing that he was an eyewitness to what was probably the most daring pilot action of the war. The rest of the combat patrol hastened to assist, downing three more of the fleeing bombers.

Brown called air operations. "Find out who fought off that last Jap wave of bombers, and send him up."

O'Hare stood respectfully before the admiral a short while later, embarrassed by being singled out.

Brown shook his hand warmly. "Lieutenant, the *Lexington* owes her life to you."

O'Hare's face flushed, and he stammered a brief thanks. Brown quickly ordered that he be recommended for the Medal of Honor. In due course, it was approved, and O'Hare eventually found himself in the office of the president of the United States, where the nation's highest award was hung around his neck.

The strike against Rabaul was a failure as far as extensive damage to the harbor and installations was concerned. The *Lexington* lost only two planes and one pilot, Ens. John W. Wilson. The Japanese air losses were severe, including two four-engine flying boats and sixteen twin-engine bombers.

The Rabaul attack did not faze the Japanese. Their advance forces encompassed New Britain and New Ireland, and landings were made on Bougainville. Japanese bombers were free to bomb all ports of New Guinea, making them untenable for any kind of Allied operations.

The *Yorktown*, Rear Admiral Fletcher's flagship, arrived to augment Brown's force. He now had two carriers, eight heavy cruisers, and fourteen destroyers. In a consultation with his staff, Brown said, "The times demand bold action. We must risk our reserves even though we face far superior forces. We plan to attack Lae and Salamaua and hope to surprise the Japs who are reported to be landing there. Here is our plan. Our two carriers will launch from the Australian side of the island, overfly the Owen Stanley Mountains, and attack the Japanese from the rear."

There were exclamations of surprise at such a bold strike with limited forces.

"March 10 is the day," he said in dismissal.

Conferences were held daily to plan for the delicate operation, whose timing was all-important. Shortly before the day of attack, Vice-Admiral Brown was appalled to learn that four cruisers and four destroyers would be detached from his task force to convoy troopships from the United States. Fully appreciative of the need to protect vital troopships, he was also aware that the loss of ships at this critical time could have disastrous consequences for his own operations.

Little seemed to be known about the interior of New Guinea, and the seas around the island were almost uncharted. Brown eventually learned of a pass in the mountains that was only 7,500 feet high. His intelligence officer said, "It's an air link between Salamaua and the Gulf of Papua. We've talked with pilots who've flown it." Brown nodded. "I'll send Commander Ault ahead to locate the pass and fly figure-eights around it. That way, he can guide the rest through the mountains."

Lexington Air Group Comdr. William B. Ault was first off. He was followed by a strong force carrying forty-eight tons of bombs and thirteen torpedoes.

Ault found the pass and made wide, sweeping figure-eights around it. For a time, he thought that the force might have missed him, but then he noticed planes heading directly for him. He counted them eagerly—103 in formation. They poured through the mountain slot and dove steeply at the target. They were thrilled to see two cruisers and four destroyers in the Lae–Salamaua bight, standing by for protection while five transports and two cargo ships unloaded.

The Japanese were caught by surprise when the *Lexington* group struck. The first bombs were dropped even before the enemy manned their guns. Wave after wave of bombers came through the slot while fighters sought vainly for enemy opposition. A single float biplane rose in a futile challenge but was easily destroyed.

The raid was a success, but Ens. John P. Johnson and his gunner, J. B. Jewell, were killed. Five transports and cargo ships were sunk, and a light cruiser and a destroyer also went down. Hits were scored on other ships and on the airfield, buildings and antiaircraft defenses were smothered with bombs.

As the planes headed back to their carriers, a report was received that a heavy enemy task force was only 25 miles away, but they were over the mountains before Japanese carrier planes could attack.

Ault was the first to return. He flew up the carrier's stern in a controlled power stall, watching the landing signal officer. When the LSO signaled that he was "in the groove" Ault cut the engine, and the SBD slammed down on the deck. He felt the arresting gear seize the plane and bring it to an abrupt stop while the tires squealed and the sturdy plane took its punishment with accustomed ease.

Ault hopped out of the plane and watched his men return. Although he had seen it hundreds of times, he still got a thrill from watching the landing signal officer directing the pilots to safe landings. The LSO reminded Ault of an orchestra conductor as each of his paddles gave the approaching pilot precise instructions.

He watched a TBD Devastator come in. The LSO's paddles warned that he was too low. The engine broke into a louder roar as the pilot lifted the nose higher while reaching for the deck. The approach now looked good to Ault, and the LSO signaled the pilot to cut his engine and land.

The Japanese were too firmly entrenched to let this raid alter their plans appreciably, but it did delay their operations against Port Moresby.

Although the Japanese did not know it at the time, the United States Navy had agreed to provide its newest carrier, the *Hornet*, as a floating air base for sixteen land-based B–25 medium bombers for a strike at Japan. After dropping their bombs, the crews would continue westward to land at Nationalist-held bases in China.

In a spectacular move to bring the war to the Japanese people, Lt. Col. James Doolittle had handpicked a group of pilots and crews to train for a specific and unusual mission. Planes the size of the B–25 had never taken off in such a limited space as a carrier deck. After weeks of training, particularly in extremely short takeoffs, Doolittle was ready.

Lt. Henry L. Miller was among those who trained Doolittle's men. During the preliminary phase, army crews learned navy procedures. They progressed to flying under standard carrier procedures with ever higher loads until they achieved the maximum takeoff weight for the mission.

Initially, fifteen days were allotted for training the Army Air Force pilots at Eglin Field in Florida. Fog reduced the number to ten and on March 24, the B–25s took off for California with Miller flying with Doolittle. The planes were taken to the army depot at Sacramento for final checks. On the last two days of March, Miller gave the army pilots refresher courses and on April 1 they flew to Alameda Naval Air Station and all sixteen planes were loaded on board the carrier with cranes. The *Hornet*, with two cruisers, four destroyers, and a fleet oiler, left San Francisco and headed for Japan.

Miller was scheduled to take off in one of the B–25s after the *Hornet* was 100 miles from San Francisco. According to plans, he would fly the bomber to the army at Columbia, South Carolina, and return to his station at Pensacola. His takeoff was designed to reassure the army pilots that a B–25 could easily take off from a carrier.

Miller and Doolittle looked out over the flight deck when the ship was 100 miles out. "This deck sure looks small to me," Doolittle said.

Miller turned to him. "Colonel, this is a breeze. I'll have four hundred ninety-five feet for takeoff, and your people have been taught to take off in two hundred fifty and three hundred feet in a forty-knot wind." He then climbed into the B–25's cockpit with his copilot. He pointed to a distant object. "Colonel, do you see where that tool kit is way up the deck by the bow? That's where I used to take off in fighters."

Doolittle looked at the tool kit. "Hank, what's the word that you use in the navy for 'bulloney'?"

Miller did not take off. Capt. Marc A. Mitscher, the *Hornet*'s commanding officer, told him he would be unable to turn up 40 knots of wind for his takeoff. Miller shrugged, saying that he would not need it and telling him of his conversation with Doolittle. Mitscher asked, "Miller, did you bring along an extra pair of pants?" He replied that all his personal gear was aboard the B–25 and that he expected to fly to Columbia, South Carolina.

Mitscher shook his head. "We will take all sixteen planes."

Miller knew that it was useless to argue with Mitscher, but he had hoped to demonstrate to Doolittle and his pilots how easy it was to fly a B–25 from the *Hornet*. He was also concerned that his original orders to help train Doolittle's men ran out on March 15, and here he was headed halfway around the world with only a phone call to back up his excuse for being on the *Hornet*.

He faced Mitscher. "Captain, would you please drop me off at the next mail buoy?" he said. "I will be traveling halfway around the world via a telephone call, and I don't want to report back to Pensacola as a lieutenant, junior grade."

He had always hoped that he could make the flight, but Doolittle had extra trained crews and he did not have a chance.

The operation was a joint army–navy endeavor, and the *Hornet* promised to take Doolittle's raiders to within a few hundred miles of Japan's coast to launch the surprise attack upon Tokyo. Since Bataan's surrender on April 9, the United States had needed a morale booster, and Doolittle and his crews had promised to give it to them.

Vice-Admiral Halsey was responsible for the operation. Inasmuch as the B-25 crowded deck of the *Hornet* made that carrier defenseless if any air attack came, he had been given the *Enterprise* task force as an air screen.

On April 18, the task force still was a long way from the agreed-upon launch point of 700 miles east of Japan on a direct line with Tokyo Bay originally selected for Doolittle's fliers. A Japanese patrol ship spotted them, and Halsey believed that their existence would be broadcast immediately to Tokyo. The raid had to be canceled or altered completely. After a conference, Doolittle and Halsey decided to launch at once, even though it was doubtful that all of the planes would have enough fuel at this range to reach their distant bases in Nationalist China. The vital task force could not be sacrificed for the squadron of bombers.

The planes were launched that day, and Halsey ordered the task force to reverse course and head east at high speed.

Halsey broke radio silence. "To Colonel Doolittle and his gallant command, good luck and God bless you. Halsey."

Miller believed, like most of the others, that Doolittle and his men did not stand a chance of coming back.

Word came first from a Japanese radio station. At some time between five and ten minutes after one, Tokyo Radio suddenly went off the air. When it started to broadcast again an excited announcer said that enemy planes had bombed the city. Tokyo Radio went dead again, and members of the task force breathed a sigh of relief. The planes had at least got there.

The raid brought new hope to a despair-ridden United States, though the bombing itself caused only limited damage. The infuriated Japanese military establishment, which had proclaimed that no American bomber would ever appear over their main islands, had some difficulty explaining the raid to their people.

China's Generalissimo Chiang Kai-shek had been opposed to the Doolittle raid because the bombers would have to land at Nationalist Chinese bases and he expected Japanese retaliation. Because they ran out of fuel, the fliers actually landed short of Chinese bases, many in territory occupied by Japanese troops. Despite their landing behind Japanese lines, the fliers managed to reach unoccupied China with the aid of the people of East China. The Chinese paid a bitter price for offering assistance. The Japanese army went on the offensive and without mercy destroyed cities and villages that had assisted the fliers to escape. Quite possibly a quarter of a million Chinese civilians were killed in retaliation.

A high price was paid for the gallantry of Doolittle's raiders, and the deaths of thousands of Chinese civilians can never be considered worth the price of the raid's limited propaganda value. Many experts claim, however, that the Doolittle raid had a great impact on the future actions of the Japanese. Admiral Yamamoto had to go hat-in-hand to the emperor and apologize because the homeland had been bombed by the Americans. There are some who say, with good reason, that the Doolittle raid even influenced the later, fateful decision to attack Midway.

6

THE BATTLE OF
THE CORAL SEA

The fall of Singapore forced remnants of Great Britain's Eastern Fleet to seek sanctuary in Ceylon. In March, Adm. Sir James Somerville, an outspoken officer but a man with a keen sense of humor, took command of the fleet. When he first saw his ships at sea, he signaled their captains, "So this is the Eastern Fleet? Well, never mind. There's many a good tune played on an old fiddle."

Privately, he was appalled by the few ships available to his new command. There were five battleships, but four of them had seen service in World War I; his three carriers included the *Hermes*, which was too outmoded to be of much use, and the *Formidable* and *Indomitable*, whose crews lacked operational experience. In addition, his fleet had seven cruisers and fourteen destroyers.

It did not take Somerville long to improve combat readiness, and he used his fleet to good advantage by countering the Japanese advance in Burma. On March 31, he divided his Eastern Fleet into two tactical units, personally taking command of fast Force *A* from the battleship *Warspite*. He turned the slower force *B* over to Vice-Adm. Sir Algernon Willis.

A Japanese raiding force made its appearance in the Indian Ocean, and Somerville decided to engage it with Force *A* by attacking at night with torpedoes from the *Indomitable*'s Albacore aircraft. The two fleets never made contact, which was fortunate for Admiral Somerville because the Japanese fleet under Vice-Admiral Nagumo included five of the six carriers that had been used in the Pearl Harbor attack, plus four large battleships with their accompanying cruisers and destroyers. If they had met, the unequal contest would have ended in disaster for the British.

Nagumo's carrier aircraft hit Colombo, a naval base on Ceylon's southwestern coast, on Easter Sunday, April 5. Dive-bombers also sank the cruisers *Cornwall* and *Dorsetshire* after they had been detached from the main Eastern Fleet. Four days later, the carrier *Hermes*, the destroyer *Vampire*, the Corvette *Hollyhock*, and two tankers were sunk by the experienced Japanese pilots.

With such overwhelming forces arrayed against him, Somerville retired his slow force to Mombasa and sent the fast force to Bombay. His fleet soon lost the remainder of its major ships to other fronts, and its activities were restricted for the next year and a half to escort duty for Indian Ocean convoys.

Yamamoto's employment of large aircraft carriers as the prime offensive weapons for a new type of war at sea had cost the Americans and British dearly. It appeared now to Allied leaders that nothing could stop the Japanese from completing their conquest of the South Pacific and then occupying Australia. Before Japanese troops could occupy Port Moresby and the remainder of New Guinea, however, the Australian–American lifeline had to be cut.

The Coral Sea, one of the world's most beautiful bodies of water, is seldom plagued by typhoons, and throughout most of the year, southeast trade winds create a balmy atmosphere. New Caledonia, the New Hebrides, and the Louisiade Archipelago are covered by almost impenetrable jungles, but the coral shores of their eastern and northern coasts are spectacular. Although it seemed an unlikely setting for a major battle, the Coral Sea's strategic value was well known to commanders on both sides. In contrast, the nearby Bismarck Sea, dominated by Japan since the earliest days of the war from a key base at Rabaul in New Guinea, has forbidding islands of lava and volcanic ash.

Admiral Yamamoto had been making long-range plans since the first of the year for conquest in the South Pacific. Now he received approval for their execution. To establish a naval air base for control of the northern part of the Coral Sea, he ordered the occupation of Tulagi in the southern Solomon Islands. After this initial step, he set in motion plans to land an invasion force at Port Moresby on the southeastern coast of New Guinea. Once control was established there, he told his staff, the northern part of Australia could be attacked by air.

Long before the start of hostilities, Yamamoto envisioned a great battle between the Imperial Fleet and the United States Navy's Pacific Fleet. He knew a decisive battle had to be fought and hoped for a great naval victory; otherwise, Japan had no hope of winning a war with the United States. He would therefore attack the island of Midway—with a diversionary move simultaneously against the Aleutians—to force the American navy into a decisive confrontation.

Beyond those two plans was a decision to overrun the Fiji Islands and Samoa, thereby cutting the lifeline between Australia and the United States.

Vice-Adm. Shigeyoshi Inouye had his Fourth Fleet Headquarters at Rabaul. He was well pleased with Japan's Greater East Asia War. He put down his latest intelligence reports and gazed intently at the crowded harbor. It seemed impossible that the armed forces of Japan had acquired 12½ million square miles of new territory in only five months of war—a momentum that the Americans would surely find it impossible to stop with their depleted forces. Further advances, particularly to gain mastery of the air over the Coral Sea, were ordered.

Inouye was not aware, however, that Rear Adm. Frank J. Fletcher's forces, totaling eleven ships, was now south of the Solomons and would shortly be augmented by another task force under Rear Adm. Aubrey W. Fitch. They joined forces at 6:30 A.M. on May 1, as the Japanese were occupying Florida Island in the Solomons and landing at Tulagi, and sailed north at high speed. By the morning of May 4, they were 100 miles southwest of Guadalcanal. Despite showers and scattered squalls, the *Yorktown* prepared to launch her attack groups. During three separate attacks against Tulagi Harbor, they sank a Japanese destroyer and a cargo ship. Five seaplanes and many smaller aircraft were also destroyed.

While Fletcher's Task Force Seventeen, built around the *Yorktown,* headed south for a rendezvous, the word went out to all ships. "Attack and reattack! Seek out the enemy. Destroy him!"

Code-room operators on Fletcher's flagship paused in their work when a message came through in the clear. It was in English, transmitted from the Philippines to Pearl Harbor but intercepted by all ships at sea. "Going off the air now. Goodbye and good luck. Callaghan and McCoy." The Philippines had fallen, and all American forces had capitulated to the Japanese. The operators had just heard the last broadcast from the navy transmitter at Corregidor.

Admiral Fletcher had received a decoded report on April 17 stating that Japanese troopships and the light carrier *Shoho* had left Rabaul and would reach an unknown objective on May 3. He also learned that two large carriers would leave Truk in the Caroline

Islands and head for the Coral Sea. These were the *Shokaku* and *Zuikaku* of the Fifth Imperial Carrier Division.

At Pearl Harbor, Nimitz believed that the Japanese destination was Port Moresby, and General MacArthur agreed because he considered the New Guinea base the key to the entire Allied defense system. He knew that when the Allies took the offensive, Port Moresby was the base from which such a countermove would have to start.

In mid-April, Nimitz and MacArthur were so alarmed by the threat to Port Moresby that there was no argument when the general insisted upon developing it into a major base. MacArthur had only two hundred Army Air Forces planes at his disposal, and their pilots were inexperienced. Reliance had to be placed on the few carrier planes available at sea.

For the first time, the problem of overlapping responsibilities had to be taken into account. Theoretically, under guidelines set down by the Combined Chiefs, this area was MacArthur's territory. It was agreed, however, that responsibility should be assigned to Nimitz because Port Moresby would have to be defended by sea power.

Fletcher was chosen to lead the forces in defense of Port Moresby. Unfortunately, his carrier strength was minimal. The *Saratoga* was at Puget Sound in the state of Washington for repairs, while the *Enterprise* and *Hornet* were still en route from Japanese waters after having launched Doolittle's raiders. Only the *Lexington* and *Yorktown* were available, and the latter was too far away to be of immediate assistance. There were no battleships in Fletcher's fleet, and only a few cruisers and destroyers.

The *Lexington* was available after it was hurriedly prepared for the trip to the South Pacific, leaving Pearl Harbor on April 16 with escorts under Rear Adm. Aubrey W. Fitch. The latter had relieved Vice-Adm. Wilson Brown in early April.

Brown was removed after having made only one South Pacific raid in fifty-four days. He had told Nimitz that raiding fortified Japanese bases was too risky for carriers, particularly in an area where seas were poorly charted. Nimitz accepted this excuse, but King did not, accusing Brown of lack of aggressiveness and demanding his removal. Fitch was not only younger than Brown, but far more experienced in carriers. (Brown was not an aviator, but he was an excellent organizer so he was given command of the new Amphibious Force at San Diego.)

Fletcher's Task Force Seventeen was built around the *Yorktown*, which was at Nouméa under Capt. Elliott Buckmaster.

A third force of three cruisers, the H.M.A.S. *Australia*, H.M.A.S.

Hobart, and U.S.S. *Chicago*, plus several destroyers, was called Task Force Forty-four and was commanded by British Rear Adm. John G. Crace.

Nimitz, although aware of the Japanese timetable because his cryptographers had broken the Japanese code, became more and more anxious, and Fletcher was ordered to proceed to Tangatabu to replenish his ships and prepare to meet the Japanese on April 14. Nimitz further ordered Fitch to join Fletcher's group on May 1 at a rendezvous 250 miles southwest of Espiritu Santo in the New Hebrides, and Crace was ordered to enter the Coral Sea on May 4, where he would be reinforced by another American heavy cruiser and a destroyer. Fletcher was given command of all forces.

Halsey wired Nimitz that the *Hornet* and *Enterprise* would arrive at Pearl Harbor on April 25 and would leave there within five days. He said that he expected to arrive in the Coral Sea on May 15 after traveling 3,500 miles. Nimitz knew his South Pacific forces were too thin, but there was nothing he could do about it. Halsey's carriers would be helpful if the Japanese delayed their invasion plans. He sent word to King in Washington on April 29 that Fletcher had been ordered to intercept the Japanese and do everything in his power to keep the lifeline open between the United States and Australia.

Meanwhile, it became apparent to the Australian cabinet that Tulagi's tiny garrison had no chance of warding off a full-scale Japanese assault. It was agreed to evacuate that island on May 1.

All commanders were advised on May 3 by MacArthur's headquarters that enemy transports were unloading troops and equipment at Tulagi, with Japanese warships standing by. The landings were unopposed, and the Japanese immediately set up a seaplane base.

Bad weather throughout the area prevented Fletcher from attacking the new Japanese base at Tulagi immediately. He still had only the *Yorktown*; the *Lexington* had not yet joined his task force. Fletcher had to decide whether to divide his command for the attack on Tulagi. He was concerned that the seaplane base there would soon be sending out patrols to locate his task force. He decided to delay the original plans to attack Tulagi—but he forgot to tell Fitch. He sent the tanker *Neosho* with the destroyer *Russell* to rendezvous near Willis Island at 8:00 A.M. on May 4. A new rendezvous was now set for all his forces to meet at dawn on May 5, 300 miles south of Guadalcanal.

Meanwhile, the *Yorktown* was headed at high speed direct to Tulagi despite bad weather.

When the *Neosho* and *Russell* rejoined the *Lexington* group and Crace's ships from the Royal Navy, Fitch finally learned of Fletcher's change of plans. Unfortunately, they placed the *Lexington* 250 miles away, so it could not possibly support Fletcher.

Fitch reduced the speed of his ships while Crace waited for Fletcher to return so that he could retrieve the American cruiser *Chicago* and reform his Task Force Forty-four.

After the Japanese landed troops and supplies at Tulagi, the transports were withdrawn, along with the covering force of warships. They headed for Bougainville while only two destroyers and auxiliary ships remained at Tulagi. The Port Moresby landing force from Rabaul had orders to arrive on the night of May 4.

The *Yorktown* was in position and launched her bombers and fighters against Tulagi before sunrise. Returning pilots made highly inflated claims; in fact, only minor damage was done to a Japanese destroyer and two minesweepers.

Fletcher broke off the attacks when an army bomber reported that Rear Adm. Arimoto Goto's force was patrolling the area with an aircraft carrier and two cruisers.

Nimitz was apprised of Fletcher's action and after he received more accurate reports of the results of the raid against Tulagi, he was deeply disappointed. He told Fletcher that the operation showed that more crew training was needed.

Rear Adm. Kuninori Marushige and Goto withdrew their forces to the north while a strike force under Vice-Adm. Takeo Takagi was ordered to the area, leaving Truk on April 20. Takagi had two large carriers and supporting warships, which he intended to use should the Americans offer any opposition at sea. He did not learn of the Tulagi attack until late on May 4 because of poor radio communication with Rabaul.

After refueling at North Bougainville, Takagi's Port Moresby invasion force headed south at high speed, reaching the northern tip of Malaita Island in the Solomons by midnight without being spotted by the Americans.

At 8:15 A.M. on May 5, the two American task groups joined forces. Fitch's and Crace's groups now headed from their waiting areas in the south for the rendezvous with Fletcher.

The *Yorktown*'s radar spotted unidentified aircraft at 11:00 A.M. The carrier was in the middle of a weather front so a Wildcat fighter, unable to find the enemy planes visually, was directed to the spot by radar. After the pilot was told that he was in the vicinity of the enemy planes, he saw a four-engine Kawanishi H6K seaplane.

He attacked and, on the second pass, shot the large airplane down in flames. It was feared at the time that the Japanese pilot had radioed the attack to his superiors, but apparently he did not have time.

When the search plane failed to report, Vice-Adm. Shigeyoshi Inouye, who commanded the Fourth Imperial Fleet, assumed that it had been shot down, although he had no idea where. He ordered his carriers to bomb Port Moresby prior to the landing of troops.

The huge weather front, covering about 300 miles, hid the American ships for the time being. When the three task groups cruised southeast and emerged into the Coral Sea, however, they left the weather front behind. Fletcher ordered a northwest heading so that his ships could take up positions to bar the Japanese from entering the Coral Sea through the Jomard Passage.

The Japanese invasion fleet, with Marushige's supporting warships, now was en route to the Louisiade Archipelago. Goto's covering force had refueled south of Bougainville while Takagi's strike force headed west after passing east of the Solomon Islands toward the Coral Sea.

Throughout May 5, MacArthur and Nimitz continued to send Fletcher messages that the Japanese apparently were headed for Port Moresby. Reports conflicted because pilots of the few army patrol planes available for searching the area were not trained to analyze ship movements. Actually, they had done a surprisingly good job of keeping MacArthur's headquarters informed, but they were spread too thin.

Fletcher formed a single naval task force with all available ships in the area on May 6 because he expected action at any moment. It was soon apparent that operational control would become a problem so he decided to give Fitch responsibility for air operations but for some unexplained reason again neglected to tell him.

The Japanese covering force under Goto was on a southwest heading from Bougainville by 8:30 A.M. on May 6, while Takagi's strike force was west of Rennell Island, northwest of Fletcher's fleet. At 9:30 A.M., Takagi headed due south to seek the Americans and engage them before they could attack his invasion forces. He had miscalculated, thinking that the Americans were farther west than they were and that they would retreat eastward if they decided not to engage his superior forces. If they did, Takagi reasoned, they would run into Goto's covering force, which was positioned as the other half of a pincer movement.

Fletcher was convinced that the Japanese were set to invade Port

Moresby even though his search planes had not found the Japanese fleet. Later, it was learned that some of Fletcher's scout planes had flown within a few miles of Takagi's fleet but had turned back without spotting it because of fuel shortage.

Takagi never did send out scout planes to locate the American ships, an action that is incredible under the circumstances. Fletcher's ships were finally located at 11:00 A.M. by a Japanese reconnaissance seaplane from Rabaul, but Takagi did not learn of the precise location of Fletcher's fleet until the next day! The typically poor Japanese communications system thus gave the Americans an edge in the coming battle. If Takagi had learned of the American position promptly, he could have attacked Fletcher's ships while they were refueling. This would have been a catastrophe for the Americans and might have drastically changed the results of the coming battle.

Four Army Air Forces B–17s of the 19th Group spotted the carrier *Shoho* at 10:30 A.M. They immediately attacked 60 miles south of Bougainville but were driven off by Japanese fighters. MacArthur ordered the word flashed immediately to Fletcher.

More reports started to come in, and the Japanese also began receiving intelligence. At 1 P.M., one of their reconnaissance aircraft saw an American naval convoy south of Rabaul on a southwest heading.

At Rabaul, Inouye knew that two of his forces had been discovered by the Americans, but Takagi was kept in the dark until the following day. Inouye knew that a large American naval force was in the Coral Sea, and he expected air attacks the following day. At 3:20 P.M., however, he ordered the invasion of Port Moresby to proceed.

About the same time, Fletcher learned that three Japanese carriers were south of the Solomons, evidently supporting an invasion of Port Moresby. According to other reports, the Japanese were also preparing to establish a seaplane base on an island in the Louisiade Archipelago. He now learned that a landing force was scheduled to pass through the Jomard Passage on May 7 and that the attack would commence the next day.

Takagi, who had neither seen nor heard reports of the whereabouts of the Americans, now turned back to refuel. At that moment, the Japanese fleet was only 70 miles from Fletcher's ships, and neither commander knew it.

Fletcher took up a position southeast of Port Moresby from which his planes could easily reach the invasion area. During refueling, his ships were cruising away from the Japanese. Then he ordered a northwest heading so that his planes could take off at dawn on May 7.

Meanwhile, following refueling, the empty tanker *Neosho* and the destroyer *Sims* turned south toward a predetermined rendezvous.

With tension mounting on both sides throughout the afternoon of May 6, opposing forces jockeyed for position, each still not knowing where the other force was. Takagi's strike force now had the benefit of heavy cloud cover—the same cover that had earlier protected the Americans. That afternoon American planes actually flew *over* his fleet but failed to see it because of the clouds.

The Japanese strike force turned north at midnight to refuel while the invasion fleet approached the island of Misima at the northern end of the Jomard Passage. Goto's covering group moved into position northeast of the island of Deboyne to protect the fleet's left flank from attack. With it, the light carrier *Shoho* was scheduled to launch its planes at dawn. Meanwhile, Fletcher's task force was moving into position near the southeast tip of New Guinea, 310 miles southeast of Deboyne.

Rear Adm. Chuichi Hara, in charge of Takagi's carriers, talked his strike force commander into stopping the refueling. He urged them to head south immediately, suspecting that an American fleet was in the area and arguing that it had to be destroyed before the carriers moved to support the Port Moresby landing force. Takagi agreed.

Hara had misgivings on the morning of May 7 when still no Americans could be located and felt somewhat vindicated when a Japanese scout plane reported an American carrier and a cruiser far to the east at 7:36 A.M. He had no way of knowing that the "task force" that the Japanese pilot had seen was actually the tanker *Neosho* and the destroyer *Sims*.

Hara set off in hot pursuit while another scout plane took off to track the two American ships. Meanwhile, pilots on the *Shokaku*, or "Flying Heron," and the *Zuikaku*, or "Joyous Heron," prepared for takeoff.

Rabaul had received a more accurate scouting report: An enemy formation, including a carrier and ten other ships, was only 200 miles south of the cruiser *Kinugasa*, and 280 miles northwest of Takagi's last known position. This intelligence from Rabaul was late in being relayed to Takagi. When it did arrive, his planes were off on the search for the ships reported earlier.

Comdr. Kakuichi Takahashi did find the *Neosho* and *Sims* at 9:35 A.M. on May 7 and ordered an immediate attack. The first two waves of planes were unsuccessful, but the third broke the *Sims* in half and sank her. The *Neosho* went down shortly thereafter. These sinkings caused a large loss of life, but they gave Fletcher time to prepare for the coming battle. As early as three hours before, he had positioned his fleet 115 miles south of Rossel Island, the easternmost point of the Louisiade Archipelago.

Fletcher was tempted to seek out the Japanese strike force and the covering force with its carriers, but his departure would leave Port Moresby wide open to attack. His orders were specific. He should defend Port Moresby.

He had decided earlier, however, to split his force at 6:45 A.M. He ordered Task Force Forty-four under British Rear Adm. J. G. Crace to continue on a westerly heading and block the southern exit of the Jomard Passage. With the remainder of his task force, he sought out the Japanese carriers.

Fletcher was taking a calculated risk that could easily end in disaster because the splitting of his fleet reduced the number of antiaircraft batteries available for the defense of his carriers. He was convinced that his action was necessary, however, because he believed that he would be attacking the bulk of the Japanese forces.

It was not until 8:10 A.M. that Takagi learned that Fletcher had split his forces. A scout plane had spotted Crace's Task Force Forty-four and reported the news immediately to all Japanese commanders. Crace was correct in his assumption that the airplanes came from the new Japanese base in the Louisiades. He remained on course, however, and as he neared his position close to the southern exit of the Jomard Passage, he saw a number of Japanese planes.

Adm. Kenzo Yamada, a commander of the Twenty-fifth Air Fleet at Rabaul, had been waiting for at least one American carrier to be reported in the Coral Sea before ordering his land-based air fleet into action. Report of Task Force Forty-four, which he believed might frustrate the landings at Port Moresby, changed his mind. He ordered bombers at Rabaul and Buna into the air.

Crace soon saw waves of Japanese bombers heading for his task force. All around him antiaircraft batteries roared into action and before his disbelieving eyes, the high-level bombers dropped their bombs and fled! Then, though torpedo bombers pressed their attacks, all his ships avoided their torpedoes. High-level bombers from Rabaul again approached the task force; still, not one bomb struck an American ship.

Crace and his men were justifiably furious when American B–26 Marauders from the air force based at Townsville, Australia, then dropped bombs on them. Fortunately, their accuracy that day was no better than that of the Japanese pilots, and no ships were hit. Crace ordered a protest radioed immediately to General MacArthur.

Crace's Task Force Forty-four had a decisive impact on the coming battle, assisting greatly the Allied cause. By blocking the Jomard Passage, it drew most of the Japanese air attacks away from Fletcher's ships.

Despite their failure to hit even one of Crace's ships, the Japanese fliers reported a brilliant victory when they returned to their bases. Japanese commanders tabulated reports that a battleship and a cruiser were sunk and that their pilots had struck a devastating blow against the Americans. As a result, no additional raids were authorized.

At dawn on May 7, Fletcher's scouts searched to the north for the Japanese ships. At approximately the same time, four scouts from the *Shoho* were also looking for the Americans. Fletcher's ships remained hidden because of cloud cover while riding high seas in a strong southeast trade wind. With each passing hour, Fletcher became more concerned that he had failed to establish contact with the enemy. He was relieved when he received a coded message that read, "Two aircraft carriers and four heavy cruisers ten degrees, three minutes north; one hundred fifty-two degrees, twenty-seven minutes east." A quick glance at the map showed him that the Japanese were a short distance north of the island of Misima, 225 miles northwest of Fletcher's force.

Fletcher and his staff agreed that this must be the strike force. Once the range was reduced, Fletcher ordered a change of course to take advantage of the southeast wind and then ordered bombers off the *Lexington* at 9:25 A.M. Once they were launched in dense cloud cover, he ordered a return to a northerly course.

When his reconnaissance planes returned, it quickly became apparent that a serious error had been made in the visual identification of the Japanese ships. Fletcher realized that the message should have read, not four cruisers, but two cruisers and two *destroyers*— and *no* aircraft carriers. He knew that this force must be neither Takagi's nor Goto's but that of Marushige's supporting warships for the Port Moresby invasion. The huge aerial armada that he had dispatched certainly was not needed against four such ships, and Fletcher was distressed by the error, so similar to the Japanese error in dispatching most of their airplanes to attack the *Neosho* and *Sims*.

Fletcher could not call back his airmen by radio. To do so would reveal his position. He hoped that the main Japanese fleet would be spotted while they were out. Unfortunately, a Japanese seaplane had been shot down at 8:20 A.M., and the pilot had managed to report the position of Fletcher's forces. Admiral Goto immediately ordered aircraft from the *Shoho* to prepare for launching. The advantage now rested with the Japanese.

At Rabaul, Inouye, apprised of Crace's position at the southern end of the Jomard Passage and fearful that his Port Moresby landing force would be exposed to full-scale attack, ordered the landing force to reverse course temporarily. Their commander was told to position his ships north of the passage and not to proceed with the attack on Port Moresby until the coming sea battle was over.

Fletcher's decision to divide his forces was now working in the way he had hoped although he did not know about the change in Japanese plans. Inouye's intelligence of the situation was poor; his decision to reverse the course of the landing force was taken with insufficient knowledge. Incredibly, he had not even heard the inflated reports about the American battleships and cruisers supposedly sunk by Japanese land-based aircraft. It would not have mattered, but he was kept in the dark about true events in the Coral Sea.

Air Group Commander William B. Ault had taken off first at 9:25 A.M., with the rest of the *Lexington*'s planes right behind him, in response to the false report about location of the Japanese carriers. The *Yorktown* group followed. They had been briefed that the enemy was approximately 160 miles away, and ninety-two planes rode in vain through a rough weather front. They listened for radio reports from the scouts but could not find the Japanese carriers, only two heavy cruisers and two light cruisers.

Comdr. W. L. Hamilton, in charge of the VB–2 flight from the *Lexington*, flew over the island of Tagula at 10:15 A.M. and headed north. At 10:22 A.M., he spotted a large naval force and a carrier. Although Hamilton did not know it, this was the *Shoho*, attached to Goto's force. He immediately radioed the news and prepared to make his dive.

Ault, listening to his radio, heard another report from an Australian base that reconnaissance planes had spotted a carrier 30 miles from the cruisers. He ordered his two section leaders to change course, and seven minutes later they found the enemy north of Misimi Island.

The Japanese ships twisted violently on the ocean's surface, and two fighters took off from the *Shoho* as the American dive-bombers began to make their dives. The first three bombers released their bombs but not one had connected. Still another Zero took off from the *Shoho* and joined its two companions in an attempt to ward off the attackers.

Lt. Comdr. Robert E. Dixon of Scouting Two led his bombers in first, and they hit the carrier on the stern and in the middle of the crowded flight deck. Bombers and torpedo planes then took over in a coordinated attack.

Lexington's Ault and two section leaders now started their dives on the *Shoho*. Lieutenant Commander Hamilton led in his SBD group at 11:10 A.M., and two of their bombs hit the *Shoho* and stopped her dead in the water with flames shooting high above her. When the bombers from the *Lexington* were finished, the carrier appeared to be in her death throes.

Lt. Comdr. W. O. Burch, commanding officer of the *Yorktown*'s Scouting Five, watched the tortured ship trying to turn into the wind to launch her planes and called Lt. Comdr. Joseph Taylor and his torpedo squadron. "We're going in Joe."

"Wait a few minutes. It will be five minutes before we can get there."

"Can't wait. Carrier is launching planes."

He led his fliers down, and they added their bombs to the carrier's woes. The damage was so severe that the last bomber pulled away without dropping.

Ens. H. S. Brown, Jr., headed for a cruiser and dropped his bomb squarely on the quarterdeck.

Five minutes later the *Lexington*'s TBDs launched low-level attacks, and new hits were scored on the *Shoho*, which was now in flames and racked by violent explosions. Within three minutes, it slipped beneath the waves.

From the ship's log, later recovered, it was learned that at least seven torpedoes and thirteen bombs had contributed to her sinking at 11:35 A.M. Only one hundred survivors were rescued, and eighteen of the ship's complement of twenty-one aircraft were destroyed. The three brave Japanese fighter pilots who had taken on the American force despite its numerical superiority tried to reach Deboyne Island but ran out of fuel. A Japanese ship picked them out of the ocean.

During the rain of bombs and torpedoes on the *Shoho*, Lt. Comdr. James Flatley shook his head in disbelief as he provided fighter cover for the bombers. The sight of the dive-bombers pouring bombs into the carrier was so awesome that he almost became physically ill. At the end, bombs seemed to plow into the shattered ship every three or four seconds while explosions tore it apart.

Fletcher and his staff tensely awaited news from the scene. They listened to their radios, but it was difficult to predict how things were going because the chatter between the pilots did not often reveal the facts. They were relieved when Dixon, who was in charge of Scouting Two called, "Scratch one flattop. Dixon to aircraft carrier: I repeat, Scrub one flattop!"

On the *Lexington*, Capt. Frederick C. Sherman paced the bridge with excitement, paused a moment as the radio blared from the fighting zone, and smiled with satisfaction as a voice shouted, "Scratch one flattop!"

The rugged SBDs had shown that they could take it. The planes were riddled with holes, wheels gone, and wings shot up, but they managed to fly home. The old TBDs, which should have long since been replaced by newer torpedo bombers, also served with distinction. Of the ninety-two American aircraft on the mission, only three were lost.

A second strike was set for 2:50 P.M. when pilots reported spotting four heavy cruisers and two destroyers. Fletcher then canceled it, saying that the aircraft should be ready to attack the Japanese carriers once they were sighted. He was aware of the air attack on the *Neosho* and *Sims* although the *Neosho*'s navigator had erred in giving his skipper a position that was too far east. As a result, Fletcher believed that Takagi's carriers were also farther to the east than they actually were. His decision to cancel the second strike until the other Japanese carriers were located proved wise.

At Rabaul, Admiral Inouye was in a state of indecision about the situation in and near the Coral Sea. Therefore, he informed his superiors that he was postponing the Port Moresby operation for forty-eight hours. This was a deliberate misstatement because he had actually ordered the landing force commander to abandon the Port Moresby landing and return to Rabaul. Loss of the *Shoho* had shaken him, making him even more cautious. Although he ordered a night action against the American ships, he even canceled that operation at midnight.

MacArthur's air force planes, which had dogged the invasion fleet, now reported that it had changed course. When Fletcher saw their dispatch, he refused to believe it. From his limited experience of the Japanese, their action ran counter to expectations. Although the course change would be confirmed later, he suspected that a trap was being set for his fleet.

Inouye remained in a state of shock. The loss of the *Shoho* was unexpected, and he had never considered that Fletcher might divide his command and place Crace's ships between the Japanese forces and Port Moresby. Unfortunately for him, he had believed the erroneous reports by his pilots that Crace's ships had been all but destroyed. When this proved untrue, he realized that his supply ships were in an extremely vulnerable position. Inouye's main problem was one that afflicted many Japanese commanders, who were thrown into confusion if there was a large deviation from an established plan.

By the afternoon of May 7, Takagi faced the same problem. He suffered doubts about the intelligence information he was receiving and unable to break radio silence following the attack on the *Neosho* and *Sims*, could not decide on his next move. He knew that he had been misled by the false information that he had received about an American carrier and cruiser, which had proved to be a tanker and a destroyer, and was convinced that the destruction of these two ships had been a waste of effort when he discovered that there was at least one American carrier in the area.

Before his planes returned from the attack on the *Neosho* and *Sims*, Takagi heard of the attack on the *Shoho*. Now he knew that there had to be *two* American carriers. Once his aircraft were recovered, he ordered their immediate refueling and in a rage demanded that they be launched again. Hara calmed his chief, reminding him that the crews would then have to return after dark without fighter escort. The Zeros, Hara told his admiral, could not fly after dark. (Fletcher was also considering launching more bombers, but had had the same problem as Takagi, that of risky night landings.) Takagi insisted that some strike be made against the American carriers, and Hara agreed that the most experienced pilots would take off at 4:30 P.M.

Comdr. Kakuichi Takahashi led the twelve Val dive-bombers and fifteen Kate torpedo planes, but they had to turn back without spotting the Americans when they ran short of fuel. Takahashi ordered them to jettison their bombs and torpedoes to lighten their loads as they headed home. The *Yorktown*'s Wildcats found them later and, close to sundown, singled out one Japanese group. Eight Kates and a Val were shot down with the loss of two American fighters.

The remaining Japanese bombers fled, but Takahashi soon realized that in the confusion they had all become lost. When he saw a carrier below, he turned on his indicator lights and sent flashlight signals. What he did not know was that the carrier was the *Yorktown*, whose captain knew that these were Japanese planes because all his own planes had already been recovered. He ordered the crew to man their guns, and the ship's landing lights were turned on.

The Japanese pilots, even though the carrier's signals looked unfamiliar, throttled their engines back and entered the landing pattern. A gunner fired from the bow as the first Japanese bomber passed close. The pilot, realizing that the carrier was American, pushed the engine throttle forward and roared away at high speed. Two others, quickly apprised of the situation, did likewise. Two more Japanese planes attempting to land were met with a hail of bullets as they made their final approach. One pulled away, but the other ran into heavy fire and plummeted into the ocean.

Japanese carriers at that time had no radar or direction-finding equipment, and some of Takahashi's pilots had been making their first night landing. To complicate their problems, Tast Force Seventeen continued to jam the frequencies on which Japanese pilots were trying to communicate with their carriers.

On his own carrier, a worried Hara scanned the blackness until he heard some of his planes returning. He ordered the lights turned on to bring in the survivors, totaling seventeen planes. All were so low on gas that they jockeyed for position to get down. In the resulting chaos, only six planes landed safely, while pilots from the others had to be picked out of the sea.

After the attempted Japanese landings on the *Yorktown*, Admiral Fitch ordered that all Japanese planes be tracked on radar in hopes of locating their carrier. The *Lexington*'s radar reported Japanese planes circling a point only 30 miles away. Actually, the distance was much farther. It was thought that the planes were landing on a Japanese carrier. Fitch immediately tried to contact Fletcher, but he was not successful until 10:00 P.M. Fletcher refused to believe the report because his own radar had picked up no signals. It was learned later that the Japanese carriers were 95 miles from the *Yorktown*.

For a time Fletcher considered a night action by his surface ships but decided to keep his fleet together for protection because he expected that he would soon face the entire Japanese fleet. Inouye was as indecisive as Fletcher, also believing that there would soon be a confrontation between the opposing fleets. He thought that the American ships were 40 to 60 miles to the west of his own ships; actually, they were at almost twice that distance.

Rear Adm. Kose Abe, in charge of the invasion fleet, called on the strike force to provide air cover at dawn on May 8. In addition, Takagi and Hara were given responsibility for providing distant cover during a night attack. The Japanese carriers therefore headed north at midnight while Fletcher's Task Force Seventeen was heading southwest in the opposite direction. With neither aware of the other's movement, it became a question of who would find the other first.

Without waiting to hear from his scout aircraft, Takagi ordered his planes aloft at 6:00 A.M. on May 8 when his strike force was 100 miles southeast of Rossel Island. At 8:33 A.M., Chief Petty Officer Kenzo Kanno, flying in a Kate from the *Shokaku* and reaching the limit of his fuel range, reported two American aircraft carriers and twelve escorts. Takagi's mixed fleet was ordered to converge on this point under Lieutenant Commander Takahashi while Kanno turned back. The two met, and Kanno thought that Takahashi's aircraft were on the wrong heading. Despite insufficient fuel, Kanno courageously turned around and led Takahashi to the American ships. Only then did he head for home. He had to land in the sea, out of fuel and a long way from help.

Kanno's report to Admiral Takagi had been picked up by the *Lexington*'s radio operator, so Fletcher was warned that they had been located. Although Crace's Task Force Forty-four was not available to protect his two carriers, Fletcher immediately sent out search planes. His fleet was in the clear, but the Japanese were hidden by the same storm front that had earlier hidden Fletcher's fleet.

Lt. J. G. Smith found the Japanese strike force at 8:38 A.M. and reported its position. He had actually seen Takagi's fleet at 8:15 but had delayed his report until he could verify all the facts. When Fletcher learned of the delay, he went into a rage. He was even angrier when he learned from Commander Dixon, who had tried to find the Japanese fleet, that Smith's position report was also in error. The Japanese were actually 45 miles north of the position given by Smith. Dixon meanwhile continued to orbit the perimeter of the Japanese strike force to give continuous reports until low fuel forced him to turn back.

Fletcher now turned over tactical command to Admiral Fitch, who ordered the dispatch of eighty-two aircraft while sixty-nine Japanese planes were heading for them. In the clouds, they passed without spotting each other.

Fletcher radioed MacArthur about the contact and asked for land-based bombers. None was available.

The Japanese had taken off earlier, but the Americans found the Japanese fleet first because they had flown faster on a more direct route. The distance was in fact closing fast because both fleets were now sailing toward each other.

Commander Burch's *Yorktown* SBDs arrived first, so he circled the Japanese fleet, waiting for the others to catch up.

Below, the men on the *Zuikaku* could hear the engines of the American planes, but they could not yet see them. Her captain immediately sent more Zero fighters aloft.

The rest of the *Yorktown* squadrons arrived just before 11:00 A.M., and Lt. Comdr. Joseph Taylor of VT–5 led nine Devastators toward the *Shokaku*. SBDs prepared to make their dives while fighters covered them.

Japanese fighters pressed their attacks against the TBDs, and the American torpedoes missed the *Shokaku*. Two SBDs dropped their bombs on the Japanese carrier—one on the flight deck, the second on her stern. Fires erupted immediately in both places. On board the *Zuikaku*, which was enveloped in a rainstorm, Hara was unaware of what had happened.

The SBDs and Wildcats from the *Lexington* got lost en route and failed to find the Japanese ships. Lt. Cmdr. James Brett's torpedo squadron VT–2 from the *Lexington* had used Smith's erroneous report and so had flown the wrong course. They did not find the Japanese ships until 11:40 A.M.

Four SBDs from VS–2 and six Wildcats from VF–2 had latched onto the torpedo bombers, hoping that they would lead them to the Japanese fleet. Once they spotted it, Commander Ault organized an attack. With eleven TBDs, he led his men through cloud cover until he saw the *Shokaku* far below. While the Wildcats tangled with the Zeros, Ault ordered his TBDs to attack. In the resulting action, Ault and several others were shot down.

While the Japanese ships maneuvered, easily avoiding the TBDs ineptly laid American torpedoes, the SBDs dropped their bombs. Lt. John J. Powers led three dive-bombers in an attack on the *Shokaku*, himself diving well below the safe altitude for release.

Before taking off, Powers had briefed his men that they should risk their lives to obtain a positive hit on a vital part of a carrier and make their release as low as possible to assure such a hit. "I'm going to get a hit if I have to lay it on their flight deck. The folks back home are counting on us."

Some thought that he was bragging, but he was as good as his word. Plummeting from 18,000 feet despite heavy antiaircraft fire that quickly found his range and flying under heavy fighter attack, Powers released his bomb at 300 feet. His wingmen, who had dropped earlier, saw his plane try to pull away, but it was aflame and crashed into the ocean.

Fitch was concerned about the vulnerability of his ships so he ordered a second attack by twenty-three SBDs. Meanwhile, Japanese attackers were sighted at 10:55 A.M., and Fitch had only eight Wildcats on combat patrol. In fact, he had only seventeen Wildcats all told, and he knew that the Japanese had a huge superiority in fighters. Fitch ordered all available SBDs to be used as fighters.

Antiaircraft guns started to fire at 11:15 A.M. Their accuracy saved the day—four Japanese torpedo bombers were shot down. Unfortunately, four SBDs were also lost.

Despite the loss of four planes, Japanese torpedo bombers succeeded in launching several torpedoes. With wooden boxes around their heads and tails to absorb the shock of landing in water from high altitudes and to keep them from diving too deep, these torpedoes headed straight for the *Lexington*. Sherman gave orders to the helm to try and place the ship's stern to the Japanese torpedoes churning toward his ship, but the parallel wakes convinced him not to change course. Incredibly, the huge ship evaded eleven torpedoes.

The first torpedo bombers had come in high, but the antiaircraft fire proved so intense that Capt. Shigekazu Shimazuki, leader of the *Zuikaku*'s torpedo plane group, ordered his men to come in just above the waves. Antiaircraft fire was still so thick that Shimazuki was convinced that he would never live through the attack. Miraculously, most of his men did, and two torpedoes slammed into the *Lexington*, one forward and another below the bridge.

Captain Buckmaster's *Yorktown* was also under attack and at 11:20 A.M., a heavy bomb went through the flight deck and exploded four levels below. Fortunately, there were no more hits, the fire was brought under control, and the *Yorktown* soon recovered her aircraft.

Earlier, the *Yorktown*'s scouts and bombers dove at *Shokaku* while Torpedo Squadron Five swung in to drop their fish. Burch led Scouting Five toward the carrier. Ens. J. H. Jorgenson followed quickly behind him, releasing his bomb at 2,000 feet. Through swirling smoke, he saw his skipper's 1,000-pounder hit flush on the carrier's deck.

Planes from the *Lexington* struck at the *Zuikaku* but no direct hits were made. When they returned to their own carrier, the fliers saw that it was doomed. In their absence, she had received mortal blows from Japanese planes. Fires resulting from attacks by Japanese dive-bombers and torpedo planes had been briefly brought under control. Then they flared out anew, more fiercely than ever.

"Abandon ship!" Captain Sherman's voice broke when he gave the tragic call. The *Lexington* was sunk by the task force's own destroyers at 6:54. The fact that 96 percent of her personnel were saved was some measure of comfort to her grieving commander.

The *Shokaku* had been seriously damaged and had to spend several months in a Japanese yard for repairs. A total of thirty Japanese aircraft were lost, including the one flown by Takahashi. The air group aboard the *Zuikaku* lost so many of its pilots that the carrier had to return to Japan to train new crews.

The Americans lost thirty-three aircraft in air battles, and another thirty-six went down with the *Lexington*.

Takagi's pilots were wildly enthusiastic about the results of their attack and reported to Takagi that *two* American carriers had been lost and the American fleet largely destroyed. Takagi sent this report to Admiral Yamamoto, but it did nothing to assuage the admiral's bitterness about the aborted Port Moresby landing.

Nimitz ordered Fletcher to withdraw and head south. Later, the Japanese abandoned their seaplane base at Deboyne Island, and an American landing force moved in to destroy it.

Admiral Inouye was ecstatic when he read Takagi's report that two American carriers had been destroyed, and he ordered Takagi to return to Truk. On the morning of May 9, a furious Yamamoto, disbelieving the reports of American ship losses, ordered Takagi to turn around and destroy the rest of the American fleet. By then, Fletcher's fleet had departed. Yamamoto agreed to suspend the chase, which had also involved Goto's covering force, two days later.

A fleet under Adm. Kiyohide Shima left Rabaul on May 10 with orders to occupy Ocean Island in the Gilberts and nearby Nauru Island on the following day. An American submarine, the *S-42*, torpedoed the supply ship *Okinsohima*, which was also Shima's flagship, so Inouye suspended the operation for the time being. Four days later, a reconnaissance plane from Tulagi reported the presence of the *Enterprise* and *Hornet*, which had been steaming at high speed to assist Fletcher. Shortly afterward, both carriers were ordered to return to Pearl Harbor, along with the *Yorktown*, for repairs. Inouye therefore canceled the entire operation and ordered Shima's invasion fleet to return to Truk.

After five days of heavy fighting, one Japanese carrier had been lost, two crippled, and smaller ships sunk or damaged. They also lost more than five thousand men. Admiral Nimitz responded to this news with a message to the fleet, "Admiral Fletcher utilized with consummate skill the information supplied him and won a victory with decisive and far-reaching consequences for the Allied cause."

Radio blackout had kept Admiral King in doubt about the outcome of the Battle of the Coral Sea. He was upset when he learned that Fletcher was heading south to refuel at Nouméa even though Nimitz had ordered him to do so. King considered Fletcher's action an unwarranted retreat from the battle zone.

King sent a blunt message to Fletcher, reminding him that he expected him to keep the pressure on the Japanese until ordered to do otherwise. When Fletcher received King's message, he wired King that he would cease refueling if the Japanese transports started to head south and would position his fleet off the northeastern part of Australia to await orders. Nevertheless, King began to distrust Fletcher and decided to take up the matter with Nimitz. Of course, this is what he should have done in the first place. King was aware from decoded Japanese cables that another attack on Port Moresby was under consideration by the Japanese. He now realized that he had erred in sending Halsey to launch Doolittle's raiders because Halsey was his best carrier commander.

After the Battle of the Coral Sea, King and Nimitz were convinced that the aircraft carrier was the prime offensive weapon in sea war. This strategic battle was the first naval battle fought entirely by air and in the future, many naval battles would be dominated by airpower.

The battle's greatest significance later came to light when it became clear that the Japanese had finally overstretched their military resources and found it impossible to occupy Port Moresby and the southeastern coast of New Guinea. From those vantage points, they could have severed the Australian–American lifeline. The battle was therefore of primary importance to Allied morale, for it was the first time that the Japanese had been turned back. The crippling of Japan's two carriers would prove a severe blow to her plans for future operations. She had to halt her southward expansion for the time being. As it turned out, she had reached the limit of her aggression against the Allies in the Pacific. Now the southern coast of New Guinea and the northern provinces of Australia would remain free of conquest and out of range of attacks by Japanese bombers.

7

THE THACH WEAVE

Admiral Yamamoto had long considered an attack on the Midway Atoll, believing that such a move would force America's Pacific Fleet to contest such an attack in a decisive battle. He told the Naval General Staff that if the American fleet were defeated, the Americans would be forced to sue for peace. They disagreed with his plan, saying that it would be difficult to keep the Imperial Fleet supplied if the American fleet was not destroyed. Yamamoto was also reminded that Midway was within the range of American long-range bombers from Hawaii.

Yamamoto persisted. The Doolittle raid on Japan had shocked the Japanese people, he said, and after losses in the Coral Sea, he knew that time was running out for a decisive sea battle.

Midway Atoll, 1,150 miles northwest of Hawaii, is comprised of Eastern Island and Sand Island, the latter only two miles long. Midway was discovered in 1859 by Capt. N. C. Brooks, who claimed it for the United States, but it was not occupied. President Theodore Roosevelt placed it under the United States Navy's jurisdiction in 1903, and Japanese bird poachers were driven off. It later became a link in the trans-Pacific cable between Hawaii and the Philippines and was commissioned a Naval Air Station in August 1941.

Prior to the Battle of the Coral Sea, Lt. Comdr. James Flatley had trained his men in a new fighter tactic and used it for the first time with great success. Lt. Comdr. John S. "Jimmy" Thach, who later became an admiral, had also experimented prior to the war with a tactic to counter the Japanese Zero. Intelligence reports indicated that this plane could fly rings around anything the United

States Navy had in operation. Knowing that his squadron—one of only seven prewar fighter squadrons in the navy—would surely be fighting Zeros if the United States went to war, Thach had developed a method to fight the Zeros even though they had a rate of climb of 5,000 feet per minute, a tight turning radius, and higher speeds than any navy fighter. Loaded with ammunition, American fighters of the period were slower, could climb at only 1,000 feet per minute, and could not turn as tightly as Zeros.

At night, using kitchen matches to represent airplanes, Thach worked out a system of reducing the advantages of the Japanese fighters. Basically, he developed a method that enabled American pilots to stay alive in inferior airplanes.

In those days, typical fighter formations consisted of three-plane sections. Thach considered such formations unrealistic because a pilot had to have three eyes—one on his section leader, another to shoot with, and a third to keep from running into his opposite wingman in case the leader made a sharp turn.

His "match" games went on late into the night and convinced him that the key to attacking Zeros was fast maneuvering. From then on he used two-plane sections, which later became standard.

Later, he explained to his squadron's pilots the advantages of flying in two sections against a fighter with superior performance and quite probably an altitude advantage. If planes flew in two two-plane sections, then the two pairs of aircraft could split apart when an enemy fighter brought his point of aim to one of the aircraft in formation. The other section would then have a chance to shoot him down while he was preoccupied with the first section. As Thach said, "If we space two sections far enough apart they will meet in a half circle if they turn toward each other. And, if an opponent attacks one section, that pilot can also take a head-on shot while his partners, in the other section, will have a free shot at the preoccupied enemy."

Thach later tried this tactic in the air, telling Lt. "Butch" O'Hare to take four planes aloft and to use full power any time he needed it. Thach himself took four planes and flying in the two-plane sections he proposed, used only half throttle. This would simulate a dogfight between Japanese Zeros and navy fighters.

The Thach tactic succeeded so well in the air that O'Hare came running up to Thach once they were on the ground. "Skipper, it really works. Every time I started to make a beam attack on one of your half-throttle planes, another one would be around pointing his nose at me."

A lookout doctrine was established in the Pacific so that pilots flying parallel courses in two-plane sections could protect one another. Normally, a base element consisted of four fighters in two-plane sections. On a signal from the section leader, both pilots in a section turned toward each other with a crossover maneuver to see whether an enemy aircraft was on the tail of either. This maneuver was repeated, first one way and then the other so that one of the fighters was always in position to make a quick turn and get a head-on shot at an attacking enemy fighter. This "weaving" action gave the maneuver its name.

The tactic was so successful during the Battle of the Coral Sea that losses were kept to a minimum. Later, Flatley wired the Navy Department to say that the only way that American planes could survive against superior fighters was to use this maneuver. He also wrote Thach to thank him, saying that from then on the maneuver would be designated the "Thach Weave."

Elsewhere on the world's battlefronts, the position of the Allies improved. Russia successfully defended Moscow and Stalingrad, and British general Sir Claude John Eyre Auchinleck won the first battle of El Alamein in the Libyan Desert.

Before the Coral Sea battle, some American newspapers had carried a story from MacArthur's headquarters that a major Japanese offensive was imminent. King used strong language to convey to General Marshall his displeasure about this breach of security. Marshall was equally concerned, and he personally warned MacArthur to tighten up his security. The Japanese did not know that their code had been broken, and any indication that it had been would immediately shut off a crucial source of intelligence.

Nimitz and King had met in San Francisco on April 25 prior to the Battle of the Coral Sea to select flag officers for future operations. King said that both he and Secretary of Navy Knox wanted younger officers promoted and older ones retired. King respected Nimitz' judgment and appreciated the job he had done in reorganizing the Pacific Fleet and supervising its operations over such a vast theater as the Pacific Ocean. Nimitz' capacity for dealing with other services and their commanders to assure unity was, he said, a great asset. But he told Nimitz that he was too lenient with his subordinates.

King stressed that he wanted aggressive young flag officers with aviation backgrounds placed in command of carrier groups. He insisted that Wilson Brown, and Fletcher were not aviators and that

Halsey was the only aviator with the fighting spirit and the seniority for top command jobs.

Although Nimitz' background was in submarines, he readily agreed with King that naval aviation commands had to be reorganized. He cautioned, however, that with the crisis confronting them in the South Pacific, this was not the juncture at which to make top-level changes. Neverthless, King advised members of the San Francisco conference that Vice-Adm. Robert L. Ghormley, senior American naval officer in London, would soon be transferred to the Pacific. King considered Ghormley to be an able man, skilled at both planning and strategy. Nimitz agreed. It was a move that both would regret.

Although they respected each other, King and Nimitz were opposites. King was ruthless when he was convinced that a subordinate was not giving his best and was quick to demand his removal. Nimitz was more inclined to see both sides of a case.

After the Battle of the Coral Sea, King and Nimitz reached a private agreement that the war in the South Pacific would be fought at sea even though technically most of the area had been assigned to General MacArthur.

Despite King's growing mistrust, Admiral Fletcher continued to enjoy Nimitz' support. Nimitz recommended that he be promoted to vice-admiral, but King refused, citing the loss of the *Lexington* and saying that he did not consider the battle a victory. Nimitz understood, although he disagreed. The *Lexington* had been King's first major carrier command, and he had once said he would never promote or decorate a man who lost his ship.

The loss of the *Lexington* was kept a guarded secret from the British at King's insistence. First Sea Lord Admiral Sir Dudley Pound was told only that she had been damaged. Three weeks later King conceded her loss. The news was also withheld from Marshall's staff because King believed that they could not keep secrets. Even Secretary of Navy Knox was often not told of losses because he had once been a newspaper publisher.

The Japanese now considered the feasibility of an all-out attack on the Hawaiian Islands, proposed by Rear Adm. Matome Ugaki, chief of staff for the Combined Fleet, to lure the American fleet into a major confrontation with the Imperial Fleet. The occupation of India and Ceylon was also considered, and the Naval General Staff recommended an attack on Australia to prevent a counteroffensive.

These proposals were all rejected. Ugaki's staff argued that no surprise could be expected if Hawaii was attacked, and the chances of success were minimal. The Japanese Army rejected an attack against Ceylon because troops were not available, and an attack on Australia was held impossible because the ten infantry divisions needed were also not to be had. Instead it was agreed to attack Midway and attempt landings in the Aleutian Islands.

The Battle of the Coral Sea had induced caution in Admiral King. With loss of the *Lexington*, he was less inclined to risk his carriers. He advised Nimitz that Halsey should not operate beyond land-based airpower. Nimitz disagreed. He decided to go on the offensive in the South Pacific and ordered raids on Tulagi and on other nearby Japanese installations. King reluctantly agreed with Nimitz' plan to utilize the First Marine Raider Battalion, stationed at Samoa, and transport marines to the New Hebrides. This was Mac-Arthur's territory, and he considered the forces there too small to be effective, so the project was canceled.

Nimitz was convinced, after reviewing intelligence data gathered from code breaking, that the Japanese planned their next move in the Central Pacific. King believed, however, that they would strike next in the South Pacific, and he ordered at least two carriers to remain there. Halsey's *Enterprise* and *Hornet* groups were selected to stay. The *Yorktown*, meanwhile, was being repaired at Pearl Harbor, while the *Saratoga* and the *Wasp* were on the west coast and unable to participate if an emergency developed. As a result, the Central Pacific was without a single carrier.

Messages went back and forth between King and Nimitz about the need to prepare for a possible major battle in the Central Pacific. Finally, Nimitz acted—without consulting King—and recalled Halsey.

Nimitz wrote King on May 16 that he was convinced that the next Japanese attack would be against Midway. He was annoyed when King procrastinated all day and refused to commit himself one way or the other. The next day, forced to agree reluctantly with his intelligence officers, King told Nimitz that his decision was correct.

King's normally aggressive stance was muted in the following days by his concern over the losses in the Coral Sea battle. He advised Nimitz to employ strong attrition tactics and "not—repeat—not allow our forces to accept such decisive action as would be likely to incur heavy losses in our carriers and cruisers." After deliberation with his staff and coordination with King's office, however, Nimitz on his own decided to take a bolder course of action.

Fletcher was recalled from the South Pacific in the middle of May and learned to his surprise that he had to defend his actions during the Battle of the Coral Sea. At first he did not realize why he was being questioned so thoroughly, but it soon became apparent that he was on the hot seat.

Fletcher responded forthrightly, and his wartime record was discussed in depth. Nimitz was so convinced of Fletcher's abilities that he attached an endorsement to Fletcher's statement before sending it to King.

Dear King,

I have finally had an opportunity to discuss with Fletcher, during a three-day stay in port, his operations in the Coral Sea area, and to clear up what appeared to be a lack of aggressive tactics of his force. I hope, and believe that after reading the enclosed letter you will agree with me that Fletcher did a fine job and exercised superior judgment in the recent cruise in the Coral Sea. He is an excellent, seagoing, fighting naval officer and I wish to retain him as a task force commander in the future.

In conclusion, Nimitz said that he was convinced that Fletcher should command the carrier forces in the coming battle in the Central Pacific.

After Halsey returned from the South Pacific, he was such a sick, haggard man that Nimitz ordered him into a hospital. The nervous strain of the last two months had been too much; he had lost 20 pounds and had a severe case of dermatitis, a skin disease that almost covered his body and itched so much that he was almost driven frantic.

For his replacement, Halsey recommended his cruiser commander, Rear Adm. Raymond A. Spruance. He noted that the meticulous Spruance had consistently displayed outstanding ability combined with excellent judgment and quiet courage. "I consider him fully and superbly qualified to take command of a force comprising mixed types, and to conduct protracted independent operations in the combat theater in wartime."

Nimitz agreed, knowing that Spruance was a tough, even brilliant taskmaster and ideal for the big battle that he knew was in the offing.

The Americans always knew when the Japanese were set for an important operation because of the quantity of radio messages that filled the airwaves. All were intercepted and, after decoding, sent to

Pearl Harbor. The target of the next major Japanese move was listed in the messages only by the letters *AF*. It was decided to trick the Japanese into identifying the target, which Nimitz guessed was Midway but King was certain would be the Hawaiian Islands. The commander at Midway was secretly ordered to broadcast in the clear that his water distillation apparatus had broken down. Sure enough, in a message from the Japanese picked up a few days later, the high command reported that *AF* was short of water. Now Nimitz was convinced that the Japanese fleet was headed for Midway.

Under orders from Admiral Yamamoto, the last ship bound for Midway left its Japanese port on May 28. The First Carrier Force under Admiral Chuichi Nagumo, the same man who had led the Pearl Harbor strike, was in charge. Although he was deprived of one third of his carrier strength because the *Shokaku* and *Zuikaku* were still undergoing repairs for damage incurred during the Battle of the Coral Sea, he was not concerned. He had the *Akagi, Kaga, Soryu,* and *Hiryu.*

A northern force under Vice-Adm. Moshiiro Hosogaya was dispatched by Yamamoto to attack American installations at Dutch Harbor and occupy Attu and Kiska in the Aleutians. He had the carriers *Ryujo* and *Junyo* under Rear Adm. Kakuji Kakuta. This northern force, Yamamoto hoped, would lure the Pacific Fleet to Alaskan waters and thereby leave Midway unprotected.

Admiral Yamamoto had transferred his staff to the huge battleship *Yamato* in February, and accompanied by three large battleships and the light carrier *Hosho* as well as auxiliary ships, he placed it 600 miles northwest of Midway. Thus, he would be in the position to send assistance to either Nagumo or the Aleutian force if it was needed.

Submarines proved to be the weak link in Yamamoto's plan. He had intended to use them as scouts, but bad weather restricted some of them, and many others were in ports being overhauled. Therefore, there were only a limited number of submarines to serve as scouts, particularly for Nagumo's force, and they failed to locate the American fleet.

Yamamoto had another problem. Because strict radio silence was maintained, he did not learn the true state of affairs in both his task forces after the battle got underway. The Americans were more fortunate. Nimitz' staff had intercepted a sufficient number of Japanese messages that, once decoded, gave him a fairly accurate picture of the intentions of the Japanese Imperial Fleet. Therefore, on May

28, the day the last of Yamamoto's ships left port, Nimitz ordered his task forces to leave Pearl Harbor and rendezvous 350 miles northeast of Midway. Spruance had Task Force Sixteen with the *Enterprise* and *Hornet*, while Fletcher was aboard the repaired *Yorktown* with Task Force Seventeen. When the task forces joined, Spruance was in charge, but Fletcher was assigned tactical command under him.

Nimitz was so convinced that the main Japanese thrust would be at Midway that he sent most of his available ships with Spruance. Rear Adm. Robert A. Theobald in Alaskan waters was left with only a token force.

Ens. Jewell H. Reid, flying a Catalina plane from Midway on June 3, spotted the Japanese invasion forces. He remained with them for two hours to send continuous tracking information back to Pearl Harbor and to Spruance's fleet. Rear Adm. Raizo Tanaka, in charge of the Japanese transports, spotted Reid's plane and radioed Yamamoto that all hope of a surprise attack on Midway was at an end.

Air Force Lt. Col. Walter Sweeney now led a formation of nine B-17 Flying Fortresses to the invasion fleet, encountering it 570 miles southwest of Midway. During the bombing run, Sweeney turned to his copilot and said that the sea appeared to be dotted with Japanese ships. After they dropped their bombs, they glanced hopefully at the ships below. Not one bomb had made contact with a Japanese ship.

The position of Admiral Nagumo's carriers and supporting ships remained unknown to the Americans, and he was grateful that they were screened by clouds. He, too, was concerned about the whereabouts of the American carriers.

Admiral Fletcher read Ensign Reid's report about the sighting of Japanese ships. He believed that these ships were the invasion fleet and not the carrier striking force. He was convinced that the Japanese carriers would strike at dawn the next day while his carriers were 200 miles north and slightly east of Midway.

Eleven navy Catalinas were ordered to search at dawn for the Japanese fleet. The Seventh Air Force's 5th and 11th Bombardment Groups were also sent out on search and destroy missions.

Although he was aware that the invasion fleet was under American surveillance, Nagumo was still convinced that his carrier force would be able to bomb Midway with little interference.

The four Japanese carriers turned into the wind on the morning of June 4 while they were 240 miles northwest of Midway. One hundred and eight planes took off first and were followed by an equal number in the second wave. The bombers were ordered to attack any American task force they located, and they were protected by Zeros up above. Finally, Nagumo sent search planes in all directions even though he did not expect that the Americans had any carriers in the immediate vicinity.

On the American side, Fletcher's scouts also were out in force. Scouts on both sides missed each other because of heavy clouds. Finally, a PBY with Lts. Howard Ady and William Chase found the Japanese carriers and radioed the news to Fletcher's command. Fletcher was livid when he was told that their message only announced that they had seen the Japanese carriers but provided no information as to their number or location. The PBY crew was, however, too busy to furnish additional information because they were under attack by Zeros and were also trying to avoid heavy antiaircraft fire from the ships below. When Ady and Chase could spare a moment they reported, "Many planes heading Midway, three hundred twenty degrees, distance one hundred fifty."

Later, they radioed, "Two carriers and battleship bearing three hundred twenty, distance one hundred eighty, course one hundred thirty-five, speed twenty-five." Fletcher issued orders to Spruance to "proceed southwesterly and attack enemy carriers when definitely located. I will follow as soon as planes recovered."

At Midway, orders were issued to the air force that its B–17s should attack the carriers and ignore the Japanese transports. Four Air Force B–26s, equipped with torpedoes, and six navy Avengers flying their first combat mission, were vectored to the Japanese carriers' last known position. Sixteen marine SBD dive-bombers under Maj. Lofton R. Henderson and eleven SB2Us under Maj. Benjamin W. Norris of VMSB–241, also took off to intercept the Japanese.

Over Midway, forming a pitifully small protective screen, were the marine fighters of VMF–221. Nineteen of their twenty-five airplanes were outmoded F2A Brewster Buffaloes. They had only six modern F4F Wildcats.

Japanese Zeros strafed all Midway's military installations while bombers concentrated on major installations. Maj. Floyd B. Parks led twelve fighter planes against the unsuspecting Japanese bombers and was soon joined by an equal number of fighters under Capt. Kirk Armistead. Most fighters were Buffaloes so after the first attacks against Japanese bombers, only ten fighters survived. At most, only six Japanese planes were shot down. With little opposition,

Japanese bombers covered the islands, flying through heavy American antiaircraft fire almost with impunity.

The forces at Midway struck back with all their strength but the Japanese were undeterred. Their eighty ships converged on the embattled island with little opposition. By now, most of Midway's fighters and bombers had been sacrificed but the Japanese carriers remained undamaged.

Admiral Nagumo received word of the bombing attack's success, but he hesitated to follow the recommendation of its leader that a second attack was necessary to complete the destruction of the island's defenses. He was aware that the Americans knew of the location of part of his fleet from Ensign Reid's spotting of the invasion force. As he stood on his bridge, weighing whether to follow up the first raid, a bugle blared—the signal warning of an enemy air raid. Then a destroyer sent a flag signal that an enemy plane was in sight.

Capt. James F. Collins led four air force B–26 Marauders from the 22nd Group. While heading for a Japanese ship, he saw six navy Avengers close to the water fighting off Zeros. These were planes from the *Hornet*'s Torpedo Squadron *Eight*, which had been assigned temporarily to Midway's defenses. In the lead, Lt. Langdon K. Fieberling fought desperately to stay alive, watching with horror as three of his bombers cartwheeled into the ocean. Grimly, the survivors continued their runs while Collins' B–26s fought their way through a hail of antiaircraft fire. Soon, he too was down to three planes as the Japanese ships depressed their large guns to bring all their firepower to bear upon the attackers. The fire was so intense that all the bombers had to release their torpedoes too soon. One of the last three B–26s released its torpedo and, aflame, flashed over the *Akagi* and crashed on the other side of the carrier. Only two B–26 crews and one Avenger survived. Not one scored a hit.

Admiral Nagumo now decided to order the second strike on Midway. The planes on the *Akagi* and *Kaga* had been armed with torpedoes for attacks against American carriers, but none as yet had been sighted. Therefore, Nagumo ordered them refitted with bombs. Planes on the *Hiryu* and *Soryu* were already equipped with bombs so they did not have to be changed.

At 7:55 A.M., Major Henderson brought his Dauntless bombers of Marine Scout Bombing Squadron 241 to the scene. En route, he had come to a reluctant decision. Ten of his pilots were new, and only three were experienced in the SBD.

"Make a glide-bombing attack," he called. "No dive-bombing."

He led them in a wide circle and then dipped the nose of his SBD at the *Kaga*, which was maneuvering on the ocean's surface. Zeros and Nakajima 97 fighters swept toward them, but they continued to the target while flak mushroomed around their small planes in bursts that rocked the formation. Henderson's SBD and eight others were hit hard and crashed, so Capt. Richard E. Fleming took over the lead and dove his plane to 400 feet before releasing his bomb. His plane was riddled by 179 hits from fighters and anti-aircraft fire as he pulled away with two minor wounds. Six of the formation's planes were so riddled they had to be scrapped.

Eleven Vindicators assigned to the second unit of the marine group under Major Norris found the invasion fleet at 8:20. Japanese fighters were on guard, flying low to stave off torpedo planes. Norris quickly realized that it was impossible to get into position to attack a carrier. Swarms of fighters ripped into his formation as he selected a battleship. He led his planes in a low approach through heavy flak and fighters and after pulling away, thought with exultation that they had made two direct hits. He had in fact scored near misses, and the attack cost them three planes.

Army Flying Fortresses under Lieutenant Colonel Sweeney now concentrated on three carriers from high altitude. Zeros ignored the high-altitude bombers on their runs, so they were free to take all the time they needed to aim properly. Although they claimed hits, the heavy bombers actually failed to make a single hit on the twisting Japanese ships.

A Japanese search plane reported to Admiral Nagumo that it had located ten ships that were considered those of the enemy but to Nagumo's rage, the pilot did not say where they were or what they were! For the first time Nagumo began to fear for the operation's success. He had not expected American ships in the vicinity of Midway for at least two more days. He, like Yamamoto, had believed that the Japanese expedition to the Aleutian Islands would draw the main American battle fleet to Alaskan waters.

At first, Nagumo thought that his attackers were all land-based planes from Midway, but a search plane from the *Tone* disillusioned him, reporting an enemy force with what appeared to be a carrier in the rear. He needed no more convincing. With the number of surface ships in the area, there had to be a carrier.

He sent wires to Yamamoto and to the commander of the invasion force announcing a change in plans. The Midway attackers were streaming back to their carriers, and the confusion was so great it took forty minutes to recover them. The carriers now were extremely vulnerable, jammed with planes topside and with fuel lines and bombs covering the decks. Below decks, chaos was even greater as crews worked frantically to get their planes airborne again.

American carriers, only 155 miles away, were also vulnerable because they lacked adequate supporting ships, and Spruance spent anxious hours waiting for the *Hornet*'s scout planes to return from their search for the enemy.

Spruance, aboard the *Enterprise*, ordered his task force, which included the *Hornet*, to steam toward the position reported by his scouts. He wanted to wait until they were 100 miles from the Japanese carriers before the planes were launched, but his chief of staff, Capt. Miles Browning, insisted on an earlier launch. He told Spruance that he thought Nagumo would make a second strike against Midway and if they launched earlier at a greater distance, they might catch Nagumo's planes on deck while they were being refueled.

Admiral Fletcher, who had earlier ordered Spruance's carriers the *Enterprise* and *Hornet* to launch attacks as soon as they came within range of the Japanese fleet, now ordered the *Yorktown* held in reserve because initial reports specified only two Japanese carriers. Spruance reluctantly agreed, and his carriers turned into the wind at a point thought to be 200 miles from the last known Japanese position. At this time, Japanese planes were returning from Midway, and the Japanese fleet was under attack by army and navy planes from the island.

Fletcher, fearful that a Japanese attack might catch the *Yorktown*'s planes on deck, ordered the torpedo squadron, half the bomber planes, and six fighters to launch at 8:40 A.M. Lt. Comdr. Clarence W. McClusky led an equal number from the *Enterprise*. The last seventeen SBDs from the *Yorktown* were kept in ready reserve. Lt. Comdr. John S. Thach, whose Thach Weave had been successfully demonstrated during the Coral Sea battle, led six Yorktown F4F Wildcats to protect twelve torpedo bombers and sixteen dive-bombers. Stanhope C. Ring, Hornet air group commander, led another thirty-five bombers and fighters.

Admiral Nagumo remained in a state of indecision. He knew that he should launch his torpedo bombers against the American fleet, but they would be without fighter support because he had sent his fighters aloft to beat back attackers from Midway.

Rear Adm. Tamon Yamaguchi, who headed the Second Carrier Division in the *Hiryu* and *Soryu*, was impatient for action. He sent a message to Nagumo saying, "Consider it advisable to launch attack force immediately."

Nagumo continued to vacillate; his concern for the lack of fighter support for his bombers growing by the minute. He had seen what his fighters had done to the American torpedo bombers when they attacked his ships, and he feared that the same could happen to his own. To the frustration of his staff, he decided to wait until the Midway attackers had all returned and were rearmed. He changed the orders he had issued just a few moments before and told the armament and ordnancemen below decks to stop rearming his bombers with bombs for a second strike at Midway and instead rearm with torpedoes. He sent similar orders to the *Kaga*. He also sent a signal to the other carriers, "After completing recovery operations, force will temporarily head northward." This meant that his fleet was actually steaming away from Midway—a new problem for the Americans who were searching for it.

8

THE BATTLE OF MIDWAY

The aggressive, colorful commander of Torpedo Eight, Lt. Comdr. John C. Waldron, had told his pilots aboard the *Hornet* prior to the mission that despite their limited training in their slow Devastator torpedo bombers, they had done all that was humanly possible to prepare for the battle. They had listened with respect, knowing that Waldron, of tough Sioux Indian descent, meant what he said when he told them if only one man survived, he expected him to get a hit on a carrier. Their hard-driving boss had drilled them unmercifully, but he had also managed to get them armor-plated bucket seats and twin-mounted 30-caliber machine guns for their rear-seat gunners.

En route, on Waldron's left, Lt. Comdr. Eugene E. Lindsey led fourteen Devastators from Torpedo Six. Above, six Wildcats led by Lt. James S. Gray provided fighter escort for the *Enterprise*'s bombers. Somehow, in the cloud cover, Gray's fighters ended up with Waldron's formation.

Waldron, suspecting that the Japanese had changed course, called for a search to the north when the Japanese fleet was not located. At 9:20, he found the carriers. Waldron signaled for an immediate attack. As they headed in, Waldron noted the vicious swipes of the enemy fighters, who came at them with all guns firing, so close that he could see the flashes from the guns on their wings.

Thach's fighters tore into the twenty or more Zeros that were destroying the Devastators one by one. When his wingman was shot down, he thought that the Thach Weave was not working. Then he realized that the Japanese were coming in a stream. He caught one Zero on the outside of the turn at exactly the right moment, and shot it down. Then another Zero slid in, and he held the fire of his 50-caliber guns until he got within range. When he was about to turn, he saw another section leader on his right turn just before he did. He thought at first that his man had made a mistake and was looking back on his own tail instead of concentrating on Thach's. He swung around and a Zero tried to follow; Thach got a good low shot and the Zero caught fire. After he moved back into position, he turned around and saw that the section leader had shot another Zero off his tail. Thach realized that he had been wrong and forgave the leader for his earlier doubts. The sky seemed filled with enemy fighters, and Thach was convinced that none of them would get home, but the Thach Weave seemed to be working and he was still alive, thanks to the Wildcat's armor plating and self-sealing fuel tanks. His fighters were being reduced one by one, however, because of the sheer numbers of Japanese fighters.

Thach had taken the fighters off their backs, but Waldron's TBDs had been falling so fast that only he and Ens. George Gay's plane survived passage through what seemed to be a wall of flak. Then Waldron winced as steel slammed into his Devastator. He lost control and sat helplessly as his plane plummeted into the sea.

Gay's TBD was thus the sole survivor of Torpedo Eight, and he held a course for the *Akagi*. That morning, this young, inexperienced pilot had made his first takeoff with a torpedo. Like most pilots, he had never seen a torpedo before; there had not even been dummies with which to practice. The Mark 3 torpedoes he carried dated back to World War I, but they had been modernized with new fins to give them a better chance of reaching a target.

Gay held his slow, outmoded TBD 80 feet off the water. He reduced his speed to 80 knots, determined to release his torpedo only 1,000 yards from a Japanese ship to assure a hit.

The Japanese fighter patrol had devastated the first American torpedo bombers because all seventy-five Zeros had come down to attack. This proved to be a fatal mistake for the Japanese, for the dive-bombers would have no opposition when they appeared a few minutes later.

While Thach's Wildcats were eliminating many of the Zeros, Gay's lone Devastator reached the release point. His plane had been hit repeatedly, mostly by small arms fire. Then he heard his rear gunner, Robert Huntington, cry, "My God! I'm hit!" Gay pushed the electrical release to drop his torpedo. Nothing happened. Frantically, he activated the emergency pull, and the torpedo dropped. His TBD, badly hit, was difficult to maneuver so he flew on toward the carrier, feeling almost as if he were flying straight down the barrels of the big guns up forward. The air was thick with exploding bursts as he tried to get a line on the gunners, who were firing hundreds of rounds. He bore straight in to give the Japanese gunners a smaller target. He was only yards above the water, and below the level of the ship's deck. He spotted one gunner and zeroed in on him, but the man jumped aside. Gay did not want to go to the far side of the carrier where all guns could concentrate on his plane so he turned and flew down the flight deck. He saw the captain on the bridge waving his binoculars. He flew past the stern and over two large cruisers, and it seemed as if the whole fleet was shooting at him. Each gun's explosion seemed to him like red tennis balls with puffs of smoke behind them.

He tried to get away from the other ships, but five Zeros homed in on him; his plane was so riddled that his engine caught fire and his rudder and aileron controls were shot out. He tried to pancake onto the ocean, but his right wing hit first and the TBD cartwheeled. He had left his canopy open during the battle but the impact of the crash landing slammed it shut. He tore at it frantically as the torpedo plane settled slowly in the water. He was close to panic, sure he would drown. Finally, the hood released and he jumped onto the rear fuselage to rescue his gunner, although he was convinced that he was dead. Despite his efforts, the plane sank before Gay could reach him.

Looking up, he saw a large carrier heading straight for him with her planes coming in to land. He dove into the water, grabbing a seat cushion quickly, and hid beneath it as the carrier passed only 1,500 feet away. Gay decided not to inflate his life raft until dark, hoping that the battle would move away from his area and that he would be rescued. He was calmer now and watched the attacks continue against the Japanese carriers.

Gay probably owed his life to the fact that he had been ordered to bring up the rear. He was the squadron's navigation officer, and Waldron wanted him there because, if anything happened to him, Gay might be able to get the squadron back safely with his navigational skill.

On the *Kaga*, a lookout yelled, "Enemy torpedo bombers, thirty degrees to starboard, coming in low!" Another yelled, "Enemy torpedo bombers approaching forty degrees to port!"

Lindsey's fourteen Devastators of Torpedo Six came in slowly. For some reason, he had neglected to call Gray for fighter support, and the Zeros had a field day, splashing ten of his TBDs before they could release their torpedoes. The remaining four dropped their torpedoes, but all missed the carrier.

A mile east of the *Akagi*, Lt. Comdr. Lance E. Massey arrived with twelve Devastators from the *Yorktown*'s VT-3. His pilots were shocked when an enemy fighter swept in close and shot Massey down in flames, but they never faltered, even when six more planes were shot down and only five remained to launch their torpedoes. During the getaway, three more succumbed to the fierce Japanese fire.

Until now, three enemy carriers had been under attack. Brave men, pressing home their attacks within a few hundred feet of the carriers, losing comrades on all sides but getting some torpedoes into the sides of the carriers, found that not one torpedo functioned properly.

To the survivors, it was galling to realize that they had risked so much only to find that their torpedoes were malfunctioning. It was a problem that rarely occurred with Japanese torpedoes but was all too familiar to American pilots at this stage of the war.

Spruance was shocked by the loss of so many planes. The *Hornet*'s Torpedo Eight was wiped out. The *Enterprise*'s Torpedo Six had only four planes out of the original fourteen. The *Yorktown*'s Three also lost heavily, with two survivors out of twelve. Worst of all, not one torpedo had found its mark.

These attacks did make it difficult for Japanese carriers to launch their own bombers because of the almost continuous evasive maneuvers demanded of the carriers themselves. Nagumo feared the torpedo bombers most, believing that they were his greatest potential threat. Zero pilots had orders to concentrate on them, and they did so with a vengeance. The American dive-bomber attacks, which had been planned to coincide with the torpedo attacks, therefore had to be made alone.

After the last torpedo attack, Nagumo ordered his fighters and bombers to get the American carriers. Just as the first Zero lifted off at 10:24 A.M., a lookout yelled, "Dive-bombers!"

To the consternation of those on board the *Akagi*, SBDs were plummeting directly toward them. They came in unopposed because Zeros were flying close to the water to ward off further torpedo attacks—which were now completed. More SBDs were heading for the *Kaga*, and they, too, were unopposed.

Bombers from the *Yorktown* were under the command of Lt. Comdr. Maxwell Leslie, who led them against the *Soryu* to the northwest even though he had lost his own bomb inadvertently before the start of his dive. He fired his machine guns as he led his squadron mates in a 70-degree dive.

Lt. Paul Holmberg aimed for the red circle on the *Kaga*'s flight deck, which was steaming to the *Soryu*'s right. At 2,500 feet, he hit the bomb release switch and then the manual lever to assure that the bomb would dislodge from its rack. The 1,000-pound bomb hit the deck near the superstructure, creating a mounting mass of flames, death, and destruction in its wake, and three more bombs quickly followed. Now, because fueled planes were on her deck, the *Kaga* became a flaming torch.

Lt. Comdr. Clarence W. "Wade" McClusky had thirty-seven *Enterprise* SBDs from VB–6 and VS–6 with him when he spotted a Japanese destroyer harassing an American submarine that was searching for Japanese ships to torpedo. He decided to follow the destroyer and sure enough, it led him to the carriers. He signaled for an approach from the southwest at right angles to Leslie's *Yorktown* formation, which was attacking the *Akagi*, causing tremendous destruction. McClusky ordered his pilot to head for the *Soryu*.

Lt. Wilmer Earl Gallaher led the attack upon the *Akagi*, scoring two hits on its deck that not only exploded the fueled airplanes but also detonated the bombs and torpedoes that were piled nearby. Japanese pilots and work crews on deck suffered agonizing deaths as flaming gasoline was flung over them by exploding bombs and torpedoes.

The *Soryu* was hit three times and so fierce was the spreading inferno that Capt. Ryusaku Yanagimoto ordered his carrier abandoned. Men leaped off her deck into the ocean to escape the tremendous heat while flames almost instantly cremated those less fortunate. The captain was urged to leave his ship, but he refused.

The *Akagi*, turning northward to launch her planes, found Dauntlesses hurtling down from 14,500 feet. The first bomb exploded in the center of a group of planes on deck, and the afterdeck became a mass of flames. The Japanese ship maneuvered wildly, but the bombs came down in a rush with five direct hits, while three exploded close along her sides.

Chief of Staff Ryunosuke Kusaka urged Admiral Nagumo to leave the carrier. Despite the burning deck, Nagumo refused to consider such a move. The *Akagi*'s Capt. Taijiro Aoki then added his pleas. "Shift your flag to the *Nagara* and resume command of the force." Nagumo reluctantly agreed. The *Akagi*'s fires were so intense that Nagumo had to slide down a rope to get away.

Admiral Yamaguchi, on board the *Hiryu*, had so far escaped attacks because his ship was farther to the north. He ordered an immediate strike at the American carriers. Before Nagumo left his flagship, the *Hiryu* launched eighteen dive-bombers and six fighters to seek out the American carriers. A veteran of the Pearl Harbor attack, Lt. Michio Koboyashi, led the flight.

It was noon when the Bakugeki 99 dive-bombers from the *Hiryu* and six Zeros tangled with the *Yorktown*'s combat air patrol 20 miles away. In a swirling dogfight, all but eight bombers were shot down, but the remainder evaded heavy antiaircraft fire and snarling *Yorktown* fighters to start their runs. Three hits were made on the carrier. Before Japanese bombers could find safety in distance, all but five bombers and three fighters were splashed in the ocean. Koboyashi was one of those who did not return. Damage to the carrier was not serious, and repairs were made quickly.

Commander Thach returned to the *Yorktown* in the midst of the battle. He noted that Japanese dive-bombers had placed one bomb right down the stack, putting the ship out of commission until engineers were able to rig temporary steam lines and get the ship up to 16 knots.

Dive-bomber attacks continued during the landing, and the *Yorktown*'s combat patrol was right on their tails. With the ship's guns blazing around him, Thach took off and turned while cranking the wheels of his F4F the more than thirty turns required to retract his landing gear.

At 2:30 the call came on the *Yorktown*, "Launch fighters."

Admiral Yamaguchi had ordered his last sixteen planes to attack the other two carriers. This time torpedo bombers, led by Lt. Joichi Tomonaga, were fighter-escorted. They found a curtain of flak walling the *Yorktown*, but half of them got through.

While gunners poured shells in their 5-inchers, 20 mm and 40 mm cannons roared incessantly, the Japanese headed straight for the carrier. Captain Buckmaster marveled at their survival. In a display of raw courage, four Japanese pilots reached their dropping points.

Thach dove at one torpedo plane and opened fire when he got the plane in his sights. One Japanese plane, possibly the one flown by Tomonaga, headed just above the waves. Its wing was on fire with its ribs protruding, but its pilot kept steadily on course until his torpedo was released and headed for the *Yorktown*. Seconds later, the stream of fire from Thach's Wildcat tore the torpedo bomber apart.

Another Wildcat took off from the *Yorktown*, and with its wheels still down, managed to shoot down another torpedo plane. The American fighter pilot, in turn, was shot down by a Zero, having been airborne for only sixty seconds. Fortunately, he survived the crash at sea and was recovered by a destroyer.

Buckmaster had been barking orders throughout the attack, and the *Yorktown* swung first this way and then sharply the other way, managing to avoid the first two torpedoes. It was impossible for the large ship to escape them all, and two caught her amidships. The shock almost threw Buckmaster off his feet. Recovering quickly, he called for an immediate report of damage. "Large holes in our port side, sir," a tremulous voice called to the bridge. Firing ceased, and the silence was almost unbearable. Buckmaster nodded grimly when someone said, "Got the last of the bombers, sir." "I'm afraid they've got the *Yorktown*," he said sadly.

The action had lasted only six minutes. The *Yorktown* was listing heavily to port, losing speed, and turning in a tight circle out of control. Fletcher left the ship to go on board the cruiser *Astoria* to keep in touch with the rest of his fleet. Buckmaster, after surveying the damage, could see that his ship was about to capsize. At 3:05, he called, "Abandon ship!"

The scouts went in search of the *Hiryu*, bent on vengeance. Lt. Samuel Adams found her, gave her position to the *Enterprise* and *Hornet*, and planes were launched immediately.

Admiral Yamaguchi now learned the true American strength. A scout plane from the *Soryu*, which was forced to land on the *Hiryu* because its own ship was on fire, reported that there were three American carriers, and the scout's pilot accurately reported them as the *Enterprise*, *Hornet*, and *Yorktown*. This news came as a shock to Yamaguchi because all three carriers had been reported sunk during the Coral Sea battle.

When Yamaguchi got a report on the second *Yorktown* attack, he assumed incorrectly that Tomonaga had hit a different carrier so now two carriers were dead in the water. He decided to expend his last five dive-bombers, four torpedo planes, and six fighters in a twilight attack. The remaining crews, however, had to have some rest. They were in a state of exhaustion. While a scout plane went out again to search for what Yamaguchi thought was the last surviving carrier, the pilots were fed rice balls.

Yamamoto was 600 miles from the battle, which was now being resolved so quickly that he had no time to speed to the rescue of his beleaguered carriers. When Captain Aoki wired for permission to sink the *Akagi*, Yamamoto delayed permission because he could not comprehend the disaster that had overtaken Nagumo's fleet. After he was apprised of the realities of the situation, he agreed to her sinking but refused to permit her skipper to go down with his ship.

Enterprise scout bombers sighted the *Hiryu* at 4:50. Far to the south, three columns of smoke were spiraling from the three Japanese carriers that had been attacked earlier. Lt. Wilmer E. Gallaher led another contingent, which had taken part in some of the earlier attacks, from the *Enterprise*.

The *Hiryu*'s lookouts spotted the attackers at 5:00 P.M. while their own planes were being readied for the third attack ordered by Admiral Yamaguchi at twilight. While the SBDs screamed down, the *Hiryu*'s captain Tomeo Kaka ordered full right rudder. Some bombs missed the carrier, but four landed on her deck and exploded among the gassed and bombed-up airplanes, adding to the horror and destruction.

A pitifully small number of Japanese fighters fought with desperation and managed to destroy three of the attackers.

Dive-bomber pilots gazed in awe as their first bombs lifted the *Hiryu*'s flight deck, throwing it back over the navigation bridge. When more bombs struck near the elevator, a huge mass of flames erupted.

Pilots from the *Hornet* now arrived, and they saw that the *Hiryu* was doomed, so they concentrated on the battleship *Kirishima*. Their bombs caused no serious damage.

Ens. Hisao Mandai directed the futile efforts of a work party that was attempting to remedy the damage to the *Hiryu*'s engine rooms. He no longer had any communication with the bridge and when it became apparent that the battle was lost, he reluctantly ordered his men topside.

They found the watertight door to the engineering department warped by the heat and jammed so tightly that they could not open it. Desperately, he and his men set about trying to cut a hole in the steel bulkhead with sledgehammers and chisels.

Air force B–17s now arrived again from Midway and as before expended their bombs on the ocean's surface.

The *Hiryu*'s crew continued to battle the flames, but the situation was hopeless. Her commander, Captain Kaka, accepted responsibility for the loss of his ship and announced that he would go down with it. Rear Admiral Yamaguchi ordered him to leave and to continue serving the Emperor, but Kaka refused to consider leaving his ship.

The first reports to Yamamoto had been misleading, saying that the American fleet was practically destroyed and retiring to the east. Yamamoto, acting on this false information, had ordered Nagumo to destroy what remained of America's Pacific Fleet. Once it became clear to Yamamoto that the battle was going against Nagumo, he ordered his decoy Aleutian carriers to rush back to Midway and ordered his own fleet, which was held in reserve, to proceed immediately to the combat zone.

When Nagumo informed him on the evening of June 4 that there were three American carriers and that they were steaming westward, Yamamoto was shocked. Nagumo now told him the truth. He was retiring to the northwest with the *Hiryu* in tow. Yamamoto now angrily removed Nagumo as overall commander. In his place, he put Vice-Adm. Nobutake Kondo, who had commanded the Midway invasion fleet.

The *Soryu* sank at 7:20 P.M. before her crew could be removed, and the *Kaga* followed five minutes later. To add to the misery of the *Kaga*'s final minutes, an American submarine, the *Nautilus*, under Lt. Comdr. William H. Brockman, Jr., dealt her mortal blows that sent her eight hundred remaining men and officers down with her.

Spruance decided to reverse course because he did not want a night battle against possibly superior enemy forces. He also wanted his fleet to be close to Midway on the next morning, June 5, to break up any landing there and to be in a position to follow the Japanese westward if they started to retreat.

The *Akagi* was scuttled at 5:00 A.M. the next morning after her interior was gutted by fire, but she had to be sunk by a destroyer's torpedo.

Ensign Mandai and his men, trapped in the *Hiryu*'s engine room, finally cut a hole in the steel bulkhead before dawn on June 5. Working their way topside, they were shocked to find the ship abandoned and to see the destruction around them. When they reached the flight deck, they joined a work party under Comdr. Kunizo Aiso who, with a party of thirty-nine men, had been left behind when the ship was abandoned. In the distance, they could see a Japanese destroyer and attempted to signal, but it drew off and vanished in the darkness.

By morning the ship was listing badly and down at the bow. Aiso and his work party scuttled the huge ship and hurriedly tried to find a means of escape. Aiso found the ship's cutter still hanging from its davits and ordered it launched. They scoured the ship for food but found only a few oranges, some sea biscuits, and a case of beer.

The cutter was not designed for the number of men in Aiso's and Mandai's parties and rode low in the water as they pulled away. Aiso ordered the rigging of a stub mast and, using a blanket for a sail, placed a Japanese flag at the top of the mast. He ordered course set for Wake Island, the nearest point of land known to be held by the Japanese, and left the area without being spotted by other Japanese ships.

Despite its scuttling, the *Hiryu* refused to go down, and it had to be sunk by a Japanese destroyer at 9:00 A.M. with a spread of torpedoes. Her skipper, Captain Kaka, went down with her. All her planes and five hundred men and sixty pilots of the ship's complement were killed in action, including one of Japan's finest flag officers, Rear Admiral Yamaguchi.

On a nearby ship, Captain Kawaguchi, the *Hiryu*'s air officer, watched her destruction with tears in his eyes. He began to realize that the Americans were about to win control of the air in the Pacific.

After Yamamoto received reports that the American fleet was retreating, he realized that there was no possibility of a night action and considered total withdrawal. In daylight, his ships would be at the mercy of American carrier planes. An aide suggested that all ships go to Midway and shell it before they withdrew from the battle scene. The *Yamato*'s guns, he said, and those of the other capital ships, could put the airfield at Midway out of action and permit the island to be occupied by Japanese troops.

"Of all naval tactics, firing one's guns at an island is considered the most stupid," Yamamoto replied sharply. "You've been playing too much shogi!"

Admiral Ugaki suggested that they wait for the Aleutian carriers and perhaps launch another attack. He said that if this proved impossible, "we must accept defeat in this operation but we will not have lost the war."

Yamamoto now learned that the *Hiryu* was sinking. He knew that he had to be realistic. He was shocked by the tragic losses of four carriers and thousands of men. He had initiated the Midway operation because he had believed that it would improve the chances of a negotiated peace with the United States. Such a thought had been uppermost in his mind from the time that he knew war was inevitable and that Japan stood no chance of winning a long war against the United States.

While his staff waited for Yamamoto's final decision, one officer, reflecting the consternation they all felt, asked who would admit defeat to the emperor. "I am the only one who must apologize to the emperor," Yamamoto replied sharply.

At 2:50 A.M. on June 5, Yamamoto ordered the Midway operation canceled.

Lt. Comdr. James S. Russell commanded the only naval air squadron in the 2,000-mile stretch of the Aleutians from the end of January 1942 to late May. Four of his planes were at Dutch Harbor, two were at Sitka, and six were at Kodiak with squadron headquarters.

The veteran pilot had been a seaman since he joined the Merchant Marine in 1918 at the age of fifteen after being turned down by the United States Navy because he was too young. Later, having graduated from the Naval Academy in 1922 and having become a superb pilot, he was first to fly from the navy's first six carriers. Russell was now one of a handful of experienced officers facing the Japanese invasion fleet.

His VP–42 had been flying PBY–5s since before the start of hostilities. They were veterans in Arctic flying, all too familiar with the Arctic winds that seemed to blow east on one side of a runway and west on the other side.

Some strategists thought that the Aleutians were the northern highway to victory. Those who had been there knew otherwise. The glamour, if there ever had been any for these men, had long since worn off as, hungry and tired from long patrol missions, fliers returned to runways whipped by winds that ripped canvas tents and snapped guy wires. Mechanics often had to service airplanes in the open with no protection from the freezing temperatures and the williwaws—or Arctic winds—that suddenly materialized as violent gusts across the bleak tundra.

Flying in the Aleutians was an experience no flier would ever care to repeat. The continually changing atmosphere could close in stormily and suddenly. For anyone who crashed at sea, survival time was fewer than twenty minutes.

VP–42 was the first squadron to get radar in the Pacific. It was equipped with the British ASV system whose numerous antennas made the patrol planes look like porcupines. The radar poles caused problems because they collected ice and frequently became so heavy that they broke off. It was amazing that the primitive radar sets worked as well as they did with so many "hay rakes" missing.

For months, while war raged in the south, efforts had been directed toward establishing the capability to service naval planes in the Aleutians. Living conditions improved gradually, but weather maintained a miserable monotony.

Japanese planes from Admiral Hosogaya's fleet carriers the *Ryujo* and *Junyo* took off at 7 A.M. on June 3 for Dutch Harbor prior to the start of operations at Midway. Yamamoto had conceived the attack as a classic feint on the flank while striking at the center of the American's strength at Midway. Only the *Ryujo*'s planes got through to their targets the first day; the *Junyo*'s planes were forced to turn back because of bad weather.

A new American squadron, VP–41, was rushed to the Aleutians in late May. Lt. Gene Cusick, one of its pilots, took off in a Catalina to search southwest of Dutch Harbor for the Japanese fleet. When Cusick's plane failed to return, squadron officials believed that he had run into the Japanese carriers.

One of Russell's VP–42 pilots, Lt. Lucius D. Campbell, found the Japanese fleet, but his radio report was so garbled that Russell was in doubt about its location. He had heard enough, however, to know that Campbell had located the enemy.

June 4, the day the Japanese struck Midway, was also the date Hosogaya sent his bombers out with orders to destroy American installations at Adak, even though Adak at this time had no facilities or garrison. The attack was canceled because of bad weather. In the afternoon, Japanese carrier planes bombed Dutch Harbor.

Six United States Army Air Force B–26 bombers, under Col. William "Wild Bill" Eareckson, took off with torpedoes strapped under their bellies. Lieutenant Commander Russell had helped to rig the B–26s with torpedoes and had also set up a temporary radio receiver to maintain contact in the air. Lt. George W. Thornbrough was the only pilot who found the Japanese fleet. He made several approaches against heavy antiaircraft fire but each time the Japanese ships turned endwise so he knew he had no chance of hitting one of them. Russell had warned the air force pilots that if they flew too fast, high velocity air moving past the impellers on the noses of the torpedoes might arm the warheads just as if the weapon was traveling through water. Thornbrough decided to try a new tactic and deliberately dove his plane at high speed, hoping to cause the impeller to spin so that he could drop an armed torpedo like a bomb on the carrier *Ryujo*.

Masatake Okumiya, air operations officer of the flagship, saw Thornbrough's B–26 fly the length of the carrier's deck and drop what appeared to be a very large bomb. To his relief, it landed in the wake of the ship with only a slight splash. Obviously, it had not armed itself because it did not explode.

Thornbrough knew that he had missed as he returned to his base at Cold Bay and reviewed the Japanese formation with Russell. A report was sent immediately to Kodiak that described the formation and its composition. Thornbrough now insisted on going out again. This time he gave orders to load his B–26 with 500-pound bombs.

Russell waited impatiently for word from Thornbrough and when it came, he learned that the air force pilot had failed to find the Japanese fleet and had returned to find his base at Cold Bay socked in. So heavy was the cloud cover that he could not get down through the overcast. Russell called the seaplane tender in the harbor and asked her skipper to get on Thornbrough's radio frequency and try to talk him down. They were not successful, and several days later the wreckage of Thornbrough's plane was found. There were no survivors.

Meanwhile, Lieutenant Campbell dogged the Japanese fleet and radioed reports back to headquarters. He continually avoided Zeros by flitting in and out of the clouds. Once, when he thought he was safe, he found a Zero on his tail with bullets spitting all around his Catalina. His radar picked up images in the air and at first he thought that the Japanese fighter pilots were being directed by radar to his position. At this time, the Japanese did not have radar on their planes and Campbell's Catalina was kept in sight only by keen-eyed fighter pilots.

Finally, Campbell's plane became so full of holes that he had to head for the dispersion harbor at Akutan. He ran out of fuel 50 miles from the island. His engines quit at 6,000 feet, and he headed down through the overcast but was unable to turn into the wind. His rudder cables had been shot away, and his hull was full of holes. He broke through the overcast at 300 feet. He had neglected to cut his engine switches when they quit and now the downwind engine caught briefly. It kicked the Catalina a little more into the wind before quitting for good. He made a smooth landing, and the holes in the hull were quickly patched. The Coast Guard was alerted to his precarious position, and he and his crew were soon picked up and returned to base.

Lt. Marshall Freerks tracked the Japanese ships that morning until he ran low on fuel. He was replaced by a plane flown by Lt. Eugene W. Stockstill. He was sent out because American fighters were weathered in. Japanese fighters shot down Stockstill's plane, and all were lost without a trace.

When the Japanese appeared to be losing at Midway, Yamamoto decided to give up the Aleutian operation as well. He radioed Hosogaya, whose Fifth Fleet was in Aleutian waters, to concentrate on the Midway force and return to Japan.

Hosogaya sent a message to Yamamoto asking for permission to let his northern force proceed with its invasion, pointing out that American territory could be taken easily and although Japan had had a reverse at Midway, he was positive that her forces would be successful in the Aleutians. Yamamoto therefore authorized the reinstatement of the Aleutian operation subject to a later modification of orders. He advised Hosogaya to occupy Attu and Kiska but not to take Adak.

(Russell and other commanders noted the heavy radio traffic between Yamamoto and Hosogaya, easily distinguishing the Japanese messages in Morse code from those of the Americans even though they did not understand them. It was easy to detect Japanese messages because they used the forty-odd characters of the Japanese language compared with twenty-six in the English alphabet.)

When Attu and Kiska were occupied by the Japanese, the United States decided not to try to retake them for the time being, but they were bombed repeatedly. Catalinas were used at first until the Army Air Forces built up their B–24 bomber strength to take on the job.

One unexpected benefit to the Americans of the Aleutian campaign was the location of a nearly intact Zero 21 fighter plane that had crash-landed in a bog, on Akutan, breaking the pilot's neck. On the third salvage attempt in late June, the plane was recovered with the pilot's corpse still in it. It was damaged only by 50 caliber bullets, which led to the conclusion that it had been shot down by Ens. Albert Mitchell's Catalina of VP–42 before he himself was shot down.

The Zero was rebuilt at the North Island Naval Air Station near San Diego and flown in October. This was the first modern Japanese plane in a flyable condition to be captured during the war. Experienced pilots who flew it were impressed by the finish of all surfaces, the close and accurate fit of fairings, and the outstanding job of design and manufacture.

During extensive flight tests and evaluations, engineers probed the Zero's secrets. It was learned that the Zero 21's engine was not as supercharged as the Pratt & Whitney engines used in American planes, and compared poorly in this regard to American. One combat pilot pointed out that such a capability was not important because American pilots in their F4Fs hardly ever encountered Japanese pilots above 10,000 feet. The supercharger hardware carried by American planes was thus extra baggage that reduced their performance.

In tests against American fighters, it was learned that the built-in incidence of the Zero's vertical surfaces was designed to counter the tremendous torque produced on takeoff by the Japanese fighter's large propeller. This incidence was designed into the Zero so that the pilot would not have to use excessive right rudder on takeoff. In flight, however—and particularly at high speeds—the Zero rolled very fast toward the right but only slowly to the left. One of Thach's new combat techniques, therefore, was to attack Zeros at high speed and roll to the left, which was the Zero's slow-roll direction.

Tests showed that a good spray of bullets would make the Japanese fighters disintegrate because they had little or no armor protection. They also showed that the Zero 21 carried numerous rounds of 7.7 mm ammunition for its two fuselage guns but only 80 to 100 rounds for each of its 20 mm guns. It was established that Japanese pilots normally used the 7.7 guns for sighting before firing their 20 mm cannon.

The fact that a Zero was available for American flight tests so early in the war was an enormous asset to later combat operations. The tests on the Zero proved so valuable that the F6F Hellcat was redesigned, becoming so effective in combat that it ended the Zero's dominance in future operations.

At Midway, Lt. Comdr. John W. Murphy, Jr., in the American submarine *Tambor*, had located Japanese warships at 3:30 A.M. on

June 5. This was the fleet under Rear Adm. Takeo Kurita that had turned around after Yamamoto canceled the Midway strike an hour earlier. The *Tambor* dogged Kurita's ships for the rest of the night, waiting until dawn so that Murphy could be positively identified. When his submarine was spotted, there was such confusion that the *Mogami* rammed the *Mikuma*. Although the *Mikuma* was severely damaged, both ships remained underway.

Once the position of the Japanese ships was relayed to Spruance's flagship and to the defenders at Midway, air force B–17s and navy bombers went out to try and finish off the *Mikuma*. They easily found her oil slick.

Capt. Richard E. Fleming, with six SBDs, found the *Mikuma* and started to attack her. Fleming's plane was hit so heavily by the ship's antiaircraft fire that it caught fire and crashed onto the ship. Both Japanese ships limped away without further damage. Fleming was later awarded a Medal of Honor.

The next day the *Mogami*, which had lost its bow in the ramming, fought off SBD attacks from the *Hornet* and *Enterprise* and limped away. Eventually, it reached Truk with its destroyer screens, but loss of life on all ships was high.

The *Mikuma* was not so fortunate. It was finished off by some of the same SBDs that had attacked the *Mogami*.

The *Yorktown*, which had been taken in tow in an attempt to salvage her, was struck by torpedoes from a Japanese submarine commanded by Lt. Comdr. Yahochi Tanabe. Captain Buckmaster had labored heroically to save his beloved ship but her hour had come. A minute after 6:00 A.M. on June 6 she turned slowly on her side and slid beneath the waves. The destroyer *Hammann* alongside broke in half and sank along with her.

Throughout the Midway battle, Ensign Gay, sole survivor of Torpedo Eight, had a fish-eye view. Trying to hide under the seat cushion that had floated free when his torpedo bomber sank, he watched three Japanese carriers lose headway and screening ships appear all around him. The *Akagi*, *Kaga*, and *Soryu* were burning fiercely. From their open ends, fire streamed like flames from a blowtorch.

At first, Gay did not think about sharks. After awhile the thought scared him, but he saw none. He guessed that the explosions all around him had scared them away.

Finally, after partially inflating his life raft, he reviewed his condition. He had a bullet hole in his left arm, a piece of shrapnel in his left hand, and his left leg was badly burned. He knew he had lost a lot of blood, and after having been in the water for thirty hours, he was becoming seriously dehydrated.

He was all alone in the area, as far as he knew. Once he saw a PBY–5A fly over and watched with despair as it continued on. Although he did not know it, they had spotted him, but they had orders to complete a search for remnants of the Japanese fleet.

The pilot, Lt. Shelby O. "Pappy" Cole of VP–43, had radioed Midway when Gay was spotted to send a PT boat to pick him up, but they told him it would take three days. Over the intercom, Cole talked to his crew after they completed their search, saying that he would like to land and pick the guy up, but he thought that such a dangerous operation should be submitted to a vote.

They all readily agreed.

He set the plane down and, as he taxied up to Gay, Cole said, "Have you seen any Zeros today?"

"No."

"Good. Let's get the hell out of here."

They hauled the weakened Gay out of the raft and took off. He was grateful, knowing that if Japanese fighters had caught them on the water, the plane would have been easily destroyed. He was taken to Midway first but transferred to Pearl Harbor for extensive convalescence.

Twelve days later, another American PBY–5 was returning to Midway from patrol toward Wake Island. It had not seen a ship of any kind for hours.

The pilot, Lt. "Speedball" Campbell, and his crew of Squadron VP–11 were exhausted after two weeks of rescue and patrol work following the Midway battle. C. R. Frieze, second mechanic on the plane, was dozing in the waist hatch. He was jolted awake by Campbell's voice on the intercom. "Gentlemen, there's a boat out there ahead of us. It's flying a Japanese flag. Rig out the port fifty. I'm going to make a pass. If they don't haul down the flag, shoot the damn thing down." He paused. "Try not to hit anyone in the boat unless they shoot at us. If they do, sink the boat."

Below, the men of the *Hiryu*'s cutter had made slow progress. They suffered from thirst, starvation, and exposure. Four had died, and their bodies had been dumped over the side. On their twelfth day at sea, the survivors saw a large flying boat approach from the direction of Wake Island. The exhausted men started to shout and cheer, waving to the plane with tears in their eyes, but their jubilation vanished when they saw the big white star on the side of the fuselage.

Someone pulled down the sail and Japanese flag, and they draped themselves with the blanket sail, huddling in despair. They watched fearfully as the American plane approached closely, noticing the heavy machine gun tracking them. One Japanese removed his white shirt and waved it, and the gun remained silent.

On the plane there were mixed emotions. Some almost wished that the Japanese would make some threatening gesture so that they could use the gun. Their base at Kaneohe had been one of those hard hit during the attack on Pearl Harbor. The squadron had lost most of its planes, and seventeen VP–11 men had died with many more wounded.

Campbell ordered the machine gun stowed, and he reported the cutter's position to officials at Midway. The destroyer U.S.S. *Ballard* was ordered to pick up the survivors and return them to the island. They were the only Japanese prisoners to be brought to Midway.

A messenger appeared at Campbell's airplane on Midway on June 17 with a small box of trinkets, including Japanese uniform buttons and insignia. Commander Aiso had sent them in gratitude because Campbell's crew had not sunk his cutter.

Spruance, who had long before earned the respect of all members of his command, took the victory with customary modesty. His experience and intelligent decisions were in large part responsible for the victory.

Admiral Nimitz' decision to face most of Japan's navy at Midway with only three American carriers had at last turned the tide of the Pacific war. It had been a decisive defeat for the Japanese; their attempt to pierce the outer defenses of the United States had met with disaster. They had lost four carriers and a cruiser. The battleship *Kirishima* and destroyer *Tanikaze* were badly damaged. The operation had cost the Japanese 2,000 sailors and 100 irreplaceable pilots, plus 322 carrier aircraft. American losses included the *Yorktown*, 109 carrier planes, 38 shore-based airplanes, and 307 men.

Carriers had proved themselves despite overwhelming opposition, and airpower reached maturity in the minds of those who had doubted its effectiveness. It was a great victory, resulting in large part from the work of the SBD dive-bombers.

During the Battle of the Coral Sea, when the carriers *Zuikaku* and *Shokaku* were damaged, the Japanese had lost one third of their airpower. Unquestionably, these losses contributed to their defeat at Midway.

The Japanese, stunned by this latest defeat, reorganized their strategic plans. They had lost five carriers, half their carrier strength, during May and June. It therefore became necessary to remove the battleships *Ise* and *Hyuga* from operations and convert them to carriers.

The Midway disaster was not mentioned in the Japanese press or on the radio, although the landings in the Aleutians were revealed. When the Japanese fleet returned to Japan, all crewmen were denied home leave, and the wounded were secretly taken to isolated hospitals.

The defeat made Yamamoto ill, and he isolated himself, although he was still revered by the Japanese people.

The Japanese had been outguessed at Midway. The breaking of their code was an incomparable asset. It enabled the United States to follow Japanese ship movements with some degree of accuracy. However, Nimitz did not dare put full reliance on decoded messages because he feared that he might be misled. Like most intelligence data, reports of Japanese ship movements were voluminous and of mixed quality.

After the battle, Spruance's fleet returned to Pearl Harbor flying the Number 2 pennant, used to mark a victory of which the fleet is proud, instead of the Number 1 pennant, which is reserved for great and decisive actions.

9

A PROFOUND LESSON
IN THE TENACITY OF
JAPAN'S FOOT SOLDIERS

Admiral King's elation about the victory at Midway was tempered by stories in the Chicago *Tribune* and the Washington *Times–Herald* saying that the United States had known in advance about the Japanese intentions. He was furious, thinking that the closely guarded secret of the Americans' breaking the Japanese code was endangered. Incredibly, the Japanese never learned that their code had been broken.

Admiral Nimitz studied a large map of the Pacific. With the occupation of part of the Aleutians, the Japanese had a battle line stretching from Alaskan waters to the Solomons in the South Pacific. He knew that they had received a severe setback during the battles of the Coral Sea and Midway, so an all-out assault against Australia was not to be expected soon. After consultation with King in Washington, he decided to commit his forces to the South Pacific, where the Japanese posed a more immediate threat. Japan's bases in the northern Solomons and New Britain posed a stumbling block to the Allied command—one which would become serious if the Japanese continued to press southward.

"The chain of islands to the east of New Guinea," he told his staff, "is the logical route to return to the Philippines."

Nimitz established a new command for the South Pacific under Vice-Adm. Robert L. Ghormley. He wired precise instructions. "Hold the island position. Continue to support operations in the southwest and central Pacific. Amphibious operations should be planned against positions now held by the Japanese. D Day is tentatively scheduled for August 1."

General MacArthur proposed a different plan. He recommended

to General Marshall that Rabaul be invaded. Marshall approved the plan on June 12, believing that Admiral King would provide the necessary ships.

Earlier, the question of theater priorities had been temporarily resolved when King assured Marshall that he would support an eventual cross-channel invasion of Europe. President Roosevelt had supported Marshall's plan because he was anxious to get American troops involved in the European theater. The president was under constant pressure by the American people and the nation's news media to send American troops to Europe despite the fact that army troops were not available in large numbers and needed extensive training. King stipulated, however, that he would withdraw support if such an invasion reduced Pacific forces to the danger point.

After the victory at Midway, King wanted to go on the offensive in the Pacific while Japanese ship losses had the Imperial High Command in a state of shock. Marshall did begin to be inclined toward starting a limited offensive in the Pacific but not at the expense of an invasion of Hitler's Europe.

After reviewing MacArthur's plans to invade Rabaul, Marshall decided the risks were too great because it was heavily defended. Instead, he proposed that American troops make an indirect approach through the eastern Solomons, where defenses were weaker. He also flatly turned down MacArthur's request to command major elements of the Pacific Fleet. He told the general that in any amphibious assault, the commander had to be one of Nimitz' officers.

King acted quickly. He directed Nimitz to prepare for the seizure of Tulagi in the Solomons with amphibious forces—an order contrary to President Roosevelt's decision not to increase American strength in the Pacific. King's order also meant that Nimitz' forces would be used in MacArthur's assigned area, which was counter to an agreement that such action would not be taken without the president's or Joint Chiefs' specific approval.

King used as an excuse the almost forgotten presidential approval—granted in March and never canceled—that a limited operation in the Solomons was permissible. The president had not specifically prohibited such operations. Also, King told Nimitz only to "prepare for an assault." Still, he was on dangerous ground.

The plan was presented to the Joint Chiefs of Staff by King on June 25 for concurrence only. Unexpectedly, MacArthur agreed to abandon his plans for an attack on Rabaul and back King's plan instead. Marshall went along but insisted that MacArthur command the operation. King refused.

He believed that Marshall, who had served under MacArthur as a staff officer, was too subservient to his former boss. Secretary of War Stimson also supported MacArthur's bid to command the operation, but King remained obdurate that command should be invested in Nimitz. King and Stimson disliked one another, and King believed Stimson's views were mainly an expression of his strong backing for the general.

Marshall was in a difficult position, and King took full advantage of the situation, saying that army officers did not understand either airpower or sea power. As always, he fought stubbornly for his position.

MacArthur was livid at King's insistence that Nimitz be responsible for the seizure of Tulagi. He sent angry messages to Washington that valuable time was being lost and that the Japanese were recovering quickly from their defeat at Midway. In a letter he reminded Marshall that the army had supreme command in Europe, and he expected no less in the Pacific. He said that, with or without support from the navy, he would invade the Solomons. How this would be done without the navy's warships and transports, he did not specify. Finally, he told Marshall that if the navy was permitted to have its way the army would be reduced to an "occupation force."

MacArthur lost the argument when King and Marshall reached a compromise on June 30: Nimitz' command was moved farther west—deep into MacArthur's territory—to encompass the eastern Solomons, including Tulagi. They also agreed that Vice-Admiral Ghormley would command the assault in the eastern Solomons.

A compromise was also reached for future assaults. MacArthur would command operations in the western Solomons, eastern New Guinea, and the Bismarck Archipelago. The Joint Chiefs approved this new Pacific stategy on July 2. The assault on the eastern Solomons would start on August 1, 1942. King was satisfied, knowing that an American counteroffensive in the Pacific was about to begin.

King came to see Nimitz and his staff in San Francisco on the Fourth of July. Nimitz almost did not make it—his seaplane hit a log on landing and he narrowly escaped being killed.

"The eastern Solomons is only the start of our counteroffensive," King told Nimitz. After they were seized, and New Guinea occupied, he wanted Truk, Saipan, and Guam invaded. Despite his compromise agreement with Marshall, King now made it clear that none of these plans included General MacArthur's forces. To a surprised Nimitz, he admitted that these were his own ideas, unapproved by either the president or the Joint Chiefs.

Rear Adm. Richmond Kelly Turner had been invited to the meeting because Nimitz had selected him to command the South Pacific's amphibious forces. Turner began to demur, saying he knew nothing about such operations, but King peremptorily told him he would soon learn, and that he was not alone—few others knew anything about amphibious operations. It was King's way of backing Nimitz' selection of Turner, believing that this brilliant, often arrogant officer would succeed.

Turner had been busy ever since he was given the command. He laid out his plans for King and Nimitz, saying that he intended first to occupy the Santa Cruz Islands and Tulagi, Florida, and Guadalcanal islands in the eastern Solomons. Then he proposed the occupation of Funafuti in the Ellice Islands and the reinforcement of the army garrison on Espiritu Santo Island in the New Hebrides. King quickly agreed.

When Ghormley was apprised of these ambitious plans, he sided with MacArthur, who said that the available forces were inadequate unless strong reinforcements were assigned. MacArthur's persuasive powers were considerable, and with great success he used them to get Ghormley to agree. Both men wrote Washington about their doubts, and King reacted with anger. This was not the first time that one of his admirals had succumbed to MacArthur's charm, and his esteem for Ghormley went down. King referred to MacArthur as vacillating and fainthearted, pointing out to his staff that the general had been ready to attack Rabaul only three weeks earlier.

Actually, MacArthur was sulking because of his downgraded position in planned operations in the South Pacific. He was not made any happier when Marshall supported King, at least in the initial operations in the eastern Solomons. Ghormley quickly changed his mind when he saw how the situation was developing in Washington, offering the excuse that MacArthur had promised him air support.

President Roosevelt recalled former Chief of Naval Operations Admiral William D. Leahy to active duty in early July as his personal chief of staff. King was unhappy with the decision, even though Roosevelt stressed that Leahy would be only a personal aide. He had no command authority and King, Marshall, and Arnold had access to the President whenever they wished. Actually, Leahy's seniority made him something akin to a de facto chairman of the Joint Chiefs of Staff.

King began to doubt that sufficient forces were available in the South Pacific for upcoming operations. He pressed Marshall and

Arnold for more men and equipment, but Marshall refused all requests because of the planned invasion of North Africa in the fall. King continued to insist that the Allies should take at least a limited offensive in the South Pacific, believing that the Japanese should not be permitted to consolidate their gains, which would give them an opportunity to make a direct assault on Australia. Therefore, he continued to resist all attempts at the highest levels in Washington and London to reduce the Pacific war to a defensive role. He recognized that Guadalcanal, centrally located in the South Pacific and ideally suited for air bases, would be the key to Japan's plans for expansion to the south, particularly after the Japanese seized Tulagi, located opposite Guadalcanal. He was also aware that Tulagi's terrain prohibited the establishment of airfields, although the Japanese quickly established a seaplane base there while they were building air bases on other islands in the area.

King's efforts to start a limited South Pacific offensive were successful when he obtained a directive from the Joint Chiefs of Staff on July 2, 1942, for Ghormley's South Pacific Force to seize Tulagi and Guadalcanal and for MacArthur's Southwest Pacific Forces to take over the rest of the Solomons and later Rabaul. Despite Marshall's objections that such actions were contrary to previously established strategic plans, King's views prevailed because of his strong arguments that the occupation of these islands was necessary to stop Japan's advances in the area and to provide bases for future Allied drives on the long road back to the Philippines and toward the eventual defeat of Japan.

Execution of King's plan took far longer than he had envisioned. Before Guadalcanal could be secured six months later, there would be seven major naval engagements and ten hard-fought battles on land.

The Japanese occupied the north central shore of Guadalcanal on July 4 and moved down the east coast of New Guinea. Ghormley, in association with MacArthur, organized three major task forces. Task Force NAN, under Rear Adm. Leigh Noyes, was assigned to provide carrier support for the counterattack, with the *Saratoga* commanded by Capt. DeWitt Ramsey, the *Enterprise* under Capt. Arthur G. Davis, and the *Wasp* under Capt. Forrest P. Sherman. A second amphibious force for the landings, a third force to supply aerial scouting, and seaplanes completed the arrangements. There was to be advance bombing by land-based planes.

The carriers departed from Wellington, New Zealand, to conduct rehearsals for major assaults on Tulagi and Guadalcanal, now scheduled for August 7. Prior to D Day, the amphibious forces split with the Tulagi force, clearing Savo Island and Cape Esperance at the northern tip of Guadalcanal.

On D Day, Task Force NAN launched planes just before sunrise, its pilots having difficulty in forming up because the carriers were so close to one another. The planes hit installations at Guadalcanal and Tulagi just as the sun rose in the east, catching the Japanese by surprise.

The operation was codenamed "Watchtower"; the marines called it "Operation Shoestring." It would be the first American amphibious operation since 1898, when American forces had stormed ashore in Cuba. Ghormley had been doubtful of its success from the start. Preparations for landings had been made in haste, and the Americans' lack of experience in such operations was exacerbated by inadequate maps of the area.

Adm. Frank J. Fletcher, responsible for execution of the operation, told Ghormley that he did not like it and predicted failure. He openly told associates that he would not expose his three carriers— the *Enterprise, Saratoga*, and *Wasp*—for more than two days while the marines were landing. He and Ghormley estimated that the landings would take five days, so the marines would be exposed without air cover for three days. Fletcher had grown increasingly cautious because he had already lost two carriers—the *Yorktown* and *Lexington*—to the Japanese.

While Ghormley remained at South Pacific Force Headquarters in Auckland, New Zealand, the marines arrived off Guadalcanal's Beach Red and Tulagi's Beach Blue on August 7. Fletcher was aboard his flagship the *Saratoga* 100 miles to the south.

Lt. Gen. George C. Kenney's 11th Bombardment Group's planes and carrier bombers made strikes on the proposed landing areas during the last week of July and the first week of August. The unfinished airstrip on Guadalcanal received the most attention because, once in operation by the Japanese, it could be used to launch strikes against targets in New Zealand and to harass Australia-bound shipping.

Marines left their transports off Guadalcanal and Tulagi at dawn and boarded their landing craft, while ships bombarded Japanese defensive positions. Carrier-based bombers swung low over the invasion fleet, striking strong blows against Japanese artillery positions.

The First Marine Division hit the beaches on Guadalcanal with little opposition and started to move inland by 9 A.M. There were only six hundred Japanese defenders on the beaches instead of the five thousand that had been predicted. Most had retreated inland, abandoning their supplies.

Brig. Gen. Alexander A. Vandegrift quickly assessed the situation. The beaches were dangerously cluttered, but he was forced to continue unloading men and supplies.

Forty-five Japanese planes, bombers with fighter escorts from the Twenty-fifth Koku Sentai, appeared at 12:30. Lt. Vincent de Poix of the *Enterprise* spotted them over Florida Island and attacked with three other Wildcats. Betty bombers succumbed to their guns in rapid succession until the Zeros bore down on the outnumbered F4Fs and halted the attacks.

Off the beaches, ships stopped their unloading and tried to maneuver to evade the Japanese bombs. Navy fighters swarmed to the area, and so tenacious were their assaults that the Japanese bombers had to retire. No ships were hit.

The ships were in Sealark Channel between Florida and Guadalcanal islands, later named "Iron Bottom Bay" for the number of ships from both sides that sank there.

Navy carriers had been alerted by a coastwatcher to the approach of Japanese planes, so Wildcats were on the scene in time to fight them off. Flight Petty Officer Saburo Sakai, one of Japan's top fighter aces, was badly wounded in the fray and barely made it back to Rabaul. The action cost the Japanese thirty planes, some lost during their return because of fuel shortages.

At Tulagi, marines ran into fierce resistance. There, unlike Guadalcanal, Allied troops were given a profound lesson in the tenacity of Japan's foot soldiers.

Carriers and other warships continued to fight off Japanese aerial attacks. The following day, forty more Japanese planes headed for the invasion areas. Wildcats met them over Savo Island in the channel between Florida and Guadalcanal islands. Japanese Betty bombers dropped down to race toward American ships, just above the water. All guns were brought to bear and a dozen Japanese bombers plummeted in, some cartwheeling over the waves, aflame from nose to tail. One plane, however, released a torpedo that hit the destroyer *Jarvis*, forcing it to retreat toward Nouméa in New Caledonia. The ship never made it; a torpedo plane sank it the next day. A stricken Betty crashed on the transport *George F. Elliott*. Her troops had already disembarked, but the decks were loaded with supplies that caught fire, and the ship was doomed. It was scuttled in Iron Bottom Bay that night.

American carrier planes fought well, but losses rose and only seventy-eight fighters were still available for combat. Task Force Commander Admiral Fletcher wired Ghormley at Nouméa, "Recommend air support groups be withdrawn because of heavy enemy torpedo and bombing attacks."

Fletcher had panicked. He justified his request for withdrawal by saying that his ships were low on fuel, which was not true. It *is* true that Fletcher's carriers were in an extremely vulnerable position, but these carriers offered the primary protection for the imperiled marine invasion troops.

Ghormley approved the action but Vandegrift, commander of the First Marine Division, bitterly opposed it in a message to Ghormley because it would expose his amphibious forces to massive Japanese air attacks. Because of his protests, Fletcher's ships remained in the area but pulled back from the invasion front.

Adm. Gunichi Mikawa, once he learned of these landings, assembled Japanese ships from Rabaul and Kavieng, a town on New Ireland in the Bismarck Archipelago, and ordered them to proceed at high speed for the Solomons. "We will penetrate south of Savo Island and torpedo the enemy main force at Guadalcanal." Every man was called upon to exert his utmost skill in what was planned as a night action.

With Fletcher's carriers pulling back from the front, Mikawa's ships were never plotted adequately and approached without opposition through the Slot, the channel between New Georgia and Santa Isabel islands northwest of Guadalcanal, even though an Australian scout plane reported their presence. The pilot's report was so mishandled by him, and later by higher authorities, that Admiral Turner received no word of the Japanese warships for eight hours. The pilot's report was, moreover, inaccurate; he misidentified two Japanese cruisers as airplane tenders.

With this misinformation, Turner assumed that the Japanese task group would not put in an appearance that night, believing instead that the Japanese would first set up a seaplane base at Santa Isabel Island, 150 miles from Savo, and make their attack on the Guadalcanal beachhead at a later date.

His assumption proved erroneous, and he compounded his error by dividing his forces into three groups to guard the sea approaches to Tulagi. Rear Adm. Norman Scott had two light cruisers and two destroyers to patrol the area between Tulagi and Guadalcanal so his ships were too far away to participate in any confrontation with Japanese ships. Rear Adm. Sir Victor Crutchley of Great Britain's Royal Navy had six heavy cruisers and six destroyers to guard two of the western approaches to Savo Island. The red-bearded officer had proved his gallantry during the Battle of Jutland in World War I, thereby winning a Victoria Cross. For unknown reasons, Crutchley failed to issue a battle plan before his ships were suddenly thrust into action, but even worse, he had divided his slim forces. Crutchley took personal charge of the group guarding the sound's south entrance in the H.M.A.S. Australia with her sister ship the Canberra, U.S.S. Chicago, and two American destroyers. The United States cruisers Vincennes, Astoria, and Quincy, plus two destroyers, were under the tactical command of Capt. F. L. Riefkohl in the Vincennes to guard the northern entrance.

Turner's obsession with his belief that the Japanese would not attack that night prompted him to summon Crutchley from his flagship the Australia to a conference on board the American flagship McCawley at Lunga Roads, which was near Guadalcanal, approximately 20 miles away. Therefore, when Crutchley's leadership was most needed in the upcoming battle with his ships and the Japanese fleet, he was miles away conferring with Turner.

Japanese cruisers opened fire off Savo Island at Allied ships on August 9 at 1:30 A.M. Their Long Lance torpedoes sank four heavy cruisers and a destroyer; another cruiser and two destroyers were damaged. The night action killed more than a thousand men and wounded another seven hundred. Yet it could have been worse. If Mikawa had pressed on to the Guadalcanal beachhead, every American transport would have been destroyed. The American command could not believe it when he slipped away, passing up the opportunity to make an even more destructive impact on the Allied invasion fleet.

In Washington, Admiral King went into a state of shock over his losses, wondering what had gone wrong. He did his best to withhold the news from the press.

At noon the next day, Turner called for his amphibious ships to withdraw. They were exposed to another Japanese foray, and he believed that this left him no choice, even though it meant leaving Vandegrift's sixteen thousand marines unprotected and only half supplied.

The Japanese did not press their advantage, but their air fleets came methodically to bomb Henderson Field, named for Maj. Lofton Henderson, who had lost his life during the Battle of Midway. Marines struggled to make the airfield ready to support land-based airpower, but Henderson was bombed relentlessly. One Japanese pilot was called "Washing-Machine Charlie" because he droned over as regularly as clockwork each night to disrupt their sleep.

The Japanese high command in the islands believed that only three thousand marines were on Guadalcanal, but more than five times that number were actually entrenched there. Col. Kiyona Ichiki was sent to the island with his detachment and made landings virtually unopposed on August 18. They were practically destroyed in the two days of fighting that followed, but they fought with a ferocity that astonished the Americans. Some wounded Japanese booby-trapped themselves with grenades. When Americans came to examine them, they deliberately destroyed themselves, hoping to kill nearby marines.

Time after time, Ichiki's men charged American positions with bayonets although they faced automatic weapons. The inevitable happened, and eight hundred brave Japanese died. At the end, Ichiki burned his regimental colors and shot himself in the head.

The so-called Tokyo Express continued to bring in small numbers of reinforcements, but there were never enough to overcome the American marines.

Finally, eighteen Wildcats of Marine Aircraft Group 23 alighted on the airstrip at Lunga Point. The F4Fs were under Capt. John L. Smith, a lean Oklahoman who would soon prove his worth. Twelve SBDs of Maj. Richard D. Mangrum's VMSB–232 also set up operations. All of them were greeted wildly by the marines of the First Division.

Aircraft Group 23 immediately supplied four Wildcats to strafe remnants of Ichiki's detachment. Later, over Savo Island Smith spotted several Zeros, and he told his pilots to follow him. When they were 2,000 feet above the Japanese fighters, Smith headed down. A Zero flashed by, scoring hits on Smith's plane. Then another got on his tail, so he rolled until he could bring his sights to bear on the belly of one of the Zeros. He pressed the button and watched 50-caliber bullets stitch the underside of the Zero until it burst into flames and headed down. It was his first of many victories to follow in the months to come.

No more Zeros attacked, although he saw some doing aerobatics in the distance. Low on fuel, he led his men back to Henderson Field, noting that one plane was missing. On the ground, he learned that Tech. Sgt. John D. Lindley's F4F had been hit during the fight but that he had safely made a crash landing.

Capt. Dale Brannon brought part of the air force's Sixty-seventh Fighter Squadron to Henderson on August 22. His pilots flew

P–400s, prewar export models of the P–39 fighter, and these airplanes proved more deadly to their five pilots than Japanese Zeros. They were called klunkers, and with good reason. They were underpowered and lacked sufficient firepower in combat against the more modern Zeros.

Although air battles were on a small scale for the next few days, the shortage of all supplies and the primitive conditions under which they lived and fought brought maintenance men and air crews almost to the breaking point.

The limited superiority of the American force soon disappeared. By August 23, the Japanese had several carriers and two battleships in the Rabaul area. They were determined to drive the invaders out of their Guadalcanal beachhead.

Admiral Fletcher had three carriers and one battleship, and the *Hornet* was en route from Pearl Harbor with additional warships. His carriers, however, needed to be resupplied. When Fletcher was told that Japanese carriers were north of Truk, he sent the *Wasp*, two heavy cruisers, and seven destroyers south to refuel. Unfortunately, his intelligence was in error: Three Japanese carriers and a strong supporting force were heading south toward Guadalcanal.

Extensive carrier searches found no sign of major Japanese fleet activity on the 24th. Fletcher was astonished, therefore, to receive word from another source that a Japanese carrier and task force was only 280 miles from his own carriers. Scouts from the *Enterprise* reported even more disturbing news. A still larger fleet was only 200 miles away. They identified the smaller carrier *Ryujo* and the newly repaired *Shokaku* and *Zuikaku*. Fletcher grimly told his staff, "The Japs will do everything in their power to destroy our landings on Guadalcanal and Tulagi."

Admiral Yamamoto had gathered a formidable number of carriers, battleships, and cruisers to protect four large transports with 1,500 troops bound for Guadalcanal. His strike force was under Nagumo, who had lost the battle at Midway, and he had the heavy carriers *Shokaku* and *Zuikaku*. Rear Admiral Hara had a smaller force with the light carrier *Ryujo*, which the Japanese hoped would draw away the American carriers from Rear Adm. Raizo Tanaka's transports.

Ghormley learned of the Japanese approach to Guadalcanal and told Fletcher to use his three carriers to cover the island's sea approaches. Fletcher's ships had been patrolling south of the Solomons and at dawn on August 23, the *Enterprise*, *Saratoga*, and *Wasp* were 150 miles east of Guadalcanal.

Weather had been so bad throughout the area for two days that the opposing forces failed to locate each other. Then a patrol plane saw a Japanese carrier after nine o'clock and reported its position as 200 miles north of Malaita, 280 miles from Fletcher's two carriers. This was the *Ryujo*, which Yamamoto was using to divert Fletcher's attention from the rest of his armada.

Fletcher fell for the ruse and sent bombers and torpedo planes from the *Saratoga* and *Enterprise*. Bombing Six from the *Enterprise* went out to locate the carrier, and was joined by Torpedo Three but neither squadron hit the carrier.

Comdr. H. D. "Don" Felt of the *Saratoga* led twenty-nine bombers and seven torpedo planes against the carrier after it was found at 4:06 P.M. Scouting Squadron Three attacked first, and the carrier smoked heavily as they swung away after exploding three 1,000-pound bombs on her deck. Felt looked back as he led his group to the carrier. The *Ryujo* seemed in a bad way, flames shooting up from her hangar deck.

Avengers of Torpedo Eight made passes at the smoking carrier, three in all because of poor visibility. Two more hits were scored, and the fate of the *Ryujo* was sealed. One torpedo that missed the carrier struck a destroyer squarely, and it quickly broke in two and sank.

The Japanese lashed back. They sent dive-bombers and torpedo planes against the American carriers. When combat patrols tangled with the bombers and Japanese fighters, a brisk battle ensued, but thirty dive-bombers got through, scoring three direct hits on the *Enterprise*. Flames shot high above the carrier, and the battleship *North Carolina* moved closer to protect her.

When the attacks ceased, only three Japanese bombers were seen streaking away over an ocean surface resembling a junkyard of airplane debris.

While the *Enterprise* fought off attackers, some of her planes were destroying the *Ryujo*. The planes suffered extensive damage and were ordered to land at Henderson Field. Lt. Turner Caldwell led them to the Guadalcanal base, where they had to remain for a month to fly missions in support of the ground fighting.

After the *Ryujo* sank, fifteen of her bombers and twelve of her fighters headed for Guadalcanal and ran into Smith's Aircraft Group 23 from Henderson. Sixteen Japanese planes were promptly shot down and the others turned back. Capt. Marion Carl, who had fought at Midway with VMF-223, personally destroyed two Kates and a Zero. Eleven other Japanese planes, after they found the *Ryujo* sinking, were ordered to land at Buka near Bougainville to the north. The entire action cost Aircraft Group 23 only two pilots.

Fletcher and Nagumo almost simultaneously ordered launches of their aircraft as they learned of each other's position.

Lt. Comdr. Mamoru Seki took off with the first fleet of sixty-seven planes. Seki located the *Enterprise*, but another group of forty-eight aircraft launched an hour later failed to locate the American carriers because of a navigation error.

"Tallyho!" Lt. A. O. Vorse called, as he spotted the Japanese bombers with their two groups of fighters—one below and the other above. Vorse led his men in a full-throttle climb to the Japanese bombers at 10,000 feet until they leveled out above them. With the advantage of altitude now held by the Americans, Vorse led his Wildcats in screaming dives, hotly pursued by Zeros. Four Japanese fighters quickly fell to the impact of 50-caliber machine guns, but the four F4Fs were quickly outnumbered. They were soon out of ammunition and low on fuel so they headed back to the *Saratoga*. Vorse did not make it, ditching his fuelless airplane in the ocean, but he was picked up by a destroyer.

Ens. G. W. Brooks was sent out by the *Enterprise*'s fighter director with three other Wildcats to investigate a suspicious radar blip. He was 60 miles from the carrier before he found eleven Vals and Kates without fighter escort. His first burst knocked down a Val and as he turned aside, a Kate appeared directly ahead of him. He pressed the button, and the Kate seemed to come apart, hitting the water and sliding over the waves until it finally sank. Three other bombers were shot down by Brooks' section, while a fourth, in panic, flew into the water. The survivors streaked for home.

Seki's bombers found the *Enterprise*, and a wild battle resulted that was costly to both foes. Seki had fired a signal flare 25 miles from the American carrier for the Kates to descend to the water to make their low-level torpedo runs while the Vals, in smaller sections, made dive-bombing attacks on the American carrier.

American fighters fought stubbornly, often braving the massed fire of their own ships to press their attacks. The Japanese pilots, with incredible bravery, never wavered on their runs, and many were shot down. Some got through to the *Enterprise*, and the carrier was hit on the aft elevator by one bomb that penetrated three decks before it exploded. That bomb killed thirty sailors instantly, and many others were thrown violently against the bulkheads.

A second bomb burst close to the first. The carrier started to list as black smoke poured out of its interior. As work parties fought to save their ship, a third bomb hit the flight deck. It was not as destructive as the first two, but it knocked out an elevator.

The *Enterprise* remained afloat after the last Japanese bomber departed, and her skipper hoped that she could be saved despite the severe damage she had sustained. He knew that was possible only if there were no more attacks. Fortunately, there were none, and an hour later she was able to turn into the wind and recover all her planes except Caldwell's flight, which had been diverted temporarily to Henderson Field. Although crippled, she was able to join Admiral Fletcher's task force when it retired southward. She had to leave later for Pearl Harbor because of limited repair facilities in the area.

Japanese pilots later reported that they had sunk the *Hornet* out of revenge for carrying Doolittle's bombers to Japan. Of course, it was the *Enterprise* that was hit, and she was not sunk, although she was out of action for two months.

The *Saratoga* was not attacked during the engagement. Planes of her second attack group struck an enemy group of four heavy cruisers, six light cruisers, and destroyers 150 miles north of Malaita Island at 6:05. TBFs, hugging the water and racing swiftly toward the ships despite heavy flak, made one direct hit on a heavy cruiser. The battle encompassed a wide area; the SBDs landed bombs on the battleship *Mutsu*.

Two heavy Japanese carriers were located, but they escaped serious damage. The *Zuikaku* received one bomb on its flight deck, but it was not of great consequence.

One final action completed the carrier battle. Five Avengers and two Dauntlesses from the *Saratoga* were led by Lt. Harold Larsen in an attack on the seaplane carrier *Chitose*. She was not sunk, but she had to return to Truk with a 30-degree list.

Once Fletcher's task force retired, Japanese surface ships were free to bombard the marines on Guadalcanal as Tanaka and his Tokyo Express continued to the island with troop transports. Tanaka's ships had approached from the north while Japanese carriers were fighting in the eastern Solomons.

In the air war, the Japanese had lost over ninety airplanes, a destroyer, and a transport besides the carrier *Ryujo*. Another aircraft carrier, a battleship, two heavy cruisers, and a light cruiser also suffered damage.

In air actions that lasted fewer than three weeks, Fletcher's command lost twenty planes. Admiral Nimitz hailed the operation as a major victory. He said, "This action permits consolidation of our positions in the Solomons."

The *Hiryu* in her death throes during the Battle of Midway. This photograph was taken by a Japanese plane.
Courtesy of Kazutoshi Hando

The *Yorktown* survives initial air attacks during the Battle of Midway, but her hours are numbered. *Courtesy U.S. Navy*

Intensity of air attack during the Battle of Santa Cruz can be seen by heavy flak bursts. *Courtesy U.S. Navy*

Main battery of U.S.S. *Maryland* shells Tarawa on November 20, 1943, prior to invasion of this Japanese stronghold in the Gilberts. *Official U.S. Navy photograph*

United States Marines storm Tarawa. *Official U.S. Navy photograph*

Vice-Admiral Mitscher aboard the carrier *Lexington* during the battle for Saipan. *Courtesy U.S. Navy*

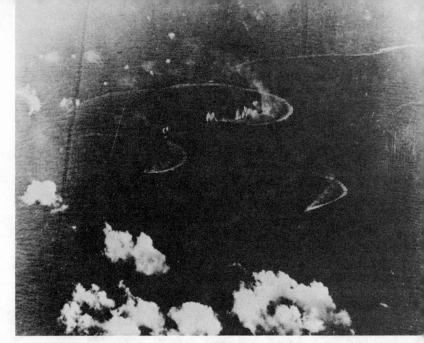

American ships of Task Force Fifty-eight maneuver to avoid Japanese bombs off Saipan, June 1944.
Official U.S. Navy photograph

Lt. James D. "Jig Dog" Ramage
Courtesy of Rear Adm. (Ret.) James D. Ramage

An F6F leaves the U.S.S *Yorktown* on June 19, 1944, to intercept Japanese bombers during the Marianas "Turkey Shoot."
Official U.S. Navy photograph

Fighter contrails mark the sky on June 19, 1944, over Task Force Fifty-eight during the Marianas "Turkey Shoot." Men in foreground are on the U.S.S. *Birmingham*. *Official U.S. Navy photograph*

The *Enterprise*, from the rear seat of an SBD that has just taken off.
Courtesy U.S. Navy

Capt. P.C. Delong of VMF–212 flies an F4U–1D on a mission during 1944.
Courtesy of Ling Temco Vought

10

"THE HOTTEST POTATO
THEY EVER HANDED ME!"

While Japanese carriers and warships were battling east of the Solomons, Admiral Tanaka brought his troopships in from the north in an attempt to reinforce the Japanese soldiers already on Guadalcanal. His twenty-five ships were discovered on the morning of August 25. Maj. Richard C. Mangrum's VMSB–232 Dauntlesses, plus a few planes from another flight, were sent out to intercept the armada.

Capt. John L. Smith and his Wildcats assigned to MAG–23 went along to protect the bombers, but they had to turn back when their fuel ran low. Therefore, Mangrum's bombers from Henderson Field were forced to proceed without fighter escort. They found Tanaka's Tokyo Express and identified the Japanese flagship, the cruiser *Jintsu*, accompanied by eight destroyers and troop transports. The marine and navy bombers peeled off and headed toward the ships far below, turning and scattering in different directions. Lt. Lawrence Baldinus placed his bomb squarely on the *Jintsu*'s deck, forward of the bridge between two turrets, knocking Admiral Tanaka unconscious. When Tanaka recovered and saw that his flagship had been hard hit, he transferred to the destroyer *Kagaro* and ordered the *Jintsu* to return to Truk.

Ens. Christian Fink of the *Enterprise* flight base at Henderson Field placed his 1,000-pound bomb on the heavily loaded transport *Kinryu Maru*. Flames shot high in the sky, and Tanaka ordered the destroyers *Mutsuki* and *Yayoi* to take off the survivors.

After the American dive-bombers completed their runs, there were no other hits. They circled above the fleet while the *Jintsu* slowly turned from Truk, and the *Kinryu Maru* burned to its waterline.

When the navy and marine pilots departed, Tanaka felt reasonably secure and ordered his force to continue toward Guadalcanal. His composure was dispelled by B–17s from Col. LaVerne G. Saunders' 11th Army Air Force Group appearing overhead. Although the 11th had frequently claimed hits on ships, in truth they had never had any. Now their bombs straddled the destroyer *Mutsuki* and sank it.

At noon on August 24, Tanaka issued orders that his fleet should retire to the Shortland Islands, one of the smaller of the Solomons group, south of Bougainville.

Thus, Japan's attempt to provide major reinforcements for her beleaguered troops on Guadalcanal failed, and the cost was heavy. The carrier *Ryujo* had been sunk, ninety aircraft destroyed, and hundreds of Japanese sailors and soldiers killed in the attempt.

The Americans had lost only seventeen planes, but the *Enterprise* was out of action for some time.

The American strategy soon became familiar to the Japanese: Seize a relatively weakened outpost and build airfields quickly so that Japanese supply lines could be cut or isolated. Generally, losses were slight. The Americans were beginning to appreciate that the war in the Pacific was different from any they had previously fought. The broad reaches of ocean prevented massive land battles and primary importance had to be given to the destruction of Japanese airpower. Once this was accomplished, Allied naval ship and ground troops could move forward on the long road back.

Fliers and ground-support men assigned to Henderson Field knew misery at its worst. Conditions were intolerable. Black dust clogged the engines. When it rained, the ground became a quagmire. Equipment and engines had to be soaked with oil to prevent their rusting in the high humidity. Aircraft engines so coated, however, created problems at high altitudes, sometimes seizing up during combat.

Malaria and dysentery were rampant, and there was often a shortage of food after the supply ships were withdrawn. During one period, ground troops lived on captured Japanese rice. To make matters worse, "Washing-Machine Charlie" and "Louie the Louse" dropped bombs or flares each night so that Tanaka's ships could shell Henderson Field and marine positions.

A few American ships managed to slip past Japanese submarines and planes to bring in supplies. Smaller ships did the same at Tulagi. It soon became apparent that neither side had the strength to bring the fighting to a conclusion.

While United States Marines stubbornly battled inland in some of the worst jungle fighting of the war, American airpower on Guadalcanal was almost destroyed by daily operations. Additional airpower did become available after the remainder of MAG–23 joined its forward echelons. Maj. Robert G. Galer's VMF–224 provided nineteen more Wildcats, and Maj. Leo R. Smith's VMSB–231 supplied twelve SBD dive-bombers.

The Japanese moved more planes into Rabaul, doubling the air strength at their strategic bases. Meanwhile, General Kenney's Fifth Air Force finally received additional planes, and a new air force, the Thirteenth, arrived in the area with new groups.

At the time, Rear Adm. John S. McCain was in command of all air operations in the South Pacific. He wrote Nimitz his evaluation of the situation: "Guadalcanal can be consolidated, expanded and exploited to the enemy's hurt. The reverse is true if we lose Guadalcanal. If the reinforcements required are not available, Guadalcanal cannot be supplied and cannot be held."

The Japanese tried to retake Henderson Field, and on September 14, marines stubbornly fought to hold the line at a point now called "Bloody Ridge." They were successful, killing a thousand Japanese soldiers for a loss of only forty marines.

Capt. Marion Carl, one of the area's two leading aces, tried to help by making sweeps in his fighter, but he was shot down at sea. After five days in a life raft, Carl was picked up by a navy amphibian, a gaunt caricature of his former self. While he was away the other leading ace, John Smith, brought his string of victories to fourteen and now Carl was three behind.

While United States Marines frequently fought hand to hand with the Japanese on Guadalcanal, seemingly over the same territory day after day, the United States Navy tried to keep the long sea-lane open from the United States. The *Hornet* and *Wasp* fought for weeks to protect this supply line, but it was a time of desperation.

The *Hornet* and *Wasp*, the only operational carriers in the South Pacific by September 15, were ordered to escort six transports with the Seventh Marine Division en route to Guadalcanal. Between Espiritu Santo and Guadalcanal, now infamous as Torpedo Junction, Japanese submarines attacked the fleet. The battleship *North Carolina* was hit by a torpedo, along with the destroyer *O'Brien*. The battleship survived the attack, but the destroyer later sank. Three torpedoes found the *Wasp*, and she quickly went down. Now the American carrier *Hornet* was the only one left to face the large Japanese carriers *Shokaku* and *Zuikaku*, along with light carriers

Zuiho and *Junyo*. The situation would have passed the point of no return if it had not been for the planes on Guadalcanal. Still, Brig. Gen. Ross E. Rowell, commanding officer of Marine Pacific Air Wings, was down to only fifty-eight operational aircraft by October 1. At Rabaul, the Japanese had three times that many available for operations.

King was unhappy with Ghormley following the August 9 Savo Island disaster, which cost the United States Navy four cruisers and a destroyer. He was persuaded that Ghormley lacked aggressiveness and therefore ordered Halsey into the South Pacific as task force commander but subordinated him to Ghormley while the latter's actions were reviewed.

Japanese warships of the Sixth Imperial Cruiser Division moved toward Guadalcanal on the night of October 11, intending to bombard the entrenched United States Marines in a sneak-and-run attack. Instead, they ran into a well-laid trap, and only one ship escaped.

Rear Adm. Norman Scott, whose ships almost wiped out the enemy force, had achieved far more than the Japanese realized. Six thousand United States Army troops, which Scott's ships were shepherding through the dangerous waters, landed successfully on Guadalcanal. The marines, who had fought so long and so well, welcomed the reinforcements because they knew that the Japanese were ready with another full-scale offensive.

The overall Japanese plan called for a joint army–navy operation to saturate the American positions and then unload thousands of fresh troops. One such attempt failed when the *Shinyo Maru* was torpedoed on October 12 with six hundred Japanese marines on board. Despite this loss, streams of Japanese combat vessels and merchant ships entered the upper Solomons and New Britain areas as the Japanese built up their forces.

Lt. Gen. Harukichi Hyakutake, commanding officer of Rabaul's Seventeenth Army, was sent in to Guadalcanal to head the twenty-thousand-man army. He planned to lead the attack himself to achieve his major goal of capturing Port Moresby.

As the Japanese built up their army on Guadalcanal with four thousand troops to reinforce the original sixteen thousand on Guadalcanal, they were able to achieve almost parity in numbers against the twenty-one thousand United States Army and Marine troops on the island. Now, the problem of revitalizing American airpower on

Guadalcanal became acute. Fighter strength rose to forty-six when MAG-14 arrived on October 9 with twenty more Wildcats assigned to Maj. Leonard K. Davis' VMF-12.

At Pearl Harbor, Nimitz ordered repairs expedited on the *Enterprise* and the carrier *Saratoga* during the second week of October. The latter had been laid up for repairs since her torpedoing on August 31, 260 miles southeast of Guadalcanal. Both ships were desperately needed in the South Pacific because the Allies had only a small task force available, built around the carrier *Hornet*, whereas the Japanese had a number of heavy and light carriers.

While repairs were rushed on the two American carriers, Nimitz ordered Allied submarines to concentrate their operations around the Bismarck Archipelago.

The *Saratoga* had been ordered to fly her twenty-four Wildcats of VF-5 to Guadalcanal's Henderson Field before she left the South Pacific, but Lt. Comdr. Leroy C. Simpler's squadron had been decimated by combat losses since they arrived. Not only had his squadron, and the few others that had been in operation there since the invasion, suffered heavy losses but its operational accidents rose, reaching as high as eight in one day.

Marine Major John L. Smith, commanding officer of 223, had seen his squadron bear much of the heaviest aerial fighting since August. His squadron was down to himself and seven other pilots. He was the first marine pilot on Guadalcanal to make a kill and had raised his total victories to nineteen. He was ordered home to receive the Medal of Honor. Under his leadership, his squadron had destroyed eighty-three Japanese planes despite their introduction into combat without adequate training. He was an outstanding squadron commander who used bold tactics although he was constantly outnumbered in the air, and it was due to the leadership of men like Smith that Guadalcanal remained in Allied hands.

Maj. Richard Mangrum's VMSB-232 had lost eleven SBD pilots and gunners, and another seven pilots and four gunners were wounded. When he was rotated home, he was the only one to depart on his feet.

VMSB-141, under Maj. Gordon A. Bell, started to arrive September 23 and by early October, had twenty-one pilots. Leo Smith's VMSB-231, plus a few strays, completed the total number available for the bombing effort to keep Guadalcanal secure.

Capt. Joseph J. Foss, executive officer of VMF-121, got his first Zero on October 13, the day that General Hyakutake opened his campaign to retake Guadalcanal. The Japanese general was prophetic when he told his troops before the start of the battle that their actions would "truly decide the fate of the entire Pacific."

Without warning, Japanese bombers struck Henderson Field and made the runway temporarily unusuable because of bomb craters. Worse, irreplaceable fuel in nearby tanks was destroyed.

The battleships *Haruna* and *Kongo* went into action, lobbing 14-inch shells on Henderson Field. The destruction rose at an alarming rate during the night, and at dawn forty-one were dead, including five pilots. Survivors viewed the devastation with dismay. Maj. Gordon Bell, who had just brought in a flight of thirty-nine SBDs, was killed during the shelling, and only four of his Dauntlesses were in flyable condition. The Wildcats suffered heavily, too, with sixteen out of forty wrecked. Those that remained all needed repairs before they could be flown. The Army Air Forces also suffered, with two of the eight B-17s from Espiritu Santo totally destroyed. The rest got out of Henderson as quickly as they could.

The ground fighting became almost unendurably ferocious. On both sides, air attacks were constant, and the Japanese moved their ships in close to bombard American lines night and day. Control of the sea changed almost hourly. At night, the Japanese were in control, but in daytime the Americans had a slender edge as both sides tried to reinforce their front-line combatants.

General Hyakutake believed Henderson could be retaken easily at dawn on October 15 because the field was a shambles and because Yamamoto had sent him five transports of troops and supplies, which now lay 10 miles off shore. Confidently, he ordered their unloading in daylight.

At Henderson Field, only three SBD dive-bombers were available, and only one made it off the bomb-pocked runway. Ground crews worked frantically to patch up other aircraft finally siphoning enough fuel from damaged airplanes to get twelve more into the air. The number was pitifully small, amounting to a handful of Wildcats and some of the discredited P-400s. A Catalina joined the retaliatory force, increasing to twenty-one the airplanes available to attack the transports.

The Catalina was the *Blue Goose*, the personal plane of Maj. Gen. Roy S. Geiger, commanding general of the 1st Marine Aircraft Wing on Guadalcanal. It was virtually commandeered by Maj. "Mad Jack" Cram, who took off with two 2,000-pound torpedoes under its wings. When Cram had asked permission to load with torpedoes, he ran into strong objections at Espiritu Santo because Catalinas were not equipped to drop them. He pointed out that no

Avengers were available to carry the torpedoes, and he got the weapons jury-rigged on his plane.

The SBDs went in first, with Cram lumbering along behind, as thirty Japanese Zeros dove at them. As Cram headed for a transport, a burst of machine-gun fire ripped off the navigator's hatch. The makeshift dropping mechanism nevertheless worked perfectly, and Cram's two torpedoes struck the transport, ripping it open.

Zeros concentrated on his Catalina as he tried to get away. Dozens of shells tore the thin skin of the *Blue Goose* as Cram put the plane through unconventional aerobatics for which it was not designed. Frantically, he headed home, arriving over Fighter Field 1 with a Zero still on his tail.

Lt. Roger Haberman of VMF–121, who had been forced out of the fighting over the Japanese fleet because of a smoking engine, arrived at the same time as Cram's Catalina. Although Haberman's wheels were about to touch down, he pushed the throttle forward and climbed away from the field to permit Cram's Catalina to land first. Soon he was on the tail of the unsuspecting Japanese fighter pilot who, concentrating all his attention on the Catalina, hardly knew what hit him when Haberman's F4F guns tore his Zero apart.

General Geiger looked at his riddled command plane with consternation, threatening Cram with court-martial for "deliberate destruction of government property." After he calmed down, he awarded Cram a Navy Cross instead.

The Japanese lost three transports in a series of air attacks, with great loss of life and the destruction of valuable cargo. B–17s from the New Hebrides destroyed one of the transports and navy and marine pilots the other two. Fighter pilots strafed the beaches as large numbers of Japanese troops tried to get ashore after their transports were sunk. The other transports fled the scene, but five thousand troops did land and were of inestimable value to Hyakutake's army on Guadalcanal.

Of the twenty-one American navy planes taking part, three SBDs and four Wildcats were lost, reducing Geiger's total strength in the area to fourteen aircraft. Only nine were fighters.

At Pearl Harbor, Admiral Nimitz, who had been following the fighting with growing concern, wrote King and the Joint Chiefs in Washington, "It now appears that we are unable to control the sea in the Guadalcanal area. Thus supply of our positions will only be done at great expense to us. The situation is not hopeless, but it is certainly critical."

Marine Gen. Vandegrift wrote Admiral Ghormley that his command must receive maximum support of air and surface units. Ghormley immediately dispatched some of VMF-212 under Lt. Col. Harold W. Bauer along with seven SBDs, which boosted Geiger's strength to twenty-eight aircraft. They arrived in the middle of an attack by nine Japanese Vals against the seaplane tender *McFarland*, which had just delivered aviation fuel and was departing with medical evacuees from Lunga Point.

Although low on fuel after his 600-mile flight, Bauer headed for the Vals. One after another, four of them succumbed to Bauer's relentless guns. With tanks almost empty, he was able to disengage safely, apparently because the Japanese thought that they had been attacked by a whole squadron. (Two weeks later, in a free-for-all action with Marion Carl, Bauer raised his total to eight, with only two of his overheated guns operating.)

Lt. Col. Kenneth Frazier knocked down two Japanese planes in the same action but got caught by cannon fire from a Zeke on his tail. Flames erupted, and his engine quit; he quickly bailed out. When Bauer saw a Zeke pilot follow Frazier down, firing at the parachute, he lined up the Zeke in his sights and shot it to pieces. He circled the ocean over Frazier until a destroyer picked him up.

Bauer's own luck was to run out in the middle of November, when he was killed after shooting down eleven Japanese planes. His courage and daring were honored posthumously with a Medal of Honor.

Maj. Robert G. Galer of VMF-224 was another pilot who heroically helped to save the situation at Guadalcanal by extraordinary personal efforts. He shot down eleven Vals and Zekes, and his squadron destroyed a total of twenty-seven Japanese planes in twenty-nine days despite constant day and night bombing of their airfield. Galer's Medal of Honor citation made particular mention of the enormous pain and exhaustion that he endured during these trying weeks.

Ghormley learned of increasing Japanese activity south and east of the Solomon Islands, particularly in the vicinity of the Santa Cruz Islands. He wired Nimitz that his forces were inadequate to meet this threat.

Admiral King had been critical of Ghormley ever since the Savo Island disaster on August 9. Now King impressed on Nimitz the urgent need to replace Ghormley. King also criticized Ghormley for inadequate night dispositions around Guadalcanal, which permitted the Japanese to maintain control after dark, although the Allied forces maintained a tenuous control by day. King was blunt in charging that the disasters that had befallen American forces resulted from Ghormley's inefficiency and lack of aggressiveness. Earlier, he and Nimitz had placed Halsey in the South Pacific as Task Force Commander but subordinate to Ghormley. On October 15, when the land and sea battles for control of Guadalcanal were at their height, Nimitz recommended to King that Halsey replace Ghormley, and King quickly agreed.

In the South Pacific, Halsey received the word the next day. Nimitz wired, "You will take command of the South Pacific area and South Pacific forces immediately." Halsey read the dispatch and said, "Jesus Christ and General Jackson. This is the hottest potato they ever handed me."

Ghormley's removal was long overdue. Losses under his command were heavy, and morale was low throughout the South Pacific. Nimitz told his Pearl Harbor staff, "For his effect on morale, Bill Halsey is worth a division of fast battleships."

One of Halsey's first actions was to get a report from General Vandegrift. "Can you hold?" he asked.

"Yes, I can hold, but I have to have more active support than I've been getting."

Admiral Turner protested that the navy had been doing all it could and that he was losing transports and cargo ships at an alarming rate. He cited lack of sufficient warships to protect them as the main reason.

Halsey listened to arguments on both sides. Then he turned to Vandegrift. "You go on back there. I promise to get you everything I have."

At last the *Enterprise* completed her repairs at Pearl Harbor and left for the South Pacific on October 16 with a task force flying the flag of Rear Adm. Thomas C. Kinkaid. He was told to proceed with all speed and soon rendezvoused with the *Hornet* group under Rear Adm. George D. Murray. Both now came under command of Admiral Halsey, and the spirits of the officers and men took an immediate uplift.

The *Hornet* and *Enterprise* groups met northeast of the New Hebrides at noon on October 24, and Halsey placed Kinkaid in charge of a consolidated group called Task Group King. Kinkaid knew that they would have trouble because his group was only half the size of the Japanese forces. Resourcefully, he told his staff, "At least we're twice as strong as the Japanese think we are."

The task group moved along the northern shores of the Santa Cruz Islands, then swung east of San Cristobal, the southernmost island in the Solomons group.

*   *   *

At Truk, Admiral Yamamoto assembled four carriers, five battleships, fourteen cruisers and forty-four destroyers to assist in an all-out effort to retake Guadalcanal. He issued orders to his commanders to prepare for a decisive battle against the United States Navy's ships located northeast of the lower Solomons in the vicinity of two small island groups—the Stewards and Santa Cruz Islands. On Guadalcanal, Hyakutake prepared to make three simultaneous attacks at widely separated points on the island. The main attack from the south, under Lt. Gen. Masao Maruyama, would coincide with Hyakutake's attack against Henderson Field.

The three-pronged assault on Guadalcanal commenced on October 23, supported by Japanese fighters and bombers from Rabaul and Buin; a Japanese base on Bougainville. They were met over the island by twenty-four marine and navy Wildcats.

Capt. Joseph J. Foss of Marine Fighting Squadron 121, a man of indomitable spirit and extraordinary skill, won the first in a series of aerial victories that eventually earned him a Medal of Honor. Joe Foss counted sixteen bombers and twenty-five Japanese fighters as he led his men against the Zeros. Foss noted one Wildcat on the tail of a Zero as they headed up to gain altitude, with another Zero behind the American fighter. He dove quickly and shot down the menacing Zero, and it disintegrated. The propeller spun off, the air was filled with debris, and the Japanese pilot was thrown from his seat. Foss had to maneuver wildly to avoid flying into the pieces. Before the day was over, he shot down four Japanese planes, and the squadron totaled twenty Zeros and four bombers.

Rains made a quagmire of Guadalcanal's battlefield the next day, and fighting came to a halt. Air strikes had to be canceled in the morning, but Foss led his squadron that afternoon. The Japanese were also out for blood, but they were the ones who lost it: Foss got five himself, bringing his total to sixteen.

October 25 was even more costly to the Japanese. They lost twenty-two more planes to American fighters and one to antiaircraft fire.

Yamamoto's support force, which included Nagumo's Third Fleet and Kondo's Second Fleet, waited 300 miles east of Guadalcanal for word to join the action. The Japanese Combined Fleet commander had positioned them to intercept American ships that came to Guadalcanal's aid and to prevent survivors of the ground fighting from escaping.

Halsey had divided his ships into three task forces. Task Force Sixty-one had the *Enterprise*, and Task Force Seventeen had the

Hornet. They were told to rendezvous north of the New Hebrides. The third task force, sixty-four, had the battleship *Washington.* All were placed under the tactical command of Rear Admiral Kinkaid on the *Enterprise,* and he had a total of 171 aircraft.

Nagumo had four carriers with 212 aircraft. There was only one American battleship—the new *South Dakota*—to face four Japanese battleships. The rest of the lineup was equally unbalanced, with twelve Japanese cruisers to six American, and twenty-four Japanese destroyers to fourteen American.

Nagumo moved into position with confidence. He was convinced that the *Enterprise* was still out of action and that the rest of the American ships would pose no problems because of his great numerical superiority.

The Japanese admiral grew more and more concerned when he failed to hear from Hyakutake that Guadalcanal had been captured. Nagumo sent him a radio message that he was running low on fuel and urged him to hurry his ground victory over the Americans. When he heard a report—erroneous—that Henderson Field had been overrun, he was elated. He refueled and turned toward Guadalcanal just as the United States Marines were forcing the Japanese to halt their drive.

While American and Japanese fleets maneuvered in search of each other, troops on Guadalcanal fought back stubbornly against waves of Japanese, who literally threw themselves against the American lines. Even worse for the Americans, Japanese reinforcements landed on the island.

Some of Nagumo's ships were located after midnight on October 25 by one of Kinkaid's Catalina search planes. Nagumo still did not know the whereabouts of the American fleet, but once his own position was known to the Americans he changed course. It was not until later that a search plane from the *Shokaku* sighted the American ships on a northwest heading. Almost simultaneously, an *Enterprise* search plane spotted Nagumo's fleet. At last, what was later to be known as the "Battle of Santa Cruz" was about to begin.

Once the Japanese fleet was positively located, Kinkaid ordered his carriers to launch planes. "Pilots, man your planes!" came the cry as ready rooms evacuated quickly and pilots rushed out across the flight decks.

Lt. Stockton B. "Birney" Strong and Ens. Charles Irvine were on a regularly scheduled vector search in their two SBDs. Strong left his sector when he heard a sighting report that identified the *Sho-*

kaku and the smaller *Zuiho*. Strong immediately ordered his wing-man to join him in an attack on the *Zuiho*, which was closer. He glanced nervously around, marveling that the Japanese had not un-limbered their antiaircraft guns and that their combat air patrol had not put in an appearance. Nevertheless, for two planes to attack a carrier alone was an act of unprecedented bravery.

Strong rolled his SBD into a dive and got his scope lined up with the yellow deck; Irvine was close behind. At 1,500 feet, Strong noted with surprise that there were no aircraft on deck. He realized that the *Zuiho*'s planes must be in the air and that he and Irvine would have to be exceptionally alert as they pulled away.

Strong released his 500-pounder, and Irvine did likewise. Both bombs struck aft, ripping open the *Zuiho*'s deck. Antiaircraft guns were twisted violently around by the blasts.

As they pulled away, they saw the *Zuiho* limping through the water. Her captain, Sueo Chayashi, had radioed Nagumo that his damage was so severe that he could not recover his aircraft and would have to leave the area.

Strong and Irvine streaked away, radioing details of the Japanese fleet to the *Enterprise*, and were soon surrounded by Japanese fighters. Strong motioned to Irvine to join him just above the waves, and their rear gunners fought off a series of attacks. Neither was sure of the exact position of the *Enterprise* as they fought their way homeward, knocking down two of the pursuing Zeros. After forty-five minutes of almost constant attacks, the Japanese fighters turned back.

The two pilots landed on the *Enterprise*, with little remaining am-munition and still less fuel, to report their success.

Lt. Comdr. Mamoru Seki had taken off at 5:15 A.M. in command of a large number of Japanese fighters and bombers. En route to the American fleet, they passed a formation of SBDs from the *Hornet* that was looking for their Japanese carrier.

Kinkaid had ordered the *Enterprise*'s Avengers, Dauntlesses, and Wildcats to head for the last known position of the Japanese fleet. A half hour after takeoff, they were attacked by Japanese fighters, and two Avengers quickly succumbed and dropped flaming into the sea. The Wildcats, caught at low altitude, were at a disadvantage when attacked by Japanese fighters orphaned from the burning *Zuiho*. The Japanese fighters quickly shot down eight of the nine-teen American planes.

The remaining American planes never found the Japanese car-riers but bombed a ship they thought was a Kongo-type battleship.

This "battleship" proved to be the cruiser *Chikuma*. Although it suffered heavy damage, it was not knocked out of action.

Seki's fighters, which had attacked the *Enterprise*'s planes, were no longer available to protect the Vals and Kates. He ordered the Japanese bombers to continue on, and they soon found the *Hornet*. Wildcats slashed at the Japanese bombers, but they began their runs.

Comdr. Lawrence L. Bean, the ship's medical officer, had gone on deck to stretch his legs after the last planes left the *Hornet*. Striding back and forth, he stopped abruptly when the loudspeaker blared, "General Quarters!" He hurried to sick bay. The phone rang, and he picked it up quickly. "Twenty-four bogies, sir. They've disappeared now in the clouds."

Seki's bomber was riddled by antiaircraft fire. He held his course for the *Hornet* even after his plane rolled over on its back, with flames streaming behind it.

The *Hornet* trembled under Bean's feet. He heard a loud explosion forward of sick bay, then another and another. The sickening third blast knocked him off balance and before his unbelieving eyes, the deck seemed to lift up. Two more blasts came, then aircraft guns stopped firing and a deathly stillness pervaded the ship.

The deck slanted beneath his feet as the ship listed. Thick smoke billowed around the deck.

Seki's plane had careened off the *Hornet*'s stack, crashed into the flight deck and exploded with its bombs. Other Vals continued their runs and bombs were dropped with great effect while Kates swept in low with their torpedoes.

Another plane now deliberately smashed into a gun gallery and exploded into a ball of flames that enveloped the forward elevator shaft. Although it is impossible to be certain, the plane probably was flown by Lt. Jiichiro Imajuku.

"Now hear this!" Bean recognized Captain Mason's voice. "Prepare to abandon ship."

He hurried back onto the deck just as a flaming suicide plane crashed into the communications tower. He was sickened as he passed the wreckage to see the Japanese pilot's body burned to a crisp on deck alongside it in the same position he had occupied in the cockpit.

Attacks continued but Capt. Charles P. Mason skillfully managed to prevent further damage by maneuvering his ship to avoid dive-bombers. Two more torpedoes now struck simultaneously, and the *Hornet* listed 15 degrees.

"Abandon ship—"

Violent explosions tore at the bowels of the ship that had carried Doolittle's raiders to Japan. Men scrambled over the side to waiting destroyers.

Lt. James E. Vose, flying with a *Hornet* formation, found the *Shokaku*, Nagumo's warship, 150 miles away and attacked. The sky above the Japanese carrier was a whirling mass of planes as Zeros, fighting with tenacious skill, ripped into the American bomber formation. Despite the Japanese fighters, four 1,000-pound bombs dropped on the *Shokaku*'s deck, and flames erupted.

Hornet TBFs, flying low across the ocean, could not locate the enemy carriers so they made attacks on other ships. Lt. Edwin B. Parker led them back to the *Hornet* at noon, noting with horror that his ship lay dead in the water, listing heavily with swirling smoke rising from her. He tried to contact the ship but she was voiceless.

The nearby cruiser *Northampton* radioed, "Land aboard the *Enterprise*."

It too was under attack, so they had to circle out of range, their fuel running low, hoping that the attack would break off. When it did not, they had to land in the sea and wait for boats to pick them up.

More than two hundred Japanese planes swarmed over the American task force in strong attacks. The destroyer *Porter*, evacuating men from the *Hornet*, was the first to go down after being hit by a torpedo.

The *Hornet* was taken in tow by destroyers, but six Japanese torpedo planes scored. The ship refused to sink, and only after American destroyers poured hundreds of rounds into her did she finally go down.

Nagumo, on board the blasted *Zuiho*, was forced to turn command over to Rear Adm. Kakuji Kakuta on the *Zuikaku* and flee with his crippled flagship to Truk.

While American pilots sought the *Zuikaku* and the *Junyo* of Kondo's advance force, Vals and Kates from these ships found the *Enterprise* and got three bombs into her despite the desperate action of her fighters and antiaircraft gunners. Raging fires spread quickly and forty-four men died. Capt. Osborne B. Hardison managed to prevent further damage by skillfully maneuvering his big ship each time Japanese bombers appeared.

The battleship *South Dakota* used her guns effectively and destroyed several Japanese planes that otherwise might have finished off the *Enterprise*. It came under repeated attack by bombers from the *Junyo*, which also attacked the cruiser *San Juan*. A Kate landed on board the destroyer *Smith* and almost destroyed her.

The Japanese claimed a great victory, but the *Hornet* and the *Porter* were the only ships lost, and Japan had suffered damage to two carriers that would put them out of action for months. Destruction of sixty-nine bombers and fighters and the loss of their crews was an even greater loss to the Japanese because they were experienced men. It would soon become apparent to American fliers that the Japanese veterans from the early days were being eliminated at an ever-increasing rate and proving to be irreplaceable.

Kinkaid ordered his ships to retire independently and proceeded on a southwesterly course. His carriers had lost seventy-four planes and with them twenty-three pilots and ten crew members. Despite these losses, a much stronger fleet had been routed and the Japanese assault on Guadalcanal brought to a halt. As it turned out, the Japanese lost their last chance to defeat the Americans on Guadalcanal.

Admiral King was disturbed by the loss of the *Hornet*, which reduced American carrier strength in the Pacific to a dangerous level that would have a profound impact on future operations. It was impossible to send reinforcements at this time because the Allies were preparing to make landings in force on the North African continent. The crippled *Enterprise* and the *Saratoga* would have to suffice for the time being.

With available Japanese naval strength in the area reduced, American reinforcements on Guadalcanal and particularly an increase in the island's air strength made the position of the Allies more tenable.

In this action, the Japanese lost the initiative and were never able to send sufficient strength to recapture Guadalcanal, although Yamamoto would make one more disastrous attempt.

11

THE SLAUGHTER OF
JAPANESE TROOPS
WAS SICKENING TO BEHOLD

Admiral Yamamoto came up with a plan that he hoped would assist the Japanese army under Hyakutake, beleaguered on Guadalcanal. Hyakutake's men were desperately in need of reinforcements and supplies.

Although the Imperial Navy had paid a high price for its assistance to the army, Yamamoto ordered a large force of battleships, cruisers, and destroyers to be assembled from Kondo's Second Fleet to bombard Henderson Field around the clock. Meanwhile, he ordered Tanaka's Tokyo Express to deliver the Japanese army's Thirty-eighth Division to relieve Hyakutake's sick and dying force.

Eleven troop transports moved down the Slot, northwest of Guadalcanal. Meanwhile, another force of Kondo's ships positioned themselves north of Savo Island to provide distant cover while a large force of battleships and smaller ships shelled Henderson Field and surrounding American troop strong points. Still another force under Vice-Adm. Gunichi Mikawa was assigned to provide backup for landings by the Thirty-eighth Division. It was equipped only with cruisers and destroyers for close support. Scouts reported the Japanese movements to Rear Adm. Daniel J. Callaghan, whose forces were insufficient to meet this new challenge because they included only five cruisers and eight destroyers.

Admiral Kinkaid's carrier task force returned on November 13 at the crucial moment with the *Enterprise*, her battle damage repaired.

Callaghan's ships searched the Savo Island area during entry to Lengo Channel during the night of November 12/13. He had received reports that three groups of Japanese ships were in the vicinity. Vice-Adm. Hiroaki Abe, on his way with his capital ships the *Hiei* and *Kirishima*, the cruiser *Nagara*, and fourteen destroyers ran into Callaghan's two cruisers and four destroyers.

In a bizarre night action, the ships fought it out. The Japanese had hoped to blast their way through the Solomons to provide a safe passage for their troopships. The thunder of hundreds of guns flashed repeatedly and the night sky reverberated with thunderous roar. At close quarters, Callaghan's ships fought back desperately. Callaghan and almost his entire staff were killed aboard the *San Francisco*, and more than seven hundred Americans died in a battle that was a nightmare for both sides. Finally, the *Hiei* was crippled by repeated hits, and two destroyers were sunk. This action forced Abe to cancel the Guadalcanal bombardment. The Japanese, who vastly outnumbered the American forces, were turned back and almost routed. Their retreat was, however, costly to the Americans; Callaghan lost five ships, and the new cruiser *Juneau* was torpedoed.

Abe's retirement infuriated Yamamoto, and he immediately relieved him. Tanaka was ordered to turn back from his express run to Guadalcanal and head for the Shortland Islands.

Kinkaid's task force, alerted by the action, rushed to the fray with the *Enterprise* to cover retirement of Callaghan's remaining ships.

Japanese troopships now turned back, but orders from Tokyo countermanded their retreat and ordered them to proceed with their original landing plans.

Marine pilots in SBDs and Avengers found the *Hiei* 10 miles north of Savo with a five-destroyer escort. While her guns blazed, ten bombers moved in to attack. Two Avenger torpedoes smashed into her side as more Dauntlesses arrived on the scene to make their near-vertical dives against the stricken ship.

While the *Enterprise* sailed north of Guadalcanal, nine Avengers and six Wildcats were dispatched to Henderson Field. En route, they, too, found the *Hiei*. While Wildcats kept Zeros away from the Avengers, Lt. Albert E. "Scooter" Coffin led his torpedo bombers down and with perfect runs, three torpedoes exploded against the battleship's sides.

Throughout the day navy and marine aircraft from Henderson shuttled back and forth between their island and the *Hiei*, destroying Zeros on each pass, until the final eight were eliminated. Finally, the huge *Hiei* sank into the Pacific, the first Japanese battleship to be sunk by Americans in the war.

Yamamoto now ordered his original plan to be put into effect. On the night of November 13/14, cruisers from Rabaul fired a thousand 8-inch shells into the American airfield. So erratic was the gunfire, possibly because the PT boats from Tulagi harassed the Japanese ships, that little damage was done although the Wildcats were destroyed and some other planes damaged. Those that were repairable were back in the air by daylight.

MacArthur sent only eight P–38s to Henderson to help out when he could have sent many more. Marines were particularly embittered because they believed that he was deliberately withholding equipment and army fighters during Guadalcanal's most desperate siege. Their accusations had some justification because he had Army Air Force planes available that could have been sent. During this period, marines first hurled at him the appellation "Dugout Doug" that was to follow him throughout the war and even into the postwar years.

Tanaka remained convinced, despite his setbacks, that the Americans were powerless to oppose his Tokyo Express and that he could bring his troopships safely to Guadalcanal. Therefore, on the night of November 14, eleven thousand troops of Lt. Gen. Tadayoshi Sano's Thirty-eighth Division were sent through the Slot. A few Zeros from the light carrier *Hiyo* acted as air cover, while a dozen destroyers were assigned as a screening force.

An *Enterprise* scout plane flown by Lt. Doan "Big Red" Carmody found the transports in the Slot 120 miles away cruising toward Guadalcanal at 14 knots.

He radioed the information and joined Lt. W. E. Johnson in an attack on the transports. Japanese Zeros immediately attacked, and both pilots missed their targets. Johnson's SBD was shot down, and Japanese pilots strafed his wreckage.

More marine and navy pilots appeared shortly thereafter as every flyable airplane from Henderson Field and the *Enterprise* was sent out.

To the north, Kondo had two carriers but kept his planes on deck until the battle in the Slot was desperate. Then he dispatched a few Zeros.

In a slaughter unlike anything navy and marine pilots had ever seen, they dropped their 1,000-pound bombs on the helpless troopships while torpedoes slammed into their sides. Wildcats, once they had accounted for the few Zeros, came in above the waves with all guns firing into the crowded decks, and the slaughter of Japanese troops was sickening to behold.

The first eighteen marine SBDs, under Maj. Joseph Sailer, Jr., of VMSB–132, joined Maj. Robert Richard of VMSB–142, and seven more SBDs under Lt. Comdr. James R. "Bucky" Lee swelled the ranks. The carnage became even worse.

Although troopships were sinking all around him, Tanaka refused to turn back. His transports, their decks aflame, lay dead in the water. Some were split open, and dead and injured men tumbled out of her open sides while destroyers tried to pick up the living and fight off American planes at the same time.

Japanese transports were so crowded that there was no escape from the torrent of bombs and the harassing gunfire delivered by the Wildcat fighters. Throughout the area, torpedoes rammed into the sides of transports and ripped them open like can openers, so sudden that ships disappeared quickly beneath the waves. Dying men flung themselves into the sea to escape from the horror coming at them from above.

Pilots, upset by the sight of helpless men trying to swim ashore, continued to fire at every bobbing head they could see, determined that Japanese soldiers would not get to Guadalcanal and provide reinforcements for their beleaguered troops.

Lt. George G. Estes of *Enterprise*'s VS–10 led the last bombers out of Henderson at 4:45 P.M. They dropped their bombs on transports that were already damaged but still might make it to the shores of Guadalcanal. Incredibly, four transports survived and, after midnight, they were beached and three thousand troops rushed ashore. At least that many had died during bombings and strafings. Another two thousand or so were rescued from the water but failed to reach the island. Although some troops got ashore, most of their supplies did not. Only 260 cases of ammunition and 1,500 bags of rice came through. Pilots from Henderson destroyed the beached transports the next day.

While these troops were going ashore, Kondo approached Henderson to shell it with the *Hiei*'s sister ship, the *Kirishima*, plus destroyers and cruisers. In a midnight battle against the American battleships *Washington* and *South Dakota* and their accompanying destroyers, commanded by Rear Adm. Willis A. Lee, Jr., the Japanese suffered another resounding defeat. The *Kirishima* was so badly damaged that it had to be scuttled and sank close to where the *Hiei* had gone down. Lee lost three destroyers, but it was a better than even exchange.

Yamamoto relieved Kondo in disgrace.

After this action, the five-day tally showed that the Japanese had lost two battleships, a heavy cruiser, four destroyers, and twelve transports and cargo vessels. Additional damage was so severe that they abandoned the field. American losses included two antiaircraft light cruisers, seven destroyers, and damage to a battleship. Only six SBDs and two Wildcats were lost.

Halsey sent word to his command. "Your names have been written in gold letters on the pages of history, and you have won the everlasting gratitude of your countrymen. My pride in you is beyond expression."

Admiral King was so elated that he asked Congress permission to raise Halsey to four-star rank, and his request was granted.

After such a series of decisive setbacks, the Japanese faced a dilemma: Should they accept defeat or continue their drive toward Australia despite the eventual necessity of further costly attempts to retake Guadalcanal. Their soldiers on the island felt betrayed and abandoned after weeks of attrition of their own forces since the Americans had invaded the island in early August and had continued to receive reinforcements. The Japanese rarely received supplies and hardly ever saw one of their own planes.

Meanwhile, the United States Pacific Fleet hoped for a respite. Many of its warships needed extensive repairs and its crews badly needed a rest.

Although the Allies did not realize it at the time, the Japanese had launched their last threat to the eastern Solomons.

King had a personal problem in Washington. November 23 was his sixty-fourth birthday, and the prewar order that all officers must be retired at this age had never been rescinded.

He wrote President Roosevelt before the date:

It appears proper that I should bring to your notice the fact that the record shows that I shall attain the age of 64 years on November 23rd next—one month from today.

I am as always, at your service.

Roosevelt returned King's letter and, in his own handwriting, wrote at the bottom:

E.J.K.
So what, old top?
I may send you a Birthday present!

FDR.

Halsey, meanwhile, despite his success in the South Pacific, was faced by an irate church group, which filed a formal protest that he was not adhering to navy regulations that no liquor should be served on board ships. Halsey wrote their spokesman, admitting that the *serving* of liquor on navy ships was a court-martial offense but that the liquor he served his pilots following tough missions was from "bonded medical stores and was administered by competent medical men in small amounts." He commented more colorfully to his staff, saying he liked his booze and, furthermore, did not trust a man who did not drink.

The Japanese command, aware that its whole strategy in the Pacific was threatened, ordered additional transports and destroyers to make the Guadalcanal run on November 30. Task Force William, under Rear Adm. Carleton H. Wright, set out in pursuit. The United States suffered extensive losses, with a heavy cruiser sunk and three others seriously damaged, but Japanese troops failed to make a landing.

Adm. Osami Nagano, chief of the Naval Staff, and Gen. Hajime Sugiyama personally appeared before Emperor Hirohito on December 31, 1942, to make their apologies for the failure of their commands to retake Guadalcanal. They asked permission to abandon the island, and it was granted.

The Japanese secretly withdrew their forces during the first week of February 1943. It was done skillfully; Allied airpower was spread too thin to detect their departure, and the Americans did not learn of it until later. Nimitz had at first been convinced that the Japanese would try again to reinforce their troops.

Maj. General Alexander M. Patch's troops found no Japanese troops on February 9 during a sweep of Guadalcanal to the west. Instead, he reported signs of a hasty departure.

Three weeks earlier the Papuan campaign had been concluded. MacArthur had told Lt. Gen. Robert L. Eichelberger "to take Buna or not come back alive." That occupation was completed on January 2 after Eichelberger personally led his troops through a malarial jungle.

The fighting in eastern New Guinea was almost over by late January. It had taken thirty thousand troops, half of which were Australian, to dislodge twelve thousand Japanese, whereas Guadalcanal had been won with considerably fewer troops under far worse combat conditions. Airpower proved the decisive factor in wresting control of Guadalcanal from the Japanese even though Allied squadrons were consistently outnumbered in the air. Allied airmen, particularly those of the United States Navy and Marines, made up for their disparity in numbers by their skill and tenacity against the Japanese in combat. The same must be said of those who fought on the ground. The superbly led United States Marines, and their army comrades who joined them during the fiercest battles starting in October, proved their mettle against Japanese ground troops who, until then, had had a reputation of being almost invincible. Now, for the first time in the war, the Japanese had been defeated decisively on land. In the final analysis, it was teamwork between land, sea, and air forces of the Allied nations that made the difference. The battle for Guadalcanal had taken six months but, like the one at Midway, it marked another important milestone in the war.

Early in 1943, some of the *Enterprise* officers decided that one of their chief petty officers had to be taught a lesson. He was an old-timer with duties on the flight deck, but for weeks he had been sneaking up to air plot to read highly classified dispatches that he was not entitled to see.

A fake dispatch was written and placed on top of the file. It said, "Japanese fleet sortieing from Truk. *Enterprise* proceed and attack."

From their hidden position, the officers saw the startled look on the petty officer's face as he read the dispatch. While they watched, he tiptoed away with a somber face. He returned to the flight deck, crawled into a corner, put on his steel helmet, and sat there huddled up awaiting the attack.

That was the last time he ever tried to see what action the *Enterprise* had pending.

The strength of the Pacific Fleet grew daily, and Halsey acquired his largest number of ships since the start of the war. His South Pacific fleet now consisted of three new battleships—the *Washington, North Carolina*, and *Indiana*—plus four older ones. With the carriers *Enterprise* and *Saratoga*, he also had three auxiliary carriers—the *Chenango, Suwanee*, and *Sangamon*—to add their potency.

Plans were expedited to initiate operations during the next three months in the Central Pacific.

During the long battle for control of Guadalcanal, other Japanese bases were built in the Solomons. A new airfield was completed on Munda Point, New Georgia, while others were constructed on such smaller islands as Kolombangara and Vella Lavella. Munda was only 175 miles from Guadalcanal, and Zeros used it for flights over Henderson Field. At the top of the Solomons, Bougainville had five airfields. The largest was at Kahili on the island's southern tip.

While major battles were underway in the South Pacific, the United States Navy's premier airman, John H. Towers, was promoted to vice-admiral in October 1942 and was given the job of commander of Air Operations in the Pacific, reporting to Nimitz. Towers had been deliberately kept by Admiral King in a subordinate position as chief of the navy's Bureau of Aeronautics while nonaviators in the field tried to build a new navy based upon the lessons learned from the Japanese, who used carriers to spearhead their Pacific conquests.

Towers' directives from Nimitz instructed him to build and to maintain a carrier air force although he was not given authority to operate it. However, as Nimitz' deputy commander for air, he was able to suggest for command positions aviators whom he had known since they were lieutenants.

Prior to the war, the old line of battle called for battleships in the lead, with carriers off to one side to support the main battleline. A veteran flier since World War I, Towers resisted efforts during the 1930s by old-line commanders to use airplanes primarily for dropping torpedoes, which they were accustomed to do from three different directions to assure hits. Towers believed then, and time proved him to be correct, that airplanes should be the fleet's main striking force, but it was not until he became Nimitz' deputy that he had a chance to fully develop the concept of fast carrier task groups. Of course, in the 1930s, while the battleship was supreme, it was difficult to obtain funds to build enough carriers to prove the concept.

Now, with carriers coming into their own, Towers established fast carrier task groups—four carriers with approximately 224 airplanes in each group—as the core for all task forces. Around the carriers, battleships, cruisers, and destroyers were used primarily for support.

Unlike Towers, Admiral King was a johnny-come-lately to naval aviation. Nimitz, in turn, was a former submariner with a limited knowledge of aviation.

Towers had long considered King his greatest enemy within the United States Navy. Before the war, at a social event at the Hotel del Coronado near San Diego, California, King became obstreperous and crude after drinking heavily. The gentleman in Towers took offense and when the two went to the men's room, Towers told King he was a pennywhistle. King strode out, angered by the remark. Towers later told a friend, "I made a mistake." He was never again on good terms with King.

Once King became head of the United States Fleet, Towers' belief that King had never forgiven him was reinforced when he was relegated to a subordinate job in Washington and denied a command at sea.

Airmen like Towers often engaged in disputes with other officers after Pearl Harbor because they felt that the debacle vindicated their long fight for the increased use of carriers over battleships. They distrusted officers without flying experience. Their attitude was unfortunate but understandable. Actually, King believed in giving aviators a greater role in fighting the war, and Towers was placed under Nimitz by King because he was convinced that Towers was needed in the job.

King was not completely sold on the value of airmen for high command positions because he was convinced that top flag officers should be generalists rather than specialists, as were aviators. He argued that a commander's duties and responsibilities were so vast that he required a broader range of knowledge than just how to best utilize aircraft.

For command of carrier task groups at sea, King trusted only Adms. William Halsey, Marc A. Mitscher, and John McCain. Nimitz basically agreed that the rest were too young. The exception, of course, was Towers, who had the experience, the age, and the flag rank but who was otherwise not high in King's esteem.

Towers' career had been checkered because of his strong advocacy of naval aviation. He had almost lost his life in an experimental plane years earlier: It had spun in as he clung to a strut. Somehow, he had survived the crush.

Few knew that he had a glass eye. Once, when removing the rubber bands from a golf ball with a knife, he had pierced the inner sack, and the milky substance had squirted into one eye and blinded him. Ever after, however, he had insisted on flying despite his bad eye.

It is generally agreed by fellow officers of the period that if Towers had been given a combat command early in the war, he would have become another Spruance, Halsey, or Mitscher.

Nimitz respected Towers and needed him as his deputy because the war in the Pacific had developed primarily into an air war, for which Nimitz as a former submariner had little background. Once Nimitz named Towers as his air deputy, Towers urged him to use carriers more effectively as primary attack forces. This brilliant airman, long denied the top combat job for which he was so well trained, did a superb job for Nimitz. Nevertheless, Nimitz had to constantly defend his deputy from tirades by King.

Towers' full effectiveness would come later. At the moment, the war called for emergency actions with whatever was available in the field. As Nimitz' deputy, Towers immediately went into action to help prepare the Pacific Fleet to fight an aero-amphibious war once more carriers became available.

In Washington, Admiral King continued to fight political battles, particularly when Secretary of Navy Knox tried to talk him into assuming command of the Pacific Fleet. Knox had brought King to Washington in 1941 but now believed that King was a political threat because he relentlessly pursued power at the highest levels. The navy secretary resented King's hostility to civilian authority and his intimate contacts with President Roosevelt. He tried to get King sent to the Pacific as commander of the Pacific Fleet so he could appoint a chief of naval operations who was more amenable to his authority. King insisted that his job was in Washington, and he would not consider such a move.

Countering Knox, King tried to get the president to agree that the Navy Department should be reorganized to make it more responsive to his own authority, but Knox went to the president to protest that his civilian authority would be further weakened. Roosevelt agreed, telling King that reorganization should await the end of the war. "Let's win it first."

Knox had been opposed to King's dual responsibilities from the beginning, believing that the jobs of chief of naval operations and commander of the United States Fleet should be held by different individuals. Now he plainly hated the fact that King held both jobs. Perhaps King was more stubborn than most chiefs of naval operations, but he stood for a traditional resistance by the United States Navy toward civilian authority.

The Joint Chiefs of Staff prepared a position paper prior to the Casablanca Conference, which was to be held on January 14 in North Africa and attended by Roosevelt and Churchill along with the Combined Chiefs. The Americans agreed to propose an offensive in the Pacific, a cross-channel invasion of Europe in 1943, and a strategic air offensive against Germany. Agreement was achieved only after Roosevelt insisted that they settle on a plan because he knew that the British would have one. At times, differences between Army Chief of Staff Marshall and King threatened agreement, and some of their arguments were petty.

At Casablanca, Marshall proposed that the available men, supplies, and equipment for Europe and the Pacific theater be divided between the two major war fronts by a ratio of seventy to thirty. King seconded the recommendation, and it was approved.

That night King became intoxicated. He had sworn off hard liquor for the duration of the war; it was an excessive amount of wine that almost proved his undoing. In a thick voice, he tried to tell Churchill and his British staff how to set up a French organization in North Africa that would be acceptable to all. His intoxicated condition, complicated by the fact that he did not know what he was talking about, displeased the British, who told him frankly that he had more trust in French politicians than they had.

The rest of the conference went more smoothly. It was agreed that the Battle of the Atlantic should have top priority so that the enormous shipping losses could be reduced. Although the Americans were against the invasion of Sicily, they reluctantly agreed to support that operation. The idea of a 1943 cross-channel invasion of the European continent was abandoned, but the Americans agreed to this position only if the British agreed to intensify the Pacific war. Churchill was adamantly opposed, saying that only a holding action should be allowed in the Pacific.

At a private luncheon, Churchill turned his charm on King to get him to agree to the British viewpoint on the Pacific. King stubbornly refused.

To break the impasse, Roosevelt invited Churchill and King to dinner that night. King did most of the talking and tried to impress the prime minister with the logic of the American position. He said that the British should reenter Burma to establish a supply route along the Burma Road to Nationalist China. He told Churchill that the president, General Marshall, and he were all committed to keeping the Chinese in the war so that the Japanese Army would be pinned down on the mainland and unable to participate in actions against them in the Pacific.

Then it was Churchill's turn to go on the attack. He accused King of not telling the truth about American losses in the Pacific and of withholding information about the landing-craft program, which was vital to the war in the Mediterranean. In his arguments, Churchill had to concede that the British were dependent on American warships, but neither convinced the other of his position on operations in the Pacific, and King had to settle for approval from the British Chiefs of Staff without the prime minister's personal commitment.

The conference concluded with three statements. Agreement was reached that operations in the Pacific would continue with forces already allocated to maintain pressure on the Japanese and attain a position of readiness for a full-scale offensive against Japan once Germany was defeated. Furthermore, no action should be taken that might jeopardize the capacity of the Allies to take advantage of any opportunity to bring about Germany's decisive defeat. Finally

Burma should be recaptured in 1943 and after the capture of Rabaul, operations initiated against the Marshalls and Carolines if time and resources permitted without prejudice to the recapture of Burma. Other decisions called for all possible aid to Russia, and a strategic bomber offensive against Germany.

King got some of what he wanted, including the phrase that adequate forces should be allocated to the Pacific and Far Eastern theaters. Later, King, interpreted this phrase to mean that anything was permissible to support Nimitz' needs in the Pacific—hardly what the conferees intended. King knew that Marshall and Army Air Forces General Arnold would prove stumbling blocks, but he intended to seek more troops and planes from them after he got back to Washington.

King was satisfied with his part in the conference and magnanimously promised Churchill that he would find the necessary warships to serve as escorts for the invasion of Sicily. To everyone, King said that their decisions would go a long way toward winning the war.

The recapture of Burma was later canceled, and Rabaul was bypassed.

Air personnel now began to get some respite from the constant danger of daily operations. After an air group had been aboard ship for about six months, it was replaced and returned to the United States for reforming. Talented men were divided among newer squadrons to put combat experience into new air groups.

Admiral Halsey's popularity with the press rose to new heights after Guadalcanal was secured, yet at times his words were beneath the dignity of an admiral. His comments, often colorful, occasionally lapsed into excess, as when he referred to the Japanese as monkeys and bastards. Similarly, when he predicted an early end to the war, his stature among associates declined several notches and subsequently his comments were not always trusted.

Capt. Jefferson J. DeBlanc, section leader for VMF–112, went out on January 31 to escort SBDs and Avengers in an attack on shipping in the Vella Gulf, north of the Japanese air base at Kolombangara. A large fleet of Japanese fighters met them at 14,000 feet, and DeBlanc's six Wildcats had their hands full. In an old-fashioned dogfight, DeBlanc dove at a formation of float planes. In rapid succession, his guns slashed through three Rufes and sent them down. One Zero attacked from behind, and DeBlanc was hit so seriously that he had to return to Guadalcanal. In trying to climb to a safer altitude, he found two more Zeros on his tail. He desperately searched the sky for his squadron mates. They were too occupied elsewhere, and he realized that he was alone. Quickly, he reversed direction and found himself on a collision course with the Zeros. One succumbed to his guns, and the other lost heart and broke off.

DeBlanc's Wildcat was so riddled with bullet holes that it shuddered each time he varied from straight and level flight. Although he was low on fuel and his plane was trying to shake itself apart, DeBlanc was unwilling to let the fleeing Zero pilot get away. With all the power remaining in his engine, he caught up with the Japanese plane and his four guns ripped it to pieces.

He turned around again, smoke pouring from his rough engine, and headed for base. He was down to treetop level as he roared over Kolombangara, trying to stay in the air. Over the ocean, he knew he was going to have to bail out, even though he was too low to do so safely. He managed to climb out of the crippled plane, and his chute snapped open just above the water. He realized that he had injuries to his back, arms, and legs. Fortunately, he still had on his life jacket, and it helped him to swim to Kolombangara, where friendly natives rescued him.

DeBlanc was awarded a Medal of Honor for his extraordinary heroism.

The F4U-1 Corsair, an inverted gull-wing fighter, made its appearance in the Pacific on February 12, 1943, when VMF-124 arrived. Early versions of this plane were bad actors aboard carriers. During three-point landings, in which the pilot had to put the tailhook onto the deck to pick up an arresting wire, the nose remained so high that forward visibility was limited. Compounding this, the plane's oleo gear, a hydraulic mechanism that absorbed the shock of landing, was too stiff, often causing the already nose-high plane to rebound into the air when the wheels struck the deck. This could send the aircraft floating over the arresting gear without catching a wire—a hazard to men and parked planes on the forward flight deck. The problem was corrected by lengthening the tailhook and reducing the stiffness of the oleo gear. Until these changes were incorporated in carrier planes, the Corsair was used to good effect primarily by marines from land bases. It was faster than any Japanese plane, and it had a longer range than other American fighters.

On Saint Valentine's Day, Corsairs and air force P-38s provided top cover for a B-24 bombing raid against Kahili airfield on

Bougainville. Fifty Zeros came up and quickly shot down two of the bombers. In a spectacular dogfight, American fighters were clearly outnumbered; two P–40s, two Corsairs, and all four P–38s were shot down.

This operation was not typical because it was evident by the spring of 1943 that many of Japan's best fighter pilots had been lost, and the level of experience and skill of the remainder declined as they were rushed into combat with insufficient training. In contrast, American training commands were turning out an ever-increasing number of pilots who benefited from instruction given by experienced veterans like Marion Carl, John Smith, and Joe Foss, who had been returned to the States.

Yamamoto now personally devised a plan to reverse the course of events in the southwest Pacific. At his Rabaul headquarters, the admiral approved a plan called "I-go Sakusen," scheduled for early April.

Nagumo had been removed from command, and Yamamoto ordered Vice-Adm. Jisaburo Ozawa's First Carrier Division to strip the *Zuikaku* and *Zuiho* of planes and come to Rabaul. The planes were sent to land bases because Yamamoto was reluctant to expose his carriers to American carrier- and land-based attacks. Planes from the Second Carrier Division's *Junyo* and *Hiyo* were flown to a base at Ballale, south of Bougainville. Yamamoto had approximately 350 combat aircraft when an attack against Guadalcanal was launched on April 7. American commanders ordered every combat airplane into the area to resist the aerial onslaught. Although the attack was repulsed, several American ships were sunk off Guadalcanal and Tulagi.

Lt. James E. Swett of VMF–221 led four Wildcats to Tulagi. This was the marine pilot's first mission. When a formation of fifteen Vals appeared, the cry "Tallyho!" sent them diving into the Japanese planes. Swett then heard a report on his radio that Zekes were diving from above. He soon found himself alone as he twisted in his dive with all guns firing at three Vals. Under heavy attack by Japanese fighters, Swett shot down the three Vals in a matter of minutes.

Pulling out of his dive, Swett spotted four more Vals and also shot these down in flames. Even though his ammunition was almost exhausted and he was under continuous attack, Swett headed for another Val, taking a hail of bullets that smashed his windshield, cut his face, and disabled his engine.

Swett knew that he was going down; his engine was out of oil and the propeller had frozen, leaving his Wildcat without power. He glided toward the water only to be fired on by American gunners. His Wildcat careened across the top of the waves until it came to an abrupt stop and his head slammed into the gunsight, smashing his nose. His fighter started to sink. Bloody and dazed, he fought to get out of the cockpit and found he could not; his parachute harness had caught on the handle of the cockpit enclosure. While he fought to save his life, the plane sank and, with one final desperate burst of energy, he broke the parachute strap and ejected his life raft. Although his partially inflated Mae West helped him to rise to the surface, he was near death when he was picked up off Tulagi by a small boat.

Swett's marksmanship, which destroyed seven Japanese Vals, made him an ace; his courage and skill under difficult combat conditions, moreover, earned him a Medal of Honor.

Japanese aircraft losses were heavy: Thirty Zekes and Vals had been shot down for the loss of only seven American planes. Yamamoto's plan failed even though new damage was done to American shipping and installations during the series of raids.

The Japanese were still unaware that their code had been broken and sent messages that Admiral Yamamoto would personally inspect bases at Ballale, Shortland, and Buin on April 18. With characteristic Japanese military efficiency, precise details were sent, giving times of arrival and departure at each base. Orders were issued to the United States Air Force that this information should be used in an attempt to shoot down Yamamoto's Betty bomber.

American P-38s intercepted the Japanese transports and six Japanese fighters on April 18 near Buin. Capt. Thomas G. Lanphier, Jr. of Maj. John W. Mitchell's 339th Fighter Squadron was credited with actually shooting down Yamamoto's transport, which crashed in the jungle along with the other bomber carrying high officials.

At first, no mention was made of Yamamoto's death in Japan, and the Americans kept silent because they were not certain that Yamamoto had been on the plane. His death was finally announced on May 21 when Yamamoto's ashes were returned to Japan. The radio report merely said, "While directing general strategy on the front lines in April of this year, engaged in combat with the enemy and met gallant death in a warplane."

Halsey wired Mitscher, "Congratulations to you and Major Mitchell and his hunters. Sounds as though one of the ducks in their bag was a peacock."

Yamamoto's loss was a great shock to the Japanese people, and he was given a state funeral. The emperor appointed Adm. Min-eichi Koga to succeed him. Though a veteran admiral, Koga lacked the imagination and drive that would have enabled him to take the place of the dynamic Yamamoto.

In the Aleutians, the Eleventh Air Force and the United States Navy's Patrol Wing 4 had kept the Japanese occupying forces in misery, bombing them without letup in continuous fogs and winds that made flights of any kind all but impossible. Admiral King, con-tinually pressed to drive the Japanese out of Attu and Kiska, said, "Since the Aleutians constitute an aerial highway between the North American continent and the Far East, their strategic value is obvious. On the other hand, that chain of islands provides as rugged a theater for warfare as any in the world."

The Joint Chiefs agreed to resolve the situation and in May 1943 sent the Seventh Infantry Division to attack Attu. Although the Japanese were outnumbered, the Seventh had to fight for each foot of ground. Finally, the Japanese made a final banzai charge, cheer-ing the Emperor as they rushed frantically at the Americans. When it failed, the survivors held hand grenades to their heads and pulled the pins.

Another invasion force headed for Kiska in the middle of August, but the Japanese had pulled out on July 28, leaving slow-burning fires. The Allies found it deserted except for the weather station's dog, Explosion, who was the sole American survivor of the occupa-tion. Publicly, the Japanese leaders said that the islands were evacu-ated because their troops were needed to defend the Kuriles.

The Japanese sent twenty-five Zekes to protect a reconnaissance plane which tried on May 13 to photograph the four American air-fields on Guadalcanal. Lt. Kenneth Walsh, who had already shot down three Japanese planes while flying a Corsair with VMF-124, flew up to join air force fighters and his squadron mates. It proved to be an unequal contest for the Japanese, who lost a total of six-teen airplanes for a loss of only three Corsairs. In the tangle, Walsh shot down three Zekes and became the first Corsair ace. Later, a Medal of Honor winner, Walsh would have twenty-one confirmed kills by the end of the war.

Allied leaders met at the Trident Conference in Washington on May 12–25, and Admiral King discussed possible ways to retake the Philippines. He enunciated three possibilities: a straight approach from Hawaii through the Central Pacific or a deviation north or south of that line. He made it clear that he favored an approach through the Central Pacific but that the Japanese fleet would first have to be defeated and the Mariana Islands occupied.

In the Pacific, he said, all operations should be directed toward the severance of Japanese lines of communication and recapture of the Philippines. He stressed that the Marianas were the key. Once these strategic islands were captured, the Allies would be in a central position, able to strike toward the Philippines, the coast of China, or northwest directly at Japan. He emphasized that the Japanese fleet would have to be forced into a showdown. It was his belief that the strategic importance of the Marianas to the Japanese would force them to commit their entire fleet. Once their fleet was destroyed, he added, the Pacific would belong to the Allies, and Japan could be defeated by attrition through blockade, bombing, and amphibious assault.

King warned his listeners not to become complacent about recent victories won by American forces. He felt that Japan was still dangerous and unpredictable, although he conceded that he was surprised that she had not done more in recent months to hurt the Allies. He could not comprehend Japan's failure to occupy all of China and to attack her historic enemy, Russia. He made particular mention of the failures of Japanese submarines to attack unescorted Allied ships. He concluded his remarks by saying that it would be incredible if Japan's loss of face from being thrown out of the Solomons and Guadalcanal did not result in a major blow-off.

British chiefs were impressed by King's remarks and by his insistence on an acceleration of the Pacific war. Although there was much debate about his plans to increase the war's operations in the Pacific, the British agreed to consider seriously any proposal King made for a major Pacific offensive. King was pleased with their understanding, and when plans were approved by Roosevelt and Churchill to increase the tempo of the war in the Far East, King was given written authority to pursue his master plan to initiate further offensives.

King resisted General Marshall's proposal that Admiral Nimitz be named supreme commander in the Pacific, and it was tabled without action. King opposed the plan because he did not trust Nimitz fully. He believed that Nimitz was too inclined to compromise with the army. Moreover, as theater commander Nimitz would be able to report directly to the Joint Chiefs.

MacArthur was upset when he learned that King's proposal for a Central Pacific drive was approved. He wrote General Marshall, objecting strongly to any release of his forces to Nimitz, including two marine divisions under his command. In denouncing the Central Pacific drive, MacArthur said that all resources should be sent to him so that he could capture Rabaul, "the great strategic prize." So vehemently did MacArthur press his case that some of King's support among the Joint Chiefs evaporated.

A planner was instructed to seek a compromise. It was suggested that MacArthur should bypass Rabaul, continue his advance along the northern coast of New Guinea, and agree to release to Admiral Nimitz only one marine division—the second—for his Central Pacific drive. It was further suggested that General Marshall should assign the Twenty-seventh Infantry Division to Nimitz' forces so that MacArthur could retain the First Marine Division. After extensive arguments, it was decided that American industry was reaching peak production and the nation could support two paths to the Philippines.

Gen. Henry H. Arnold of the United States Army Air Forces agreed to provide additional air force groups to the Central Pacific to permit Nimitz to seize the Gilbert Islands on November 1, 1943. The Gilberts were given priority over the Marshalls because air bases on Tarawa and Makin were needed to support an invasion of the Marshalls.

Once it was agreed, July 20, that two independent routes should be taken to the Philippines, King had his formal directive to open a Central Pacific offensive. He suggested that the attack on the Gilberts be moved up to November 14 to coincide with MacArthur's plans for moving along the New Guinea coast.

King submitted new plans to the Joint Chiefs on June 11 that further reduced the importance of MacArthur's theater of operations. These plans called for an invasion of the Marshalls and established dates for future assaults. In effect, these plans forced MacArthur to specify his future operations so forces could be allocated between the independent commands.

MacArthur did not encourage outsiders at his headquarters and took steps to assure that long conversations in his office would be impossible. He ordered all but the most important visitors to be given a chair whose front legs were shortened by at least a half inch and whose seat was kept highly polished, directly facing the sun streaming through undraped windows. A visitor, sliding off his chair while the sun blinded him, could barely see his "Imperial Highness MacArthur" and often as not left in a hurry with most of his remarks unsaid.

12

A MASTER PLAN
FOR JAPAN'S DEFEAT

While battles raged in the southern and eastern Pacific following the Battle of Midway, the Central Pacific had remained quiet for almost a year, perhaps in part because of Yamamoto's demise. All that was changed now as Nimitz prepared his forces for a drive aimed ultimately at the main islands of Japan.

A Fifth Fleet was organized on August 5, 1943, under Vice-Adm. Raymond A. Spruance. It was scheduled to build up to eleven carriers by late fall, including the new heavy carriers *Lexington* and *Yorktown* to replace the older ones, and the newly commissioned *Essex* and *Bunker Hill*. The veteran carriers *Saratoga* and *Enterprise* joined the Fifth, along with five new light carriers: the *Independence, Princeton, Belleau Wood, Monterey,* and *Cowpens.* For close support, eight escort carriers were assigned to Spruance so that he would have a total of nine hundred combat aircraft for operations against the Gilberts, Marshalls, and Marianas.

Spruance had been Nimitz' chief of staff since Midway, and now he was in command of Central Pacific Forces under his former boss. This modest officer had a remarkable capability of applying his experience and attention to detail and then making intelligent decisions. The appointment received King's whole hearted endorsement because he considered Spruance the best flag officer in the navy, and Spruance received his third star as a result of King's strong backing.

Rear Adm. Richmond Kelly Turner was named amphibious force commander. This brilliant tactician was ideal for the job and was admired by both Nimitz and King.

When Lt. Gen. Holland M. Smith's name was mentioned for landing force commander, Nimitz had his doubts although King readily agreed that Smith was the top expert in the field. Nimitz went along, but Smith's contentiousness concerned him.

The plan approved by the Joint Chiefs for Pacific operations in early June provided for Nimitz to make landings on Rendova Island in the New Georgias by the end of the month and on New Georgia at Viru Harbor, Segi Point, and Wickham Anchorage. Although the Viru landing was delayed a day, the other landings proceeded on schedule, and the whole operation was completed on August 5.

The Japanese were on the defensive, and they knew it. They could only reinforce their garrisons ahead of the Americans and fight a war of attrition. They had underestimated the tenacity of the Allies and the tremendous pace of American industry, which was now producing war material at an unheard-of rate. The Japanese could only hope that the Americans would not be able to risk their naval power at the rate it had been used up in the Solomons.

Before his death, Admiral Yamamoto had recognized the strength of America's industrial power. He once said that when the great American industry got production rolling that it would "uncoil like a massive spring." America's mass production techniques now showed its strength. Inasmuch as it takes five years from start of design for a new aircraft until it is delivered to the fleet, navy officials for the most part froze all aircraft designs, concentrating production on aircraft that were in the design and development stage during the 1930s to get the maximum number of airplanes into service at the earliest possible time. Aircraft were, however, improved throughout the war with protective armor, self-sealing fuel tanks, and more horsepower for their engines to permit greater combat loads.

The decision to freeze designs had one adverse effect: Jet engine development had to be turned over to the British so the United States could remain the "Arsenal of Democracy." This was necessary because production of reciprocating engines remained critical until near the war's end. As a result, the United States postwar development of jet engines was delayed.

Bougainville, gateway to Rabaul, was within reach after Munda, in the Central Solomons, was captured with its important air base and forces on New Georgia were consolidated. Kolombangara with its ten thousand troops was bypassed by Halsey. Vella Lavella was needed to establish another major airfield so it was successfully invaded on August 14. While ground action was light, air action above the battlefield was fierce.

Lieutenant Walsh, the United States Navy's first Corsair ace, found himself in a furious dogfight and quickly raised his score to ten kills when he knocked down a Zeke fighter. He added two more when he unexpectedly ran into nine Vals. Now he was in a jam, under attack by Zekes above with Val rear gunners firing up at him from below.

While 20 mm shells tore his right wing to ribbons, other Japanese planes raced up to add their firepower. Just as Walsh decided he had no chance of surviving, friends came to his rescue, and he expertly guided his shattered Corsair to Munda. He landed to the cheers of ground troops.

During a lull in the fighting, Admiral Halsey met MacArthur in Brisbane. He was captivated by the general's charm, saying afterward, "Five minutes after I reported, I felt as if we were lifelong friends. I have seldom seen a man who makes a quicker, stronger, more favorable impression." Halsey and MacArthur got along well together, and there was never friction between them. Their camaraderie made it possible to resolve differences quickly.

A nagging technical problem was finally overcome when American torpedoes were equipped with new firing pin mechanisms that assured more certain detonation. Since the war's earliest days, torpedoes tended to explode prematurely or not at all despite close runups against enemy ships by pilots of torpedo planes or submarine commanders. The early Mark 6 exploder in fleet-type submarines was activated by contact or by magnetic detonation. After extensive tests were done during 1943 it was determined that these early torpedoes were running 11 feet deeper than they were set.

Prior to the meeting of the Quadrant Conference at Quebec in late August and September 1943, the Joint Chiefs were more than ever convinced that an island-by-island campaign in the Pacific would needlessly prolong the war and that many islands could be bypassed. Halsey was moving ahead in the Solomons and MacArthur along the coast of New Guinea in separate drives while American submarines were taking an ever-increasing toll of Japanese shipping.

At a meeting of the Joint Chiefs, King announced that he would press for a speedup of operations in the Pacific, saying that this theater was receiving only a 15 percent allocation of America's men and material. He pointed out that Pacific forces were six months behind schedule because they had received only half the allotment previously promised by the Joint Chiefs of Staff: 30 percent of total resources to the Pacific.

President Roosevelt met with his Joint Chiefs on August 14 before they went to Quebec. They agreed on basic strategy, which was to insist upon a cross-channel invasion of Europe in 1944 despite the expected British desire to postpone such an invasion. They agreed that the British should be encouraged to remain active in the China–Burma–India theater to help keep Japanese forces there occupied—and out of the Pacific fighting.

When Allied leaders met in Quebec, Sicily had been secured by invasion on July 10, and the Italian government was in a state of disarray. Prime Minister Churchill urged the conference to agree on an invasion of Italy, implying that this would be a way of getting to Central Europe before the Russian armies could move in.

All Americans were opposed to an invasion of Italy, but King used the most undiplomatic language. He charged that such an invasion would deprive American forces in the Pacific of carrying the war to Japan. He tried to reason with Churchill by saying that only a slight decrease in the men, supplies, and equipment sent to Europe would have a dramatic impact on operations in the Pacific. The rest of the American delegation joined King in support of a master plan for Japan's defeat.

Finally, on August 16, a unified statement was approved. Although some of it was ambiguous, in general it followed the American plan that an invasion of the European continent should take place on May 1, 1944, and that it would have priority over the Mediterranean theater and the campaign for Italy. The final Combined Chiefs' agreement called for a concurrent invasion of southern France along with the channel invasion. It was agreed that operations against Japan would be intensified within twelve months of Germany's defeat.

King was bitter because the agreement perpetuated the secondary status of the war in the Pacific and because the British had not more strongly supported Vice-Adm. Lord Louis Mountbatten's British Southeast Asia Command. King did get permission to invade the Gilberts, Marshalls, Carolines, Palaus, and Marianas; MacArthur was ordered to bypass Rabaul and move instead into northwest New Guinea.

Although King did not get his master plan approved, he claimed to have done so.

The Allies were on the march around the world. Salerno was scheduled for invasion on September 9, even though the Mediterranean theater, like the Pacific theater, had been downgraded to secondary status. MacArthur's men were advancing in New Guinea, and Nimitz was preparing to invade Tarawa. The Battle of the Atlantic was at last being won, and supplies and reinforcements were getting to Europe in ever-increasing quantities. Allied bombers were hitting Germany in the first important strategic air strikes of the war. And, on the Eastern Front, the Russians were mauling the German armies and preparing to make counterattacks.

Major Gregory "Pappy" Boyington moved his Marine Squadron 214 to Munda in October. This former pilot with the American Volunteer Group in China was to lead his unconventional squadron to victory even though they were consistently outnumbered.

Boyington, a poor disciplinarian during two uneventful early tours, was given a chance to form a squadron of "misfits" he called the "Black Sheep." He stressed small formations and accurate shooting, which required tremendous coolness and achieved results against Japanese Zekes. With the air war heating up as the Japanese withdrew up the Slot through the central Solomons, Boyington's squadron was constantly in the air shooting down Japanese planes in large numbers and wreaking havoc on Japanese shipping and shore installations.

On October 17, he led a formation of twenty-six fighters over Kahili, where sixty enemy fighters were based. Japanese fighter pilots at first refused to come up so he circled their airfield and challenged them. They should have stayed on the ground. Once they were airborne, twenty aircraft were shot down by Boyington and his pilots without the loss of a single marine plane.

He was not always so lucky, and sometimes VMF–214 losses were heavy despite its skill. Boyington's own fortune gave out on January 3, 1944, when he was shot down. It was reported that he had been killed; he had been seen to parachute from his burning Corsair into Saint George Channel near Rabaul but had been followed down by four Zeke fighters in a hail of bullets. In fact, he ended up in a prisoner-of-war camp, having made six kills with the American Volunteer Group and twenty-two kills as a marine pilot. Boyington received a postwar Medal of Honor in recognition of his bravery and skill.

Since the spring of 1943, Admiral Towers, Nimitz' commander for aviation in the Pacific, had reiterated his belief that aircraft carriers had been used primarily for defensive purposes and that such use was self-defeating. He had continued to insist that all major command staffs in the Pacific theater should be headed by an aviator, but King and Nimitz rejected this thesis. Now that the aero-amphibious phase of the war was set in motion, others in the United States Navy joined Towers in pressing for major command changes. Capt. Harold Sallada, who worked directly under Admiral King in Washington, flatly stated that unless such changes were made the "mobility of naval aviation will be wasted." Commander John Thach, the veteran fighter pilot who had developed the Thach Weave, spoke out strongly, insisting that naval aviation was not an auxiliary or arm of the navy but its primary offensive and defensive weapon. Rear Adm. Calvin T. Durgin, who commanded the fleet air arm at Quonset Point, Rhode Island, was equally emphatic: "Our aircraft carrier task forces, despite their victories, have been handled with a lack of full aggressive effectiveness." He stressed that this was because the nonaviators who were in tactical command during these battles lacked experience and knowledge in handling air groups.

Other voices joined in. Capt. C. R. Brown of the Joint War Plans Committee recommended that "either the commander or chief of staff in all echelons should be a naval aviator." Capt. Matt Gardner in Admiral King's office complained in August that Nimitz' staff had only one naval aviator, Capt. Ralph A. Ofstie; the Atlantic Fleet had only one, a commander; and Admiral Halsey in the South Pacific had only a lieutenant commander who was an aviator. The staff of the new Central Pacific Force, he added, also had but one aviator, and his rank was only that of commander.

Admiral Nimitz heard about these comments indirectly. Adm. Harry Yarnell, the former commander of the Asiatic Fleet, had returned to the Navy Department in the summer of 1943 after four years of retirement. Nimitz first learned about the rising tide of opposition to some of his practices after reading a form letter that Yarnell had sent to all aviators, soliciting their views on the most effective way to employ naval aviation. At first, Nimitz remained out of the fray, disassociating himself by saying that his background was not in aviation and that he did not have the expertise to make a worthwhile contribution to the controversy. But Yarnell's poll opened the floodgates of criticism by airmen throughout the navy, and Nimitz was upset. He blamed Towers for the rising tide of opposition.

Towers' chief of staff stepped in to calm the situation. Nimitz listened as Captain Forrest P. "Ted" Sherman, whom he admired, recommended that he draft a letter for Nimitz' signature to get the controversy under control. Nimitz readily agreed with the contents of the letter drafted by Sherman. The letter acknowledged the aviators' views and stated that aviation units should be operated by commanders with extensive aviation experience or by commanders whose staff members had such experience. But it emphasized the need for the integration of air and nonair commands as preferable to the wholesale removal of present commanders and their replacement by airmen. Sherman and Nimitz were correct in believing that there were not sufficient qualified aviators of flag rank to suddenly assume all the top jobs in the Pacific Fleet.

The letter was well timed. Vice-Adm. Frederick J. Horne, vice-chief of naval operations, had already approved of the more extreme findings delineated by Yarnell's poll.

Towers added his personal thoughts in a memorandum sent to Admiral Nimitz on October 4, 1943. He said that aviation in the Pacific Fleet was sound, but he recommended that a deputy commander in chief with a rank directly below that of commander should be established in each major command in the Pacific theater. He recommended that either the commander in chief or his deputy be a naval aviator. "I contend that the navy as a whole has not been progressive in its attitude toward application of aviation to naval warfare," he said. He recalled that a few farseeing aviators had more or less forced the navy to adopt naval aviation. He acknowledged that resentment had been aroused by these officers and regretted that such resentment was still in evidence. "This is not conducive to good teamwork." In speaking of aviation-oriented officers, Towers told Nimitz that these officers would have been outstanding in any capacity in the navy regardless of their specialty. He asked Nimitz to use his influence to give such officers positions in which their views could be translated into policies and actions.

Admiral Yarnell, whose aviator poll had started the controversy, raised his voice to condemn navy officialdom for not using airpower as effectively as it could. He recommended that the deputy chief of naval operations for air be given the full rank of admiral and that he be given a seat on the Joint Chiefs of Staff like the one held by Air Forces Chief of Staff Gen. "Hap" Arnold, with full authority to direct naval air forces rather than simply advise the chief of naval operations. He even went so far as to recommend Nimitz' removal and replacement by an aviator, or at least that Nimitz' operations officer for air be raised to the rank of rear admiral.

Admiral King's views on top command positions—that such officers should not be specialists but have general navy backgrounds—

remained unchanged by the controversy. Nimitz compromised to the extent that he accepted the appointment of two key staff members; one a deputy commander in chief to advise on air matters and the other an operations officer for air.

Airmen had won a limited victory, but Towers believed that they had at last had a chance to present their views to top authorities about airpower's proper role in operations. In the great Central Pacific drives now in the planning stages, aviators were given a greater role than they would have had without this candid airing of their grievances.

While preparations were underway for a series of amphibious landings to be spearheaded by fast carrier forces, Towers wrote Nimitz on August 21 that fast carriers should be the principal offensive elements in the fleet, providing direct air support to amphibious operations. In other words, he was asking Nimitz to use fast carriers not only to gain superiority in the air by destroying enemy air forces but also to provide support to ground troops. "Carrier operations are highly specialized," he said, "and should be conducted by officers thoroughly trained therein. To be 'air minded' is no substitute for long aviation experience." Towers emphasized that in his position as commander, Air Pacific, which gave him no authority over air operations, he could not possibly handle logistics and maintenance without some authority over air operations. He concluded, "Operations and logistics cannot be divorced."

Nimitz was unhappy with Towers' letter. Towers had hoped to get a combat command, or barring that, see an aviator like Admiral Fitch placed in command of the Central Pacific Force, which was now under Spruance. But Nimitz disagreed even with Towers' suggestion that Spruance's chief of staff be an aviator.

Towers gained another important ally when Rear Adm. Kelly Turner, Nimitz' amphibious commander, supported his views. Towers wrote Nimitz again on October 4, citing the continued resentment of nonaviators toward fliers. He pressed again for the recommendations in his earlier letter.

The fast carriers proved so successful in operations during the summer and early fall of 1943 that Nimitz softened his stand. On October 12, he asked Towers to recommend an officer that he could appoint as CINCPAC's planning officer. Towers submitted the names of several top fliers, but he gave his strongest support to Capt. Forrest P. Sherman, whom Nimitz selected for the post.

Bougainville, last and largest Japanese stronghold in the Solomons, was invaded on November 1. Landings were supported with an all-out attack by planes from Rear Adm. Frederick C. Sherman's carriers, the *Saratoga* and the new *Princeton*.

Prior to the amphibious landings, Halsey decided that the occupation of all of Bougainville would be too costly because forty thousand Japanese troops occupied the northern tip of the island near Buka's airfields. Therefore, after marines waded ashore at Empress Augusta Bay in the center of the island, they established perimeters for airfields only. The Japanese strongly resisted the landings on Bougainville and their losses in the air were heavy whereas not one American pilot was lost.

Now Halsey became worried that the enemy might strike from its base at Rabaul only 210 miles away, imperiling the marines. His concern was justified; the Japanese did send in ships but, in three separate actions, they were all driven off.

Lt. Robert M. Hanson of Marine Fighter Squadron 215 single-handedly attacked six Japanese Kates on November 1, forcing them to dump their torpedoes. He destroyed one and forced the others to flee. Hanson, the son of Methodist missionaries, had been born in India. Before the war ended, he was credited with downing twenty-five Japanese planes and earned a Medal of Honor.

While the majority of Halsey's ships were in the Central Pacific for attacks against the Gilberts, he had only two carriers available. The old *Saratoga* and the smaller *Princeton*, plus their supporting warships, would have to suffice for an attack on Kurita's fleet.

Halsey flashed orders to Admiral Sherman aboard the *Saratoga*. "Attack Rabaul!" After the task force proceeded to launch position, scouts reported, "Simpson Harbor is jammed with ships refueling."

"It's a perfect setup," Sherman said with jubilation.

The *"Sara"* launched planes first, then the *Princeton*. As the planes neared Rabaul, a hundred Japanese fighters bore down on them, and Hellcat fighters fought savagely to protect the American bombers.

Rabaul harbor is surrounded by mountainous terrain, which forced torpedo bombers to come down to masthead height. TBF Avengers roared across the water barely 30 feet off the surface and headed for a group of ships. After their "fish" were dropped, they climbed steeply to clear the hills. They kept their throttles to the firewall as engines labored mightily under maximum power. The horseshoe-shaped harbor was covered with antiaircraft sites on both sides, and torpedo planes took a beating.

The scene was one of confusion as planes twisted high in the sky to evade Japanese Zeros while others dove steeply toward the crowded harbor. When the attack was over, nearly half of Kurita's ships had been hit. None was sunk, however, and ten American planes failed to return to their carriers.

Halsey wired Nimitz that he wanted to strike Truk next, but his request was denied. Instead, a week later, Rear Adm. Alfred E. Montgomery's carrier group returned from the Central Pacific and stood by at Bougainville to join Admiral Sherman's group for another attack on Rabaul. Commander Paul E. Emrick of Air Group 9 aboard the *Essex* warned his pilots, "Teamwork is the keynote. I don't want any 'burning of the blue' for personal glory."

This time bad weather so hindered operations that only limited damage was done to ships and facilities at Simpson Harbor. Still, Admiral Kurita had a badly damaged fleet and had to forgo plans to attack the marines at Bougainville.

The Japanese on New Guinea now found themselves in the uncomfortable position of being outflanked. While Japanese commanders wondered when their turn would come, Allied commanders turned toward the Central Pacific as a more promising battleground for future operations.

The Japanese had won vast territories early in the war, including French Indochina, Malaya, the Philippines, the Netherlands East Indies, and most of Burma. The Imperial High Command was now divided about the future course of action. The Japanese army recommended holding the line, but the navy vigorously opposed such defensive operations. Admiral Mineichi Koga, commander in chief of the Combined Fleet since Yamamoto was shot down, told the command, "Our only hope lies in a decisive naval engagement." Fleet Admiral Osami Nagano disagreed. "With our limited forces, Japan can fight for another two years. Beyond that the outlook is bleak." The views of the navy prevailed, and plans were made for a showdown with the United States Navy. It was exactly what King had hoped they would do.

Admiral Koga decided to keep his fleet at Truk, hoping that the Americans would seek them out and be destroyed.

After Halsey's South Pacific forces established airfields on Bougainville and General MacArthur's southwest Pacific forces took Finschhafen on New Guinea, Rabaul was in jeopardy. Until now it had been an important bastion in Japan's Greater East Asia Co-Prosperity Sphere.

Land warfare became more bloody as troops advanced along the

New Guinea coast and in the Solomons. Japan found it difficult to reinforce her advanced positions, and losses became increasingly critical.

While the Fifth Fleet prepared to soften up the defenses of Tarawa and Makin in the Gilberts, air attacks were made against Wake and Marcus islands in the north as a diversion. Admiral Koga sent Ozawa's Third Air Fleet and Kurita's Second Air Fleet to the Marshalls, which he expected would be attacked. After they were, he ordered the aircraft back to Rabaul. Seventh Air Force B–24s bombed the Gilberts and Marshalls starting November 13 even though such flights were at the fringes of these aircrafts' range.

The Twenty-seventh Infantry Division went ashore at Makin in the Gilbert Islands on November 20 and occupied it in four days. Marines of the Second Division invaded Tarawa the next day. There the marines encountered massive resistance. Preinvasion bombings and shellings had not dented Japanese defenses. Rear Adm. Keiji Shibasaki had five thousand hand-picked troops on Tarawa in stout underground defenses that were impervious to shells or bombs. He had boasted that "a million Americans could never take the island in a thousand years."

He was wrong, but the cost was awful. A thousand American marines died on Tarawa out of a total 3,301 casualties. The marines found underground bunkers all but impregnable and were forced to attack each individually, killing their occupants by tossing grenades through the gun ports or pouring ignited gasoline into them. All but 146 Japanese died, their boastful commander among them. It was the United States Navy's first large-scale amphibious operation in the Central Pacific, and lessons were learned the hard way.

Fast carrier forces under Rear Adm. Charles A. Pownall swept the seas as far south as the Marshall Islands, keeping reinforcements from the islands, while attacks were made against Japanese airfields in the Marshalls. As a result, Japanese air activity was slight, but a Japanese submarine torpedoed the escort carrier *Liscome Bay*, which burst into flames and sank with 644 of her men.

Ground fighting on Tarawa was particularly bitter because of the lack of continued close carrier support, but the key atolls of Makin, Tarawa, and Apemama finally fell. The Central Pacific drive toward the Philippines and Japan was underway.

The new Hellcat got its baptism of fire in its first raid with VF–5, launched from the *Yorktown* on August 31, 1943, during a carrier strike against Marcus Island. The Japanese Zeke was lighter and more maneuverable but the Hellcat was a tougher, faster airplane.

With no armor protection for the Zeke's pilot, the Japanese fighter flamed quickly once it was hit. The Hellcat also had the advantage of better performance at high altitude.

Lt. Comdr. Edward H. "Butch" O'Hare, who had been awarded a Medal of Honor for singlehandedly saving the *Lexington* off Bougainville in early 1942, was lost during the invasion of the Gilberts. He and others had been sent aloft at night as part of a three-plane team to counter a Japanese bomber attack. He never returned, and whether he was shot down by the Japanese or by his own men firing in error will never be known. The unit was composed of an Avenger torpedo plane that had a rudimentary radar used to direct the two Hellcat fighters in intercepting incoming attackers.

Allied leaders met in Cairo on December 3, 1943, for the Sextant Conference. China's Chiang Kai-shek this time joined Roosevelt and Churchill. This was their second meeting in Cairo, and it was held to determine grand strategy for the final years of the war. Gen. Dwight D. Eisenhower was given command of the invasion of the European continent, now scheduled for June 1944. General Marshall, who had hoped to lead the invasion, was told he was needed more in Washington.

Earlier conferences at Cairo and Teheran had dealt with the war in Europe. At this meeting it was reaffirmed that a two-pronged advance would be made in the Pacific with Admiral Nimitz leading the Central Pacific drive while General MacArthur continued his advances along the coast of New Guinea toward the Philippines. Such moves had been agreed to at the Quadrant Conference in Quebec, so the Cairo agreements were merely reaffirmations. King again had to resist suggestions that the war in the Pacific be turned over to MacArthur as supreme commander, and again his view prevailed.

According to the agreement, MacArthur's forces would advance along the New Guinea–Netherlands East Indies–Philippines axis, and Admiral Nimitz' forces would participate in an island-hopping campaign through the Central Pacific. It was also agreed by the conferees that after they were occupied, the Marianas would be used for strategic bombing bases once the Twentieth Air Force was formed in the Far East.

The United States was now producing almost unlimited war material for itself and its Allies, making the agreed-upon major offensives possible on almost all of the world's battlefronts.

With Eisenhower's invasion of France across the English Channel now set for early June, it was agreed that American and British strategic bomber strength should be increased so that massive raids could be made against German cities and industrial areas. It was also agreed that amphibious forces would attack Anzio on the coast of Italy in an outflanking maneuver designed to trap German forces and begin a march toward Rome.

Admiral King continued to insist that Pacific strategy should be flexible to take advantage of either an early defeat of the Japanese fleet or unexpected Japanese withdrawals from the South Pacific. He emphasized that either event would change the Pacific war picture dramatically.

The Japanese knew that the Marshalls were next on the Americans' list. During February 1942, the third month of the war, Admiral Halsey's carrier task force had dealt a stinging blow to bases in the Marshall Islands. December 4, 1943, was a repetition for many in the task force as they staged another field day at the expense of the Japanese.

In carrier ready rooms that morning, dive-bomber pilots sprawled nonchalantly in their reclining leather chairs, trying to disguise their tension. Nervous younger pilots were up and down every half hour to make trips to the head. For nights, many had been unable to sleep and had gone up to wander around the flight deck.

On the fourth, as intelligence officers briefed them, they were eager to get the waiting over. They paid particular attention as their commanders drew formations on the blackboards.

Lt. Comdr. I. M. "Ike" Hampton told his Bomber Squadron Six aboard the *Enterprise*, "We have our targets assigned. Make every bomb count."

The horizon gave only an intimation of tropical dawn as loudspeakers rattled, "Pilots, man your planes!" Sober-faced men hurried to the after decks of the carriers. A fighter plane on the *Enterprise* moved up to the line and unfolded its wings. The pilot turned on his running lights. The flight-deck officer swept his signal flashlight in a forward motion and the pilot released his brakes and roared into the night.

At intervals other fighters followed, then torpedo planes. Finally, the dive-bombers, which would be used as long-range artillery on precise targets, took off. Leaving their carriers riding the long swells, the planes winged toward heavily defended Kwajalein atoll.

After the last plane left the carriers, one officer said, "It's almost uncanny. Either we're damn good or the Japs are damn stupid. Here we are right on top of one of their biggest bases in the Mar-

shalls and they apparently aren't putting up their full opposition."
For those in the task force, it was a period of tense waiting and
wondering. An hour later, word flashed back, "The enemy has been
taken by surprise and the harbor is full of ships."

The first wave of planes struck enemy ships in the lagoon, a huge
anchorage able to accommodate a large fleet. SBDs, assigned to
knock out the Japanese shipping that brought vital supplies to the
island bases, were loaded with 1,000-pound bombs. They dove
through heavy flak from ships and shore batteries, releasing close to
the ground to insure direct hits. Some planes attacked enemy aircraft and installations at Roi airfield on the heel of the boot-shaped
Kwajalein, but those who arrived first found the lagoon such a
choice target they passed up shore installations.

Off Roi, a large tanker and a light cruiser rode peacefully at anchor. In the toe of the boot, just off Kwajalein, and elsewhere 40
miles away, a dozen large merchantmen rode at anchor beside inter-
island vessels and ships.

"Ike" Hampton eyed the huge assortment of ships and decided
that the Japanese must have rushed a large group of men and supplies to the Marshalls after the American raid on the Gilberts. "It's
a dive-bomber's paradise," he said over the radio to pilots behind
him. For the next forty-five minutes, the Japanese found it an exploding hell.

Flak burst heavily all around Hampton. He saw a light cruiser
anchored off Roi shudder and explode as an SBD made a direct hit
on her stern. Seconds later, another violent explosion came from
the ship as a torpedo connected. Hampton watched with awe as a
sheet of flame rolled over the cruiser's deck and she began to list.
Bombs from other SBDs slammed into a tanker nearby, and it exploded with a roar.

Hampton saw another light cruiser heading north as he arrived
midway between Roi and Kwajalein. He watched its desperate maneuvers and just as it turned to the left, a big thousand pounder
caught her on the stern. After the cruiser completed the turn, two
more explosions ripped her insides. She lay in the water without
moving; not one gun was able to reply to the steady attacks.

Arriving off Kwajalein, Hampton figured there must be 70,000
tons of shipping in the harbor. The flak was intense, but none of the
ships was underway. It was a perfect setup. He gave the signal to
attack. Lt. Comdr. Donald B. Ingerslew followed closely, as did the
others. When they pulled out, fires blazed on five ships.

Lt. John F. Philips planted his bomb on the stern of a large cargo ship. When he circled away, it was going down fast with only its bow above water. Philips followed an oil slick that seemed a mile and a half wide in the center of the lagoon until he came to the much bombed light cruiser, whose fate seemed sealed. His attention was diverted to the north by a tremendous explosion, and he went to investigate. Flames from a burning tanker off Roi shot a thousand feet into the air while black smoke formed an anvil-shaped thunderhead at 10,000 feet.

Bombers winged back to their carriers, protected by the fighters. Only a few Japanese Zeros appeared toward the end of the strike.

Admiral King told Nimitz and Halsey to meet him in San Francisco on January 3, 1944, to discuss future operations.

At the two-day meeting, King emphasized again that the Marianas were the key to victory in the Pacific. Their occupation, he said, would block Japanese lines of communication to the Caroline Islands, and their central position was ideal for advancing westward to the China coast. Forrest P. Sherman, Nimitz's war plans officer, suggested that Truk be bypassed altogether.

Nimitz and his staff disagreed with the importance King attached to the Marianas, and MacArthur and his staff concurred with them. When Nimitz and Sherman met with MacArthur's staff later in the month, Lt. Gen. Richard K. Sutherland, MacArthur's chief of staff, argued that all Pacific resources should be pooled. He repeated what his boss had said many times: Such action was necessary for a quick return to the Philippines and would enable them to move on to the coast of China.

Sutherland thought that he had won over Nimitz and Sherman to MacArthur's viewpoint, and his boss was delighted with the meeting. Minutes of the exchange were forwarded to Washington.

King read them and was irate. He believed that Nimitz had betrayed him. "I have read your conference notes with much interest," he wrote Nimitz, "and I must add with indignant dismay." He told Nimitz, that advocates of pooling failed to consider when Japanese occupation and use of the Marianas and Carolines was to be terminated. "Southwest Pacific advocates," he said, "failed to admit that sometime this thorn in the side of our communications to the western Pacific must be removed."

King also refuted Admiral Towers' comment that the purpose of taking the Marianas was primarily to provide B–29 bases for bombing the home islands:

That was merely one of the results that would ensue from this operation, which was to be taken to dry up the Carolines, facilitating the capture or neutralization of the Carolines, and to speed up the clearing of the lines of communications to the northern Philippines.

The idea of rolling up the Japanese along the New Guinea coast, throughout Halmahera and Mindanao, and up through the Philippines to Luzon, as our major strategic concept, to the exclusion of clearing our Central Pacific line of communication to the Philippines, is to me absurd. Further, it is not in accordance with the decisions of the Joint Chiefs of Staff.

King somewhat petulantly said that he had thought that Nimitz agreed with his views. To reemphasize them, he outlined his own plan for Japan's defeat. Basically, Japan should be forced into her inner ring of defenses, which included her home islands, Korea, Manchuria, and Shantung. He emphasized that actions had to be taken to acquire Chinese bases and manpower, which meant acquiring ports. This last viewpoint had a familiar ring to Nimitz because King had enunciated it so often. He believed, however, that King had become unnecessarily obsessed with the need for Chinese manpower if the Allies were to make a final assualt on Japan's home islands. Nimitz remained in total disagreement with this view.

King advised Nimitz to make Luzon the objective of his forces, but first the Japanese had to be cleared from the Carolines and Marianas and from Peleliu in the Palaus. Once this was done, Japanese lines of communication to the Netherlands East Indies and east of the Philippine Islands would be cut, permitting MacArthur's forces to advance without threat to their flanks during an attack on Mindanao. King concluded that Mindanao was valuable primarily to permit occupation of the rest of the Philippines, but he foresaw many difficulties in total occupation.

MacArthur meanwhile pressed his case for a single southwest Pacific drive. He considered independent drives in the Central Pacific and the South Pacific a weak strategy, saying that victory over Japan would be delayed for six months as a result. In reference to the occupation of the Carolines and Marianas, MacArthur told General Marshall that neither would attain a major strategic objective or help in an assault on the Philippines. He concluded his remarks with his by now familiar refrain that all assault forces should be given to him if Japan was to be defeated in the shortest possible time.

Marshall brought up the matter at a meeting of the Joint Chiefs, and King noted that they were indecisive even though a dual drive in the Pacific with priority given to Central Pacific forces had already been accepted by the Combined Chiefs of Staff at Cairo. King wrote Marshall a memorandum, reminding him that the Combined Chiefs had approved a dual drive and recommending that Marshall tell MacArthur to obey orders.

Marshall was in a quandary. He had heard so many conflicting arguments that he decided to refer the matter to planners.

American airpower became supreme in the South Pacific at the beginning of 1944. Japan continued to reinforce her great bastion at Rabaul, but pilot losses rose to levels that were impossible to overcome.

Lt. Robert M. Hanson of VMF–215 was one of those who had consistently run up victories during the previous fall and whose success continued into the new year. "Butcher Bob," as he was admiringly called by his shipmates after he shot down twenty Japanese planes in six successive flying days, singlehandedly fought off a number of Zeros who tried to corner him over New Britain on January 24. With his back to the wall, he shot down four of them. Six days later, Hanson escorted some Avengers to Rabaul, raising his total kills to twenty-five by shooting down four more Japanese planes out of twenty-one encountered along the way. Hanson's luck ran out on February 3 when he volunteered for a strafing mission to Rabaul. A lighthouse, used by the Japanese as a lookout, was filled with guns, and Hanson's attack against it cost him his life.

American attainment of air superiority resulted from the skill and courage of men like Hanson, whose individual feat of destroying twenty enemy aircraft in six days was unmatched in the war. It alone would have been reason enough to earn him his Medal of Honor.

As the air war in the South Pacific intensified, Admiral Nimitz called a meeting of senior officers on January 27, 1944, at Pearl Harbor. MacArthur's air boss, Gen. George C. Kenney, spoke out against using the Marianas for basing B–29 Superfortresses with which to bomb Japan. In his opinion, he said, that would be just a stunt. In general, among Pacific commanders there was little support for occupation of the Marianas. They wanted to invade the Philippines.

Surprisingly, Admiral Towers, who had recently been named Nimitz' deputy, agreed with MacArthur when he said that the Central Pacific drive should proceed by way of the Bismarcks, Admiralties, Palaus, and Philippines. Towers said that air and submarine bases in the Philippines, once they were reoccupied, could intercept Japanese shipping more easily and that any invasion of the Chinese mainland could best be mounted from there. These views were shared by Nimitz, but Admiral King did not agree, insisting that the Central Pacific drive should continue through the Marianas chain of islands.

Since the start of the war in the South Pacific, General MacArthur had sought a large American fleet, along with elements of the British fleet, to assist his drive toward the Philippines. Once, when he thought he would get all that he wanted, he had told his friend Admiral Halsey, "I want my naval operations to be in the charge of an American. Whoever he is, he'll have to be senior enough to outrank the Britisher, or at least be equal to him. How about you, Bill? If you come with me, I'll make you a greater man than Nelson ever dreamed of being."

Halsey wisely avoided a direct response. He said that he was flattered by the offer and promised to discuss it with King and Nimitz. In truth, he had little interest. His path to glory lay not with MacArthur but with Nimitz and King, and he knew it.

When King realized how little enthusiasm most Pacific commanders had for the occupation of the Marianas, he turned to General Arnold for support, knowing that the Air Forces chief of staff wanted the Marianas for his B-29 Superfortresses. Arnold readily supported King's plan to invade the Marianas because their occupation would further his plans to base large numbers of B-29s on the islands, which were only 1,500 miles from Japan's home islands.

D Day for the Marshalls was January 31, but fast carriers were in position two days early to strike installations at Majuro, Roi, Kwajalein, Taroa and Wotje.

Seventh Air Force B-24 and B-25 bombers had been participating for days in preinvasion strikes from their new bases in the Gilberts. In one incident, several B-25 medium bombers came into the range of fleet gunners from the direction of the enemy. They were retiring from a raid over enemy targets and looked very much as if they were making torpedo runs on the fleet. American guns opened up; then the frantic call came over the loudspeakers, "Cease firing! Cease firing!" One B-25 was shot down.

After days of continuous air and sea bombardment had killed at least half the Japanese defenders on the ground, United States troops of the army's Seventh Division landed on February 1 at Kwajalein's Red Beach. The entire atoll was secured only after 7,870 Japanese died in its defense. The Japanese had fanatically defended Kwajalein from interior positions dug deep into the ground, and only thirty-five had surrendered.

American casualties totaled 372 soldiers and marines, a less bloody battle than at Tarawa because Kwajalein had received a thorough softening up before amphibious forces landed.

King called the occupation of the Marshalls the most successful of all Pacific operations, with almost perfect timing in the execution of joint plans. Nimitz was particularly pleased with their seizure and with the small losses incurred to secure them. Although not completely sold on the invasion of the Marianas, he agreed to this operation because these islands would provide the necessary bases for his straight—straight in comparison with MacArthur's longer approach from the west—drive to the Japanese mainland, which now appeared to be more promising than ever.

Japan's outer ring of defenses was now cracked beyond repair, permitting further expansion of the Central Pacific forces. Moreover, Japan now found it impossible to fortify her inner defense line, which ran through the Marianas.

The invasion of the Marshall Islands demonstrated that the United States Navy had finally mastered the delicate science of combining all available forces—land, sea, and air—to reach out far into the Pacific and complete an amphibious landing against strong opposition. Aviators had long tried to convince surface officers that the key to success in such operations lay in the effective use of pre-invasion aerial bombardment.

In February, word came to the skipper of a patrol squadron that rescue personnel of the Fifth Air Force had been shot down in the vicinity of the Vitu Islands in Kavieng Harbor at New Ireland in the Bismarck Archipelago.

Lt. Nathan Greene volunteered to fly his patrol plane into the harbor and land near the men in a rescue attempt made under the very noses of the Japanese. In full view of the Japanese on shore, and despite withering gunfire, Greene made three landings to pick up the air force men. On his last flight, with nine men on board, he took off with his flying boat dangerously overloaded, in heavy swells and with no wind to provide additional lift.

En route home, he learned over the radio that another group of Americans was stranded in a rubber life raft, and he returned to rescue them as well. He landed the cumbersome flying boat within 600 yards of the enemy-occupied shore as Kavieng's guns sought to destroy it. Coolly, with six new survivors on board, in addition to the nine he had picked up earlier, Greene headed across the bay with what seemed like every gun trained on them. His daring and valor in saving the airmen from capture and probable death earned him a Medal of Honor.

United States Marines and New Zealand troops captured the Green Islands north of Bougainville on March 6. MacArthur's command meanwhile occupied Cape Gloucester on New Britain. After Emirau Island, 90 miles north of the big Japanese air base at Kavieng in New Ireland, was taken in April, Rabaul was completely bottled up. Nimitz and King decided that no invasion of Rabaul was necessary but Japanese troops were kept under periodic attack for the rest of the war.

With the occupation of the Marshalls, Nimitz was anxious to press on to take Eniwetok. At first, the Joint Chiefs of Staff procrastinated. King had to use all his persuasive powers to eliminate delays in getting operations approved, telling the Joint Chiefs that the Japanese would now be forced to fight a major naval battle if they were to stop the Americans' inexorable advance toward the Japanese homeland.

Still, King's continued insistence on the occupation of the Marianas threatened to delay important decisions. Many associates in Washington disagreed with his position. They argued that no harbors in the Marianas were suitable as fleet anchorages, which was true. But far too many opposed occupation of the Marianas because they believed that those islands would be used primarily for B–29 operations that would not shorten the war. They were also reluctant to give the United States Army Air Forces an advantage its strategic war advocates had long sought. For others, this position was too shortsighted and parochial.

13

"SPLASH SIX!
GOING FOR SEVEN!"

Eniwetok, 325 miles northwest of Kwajalein and 1,000 miles from the Marianas, was set for invasion on February 17. After the Marshalls campaign, many air crews who had expected to return to Pearl Harbor headed instead for Truk in the central Carolines to support landings there, also set for the 17th.

For thirty years, Truk had been a mysterious place where the Japanese based their southwest Pacific fleet. Japan had acquired it from Germany in 1914 and even as early as World War I, had secretly developed it into a great naval base. No American had seen it in all those years, but naval commanders knew that there was no better base in the world.

Truk, a group of two hundred islands enclosed in a 40-mile-wide lagoon, has low-lying coral reefs. Only five entrances permit ships to enter, but once inside, the largest fleet in the world can be accommodated with ease. The eleven main islands are relatively flat, and the Japanese found them ideal for airfields. The forest-covered mountains concealed coast artillery and antiaircraft guns.

Truk lies 1,800 miles southeast of Tokyo, 915 miles west of Eniwetok, and 750 miles north of New Guinea. It was in an ideal position to bar the Allied path to the Philippines, the China coast, or Japan.

Admiral Mitscher's forces attacked at dawn on February 16 as the task force lay 90 miles to the northeast. The fighter sweep caught the defenders by surprise, and 75 percent of the fifty enemy fighters shot down were destroyed below 1,000 feet, many even before their wheels lifted off the runways. Now the Japanese had fewer than one hundred operational planes on Truk. At the conclusion of dive-bombing attacks, the Japanese had lost 2 light cruisers and a destroyer, 26 cargo ships, and 275 planes.

When his pilots reported back, Mitscher was astonished to hear them say, "The Jap fleet has gone! There are about fifty ships at the anchorage but they are mostly cargo ships. We spotted only two light cruisers and four destroyers."

Once-powerful Truk was now finished as a first line of defense for the Japanese, so impotent that it was not even invaded. With these attacks, the South Pacific ended its tenure as the primary area of operations. The Japanese now had to rely upon the Marianas and the western Carolines.

Preinvasion aerial bombardment and heavy shelling by units of Spruance's Fifth Fleet helped to soften up the Japanese defenses at Eniwetok, and most of the atoll was in American hands by February 20. Some smaller islands that were not invaded because their few defenders posed no threat were kept under intermittent attack in the months that followed.

With the capture of Eniwetok, the Marshall Islands became an important asset for the continued prosecution of the war. Admiral Spruance now split up his forces, sending a task group under Adm. John W. Reeves with the *Enterprise* to strike Jaluit, a seaplane base in the western Marshalls. The island had been bypassed repeatedly, but planes from the *"Big E"* gave it a thorough lashing on February 20.

It was now the turn of the Marianas. Mitscher enthusiastically messaged all ships, "D Day is Washington's birthday. Let's chop down a few Nip cherry trees."

The element of surprise was lacking when the fast carriers struck the Marianas for the first time in the war, and some of the Japanese planes rose to fight it out. American pilots dropped their bombs all across the revetment areas on Tinian, a central main island that held several airfields, and had the satisfaction of seeing planes still on the ground exploding as they rushed past. While photographic planes droned above, taking precise strip photographs of each of the main islands, navy fighters and bombers pummeled military targets.

Three waves of Japanese bombers attacked the American ships on February 21, but most were either shot down or driven off by navy fighters. The following morning, Hellcats returned to strafe Japanese airfields against only limited opposition, resulting in part from the heavy Japanese losses of planes the day before.

Since August 1943, the combination of air and sea power had brought vast destruction to the perimeter defenses of the Japanese Empire. Amphibious forces had freed 800,000 square miles of Japanese-held territory. The islands now in Allied hands had three good fleet anchorages and countless airfields that would soon be put to good use. Japanese airpower had lost supremacy, and its fleet had to remain in the extreme western portion of the Pacific Ocean. Success had come in spite of the overall advantage in numbers that the Japanese held in the Pacific theater. Through the effective use of mobile airpower, in most cases United States pilots defeated Japanese airmen in local contests.

After their inner defense line was breached in the Marianas for the first time, Japanese naval leaders viewed the future with consternation. Admiral Koga ordered his fleet to evacuate Truk and to move westward to the Palaus, which were closer to the Philippines.

Koga then flew to Japan for consultations with government leaders. He advised officials that the new defense line had to be held because the Palaus lay across MacArthur's path as he moved north along the coast of New Guinea. He also warned that maintenance of this defense line was vital to prevent Admiral Halsey's ships from moving toward the home islands.

The fact that the Marianas now faced invasion, and that they were within bombing distance of Japan's cities, was not lost on Japanese government leaders.

When Koga returned to the fleet, he ordered the destruction of American aircraft to take top priority, and he devised a new plan to destroy America's Pacific Fleet.

After a high-level conference held in early March in Washington, Nimitz received direct orders to seize more Japanese-held territories. MacArthur had been invited to discuss future operations but he had declined. Instead, he made the mistake of sending his Chief of Staff Gen. Richard Sutherland—no match for Admiral King, who dominated the conference. With Air Forces General Arnold's strong support for occupation of the Marianas, this operation was approved by the Joint Chiefs.

For once there was quick agreement about future operations. The Joint Chiefs agreed with King that Rabaul should be isolated and that MacArthur should proceed westward along the northern coast of New Guinea to seize Mindanao by November 15. Nimitz was ordered to bypass Truk, seize the Marianas on June 15, isolate the Carolines, and invade the Palaus on September 15 in support of MacArthur's Mindanao attack. Further, Nimitz was ordered to invade Formosa on February 15, 1945, and if necessary attack Luzon by air that day. The Joint Chiefs further agreed that the next objective should be the China coast.

The plan to invade Formosa was not realistic. The Japanese were dug in along defensible shores, and the losses necessary to dislodge them would have been prohibitive. King's plan to occupy parts of the China coast was even more unrealistic because the Japanese were rapidly extending their control of China all along the coast.

The Palaus, a main refueling stop for Japanese tankers en route to Japan from Indonesia and the East Indies, was swept by one thousand planes from Mitscher's carriers on March 30. He had ordered his air groups to hit everything that floated. Ever since the success of the earlier raid on Truk, these attacks had been known as the "Mitscher Shampoo." They began early in the morning with a fighter sweep by two hundred F6Fs, followed by the strike forces. This time there was a new wrinkle. Torpedo planes went in first to mine the harbor entrance and keep any ships from escaping.

Prior to the attack, it was believed that the Japanese fleet had arrived there from Truk. Once again, the fleet was not where it was expected to be, but targets were still plentiful.

Lt. James D. "Jig Dog" Ramage was with the *Enterprise*'s second launch at 8:30. He had listened with satisfaction to reports of the excellent job the first group had done against ships in the harbor. En route, Ramage noticed two large tankers near Karst Island, which made up a part of the Palaus. Both were heavily loaded, so he told his strike group to break into two sections.

SBD dive-bombers, still used by at least a third of the Pacific carriers despite the introduction of the more modern SB2C Hell-diver, made up the base element. Underneath were TBF torpedo planes, and a fighter escort of F6Fs completed the combat group as a protective screen.

Ramage positioned the group, and the lower F6Fs started their strafing runs ahead of the dive-bombers, who maintained their 10,000-foot altitudes. Then, he signaled the dive-bombers to follow him. He opened his dive brakes and nosed over into a 70-degree dive toward the tankers. The SBD was so stable as he hung in his straps that he felt he was riding down on a pillow. The torpedo planes, meanwhile, went into a spiral, waiting for their turn to strike in 45-degree glides after the dive-bombers completed their runs.

Ramage was pleased with the smoothness of the operation, knowing how important it was for the strike group to get on and off the target in less than a minute. The Midway battle, in which torpedo planes had gone in low and alone and been largely destroyed, had demonstrated the importance of timing in such compact operations.

Ramage released his bomb and pulled away, knowing that they

had had clean runs at the tankers and hit them squarely.

In the next two days, two destroyers, four escort ships, and twenty auxiliary vessels were sunk with the loss of twenty-five American planes. At the end of the first day, Mitscher had sent out planes to locate Kurita's fleet, but it had fled to the north, once more evading detection.

Ramage was proud of the men in his squadron, knowing how hard they had worked to perfect their dive-bombing. Each pilot had to bomb within a 50-foot error before he qualified for the SBD. Most pilots had done better than that, averaging 25 feet. Each had been reminded countless times that a single 1,000-pound bomb was all that was needed to sink a ship if the aim was accurate. No one could dispute this fact after only seventeen or eighteen bombs had destroyed four Japanese carriers at Midway.

Poststrike reports indicated that torpedo bombers had done an excellent job. Early in the war, the use of aerial torpedoes had been unpopular among pilots because torpedoes had often bounced off Japanese ships without exploding.

Admiral Koga never had a chance to put into operation his plan to destroy the American's Pacific Fleet. While flying from Saipan to Davao in the Philippines on March 31, his plane was lost in a storm.

Adm. Soemu Toyoda was selected to replace him. Unlike Koga, Toyoda was an aggressive officer. He was also a realist, saying, "The war is approaching areas vital to our national security. Our situation is one of unprecedented gravity. There is only one way of deciding this struggle in our favor."

Toyoda had been opposed to war with the United States, agreeing with Yamamoto that Japan could not win a prolonged war. As head of the Combined Fleet, he told his superiors that the Americans must be stopped in the Marianas.

Gen. Hideki Tojo, Japan's prime minister, ridiculed Toyoda's comments, calling them hysterical. He refused to permit army aircraft in the Marianas to take part in a showdown with the Americans.

Toyoda went ahead with his plans for defense of the Marianas by placing 90 percent of Japan's ships under Vice-Adm. Jisaburo Ozawa as the First Mobile Fleet. His carrier aircraft were coordinated with naval aircraft on Tinian under Vice-Adm. Kakuji Kakuta. Toyoda had approximately one thousand planes at his disposal in the Marianas and Carolines, particularly at Truk, and at Iwo Jima in the Volcano Islands north of the Marianas.

The largest Japanese fleet since Pearl Harbor—seventy-three ships with nine carriers, including the new heavy carrier *Taiho*—was assembled by Ozawa. Aboard were 450 planes, including the new Nakajima Tenzen or as the Americans called it, the Jill torpedo bomber. Ozawa divided his carriers into three divisions, placing his flag aboard the *Taiho* in the first division, which was supported by the carriers *Shokaku* and the *Zuikaku*. The second division included the light carriers *Hiyo* and *Junyo* under Rear Admiral Takagi, while the third was commanded by Rear Adm. Sueo Obayashi with the light carriers *Chiyoda, Chitose,* and *Zuiho*. This last division was part of the main force, which included battleships and support ships.

Included in this vast assemblage of warships were the world's largest and most modern battleships, the *Yamato* and the *Musashi*. Vice-Adm. Takeo Kurita, who commanded this force, was confident that the American fleet would be destroyed. The Japanese were, however, short of experienced pilots. Most of their pilots were young and had only two to six months of flight training. Although Ozawa was an excellent seaman, he had no experience in the use of carriers in battle.

Spruance, the man who had proved his worth at Midway, also had a mighty fleet under his command, backed by proven aircraft and pilots with long experience. And, Spruance had under him the shrewd Vice-Adm. Marc A. Mitscher in charge of the fast carriers of Task Force Fifty-eight.

A revitalized British Pacific Fleet under Adm. Sir James Somerville, strengthened by the addition of the United States carrier *Saratoga* and three American destroyers, went on the offensive on April 19, 1944. Aircraft from the British carrier *Illustrious* and the *Saratoga* attacked the harbor at Sabang, an island off the north coast of Sumatra, causing extensive damage to oil storage tanks.

A similar attack against the Wonokromo Oil Refinery at Soerabaja on Java was equally successful. There was little opposition, but it was quickly obvious to Somerville that the crews on his British carrier would be able to learn from the more experienced Americans on the *Saratoga*. Later, a larger all-British force, including the carriers *Victorious* and *Indomitable*, raided Sabang on July 22.

While major battles were fought until the end of the war in the North Pacific, the British East Indies Fleet under Adm. Sir John Power cut the Japanese supply line to Burma and to Japan's garrisons in the Andaman and Nicobar islands. Once his fleet had cleared the Indian Ocean of Japanese navy ships, the Japanese limited their sea operations to small coastal convoys, but these were largely wiped out by the end of the war.

Gen. Douglas MacArthur had been anxious to neutralize the Admiralty Islands so that they could be converted into an Allied naval and air base to cut off a Japanese supply center that was hampering his operations to the south. The mountainous islands at the head of the Bismarck Sea would provide him with the operational base he needed to return to the Philippines. Capture of the largest islands, Manus and Los Negros, would, as he described it, "cork the bottle."

Seizure of these islands came at high cost in casualties, but with their capture on May 12 the entire Bismarck–Melanesia area, with 100,000 battle-hardened Japanese veterans inside, was effectively bottled up.

MacArthur next decided to leap his forces 400 miles up the New Guinea coast to capture Hollandia. The isolation of Rabaul and the recent occupation of the Admiralties made this bold stroke not only sensible but appealing.

"I need maximum naval and air support," he told Nimitz.

Nimitz agreed. Kinkaid's Seventh Fleet was reinforced by ships from the Central Pacific. He also ordered Mitscher to assign his fast carriers to direct air support before and after landings at Hollandia were made.

Task Force Fifty-eight arrived off Hollandia on April 21, a day before Lt. Gen. Walter Krueger's Sixth Army planned to land. Targets were scarce because army bombers had given the area a saturation bombing.

The following day, carrier planes provided close support for the Southwest Pacific Forces, the first of its kind for MacArthur's troops. While the Sixth Army landed unopposed, carrier planes destroyed sixty-seven planes at Hollandia and another twenty-one at the Wakde Islands off the coast of New Guinea.

Following that action, Admiral Mitscher withdrew his carriers and put them to better use in another strike against Truk. Shore installations were primary targets, but he also hoped to further reduce enemy airpower.

Fighters swept Truk on the morning of April 29. Commanders of the Japanese Twenty-second Air Flotilla, with 104 planes available, were appalled when only 11 came home. Truk received its worst pummeling of the war when bombers dropped 748 tons of high explosives, almost devastating the base. Later, reconnaissance photos showed that 423 buildings were destroyed.

Supply lines to the southwest Pacific remained critical so three weeks later carrier planes were ordered to strike Marcus and Wake because both islands had large concentrations of Japanese patrol and bombing planes. Mitscher hoped that the Japanese had become complacent, particularly at Marcus, which was fewer than a thousand miles from Japan. He felt confident that the Japanese would expect the Pacific Fleet to remain in the southwest Pacific for some time after the Hollandia raids.

Before dawn, the men took their battle stations. The planes, jammed tightly on aft flight decks, trailed purple flames from their exhausts. At short intervals, they took off and headed for Marcus.

While men on the carriers anxiously watched for the return of the first planes, every eye was alert for an attack by Japanese bombers. The first formation of American planes landed, refueled, and headed back with more bombs. For hours planes ran a shuttle service between their carriers and the island until Japanese installations appeared to be shattered. Huge fires and explosions rose above the tiny island that could be seen by crews 20 miles away. Unlike the dramatic strikes at the great bastions of the Pacific, this operation was limited, using only a small portion of the main carrier task force. But it was the kind of attack that provides a slow attrition that eventually wins a war.

Admiral Toyoda issued stern orders to his Combined Fleet. "Concentrate majority of our forces for a decisive battle. The enemy's fleet must be smashed with one blow south of Truk."

During the middle of May, the Japanese First Fleet assembled in open anchorage in Tawitawi between the Philippines and Borneo. It was an impressive sight. Ozawa had nine carriers and five battleships.

When King learned that the Japanese fleet was concentrating near the Philippines, only four days steaming from the Marianas where Spruance's fleet was preparing for an invasion, he voiced his concern to Nimitz, who replied that he was not perturbed. He did, however, ask General MacArthur to send his submarines into the area.

King was also upset that neither Spruance nor Mitscher seemed to have comprehensive plans for a decisive battle against the Japanese fleet, having decided that they would see how the situation developed. His primary concern was that Spruance's Fifth Fleet, with its preponderance of older battleships, would not be able to take decisive action because the old and new battleships would have to be mixed together. Such mixing, he feared, would cause problems in maneuvering during the formation of a battle line. Nimitz admitted sharing some of the same concern but said he was confident that Mitscher's carriers in Task Force Fifty-eight could handle anything that developed.

King was advised in Washington on May 24 that most of the Japanese fleet, which had been based at Singapore, had now definitely been moved to the Philippines. Four days later, Nimitz assured King that destruction of the Japanese fleet was his primary objective. What neither knew was that Spruance did not anticipate Japanese resistance to landings in the Marianas. Spruance's primary objective was protection of his landing force and not destruction of the Japanese fleet, which unbeknownst to him, was preparing for a showdown battle. King thus had more reason for concern than even he himself realized, for Nimitz' assurances had been based on false premises. Also, he now had a tougher adversary as secretary of navy. Undersecretary James V. Forrestal had been nominated to succeed Frank Knox, who had died of a heart attack on April 28.

Task Force Fifty-eight, with Mitscher in charge, left Majuro on June 6 to join the rest of Admiral Spruance's Fifth Fleet of 644 ships. Spruance told him, "Your job is to clear the air over the islands."

Mitscher's huge armada had 890 combat airplanes aboard seven heavy carriers and eight light carriers. In addition, he had seven new battleships, eight heavy cruisers, and numerous smaller ships.

Vice-Admiral Turner's amphibious forces, which would invade the islands of Saipan, Guam, and Tinian, were supported by numerous ships. Several old battleships that had been sunk or damaged at Pearl Harbor on the first day of the war were ready again for action.

The fleet had left Majuro on the same day that Eisenhower's forces landed in Normandy to begin the invasion of Hitler's Fortress Europe and the day after the new B-29 command made its first mission in the Far East, attacking Bangkok, Thailand.

Japanese patrol planes located the huge fleet on June 10 headed toward the Carolines. Admiral Toyoda now believed his suspicions confirmed: The Americans intended to invade the Palaus, and any landings in the Marianas would be made only to divert attention from General MacArthur's moves in New Guinea. He therefore instructed his commanders to prepare for an annihilating battle off the western Carolines, southwest of Guam near the Palau Islands, where they could be supported by Japanese bases at Yap and Woleai.

Spruance's destination, of course, was not the Palaus but the Marianas. Near the Carolines, therefore, his fleet, with two American heavy cruisers and destroyers under the command of the Royal Navy's Rear Admiral Crutchley aboard his flagship the H.M.A.S *Australia*, turned toward the Mariana Islands of Saipan, Tinian, and Guam.

Mitscher's first fighter sweeps were launched 200 miles from the Marianas at 1:00 P.M. on June 11. Avengers navigated for the Hellcats, and two torpedo planes went out carrying extra life rafts in case any fighter pilots went down at sea.

The Japanese were caught by surprise, and Hellcats destroyed 150 Japanese planes on the ground. Toyoda was astonished to learn that Task Force Fifty-eight was attacking the Marianas, and his carefully laid plans to trap Spruance's Fifth Fleet had to be hastily revised.

Because they lost so many planes the first day, the Japanese were unable to launch attacks against the American fleet. When attacks devastated island installations on the 12th and 13th and Spruance's battleships also moved in on the 13th to shell the beaches, Toyoda ordered his fleet to leave Tawitawi on a northerly course and head for the Marianas. The Japanese plan to retake the strategic island of Biak off the northwest coast of New Guinea was likewise hastily abandoned, and Ozawa was ordered to rush with his carriers at full speed to the Marianas.

Admiral Kakuta's land-based navy squadrons were decimated during the preinvasion American attacks, losing five hundred aircraft. He was advised to hang on as best he could until Ozawa's carriers arrived.

On June 15, air force B–29s struck Japan for the first time from bases in China in an attack on Kyushu's Yawata steel mills. That same day, Saipan was invaded by the army's Twenty-seventh Infantry Division and the Second and Fourth Marine Divisions.

The 30,000 Japanese troops at Saipan under Lt. Gen. Yoshitsuga Saito were ill equipped to face the Americans, whose submarines had sunk so many Japanese supply ships.

In overall charge was Vice-Adm. Chuichi Nagumo, who had led the raid on Pearl Harbor. He had told his troops the day before the landings that the Marianas were the homeland's first line of defense but that he did not expect the Americans to land until later that month or in July. The Americans landed the next day, proving that his intelligence information was tragically unreliable.

Mitscher had moved Task Force Fifty-eight around to the west so that it could counter any Japanese attack from the Philippines.

Meanwhile, over 1,400 carrier planes took off before dawn on June 15 to hit targets on Saipan ahead of the amphibious forces coming in from the sea.

Lt. Comdr. "Jig Dog" Ramage, now commanding officer of Bombing Squadron Ten aboard the *Enterprise*, led his strike group as ground troops prepared to land at 8:00 A.M. on the 15th. He was assigned to work under Air Group Comdr. William "Killer" Kane, who would circle the area in an F6F as target air coordinator of all support aircraft.

As they flew over the landing forces, Ramage heard Kane shout over the radio, "Hey, you're shooting at me!" Of course, no one on the amphibious ships could hear him on that radio net, and trigger-happy American antiaircraft gunners shot Kane down.

Ramage took over as airborne coordinator as Kane headed down, cursing all the way. Ramage cruised back and forth over the beach, directing the strike group to targets on the ground. Occasionally, he caught glimpses of marines as they hit the beach, marveling at how quickly they moved inland to get a defensible position.

Ramage repeatedly called out targets of opportunity. Bunkers, gun positions, and suspected targets in the brush and sugarcane were bombed and strafed.

Every pilot wondered about the location of the Japanese fleet. They could not understand why it did not appear. Each was anxious to get a crack at a carrier, and many felt that what they were doing was unimportant compared with a major fleet action. Because they believed that Japanese carriers posed the greatest threat to the landings, they could not understand their secondary role of providing close support to landing forces.

After the first troops landed and moved inland, carrier planes continued to concentrate on knocking out small machine-gun nests, big guns, and the small tanks used by the Japanese. Spruance was pleased with the start of the operation, but he grew more concerned about the lack of reports on the location of the Japanese fleet. Ships and submarines were constantly on the prowl in the Central Pacific to report Japanese ship movements, and they should have reported to him by now.

Finally, Spruance received a dispatch on June 16 from the submarine *Flying Fish*, "Large enemy task force sighted. Headed east from San Bernardino Strait at twenty knots."

"Looks like they're coming," he told his staff.

Spruance sent a message to Mitscher. "I'll give you all the cruisers and destroyers we can spare. Your fast carriers will have to go out and meet them."

Mitscher prepared for battle on board his flagship, the new carrier *Lexington*, which had replaced the one lost during the Battle of the Coral Sea. In a communication to all ships, he said, "Believe Japanese will approach from a southerly direction under shore-based air cover near Yap and Ulithi. Probably will attempt to operate near Guam. May come from the west. Scouts should consider all contingencies."

The next day the submarine *Seahorse* reported additional Japanese ships off Surigao Strait north of Mindanao in the Philippines. Spruance now knew that the Combined Fleet was on its way to the Marianas. He canceled the June 18 landing on Guam for the time being and ordered carrier strikes against Iwo Jima in the Volcano Islands and Chichi Jima in the Bonins south of Japan's main islands. Meanwhile, army and marine troops under Marine Lt. Gen. Holland M. Smith fought their way inland. The Japanese contested every foot of ground.

Spruance released his major battle plan on June 17. "Our air will first knock out enemy carriers, then attack battleships and cruisers." That night, Spruance received new word about the enemy fleet and ordered Mitscher to position his force 160 miles west of Tinian and attack with three of his four carrier groups.

On the ground at Saipan, the fighting grew in intensity, and waves of suicidal Japanese charges assaulted the Americans as they fought toward Aslito airfield. At night, the screaming banzai attacks made the fighting the worst yet encountered in the Pacific. Despite the opposition, Aslito Field was taken on the day Spruance released his battle plan. It was quickly renamed Isley Field in honor of Comdr. Robert H. Isley, who lost his life near it in an Avenger crash.

Admiral Ozawa's carriers now were 500 miles west of Saipan, and the distance was reduced by another hundred miles by the 18th of June. Although his planes were equipped with neither armor for the pilots nor self-sealing fuel tanks, their range now made it possible for Ozawa to launch fighters and bombers at this extreme distance with instructions to land on Tinian and Guam.

Mitscher sought permission to steam out to meet Ozawa, but Spruance refused, saying that his primary job was to protect the landings. Mitscher was angered by the refusal and voiced criticism of Spruance's orders.

Mitscher told his air commanders to hit the airfields on Guam on the 19th to keep them neutralized. Only a few Japanese planes could be assembled to counter the attack because the remainder had been either destroyed or damaged too severely for flight. Hellcats caught many Japanese planes on the ground, but some got into the air. American fighters quickly dispatched thirty-five of them. Mitscher, continuing to worry about Ozawa's exact position, paced the flag bridge of the *Lexington* in his anguish.

Ozawa, his force out of range of American carrier planes, had actually launched seventy-three planes at dawn on the 19th despite the bad weather. They were led to the Marianas by Lt. Comdr. Masayuki Yamagani. Ozawa watched them take off from the bridge of the *Taiho*, a 64,000-ton ship launched three months before. As wave after wave of his planes headed east, he felt confident that his ship was unsinkable.

With shocked surprise, Ozawa heard a warning that a torpedo was heading toward his flagship. He watched almost with disbelief as Warrant Officer Sakio Komatsu dove his plane into the torpedo and detonated it. This selfless act, which for the moment saved the ship, cost Komatsu his life.

Other torpedoes now raced toward the *Taiho* from Comdr. J. W. Blanchard's submarine *Albacore*. Despite a last minute turn, the ship was struck by a torpedo. An elevator was jammed, fuel lines ripped open, and the hangar deck quickly engulfed in flames.

The *Taiho* remained afloat for six hours, but the fires spread throughout the ship. It was wracked by explosions until it sank, a mass of flames.

Ozawa had transferred his flag to the heavy cruiser *Haguro* soon after the *Taiho* was hit. Now he saw that the *Shokaku* was under attack, and it sank even before the *Taiho*, a loss later credited to Comdr. H. J. Kossler's submarine *Cavalla*.

Despite the loss of two carriers, Ozawa's four hundred airplanes were heading away in four waves to attack the American fleet. They had been told to land at bases in the Marianas for reloading and refueling and to hit the American ships on their return to their carriers.

Japanese planes were spotted by American radar 150 miles from their carriers. Then, a pilot called in the clear, "Hey, Rube!" All ships were immediately alerted to prepare for battle by this old American circus cry.

Destroyers and cruisers ringed the carriers as gunners rushed to their stations. Hellcats, hastily recalled from their sweep over Guam, raced back to meet this new threat. Meanwhile, bombers and torpedo planes continued their attacks against Guam's defenses.

At 10:07 A.M., Mitscher was handed a message. "Unidentified planes have been picked up bearing three hundred thirty-three degrees, one hundred forty-five miles away. He ordered carrier decks cleared, and all loaded bombers and fighters were sent aloft. Now, strike planes were in the air, carrying loaded bombs with which they could do nothing. They were sent to Guam to attack airfields and told to pockmark the runways. Normally, runways were considered poor targets, but it was now appropriate to bomb them because Japanese planes would have to land on them to refuel.

Comdr. David McCampbell, in charge of the *Essex*'s Air Group 15, met the first wave of Japanese planes 90 miles west of Task Force Fifty-eight. He and his pilots tore into forty-eight Zeke fighters flying as escorts for Jills and Judys. When a Judy appeared in McCampbell's sights, he shot it down, following so closely that he had to maneuver his Hellcat violently to escape a torrent of debris. With his attention momentarily withdrawn from other Japanese fighters, he found himself under attack by two Zekes. They failed to shoot him down, and he was able to get the Japanese flight leader's Zeke square in his sights for a second kill.

Meanwhile, two Judys were shot down by McCampbell's wing man, Ens. R. E. Foltz. They suddenly found themselves all alone in the sky.

Elsewhere, thirty Japanese bombers broke through the American fighter screen and headed for Mitscher's carriers. Each carrier was now ringed by cruisers and destroyers out to a diameter of 15 miles. The sky above Task Force Fifty-eight was filled with planes. American fighters ripped at Japanese bombers, and not one managed to get a hit on a carrier. Only the battleship *South Dakota* was bombed. Out of the first wave of seventy-three Japanese aircraft, only twenty-four survived to streak for Guam and refuel for the return flight to their carriers.

That afternoon, McCampbell took some of his air group to Guam and joining other units, they quickly shot down thirty more planes. Another nineteen crash-landed in their haste to get away from those relentless guns. McCampbell's seven victories, which helped to earn him a Medal of Honor, contributed to the virtual annihilation of Ozawa's carrier planes.

McCampbell learned that he, like other fighter pilots who survived combat, had gone through three stages. At first, he had been too eager, too anxious, and had missed with his guns more often than he connected. Then, after shooting down several Japanese planes, he had arrogantly assumed that the Japanese pilots were inferior. He left that impression behind after he was chased by experienced Japanese pilots who shot up his plane. Now his operations were methodical; he took risks only when absolutely necessary and balanced military necessity against the chance of surviving for the next mission. McCampbell, who had originally been turned down for pilot training because of eye trouble, ended the war as the navy's leading ace.

Lieutenant Commander Ramage was also over Guam with his SBD Squadron as Japanese planes tried desperately to reach their airfields. It was an incredible sight to see American fighters chasing Zeros up and down Guam's hills and valleys.

The Japanese First Carrier Division, with 129 fighters, bombers, and torpedo planes, had been intercepted west of Mitscher's carriers and in a merciless battle, one hundred Japanese planes were sent flaming into the sea. Vapor trails, which had alerted American pilots to the Japanese contingent headed for Task Force Fifty-eight, filled the sky as the battle reached its climax.

Lt. Alexander Vraicu of Lexington's Squadron Sixteen was on combat air patrol when he spotted Japanese bombers that had survived earlier air battles. He alerted the patrol. "Tallyho! At least thirty rats!" (This was the term used to identify Japanese fighters. Actually, they were mostly Jill and Judy bombers.)

Hellcats dove to the attack, and Vraicu headed for a Zeke on the fringe of the battle. He started his dive but quickly realized that another Hellcat was closing in on the Zeke's tail. He spotted a Judy and, although his windshield was covered with oil from his bad engine, he dove to within 200 feet to insure a kill before he opened fire. His six guns tore the bomber apart.

"Scratch one Judy!" he radioed.

Finding two Judys flying in formation, he leveled his guns at the one on the right. The Japanese rear gunner fired at Vraicu until his guns shot down the bomber. A moment later, Vraicu found himself behind another Japanese plane. He set it afire and watched as it headed down, flaming like a torch.

Vraicu reported his latest victory. "Scratch three! Don't see how we can shoot 'em all down. Too many!"

He was now momentarily in the clear as the Japanese formation spread apart. The fight became a free-for-all as the combat air patrol was increased to seventy planes in the air.

He quickly added another Judy to his score as Jill torpedo bombers unsuccessfully tried to attack the *Lexington*. Two battleships were hit by Judys, however, and a third by a suicide attack.

A team of Judys headed for a destroyer, and Vraicu flew down through his own flak until his guns slashed the last Judy to pieces. Still in a steep dive, he sought the lead Judy, which was flying directly toward a destroyer. He overtook the Japanese plane and fired all guns. The Judy flamed, and her bomb exploded, throwing Vraicu's Hellcat into a violent roll and forcing him to fight for control.

Back on an even keel, he radioed, "Splash six! Going for seven!" This time, however, the guns of a battleship got the Judy before he could reach it.

The sudden quiet was nerve-racking. To Vraicu, it was eerie to look around and see nothing but the Hellcats that had dominated the air battle. He decided to land and was infuriated when he was enveloped in American antiaircraft fire. He realized that his IFF (radio instrumentation that *I*dentifies *F*riend from *F*oe) must have been shot out. He called and cursed the gunners for their stupidity in failing to see that they had an American plane in their sights.

On deck, Vraicu held up six fingers to Mitscher, who grinned with pleasure.

The third Japanese wave never found the American fleet because of faulty navigation. The fourth wave also missed the American ships and tried to land on Guam, where Hellcats shot down thirty of them. Of the nineteen that managed to land, most either crashed on landing or were so badly shot up that they had to be junked. Of the fourth wave's eighty planes, only nine returned to their carriers at 6:45 that night.

Ozawa's fleet was a shambles. In addition to the loss of two of his carriers, 346 planes failed to return. He reported these facts to Admiral Toyoda at Combined Fleet Headquarters at Hiroshima and was ordered to withdraw to the west. He was bitter about the battle's outcome and resolved to refuel his ships and resume the attack on the American fleet the next day.

14

"TURN ON THE LIGHTS!"

Admiral Ozawa ordered his battered fleet to sail northeastward for 250 miles to rendezvous with his supply ships. Additional losses during his retreat brought down his total complement of aircraft to only seventeen fighter bombers, eleven torpedo bombers, forty-four fighters, and thirty nonbombardment types.

He was outmatched by the Americans' strength. He expected to be pursued and was hoping to forestall an engagement until June 22 so that he could build up his attack capability.

Spruance finally issued orders to Mitscher to set out in pursuit with three carrier groups, (but to leave one carrier group—TG 58.4—for close support) before Ozawa could reinforce his fleet. Although Ozawa's ships were dogged by American submarines, by afternoon Mitscher and Spruance had not been able to determine Ozawa's precise location.

The *Enterprise*'s Lt. R. S. Nelson found the Japanese fleet at 3:40 P.M. in a refueling disposition. Unfortunately, his message to Mitscher was garbled and with only four hours of daylight remaining, Mitscher hesitated to give the attack order to his carrier groups.

The Japanese, hearing Nelson's calls, surmised that they had been discovered, and Ozawa ordered refueling discontinued immediately. They beat a hasty retreat to the Philippines.

Meanwhile, Nelson's message to the fleet had been clarified, and although it was late, Mitscher ordered air groups to stand by for possible takeoff. He had detached the carriers *Essex*, *Cowpens*, and the new *Langley* of Task Group 58.4 to cover the Marianas landings and now headed westward with the rest of Task Force Fifty-eight to reduce the 275-mile distance between his fleet and Ozawa's. He knew that his planes would have to be recovered after dark and that they would be launched at the limit of their range. He also knew that many pilots had been trained only for daylight landings and that they were all fatigued by the long day of operations. The risks weighed heavily on his mind. Losses could be heavy.

After a somber discussion with his staff, Mitscher said, "We can make it." He paused thoughtfully. "It will be a tight squeeze."

Comdr. Bernard M. "Smoke" Strean in the *Yorktown* climbed into his fighter at 4:30 P.M. to lead the first wave of 216 planes. Another deckload was scheduled to follow after the first wave cleared.

On board the *Enterprise*, Ramage, commanding officer of VB–10, completed briefing his strike group and was ready for immediate launch. As his pilots hurried out of the ready room, Ramage took a last look at the board, which showed Ozawa's fleet at 15 degrees north latitude, 134 degrees 25 minutes east longitude—some 275 miles away.

When the call came from air plot at 4:15, "Pilots, man your planes!" Ramage had a final word for his twelve pilots. "You'll have to be gas misers. Lean your engine settings to the maximum, or you won't have a chance of getting back." He told them soberly that he thought that they were going on a one-way mission—their SBDs had an attack radius of only 250 miles—and that they would all end up "boating." He noted that his grim words had no apparent effect on their enthusiasm. The squadron was experienced, nearing the end of its second combat cruise, and there was little nervousness. These pilots had waited a long time for a chance at Japan's carriers.

Ramage warmed up the engine of his SBD Dauntless and went through the checklist with Aviation Radioman D. J. Cawley in the rear seat. He reflected again that there was little chance of his returning aboard. He knew that the others were thinking the same thing but that their loss would be worth it if they sank key carriers of the Japanese fleet.

They took off and rendezvoused quickly, taking up a course of 284° magnetic. Five Avenger torpedo bombers swung in behind, and "Killer" Kane and 11 other Hellcat fighters took their positions above. With carburetor settings leaned down, they were averaging only 125 knots indicated air speed as they formed the base element. Each pilot kept a close watch on his instruments, constantly checking gauges to assure that engines were operating most economically.

After the first wave was airborne, Mitscher received sobering news from scout planes. Ozawa's ships were 60 miles farther west than first reported and retreating. He immediately canceled the second strike.

Meanwhile, the groups already airborne used a running rendezvous into the setting afternoon sun. There was no time or fuel for the luxury of the standard orbit of the force. Fuel meant everything to the SBDs of the *Lexington* and *Enterprise* because they were the shortest-legged aircraft in the air.

For two hours Strean's radio was quiet, not a voice cracking a joke or asking for instructions. Then, at 6:40, he heard, "Ships sighted. Look at that oil slick!"

A few Japanese fighters headed in for an attack on the American bombers. They seemed uncertain and at first avoided tangling with the Americans.

Strean called, "Leave them to us."

While fighters attacked the Zeros, torpedo bombers headed for the ships, pilots wincing at the flak streaming toward them, some even from the big guns of the fleet.

Lt. Charles W. Nelson of the new *Yorktown*'s torpedo group picked out an enemy carrier and with Lts. John D. Slightom, James R. Crenshaw, Jr., and Carl F. Luedemann, swung in for the kill.

Lt. (jg.) George B. Brown, temporary commanding officer of the *Belleau Wood* torpedo squadron, had said prior to takeoff that he would get a carrier at all costs. He swung in against the *Hiyo*, signaling Lts. (jg.) Benjamin C. Tate and Warren R. Omark to follow.

His small section had been left alone while other squadron planes were engaged in glide-bombing attacks. He decided to seek safety in the clouds until they could get closer to the carrier, but when the clouds drifted away he found that they were headed for a large group of battleships, cruisers, and destroyers only 5,000 yards away.

Their TBFs shook violently as a hail of steel ripped into wings and fuselages. "Break it up!" Brown called quickly to his comrades. "Come in at different angles."

A carrier, fully alerted on the far side of the warships, turned in a tight circle while the massed fire of her guns was brought to bear upon the three Avengers. The sturdy airplanes took terrible punishment, explosions rocking them repeatedly. Tracers tore through Tate's cockpit, slashing his right hand, and a large shell ripped open the fuselage. Tate hung grimly to his prescribed course. Brown's plane looked to be in bad shape as shells exploded on all sides.

"Fire!" Tate's rear gunner called, pointing to Brown's airplane. Tate blanched in horror as flames licked the fuselage of Brown's TBF. He saw the crew bail out, but Brown dove the airplane until the flames died down and then released his torpedo straight at the *Hiyo*. It connected with devastating impact.

As Brown's fire-blackened Avenger roared across the fleet, it seemed as if every Japanese gun was trained on it. When Brown saw that Tate and Omark had not yet made their runs, he turned back and flew down the length of the carrier to draw its fire away from his comrades.

Tate and Omark, electrified by Brown's heroic action to help them, swung in and dropped their torpedoes, one of which hit the *Hiyo*. They ran the gauntlet of antiaircraft fire almost without opposition and then searched for Brown. To their astonishment, his charred and riddled plane had cleared the area and was headed due west toward empty ocean.

Omark overtook him. After almost touching wing tips, Omark signaled for Brown to turn back.

Brown waved a bloodied and shattered arm. Omark felt a sick sense of futility; Brown's khaki shirt was covered with blood and he seemed about to pass out. While he watched in anguish, the plane fell off steeply and headed down. Miraculously, Brown managed to land his airplane in the water, but he died soon afterward. For two hours before they were picked up, his crewmen, Ellis C. Babcock and George H. Platz, drifted in their life raft in the middle of the battle as attacks continued against the *Hiyo* only a short distance away.

Ramage had been listening to the groups ahead as he slowly climbed to 10,000 feet, turning on oxygen to clear his head while he listened to continuous radio reports. He knew that his group was on the right track, and as they leveled out at 13,000 feet, he grew impatient to locate Ozawa's fleet.

"Tallyho ahead!" The call came from Lt. Donald "Flash" Gordon of VF–10 at 6:30.

Ramage looked down, spotting six large oilers with seven escorting destroyers. He ordered his pilots to ignore them. They were out for bigger game. He was angry when he noticed one of the strike groups attacking the oilers. Their orders had been specific, "Get the carriers!"

Ramage noted twelve SB2C Helldivers from another strike group attacking the oilers and called, "Are you trying to sink their merchant marine? Charlie Victors [referring to CVs, the designation for carriers] are about 40 miles ahead."

The attacks continued, and he received no reply. Although the leader of the group was criticized for his action, he excused it by saying that his airplanes were low on fuel. (They were all low on fuel. Actually, the SB2Cs had more fuel than Ramage's SBDs.) Despite the leader's action, contrary to the orders of the task force commander, he later received a medal for sinking three or four of the oilers.

Ramage now spotted a number of dots on the ocean's surface 30 miles ahead. Those specks quickly increased in size; he identified carriers, cruisers, and destroyers. The sky was filled with antiaircraft puffs as Japanese ships zeroed in on American planes attacking from above.

Ramage turned his squadron toward two Japanese carriers in the center of a large screening force. Before takeoff, he had stipulated that he would lead six of his pilots in an attack on the nearest carrier, while Lt. Lou Bangs and his men took on the next.

Hundreds of black puffs materialized to their right as Japanese gunners sought them. His rear gunner said that the shells were exploding at the correct altitude as usual but were off in bearing.

Ramage nosed his SBD down. As he pushed over, Lt. Oliver W. Hubbard joined him in a fast glide.

Cawley called, "Zeke overhead." After a pause, he said with a chuckle, "No guts," as the Japanese fighter pilot made an ineffectual pass and backed away after seeing Kane's F6F fighters weaving above.

Ramage, concentrated on his dive. There was a twisting throng of ships on the ocean's surface. He turned left, and for a moment the carrier he was aiming at disappeared under his plane's nose. He opened his dive brakes and rolled over into the standard 70-degree dive.

To his surprise, the carrier—identified later as the *Ryuho*—stopped turning. He could scarcely believe the perfect shot he had as he headed down in an almost perpendicular dive. The Japanese ship's flight deck seemed to be outlined by tiny, flickering candle lights that blinked when the ship's large caliber guns went off.

Intent on maintaining his cross hairs on the carrier's deck, Ramage ignored antiaircraft shells that were passing beneath him.

The dive seemed to take an eternity. At 6,000 feet, he opened fire with his twin-fifty nose guns. The carrier's deck expanded to fill his sight while he held the aiming point steady on the forward elevator. He had never been this close to a Japanese carrier before and noted that unlike American ships the Japanese hulls narrowed at the bow and stern.

Twenty-millimeter tracers seemed to be rising directly into Ramage's gunsight; fire from smaller caliber guns had increased in intensity. Despite heavy antiaircraft fire, Ramage was determined to ride the plane down so low that his 1,000-pound bomb couldn't miss. As his altimeter passed 1,500 feet—its built-in lag meant that he was actually 200 feet lower—he released his bomb. As he did so, he could see the carrier turn sharply to port, while her stern swung to starboard. He feared he would miss due to the ship's sudden movement.

Ramage pulled out of his dive, and before he could get his dive flaps closed he heard Cawley fire. He looked back into the face of a surprised Zero pilot. The Japanese plane was so close that they almost collided. Ramage headed for the water as the Zero passed beneath him and climbed in front at an incredible angle.

He felt a jar, and knew it was his bomb going off. Cawley was shouting wildly that their bomb had hit the *Ryuho*'s stern. (Later, it was revealed that their bomb had actually been a near miss.)

Then Cawley called out, "Turn around, sir! Look back! There's a carrier burning from asshole to appetite." He reported that black smoke was coming from the left side of the *Hiyo*, which had just been hit by bombs dropped by Lts. Lou Bangs, Carl de Temple, and Cecil "Tip" Mester.

Ramage looked back to see smoke pouring out of the *Hiyo*'s stacks on the starboard side, and he knew she had evidently been hurt badly because white smoke belched from her hangar deck.

The air around them was thick with antiaircraft bursts, and tracers crisscrossed their path. He was down to 300 feet, and two destroyers had him bracketed. He headed lower, and the bursts passed overhead. Close to his left side an *Atago*-class heavy cruiser flung everything in her inventory at them, including shells from her eight-inch main battery. He led his squadron up to 500 feet as shell splashes threw up huge geysers of water. They had to fly directly over the Japanese fleet, and the *Mogami* and a *Tone*-class heavy cruiser opened up with all guns. Their main batteries were firing volleys of phosphorus particles that looked to Ramage like salvos of confetti.

Cawley kept watch, and when a volley was on its way to them, he told Ramage to either dive or climb as the situation warranted.

Ramage relaxed as they penetrated the last screen of ships. It had taken five minutes to run the gauntlet but now the sky above was a tangle of dogfights as American fighter planes tore into the Zekes. Soon, to Ramage's satisfaction, the Japanese fighters looked like torches falling into a receptive ocean.

Away from the battle for the first time, Ramage circled to pick up his planes, hoping to lead them home despite the nearly hopeless shortage of fuel. On his right, he watched what at first he thought was a dogfight. Fighters rolled, looped, and went into fantastic contortions in the sky. He quickly realized, to his surprise, that only Zekes were involved: All of the planes had rounded, tapered wings.

He had been lulled momentarily and had almost fallen for an old Japanese trick of diverting attention with aerobatics while unseen planes attacked from a different direction. He understood what was going on as one Zeke rolled over and headed for an American dive-bomber that was straggling in the rear, obviously not following the safety-in-numbers doctrine. The Zeke pilot's aim was accurate, and the dive-bomber was soon in flames.

Now six Zekes headed toward them. Ramage, who had tightened up his formation when he first saw the Japanese fighters, was grateful when the Japanese pilots decided that his formation was too formidable and attacked another. "Killer" Kane and his fighters scissored in on the Zekes, quickly downing two of them. Two more soon dropped in flames; the remainder dove for the waves and headed for their carriers.

Ramage surveyed his nine-plane formation as they circled in the gathering darkness, hoping the other three would turn up. Attacks by Zeros intensified, and Ramage surmised that they were trying to make up for their lack of aggressiveness at the beginning of the battle. Kane and his fighters finally eliminated all of them.

Ramage knew that he had to abandon the search; precious gasoline was methodically being fed every minute into the cylinders of his engine. His only hope was that his two missing pilots, Lts. Lou Bangs and "Tip" Mester, had joined another formation, along with the third missing pilot, Lt. Jack Wright from the *Lexington*.

The formation included a dozen or so stragglers, but Ramage could not identify them in the moonless night. As he turned back, he recalled with a pang that he had seen a dive-bomber aflame at 4,000 feet over one of the Japanese carriers. He hoped that it was not one of his ducklings.

In the darkness, the formation tightened, the youngsters pressing close so as not to lose the "old man." Air Group 10 was qualified for night carrier landings; gasoline was the major problem. Ramage figured that they had flown 300 miles on the way out, and should only have to cover two hundred and seventy on their way back if Mitscher's fleet kept to its westerly heading. Still, it would be a miracle if they survived.

The night was pitch dark, with no moon. Suddenly, there was a flash of light to starboard. Ramage wondered whether it could have been gunfire or a signal flare. He decided that it was the only thing he had to go on, so he altered the formation's course twenty degrees to the right. He had no way of knowing that the flash he had glimpsed was distant lightning.

On the bridge of the *Lexington*, Admiral Mitscher's hands gripped the arms of his swivel chair until the knuckles showed white. Task Force Fifty-eight was blacked out, not a light showing, because Japanese submarines had been detected.

His eyes were red-rimmed and his face haggard with worry about his pilots and crewmen. Mitscher gazed into the dark as the radio crackled with reports from the first planes. He swallowed tightly as one pilot reported, "Almost out of gas. Going in."

Agonizing calls came from several pilots lost in that awesome black void to the west. They needed position reports to home in on. Mitscher's leathery face showed the agony he felt. The thousands of men in the huge task force and the vital carriers needed to pursue the war against Japan should not be sacrificed even to save the carriers' pilots. Prior to the mission, he had secretly ordered that the fleet's lights be ready to be turned on if his men returned after dark, but while the ships' lights might save scores of men struggling to get back safely, they also might make the carriers easy pickings for lurking Japanese submarines. The pilots had not been told about the lights because it was feared that they might depend too much on them and ignore strict navigation discipline and fuel conservation measures. In additon, Mitscher ordered all task groups to keep at a distance so that their lights would not blind pilots trying to land on their carriers. Searchlights on the carriers were ordered to be pointed straight up. Other ships were told to keep their lights to a minimum, and only those on the fringes were permitted to run with all lights. Finally, destroyers were sent far in advance to help rescue downed pilots.

Mitscher's slight 125-pound frame shifted uneasily in the skipper's chair, and his jaw was set stubbornly to control his quivering lips as he listened to the frantic cries for help coming in over the radio. These were his men. He was the one who had sent them out on this dangerous night attack, and they had fought well. He knew, however, that the safety of his task force had to come first, so he delayed his decision until the first large group of returning planes appeared on radar.

His normally soft voice vibrated with emotion as he said, "Turn on the lights!"

The fleet lit up like Times Square in New York. Starshells were fired, exploding high above the ships, so pilots could see them from afar.

Destroyers prowled through the fleet, searching for enemy submarines and hauling wet pilots out of the sea after their planes crash-landed short of the carriers. Planes streamed in, dozens dropping into the ocean so low on fuel that they could not make the last mile. The sea was covered with flickering lights as pilots waved their waterproof flashlights so that destroyers could find them more quickly.

Bringing up the rear, Ramage realized that though the flashes of light he had seen were lightning, his turn to the right had proved correct. He could see a huge searchlight beaming from one of the ships.

With only 15 gallons of fuel sloshing in his tanks, Ramage brought his formation back to the *Enterprise*. He wished Mitscher had not ordered the lights of all ships turned on because it was difficult to pick out the carriers, but he was grateful to be alive. His strike group could not land on its ship because a plane from some other carrier had crashed on deck. Ramage broke up the formation and with almost empty tanks, they split away and landed on other carriers. Ramage landed on the *Yorktown*. He later learned that only one plane from his squadron—the one flown by Lou Bangs, who had got a hit on the *Hiyo*—had been forced to ditch. Bangs was later picked up by a destroyer.

Aboard the *Yorktown*, there was deep gloom because her strike group of SB2C dive-bombers had not returned. A preponderance of the SB2Cs, new in comparison with the tried and tested SBD dive-bombers, which were going out of production, had gone on the raid. Although some SB2C Helldiver pilots landed safely, many of the rest had to be picked up that night and the following day.

Ramage was not pleased with the mission. He believed that the bombing had been poor and felt that sinking two carriers by planes was no great victory. He was amazed at the claims of battle damage made by several of the air groups.

Capt. John Crommelin, the carrier division's chief of staff, came in to the wardroom to talk to Ramage. Crommelin had been the executive officer on the *Enterprise* during a previous tour, and had come to know Ramage well and respected his judgment.

"Well, Jig Dog, looks like we really got 'em this time."

"Captain, I don't believe it's all that good. Take a look at these battle claims. I was the last one in there, as far as I know, and they simply aren't so."

Crommelin looked at him appraisingly, then nodded and walked away.

Ramage returned to the *Enterprise* the next day. After some figuring, he was astonished to find that the night before he had been in the air 5.8 hours, something the SBD's designers would say was impossible. The long flight had been carefully planned to get every mile out of each gallon of gasoline, and it had been remarkably successful.

Ramage was relieved that all his pilots were saved. Sailors who rescued Lieutenant Bangs by pulling him on board their destroyer claimed that he weighed 300 pounds. When Bangs came back aboard the *Enterprise*, Ramage kidded him, saying that it was his ample posterior that had put him into the drink.

Task Force Fifty-eight was ordered to steam to Eniwetok and upon arrival Admiral Mitscher called Ramage to the *Lexington*. John S. McCain was also in attendance, and Ramage, who had never been in an admiral's cabin before, was nervous. When he saw the kind look in the 5-foot, 6-inch Mitscher's eyes—deep appreciation for the efforts of the pilots he truly loved—Ramage felt a warmth creep through him. Now he fully understood why Mitscher's men respected their self-effacing commander. He was concerned for his pilots' welfare like no other man in the fleet.

Mitscher motioned Ramage to a seat and asked him to give him his thoughts about the battle. When he was done, Mitscher said, "I think you're probably right. It wasn't a great victory."

The admiral turned to another subject, the retention of SBDs in the fleet. "You and Ralph Weymouth brought all your planes back. Your SBDs probably got most of the hits. What can we do about keeping the SBD in the fleet?"

Ramage said, "It would be very simple to train SB2C pilots to fly SBDs because most started out in them. The SB2C is more difficult to operate. They could transition right aboard ships."

Ramage explained that transferring back from the SB2C to the SBD was feasible as far as pilot skill was concerned. Logistic support was another matter. Ramage pointed out that there would be no spare parts, handling equipment, or other operating gear readily available.

Although nothing further came of their conversation to get SBDs back into the fleet—it was too late for that—Ramage found it interesting that Mitscher was so concerned about the veteran Dauntlesses so late in the war. Ramage decided that both admirals were resigned to losing the reliable SBDs and would have to make do with the less-than-reliable SB2Cs.

The SBD had an additional distinction. On a previous cruise, Chief Aviation Radioman Wayne C. Colley had, as a rear gunner, destroyed five Japanese planes. Although many gunners shot down Japanese planes, this Virginia farm boy was the only one to become an ace.

Approximately one hundred planes failed to land safely after the attack, but Mitscher's prompt and heroic use of the lights, plus outstanding rescue efforts saved all but sixteen pilots and thirty-three crewmen. Total American losses for the two-day battle were 130 American planes.

In contrast, Ozawa lost 480 planes, and their air battle became known as the Marianas' "Turkey Shoot." The Japanese had lost most of their best pilots and crew members, and their carrier aviation declined steadily after this action. The loss of planes was bad enough, but they could be replaced far more readily than the experienced airmen.

Admiral Towers' insistence that the fast carriers be given extreme mobility now paid off in a great victory. Not only was Japan's airpower destroyed, but her navy was proven helpless to interfere with a large American amphibious landing.

Spruance decided not to press after Ozawa's fleeing ships. His first responsibility, he said, was to the amphibious operation in the Marianas.

After the war, when Spruance's decision was questioned, he said, "You may be right. I may have missed a chance to shorten the war. Let me explain, however, the information I had at the time. I knew Ozawa, and I feared that the Japanese habit of dividing their forces might take place. My mission was to seize and occupy the Marianas. Until I had a definite location of that entire Jap fleet, I didn't feel I could go after them."

Marine Lt. Gen. Holland M. Smith, in command of the ground troops on Saipan, had a stubborn battle on his hands. The Japanese continued to contest every foot of ground. For days, troops encountered heavy fire while they fought off suicidal Japanese daylight charges and even worse, screaming banzai charges at night. For the foot soldiers, it was as bad as anything they had experienced in the Pacific.

On June 22, Thunderbolts from the Seventh Air Force's Nineteenth and Seventy-third Squadrons joined navy planes after the Japanese Aslito airfield was secured and renamed Isley Field. The Thunderbolts now began to use a new weapon against strong points like caves and heavily constructed defense positions. It was called napalm, a gel of chemicals and gasoline, and it proved to be a horrible weapon.

The battle for control of Saipan lasted twenty-four days. Tinian was secured on August 1 with heavy losses on both sides but with the Japanese losing by far the greater number. Guam was retaken on August 10. Vice-Admiral Nagumo, the officer who led the Pearl Harbor attack, was one of those who committed suicide rather than surrender to the Americans.

The four groups of Mitscher's Task Force Fifty-eight, plus two divisions of escort carriers, had been instrumental in the early conclusion of the Marianas campaign. Guam, in particular, received the heaviest aerial bombardment ever meted out to a Pacific stronghold.

Close aerial support on all three islands was exceptional. Planes bombed enemy concentrations and artillery posts and strafed infantry positions heavily. The marines took all this for granted, but army troops greeted warmly the novelty of close support.

General Tojo, Japan's prime minister, was shocked by the loss of the Marianas. He told the Japanese people that they were now threatened by a "national crisis without precedent." The Emperor, when advised by his elder statesmen that Tojo and his cabinet had to be removed, readily agreed. Tojo's resignation was accepted on July 18, 1944.

With the fall of the Marianas, Hirohito's naval advisor, Admiral Osami Nagano, said, "This is frightful. Hell is on us."

Meanwhile, bases like Truk and others in the central and eastern Carolines, were neutralized. Like Kavieng and Rabaul, they were now left in the backwash of the war.

In mid-July, Admiral King flew from Washington to Pearl Harbor for a conference with Nimitz and then flew on to Saipan. King met Spruance and said, "You did a damn good job here." This was in reference to Spruance's decision not to send Task Force Fifty-eight in pursuit of Ozawa's battered fleet. "No matter what other people tell you, your decision was correct."

In a discussion on future strategy, King again brought up the subject of an invasion of Formosa. Spruance and Turner both objected that such an invasion might interfere with the occupation of the Philippines. Spruance told King that if Formosa had to be taken, Luzon should be invaded first to provide a fleet anchorage at Manila Bay. He explained that there were no suitable harbors in the Marianas.

King asked Spruance, "What do you recommend now that the Marianas have been taken?"

"Okinawa."

King lifted an eyebrow. "Can you take it?"

"I think so if we can find a way to transfer heavy ammunition at sea." He explained that Okinawa, in the Ryukyu Islands just south of Japan, was 1,400 miles from Saipan and that there was no suitable anchorage at which such a transfer could be made.

Spruance also brought up the subject of Iwo Jima, claiming that it should be seized before Okinawa. He said that the occupation of Okinawa would complete the blockade of Japan and that in his opinion the war could then be won without an invasion.

President Roosevelt, who had been renominated by his party for a fourth term on July 20, announced that he would meet with Nimitz and MacArthur six days later at Pearl Harbor.

King decided to return to Washington before the president arrived, and Nimitz was named as his spokesman for the presidential conference. King told Nimitz to make up his own mind about an invasion of Formosa, but as Nimitz stubbornly resisted, he continued to try to convince him of its merits.

Before King left, they discussed for the first time the possibility of carrier strikes against Japan's main islands. Towers had been urging such strikes for some time, and now Nimitz proposed that they be started in late January 1945. King insisted on late 1944.

Roosevelt arrived promptly on July 26, but much to the president's annoyance they all had to await MacArthur's arrival. MacArthur deliberately arrived several hours late to upstage the president and was escorted to the conference with considerable fanfare. Earlier, MacArthur had told intimates that the conference was just playacting for political reasons and that he resented the need for his appearance.

At the conference, MacArthur passed out a copy of a letter from King saying that once MacArthur's forces moved into the Philippines, an independent British command would take over defense of Australia and the East Indies.

That night they had dinner in Roosevelt's quarters, and the president entertained MacArthur, Admiral Leahy, and Nimitz. Later, they went into the living room, which had a large map of the Pacific.

Roosevelt moved his wheelchair close to the map. "Douglas, where do we go from here?"

"Leyte, Mr. President, and then Luzon."

Nimitz briefed the president, pointing out the strategic advantages of Formosa and its importance to the flow of oil and other strategic materials from the East Indies to Japan. He pointed out its proximity to China and expressed the hope that the Chinese army might secure bases from which the Japanese home islands could be bombed and possibly invaded.

MacArthur replied, "You cannot abandon seventeen million loyal Filipino Christians to the Japanese in favor of first liberating Formosa and returning to China. American public opinion would condemn you, Mr. President, and it would be justified."

MacArthur continued to speak about the humanitarian aspects involved in the deliverance of the Filipinos from Japanese occupation and the freeing of American prisoners. He said that Japanese airfields on Luzon were too distant to be neutralized from Mindanao. MacArthur said that American airfields were needed on Leyte or Mindoro, or both. His forces, he claimed, would then be able to land at Lingayen Gulf and be in Manila in five weeks.

Roosevelt protested that the United States could not stand the heavy losses involved in retaking Luzon. "It seems to me we must bypass it."

MacArthur disagreed, saying that he did not believe that losses would be high. In an obvious dig at Nimitz, he said, "Good commanders do not turn in heavy losses."

It was true that MacArthur's losses had been light when compared with Nimitz' drive up the Central Pacific. That was true because, for the most part, MacArthur's forces had encountered light resistance, and the Central Pacific drive had kept the Japanese from massing on his flank.

Roosevelt refused to commit himself to an attack on the Philippines and expressed his concern about the differences between the two top commanders in the Pacific.

MacArthur disingenuously assured the president that he and Nimitz had resolved any dispute between them. "We see eye to eye, Mr. President."

En route back to his command, MacArthur was for some reason enthusiastic about the meeting. He believed that he had won all the arguments about future operations and told an aide, "We've sold it!"

He had, however, underestimated King's influence with the president. When Roosevelt returned to Washington, he told King that he now favored an attack on the Philippines. King was unhappy with Nimitz, feeling that his Pacific commander had let him down. He was even more disturbed when he learned that General Marshall now seriously doubted the merits of occupying Formosa.

While these conferences were going on, the program for controlling the Central Pacific went into high gear. Mitscher's fast carriers struck targets in the western Carolines during the latter part of the month.

During the first week of August, Mitscher's forces again raided the Bonin Islands, which had been under periodic attack since June 15. This chain was important because it was on the direct air route to Japan.

In mid-August, Nimitz acted on his own and moved his Pacific headquarters to Guam. King opposed the move at first but accepted Nimitz's ex post facto explanation that he would now be closer to the war front.

By early September, while the Octagon Conference was in session in Quebec, American and British armies in France reached the German border, and the Red Army continued advancing from the east. Germany's defeat seemed imminent.

Churchill was now determined to get British armed forces involved in the Pacific war, and on September 14, he offered King his nation's newer battleships and carriers. He was surprised when King showed no inclination to accept them.

Churchill turned to President Roosevelt. "The offer has been made. Is it accepted?"

"It is," the president replied.

Despite Roosevelt's words, King was unwilling to have elements of the British navy join his forces in the Pacific even though other members of the Joint Chiefs agreed to their participation. He was forced to concur but insisted that his approval was contingent upon their being balanced forces that were self-supporting.

King was reluctant to accept Churchill's offer because the American navy had so far been successful in the Pacific despite continual British efforts to limit its forces in favor of the war in Europe. In retrospect, King was wrong, and the Royal Navy made a significant contribution to the war in the Pacific from then on.

Before the invasion of the Philippines could get underway, MacArthur asked for the invasion of Peleliu in the Palaus and Morotai in the Moluccas. A surface bombardment force, plus six escort carriers, prepared the way for ground troops at Morotai. The fast carriers of Vice-Adm. John. S. McCain's Task Group 38.1 stood by in case of a Japanese foray. Landings were made with only token opposition on September 15.

Halsey's carriers struck the Philippines during the Morotai operation, encountering little opposition.

A navy pilot, shot down over Leyte, was rescued by guerrillas and reported that his rescuers said that there were no Japanese troops on Leyte. Halsey talked to the pilot and wired Nimitz in Canada, where he was attending the Octagon Conference in Quebec and reported what he had learned. He recommended that the Pacific timetable be changed, suggesting that the Palaus be bypassed and that a landing should be made in the middle of the Philippines instead of on the southernmost island of Mindanao.

Nimitz was in partial agreement but believed that the invasion of the Palaus was too far along to be canceled. He did decide that Yap, a lesser stronghold, could be bypassed. He made his recommendations to the Combined Chiefs, who agreed with him, as did Roosevelt and Churchill.

MacArthur, at the front during the Morotai invasion, could not be reached, but Chief of Staff Sutherland agreed on his behalf. Sutherland disagreed, however, with Halsey's comment that the Japanese Air Force in the Philippines was a "hollow shell operating on a shoestring." Sutherland pointed out that Allied ground-based fighter cover would not be able to protect the invasion fleet off Leyte, so carriers would have to take over the assignment.

The invasion date for Leyte, the eighth largest island in the Philippines, was moved up to October 20 from December 20. Approval by the United States Joint Chiefs was quick and appropriate orders were issued.

Peleliu in the Palaus was captured, but at great cost.

The Imperial High Command in Tokyo now viewed the future with grave concern. Many navy officers already realized that Japan had lost the war. The United States Navy, now far more powerful than the Japanese navy, would soon be able to steam up to the main island almost without opposition.

What caused the high command and the Emperor most concern was loss of the Marianas. These island bases, only 1,500 miles from Japan, were already being converted into B–29 bomber bases. Japanese militarists knew that every Japanese city was vulnerable to mass raids, and to eventual destruction.

15

A CLEVER PLAN

King had been fighting for the invasion of Formosa for a long time. Actually, his arguments long since had lost their validity, but he was reluctant to admit it.

At a meeting on September 29 in San Francisco, Nimitz finally convinced King that Formosa should be bypassed. He also told his commander that the army could provide adequate troops for an assault on Okinawa, leaving him with sufficient marines to invade Iwo Jima.

At first, King resisted any thought of assaulting Iwo Jima. He reluctantly conceded when advised by Nimitz' war plans officer, Forrest P. Sherman, that the air force needed it for a fighter base to escort B–29s over Japan.

On September 23rd a combat team of the 81st Army Division landed on Ulithi, largest atoll of the western Carolines, but found the island unoccupied by the Japanese who, natives said, had fled a month before. The magnificent lagoon formed by Ulithi's reef of thirty islands was perfect for anchoring a large fleet, and the United States Navy quickly established an anchorage at its northern point.

Meanwhile, Mitscher's task groups made a high-speed run to a launch position 70 miles off central Luzon in the Philippines. The ships steamed warily, and at midnight on September 30, they arrived undetected.

Comdr. Jackson D. Arnold, the new *Hornet*'s Air Group 2 commander, led the attack. While Comdrs. Jack Blitch and Grafton B. Campbell of the new *Wasp* headed the dive-bombers, torpedo planes circled the bay, then swept in against shipping.

Bombers from the *Wasp*'s Air Group 14 concentrated on the old Dewey dry dock that the navy had once brought through the Panama Canal from the east coast of the United States for use in the Philippines. It was hit seven times.

In coordinated attacks, Rear Adm. Gerald F. Bogan's fliers from the *Intrepid*'s Air Group 18 and the *Bunker Hill*'s Air Group 8 struck Clark Field. Meanwhile, Admiral Sherman's crews, including the *Essex*'s Air Group 15 and the *Lexington*'s Air Group 19 headed for Nichols Field.

Halsey and Mitscher gave a masterful performance. The Japanese lost sixty-six aircraft in the air while Task Force Thirty-eight lost six.

Nimitz read Halsey's report with great satisfaction following the attack. "Approach to Luzon apparently undetected," it said, "and surprise complete thanks to convenient weather front. Weather over target good but foul in launching area. Operations possible only because of superb judgment, skill, and determination of Task Force Thirty-eight and its commander Vice-Admiral Mitscher."

American carrier aviation had destroyed over 1,000 Japanese planes and 150 ships since August 31, while their own combat losses were only 54.

These raids proved that the Philippines were susceptible to approach by invasion forces. The separate drives by Southwest Pacific and Central Pacific Forces now would be joined in the Philippines.

With Angaur in the southern Palaus in Allied hands, the Seventh Air Force's 494th Bombardment Group moved into new bases that were within range of Japanese fields in the Philippines. Clark Field, near Manila, had not seen Allied action since the earliest days of the war.

Col. Laurence B. Kelly arrived with B–24 bombers in October after a mass flight from Hawaii. The next day, Kelly's Cobras bombed Yap and Koror, near the Palaus, without loss.

Despite heavy losses of airplanes and crew members, Japanese combat aviation was far from powerless. Plans for its use in a new Sho Plan—the Japanese word for victory—in defense of the Philippines, which the Japanese high command expected the Americans to invade next, were extensive. They had brought in ground and air reinforcements during September and stiffened their top leadership by placing the "Tiger" of Malaya in charge of the defense of the Philippines. Tomoyuki Yamashita, the general who had captured Singapore at the start of the war when the fortress there was believed to be impregnable, was a far tougher adversary than the former commander, Lt. Gen. Shiganori Kuroda.

Commander in Chief of the Combined Fleet, Admiral Soemu

Toyoda, by now had lost all confidence in the Japanese army. In Tokyo, he told his staff that if the Americans gained a foothold in the Philippines, Japan's lifeline to the south for fuel and raw materials would be cut. He was ready to sacrifice his entire fleet in one bold stroke because there was no sense in saving it if it was to become impotent if fuel and ammunition supplies could not be obtained from the South Pacific and the mainland.

In preparation for the landings on Leyte scheduled for October 20, Admiral Halsey sent Mitscher's carriers to the north on October 4 to attack Okinawa and an air base on Luzon. The following day, his carrier planes swept across Formosa. They attacked airfields and harbors, and only a few Japanese fighters rose to combat the strike.

Three hundred and forty planes participated in the attack on Formosa, and extensive damage was done. In conjunction with the bombing attacks, photographic planes covered both islands extensively with their cameras.

Halsey was with his ships to the north of the Philippines, in case the Japanese left the home islands to strike when the invasion forces moved to Leyte Gulf. He moved south, feinting toward the Philippines, then heading instead for Formosa to engage in a three-day attack to reduce the enemy's air strength, which otherwise might be thrown into the coming battle of Leyte.

The Japanese Second Fleet had hundreds of airplanes. Despite Ozawa's protests, 150 were taken from his depleted carrier squadrons and rushed to Formosa. Therefore, when Halsey's planes attacked on October 12, they received a fiery reception. Over a thousand airplanes rose to fight it out with Halsey's planes.

Air force B–29s made three successive strikes on the 14th, 16th, and 17th from bases in China. The Japanese reeled under attacks from all sides. The United States Third Fleet did not complete the operation unscathed—the Australian cruiser *Canberra* and the American cruisers *Houston* and *Reno* were all damaged by torpedoes. Halsey had a good laugh when Tokyo Rose gave the Japanese version of the action. "All of Admiral Mitscher's carriers have been sunk tonight instantly." He recommended the issuance of a press release. "All Third Fleet ships reported by Tokyo Radio as sunk have now been salvaged and are retiring in the direction of the enemy."

It was estimated that the Japanese had lost five hundred planes in the air and on the ground; Third Fleet losses totaled seventy-nine planes and sixty-four pilots and crewmen. Because of those losses,

Japanese planes in the Philippines were reduced to a minimum by the eve of the Leyte invasion. At home, the Japanese continued to claim an overwhelming victory, saying that the Third Fleet had ceased to be an organized striking force. These announcements created wild celebrations throughout Japan.

The main attack force of 130,000 troops remained off the entrance to Leyte Gulf on October 19 while bombardment ships of the Seventh Fleet under Vice-Adm. Thomas C. Kinkaid moved closer to shore. At dawn, the big ships belched steel at enemy positions while Rear Adm. Clifton A. F. "Ziggy" Sprague sent planes from his six escort carriers to bomb and strafe the invasion front.

At 10:00 A.M. the next day, General MacArthur watched from the deck of the cruiser *Nashville* as his troops waded ashore. The general later waded ashore at the same spot he had stood forty-one years before when he had participated in his first Philippine mission as a second lieutenant in the United States army.

The Japanese had retired to more entrenched positions, so landings were made against only light opposition. Meanwhile, Halsey returned to a position to the north of the Philippines in case Toyoda's ships elected to come south to contest the landings.

Toyoda's Sho Plan for defense of the Philippines was not activated until after landings were made. Elements of his fleet were operating almost blind without adequate reconnaissance aircraft, and they were nearly defenseless against American air attack. Ozawa's carriers were down to 108 aircraft, and most pilots were inexperienced. In contrast, the average complement of a single American carrier was eighty planes.

All told, the Japanese had seven hundred aircraft available in the Philippines, but most were obsolete and their pilots young and unseasoned. Although Adm. Shigeru Fukudome's Second Air Fleet had returned to the Philippines from Formosa, it was reduced to 350 planes of all types. The First Air Fleet, under Vice-Adm. Takijiro Ohnishi, who had helped in the planning of the Pearl Harbor attack, was in even worse shape. His sixty pilots were so demoralized by recent heavy losses and by inadequate aircraft that had been patched up time and time again, that they were of little use.

The Fourth Air Army had about 150 airplanes of all types, but they were scattered at bases all over the Philippines. Pilots had a record of poor performance, and were not known for their aggressiveness.

In an act of desperation, Ohnishi recommended that a Kamikaze Corps be formed because his pilots were too inexperienced for normal combat duty. Such an air attack corps, he said, could use pilots to make suicidal crashes on American ships and, acting as "divine winds," destroy their enemy.

On the American side, Kinkaid's Seventh Fleet had more than seven hundred ships, including eighteen baby flattops with five hundred planes available for ground support of the troops on shore. In addition, Halsey's Third Fleet had eight large carriers and eight light carriers, with a total of one thousand planes, plus six battleships and scores of smaller warships. He had come to Leyte Gulf to support the landings even though his fleet had been fighting continuously for two weeks. There had been no time for replenishment of his command or time to give the carrier crews much needed rest.

Capt. James S. Russell, who had been assigned to Navy headquarters in Washington since the fall of 1942, finally persuaded his superiors that he wanted to get back into the fighting. He knew that he was too senior to command an air group and too junior to command a combat carrier, so he was delighted when Rear Adm. Ralph E. Davison, commander of Task Group 38.4, asked him to become his chief of staff on board the *Franklin* in early June. He replaced Capt. John Crommelin, who had long been overdue for rotation following months of combat and who had been blown over the side of the escort carrier *Liscome Bay* in a sheet of flames when the ship was sunk.

In the weeks after the invasion of the Palaus, Davison's task group had made a number of repetitive raids in support of major invasions. They had alternately been part of the Fifth or Third fleet, which actually was one and the same. They would watch Halsey depart for Pearl Harbor to plan the next operation, and the fleet's designation would change from the Third to the Fifth as Spruance took over. Then Spruance would leave on Halsey's return, and the fast carrier task force designation would change from Task Force Fifty-eight to Thirty-eight. In other words, the jockey was changed, but the horse remained the same.

After the Palaus was secured, Davison's group had retired to Ulithi to prepare for the assault on the Philippines. In preparation for the invasion of Leyte, they sallied again and struck Okinawa and Formosa to the north with attacks also against fields on Luzon.

In the vicinity of Okinawa, they had been attacked by Betty bombers that positioned themselves over the horizon, using a rain shower as protection to coordinate their attack. Russell watched as Japanese bombers got through the fighter screen and approached the *Franklin* from three directions. They rode just above the waves, the wash from their props kicking up the ocean's surface while tracers from American fighters sought them in vain.

Russell watched with amazement. When tracer bullets started to reach their mark, Japanese pilots would lift their planes slightly, and the tracers would go beneath. As the tracers also moved up, Japanese planes ducked underneath them. The American guns on the *Franklin* and those from the combat air patrol at last reached the Bettys, and five were soon burning in the water within the task group's formation.

Looking over the side from the flag bridge, Russell marveled that the *Franklin* had not been hit. One torpedo missed the bow by a few feet. He watched the rising bubbles left by the torpedo as the ship passed through its wake.

Another time, north of the Philippines, they had been harassed by Japanese search planes at night. Russell turned to Davison to ask if he would like to launch a night fighter.

"Let's see whether they really find us or not."

The Japanese planes could be seen on radar as they passed on either side of the task group before disappearing to the south. A few minutes later, on their return, search planes moved over a half space, and Russell pointed out that one was coming right for the group.

Davison said, "Okay. Launch night fighters."

Russell ordered two aloft, and soon there was an orange flame over the horizon as an Emily reconnaissance flying-boat was destroyed.

Halsey now sent McCain's Task Group 38.1 to Ulithi because its supplies were so depleted that they could not engage in sustained operations. The *Bunker Hill*, which needed a replacement group after heavy losses, was sent to the Admiralties and escorted by two destroyers. The three remaining groups speeded toward the Philippines on the night of October 23.

Admiral Sherman's carriers, with Mitscher on board the *Lexington*, went north to search an area near the island of Polillo, 150 miles from Manila.

Lt. Gen. Walter Krueger's Sixth Army had now been ashore three days, and the success of the invasion seemed assured. A series of miscalculations now almost brought disaster to the Americans. Admiral King must share some of the blame for what was about to happen. He had insisted that Halsey should report only to Nimitz and not to MacArthur, who was in charge of the invasion. Thus, all the evils of a divided command were established.

In addition Nimitz, with King's concurrence, told Halsey, "In case the opportunity for destruction of a major portion of the enemy fleet is offered or can be created, such destruction becomes the primary task."

Halsey was a fighter, much admired by King even though he was jealous of Halsey's popularity—something he himself had never enjoyed among the navy's rank and file. Halsey was also impulsive. In the invasion of the Philippines, the vital element of unity of command was lacking, and mistakes were inevitable. Although Admiral Kinkaid reported directly to MacArthur, Halsey reported to Nimitz, and there was too little contact between all of them. As a result, while MacArthur believed that Halsey's fleet would protect his troops at the beachhead, Halsey viewed his role in support of the Leyte landings as one of finding and sinking Japanese carriers if Japanese naval forces tried to intervene.

Prior to the invasion, Vice-Adm. Takeo Kurita had been told to maintain his heavy ships at Singapore because of limited oil reserves in the Empire's main islands. Kurita was ordered to put to sea on October 18. His impressive fleet, composed of the huge battleships *Yamato* and *Musashi*, heavier than any American battleships and furnished with 18-inch guns, plus heavy and light cruisers and destroyers, headed north.

Kurita moved at high speed with only cruiser and battleship float planes to scout ahead of his central force. When his scout planes came within range of American carrier planes, however, they were all shot down. Thereafter, he traveled almost blindly through the Philippines.

Halsey's Third Fleet had three fast carrier task groups plus McCain's group, which was hurrying to join the coming action; six new battleships; seven light cruisers; two heavy cruisers; and forty-six destroyers. Kurita's five battleships, ten heavy cruisers, two light cruisers, and fifteen destroyers would obviously be no match for Halsey's fleet if the two met while Kurita was headed for Leyte Gulf. Toyoda was aware of this, so he had decided to lure Halsey away by dangling in front of him Ozawa's almost planeless carriers en route from Japan. They probably would be sacrificed, he knew, but they were of little value without trained pilots and planes.

Meanwhile, American submarines followed Kurita's fleet. After it left Brunei Bay, the submarine *Darter* torpedoed Kurita's flagship, the *Atago*. He tried to avoid further torpedo attacks, but the *Maya* was sunk next, and the *Takeo* hit. Three of his best cruisers were out of action, and Kurita himself had to shift flagships twice, ending up on the *Yamato*.

He grinned wryly to himself when he read the latest orders from Fleet Admiral Toyoda in Tokyo. "Probable that enemy aware of concentration of our forces."

Toyoda informed Kurita that the Americans probably would concentrate themselves in the straits of San Bernardino and Surigao. He instructed Kurita to proceed east of San Bernardino Strait and Tacloban and destroy the transports. Toyoda warned him to be in position to attack the invasion fleet by the afternoon of October 24. "Carry through our original plans," Toyoda concluded.

Kurita was advised to increase his alertness against the submarine menace and utilize particular caution when penetrating the narrow strait. Shore-based planes, Toyoda assured him, would destroy the American carriers.

Ozawa received orders to leave the Inland Sea, thereby luring Halsey from Leyte Gulf and permitting Kurita's central force to attack the transports and supporting warships. He told his subordinates sadly, "Our fleet is so weakened, I expect total destruction. If Kurita can destroy the invasion fleet it will be worthwhile."

Ozawa led his decoy ships through Bungo Strait on October 20. His flagship, the *Zuikaku*, had been in the attack on Pearl Harbor. Three light carriers—the *Chitose, Chiyoda*, and *Zuiho*—and the converted battleships *Ise* and *Hyuga*, with only aft flight decks, made up the main part of his force, although three other light cruisers and eight destroyers completed it.

The converted battleships had no planes. Their aft turrets and some of their superstructure had been removed, and they were used to carry replacement carrier planes, which were hoisted on and off by cranes. The carriers had only 80 fighters, 31 torpedo planes, and 7 dive-bombers for a total of 118, but the crews were inexperienced, hardly able to land and take off from the carriers.

After fewer than two years of war, little else remained of Japanese carrier aviation, yet the Americans had no way of knowing this. Halsey considered the Japanese carriers the main threat to a successful invasion of the Philippines. If they had been up to full strength, with trained crews and airplanes, he would have been correct in the decision he was about to make.

Toyoda had devised a clever plan. He split his other available naval forces in three parts, so that one under Vice-Adm. Shoji Nishimura and another under Vice-Adm. K. Shima would approach

Leyte through the Surigao Strait from the south, while the largest force under Admiral Kurita came through San Bernardino Strait to hit Leyte from the north. Under the circumstances, it was a good plan, but its success hinged on timing and on luring Halsey away from the beachhead, with Ozawa's carriers as bait.

It was evident to American commanders that the Japanese were up to something, but no one knew just what. A United States submarine gave the first indication of possible action when it reported fifteen to twenty warships west of Mindoro on an easterly heading.

Halsey ordered his three carrier groups to launch at dawn, searching every square mile of the western approaches to the Philippines. A search plane from the light carrier *Cabot* spotted Kurita's attack force and radioed word back to flag plot aboard the fleet's flagship, the battleship *New Jersey*: "Four battleships, eight cruisers, and thirteen destroyers are off the southern tip of Mindoro."

Orders went out from Halsey to task group commanders. Rear Adm. Ralph E. Davison had his group to the south. Rear Adm. Frederick C. Sherman was off Luzon, and Rear Adm. Gerald F. Bogan's group was in the center.

"Concentrate your forces with Bogan," Halsey said.

Halsey wired McCain, en route to Ulithi, to return immediately even though he was 635 miles from the coast of Samar, an island to the northeast of Leyte.

Halsey continued to worry about enemy carriers because none had been reported. Ozawa's carriers were approaching from the north and would soon launch their planes to fly to bases in the Philippines, but they still had not been detected. Halsey sent Mitscher top secret instructions to keep the area north of Task Group 38.3 under close surveillance.

Capt. William H. "Bill' Buracker's light carrier *Princeton*, steaming with Sherman's group, ordered his men to battle stations at dawn on October 24 to attack Kurita's center force. This attack was canceled when radar spotted a large number of unidentified planes approaching from the direction of Manila. Then, radar plot called again. "There's a second group the same size, fifteen miles behind the first one." Buracker immediately ordered his ship's fighters into the air, and Sherman made the order universal while he maneuvered his ships into rain squalls for better protection.

Princeton's Fighting Twenty-seven ran into Japanese attackers from Vice-Admiral Fukudome's air fleet first and, with only eight Hellcat fighters, tore into the second formation of eighty planes.

Twenty-eight attackers fell, streaming flames into the ocean, but a Judy got through and dropped a bomb among loaded torpedo planes on the *Princeton*'s hangar deck. Damage control parties quickly went to work to put out raging fires.

Sherman now received orders to take his task group to the San Bernardino Strait to attack Kurita's ships, so he reluctantly had to leave the flaming *Princeton* behind. Just as it appeared that the flames were coming under control, a tremendous explosion killed many on the carrier and even crew members in the *Birmingham*, which was alongside evacuating men. The cruiser now also became an inferno, and blood literally covered her decks.

Captain Buracker aboard the *Princeton* gave the order, "Abandon ship!"

After rescuing the survivors, destroyers sent a spread of torpedoes into the doomed carrier. One of the casualties was Capt. John M. Hoskins, the *Princeton*'s prospective commanding officer, who was scheduled to take over in a few days. He lost a foot to a bomb fragment. When he later recovered, he was assigned to command a new Essex-class carrier renamed the U.S.S. *Princeton*.

Comdr. David McCampbell, commanding officer of *Essex*'s Air Group 15, had been told not to participate in scrambles if Japanese planes attacked. But when word of a large group of enemy planes was received and the *Princeton* requested assistance, he heard the call, "All fighter pilots man your planes!" There were only seven fighter pilots available, so McCampbell called the air officer and asked if that meant him, too.

He was told yes and started to strap on his parachute harness. The air officer called back, "No, you can't go on this flight."

"My plane is already on deck," he said in protest.

"Wait a minute."

The air officer spoke to the ship's captain and called McCampbell back. "Yes, by all means. With only seven planes available, we've *got* to intercept this Japanese flight."

As McCampbell dashed out to where his plane was being gassed up, he heard the air officer say over the bullhorn that he, the air group commander, was to report to him if his plane was not ready to go. McCampbell's tanks were not full, but he hurriedly dismissed the fueling detail and took off.

He knew that Sherman's task group was the most northern, only 130 miles or more from Manila across the island of Luzon. Most of his Hellcats had been sent out earlier to strafe fields, and now there were only seven available.

With Lt. Roy W. Rushing on his wing and five others behind, McCampbell saw a large formation in the distance in an area where Japanese planes had not been reported. At first, he thought they were American so he queried control and was told there were no American planes in that area.

He called back, "I have the enemy in sight."

What he did not realize was that these planes, approximately sixty in all, were from Ozawa's carriers to the north, heading for bases in the Philippines.

With only seven Hellcats to face almost nine times that number of Japanese planes, he radioed the *Essex* 30 miles away: "Please send help." Back came the response that there was no help available. They were on their own.

McCampbell was grateful that at least they were above the Japanese planes. They turned to the left, and McCampbell ordered his men to attack. Japanese bombers immediately dove through the overcast as McCampbell and Rushing headed into the formation while the other five were ordered to start at the top and hit stragglers or bombers. His orders were not understood and McCampbell and Rushing remained alone while the other five went down after the bombers.

The Japanese immediately went into a Lufberry Circle, a World War I-vintage trick of flying nose to tail for mutual protection. Soon the ring had forty airplanes in it. McCampbell signaled Rushing not to attack but to wait for the Japanese to make the first move. Occasionally, a Japanese plane would get too high and McCampbell would shoot it down. As the Japanese continued their merry-go-round, McCampbell called Rushing to say that the Japanese would soon run out of gas and to hold his fire. Sure enough, they broke the circle ten minutes later and headed in single file for Manila.

McCampbell advised Rushing that they would follow the Japanese planes all the way to Manila, and they shot down one here and there as it straggled, while he continually called for help. McCampbell finally got one American plane, but it quickly ran out of ammunition, and the pilot had to return to his ship.

McCampbell and Rushing bided their time, holding their fire until they could get a good shot. After downing fifteen Japanese planes between them in an hour and thirty-five minutes, they found themselves over Manila, low on gasoline and ammunition.

On their return to the *Essex*, they discovered that they could not land because their carrier had a full deck. McCampbell got down onto the deck of another carrier, his engine coughing just as it came out of the arresting gear. In its three-point attitude on deck, the engine was not receiving sufficient fuel.

McCampbell's seven Hellcat fighters had shot down twenty-seven Japanese planes that morning, and possibly eight more. He had personally shot down the highest single number of planes downed by a pilot in one day during the war.

McCampbell, who would soon receive a Medal of Honor for his exploits, was called in by his irate admiral, who demanded to know how he had got permission to participate in a flight against express orders. McCampbell explained the circumstances, and the admiral said, "All right, McCampbell, but don't let it happen again." He reminded him that he was not a fighter pilot but an air group commander.

Planes from the *Princeton* claimed an additional thirty-four Japanese planes, the *Lexington* thirteen, and the *Langley*'s Hellcats five more.

Kurita proceeded toward Leyte Gulf and sought air cover, but Fukudome's air fleet was now so devastated that he could offer no assistance. Kurita still had a considerable distance to transit in Philippine waters to pass through the San Bernardino Strait and arrive in Leyte Gulf. The sensible Japanese practice of attacking with their ships under a protective umbrella of land-based airpower in this case was therefore not possible

Early on the morning of the twenty-fourth, Lt. Gen. Kyoji Tominaga sent 150 of his planes against Sprague's baby flattops in Leyte Gulf. Encountering the massed fire of the warships surrounding the escort carriers, Tominaga's planes were driven off, and half were lost in action because of heavy antiaircraft fire and the skill of Sprague's Wildcat pilots.

About this time, Nishimura's seven warships entered the Sulu Sea, 300 miles south of Leyte Gulf, and were attacked by Davison's Task Group 38.4, which had been assigned to that area by Halsey's orders. The battleship *Fuso* and the destroyer *Shigure* were damaged in this encounter.

Reports to Halsey had identified two Japanese forces, but he was concerned about the failure to locate the Japanese carriers. He was only aware of Kurita's force in the Sibuyan Sea and of Nishimura's small fleet to the south.

As Nishimura continued north, more and more concerned about his lack of air cover—there was only one reconnaissance plane available—he came to expect the worst, but he had been ordered to hit the center of Leyte's eastern shore at 4 A.M. the following morning.

Kurita continued toward Leyte Gulf, heading in a zigzag course through the islands of the Philippine archipelago. He had divided his forces by the time he passed the southern tip of Mindoro, placing his flagship *Yamato* in the lead of the first formation and with the *Kongo* leading the second. The *Yamato* and her sister ship the *Musashi*, two of the world's largest battleships, composed the main striking elements of Kurita's fleet as it headed north through the Tablas Strait. Kurita, who was engaged in a desperate gamble to get at the American invasion ships, felt a keen sense of frustration because of his lack of air cover.

At 10:15 A.M. on October 24, his radar picked up a large group of American planes heading his way. These planes were from three of Bogan's carriers off the San Bernardino Strait.

Air Group Comdr. William E. Ellis led thirty-five planes into battle against Kurita's ships in perfect weather. Once they got within range to drop their torpedoes and bombs, however, antiaircraft fire grew intense, resulting in the loss of the torpedo planes and a Hellcat fighter whose pilot was later rescued.

As his ships fought off the attack, Kurita feared that he was in a desperate situation and became convinced of it after the first torpedo attack badly damaged the huge *Musashi* and the heavy cruiser *Myoko*. The *Myoko* was in such bad shape that Kurita ordered her to proceed alone to Brunei.

At 12:45, another wave of American planes attacked, seeking out the damaged *Musashi*. The mighty ship, whose steel blister-protected sides were designed to reduce the havoc caused by torpedoes, was struck three times. American fliers watched in awe as she slowed down, evidently badly hurt because she drifted in circles.

Kurita suspected correctly that he was facing Halsey's fast carriers, which were supposed to have been lured north by Ozawa's tempting carriers. He wired Ozawa, "Subjected to repeated enemy carrier-based air attacks. Advise immediately of contacts and attacks made by you on enemy." Next he called for fighter protection from Manila, but they had none to spare. At this time, of course, Fukudome's air fleet had all it could do to stand off Sherman's group near Luzon.

Admiral Davison's carriers worked over the Japanese ships, which eventually came south around Leyte, making their first contact at 9:18 A.M. in the Sulu Sea. The ships were at extreme range and as they got closer, the American strikes became more effective. The men in Davison's task group were therefore disappointed when they were called north at 9:00 P.M. on October 24 to concentrate with the other task groups. Before Halsey's order came, however, Davison's air groups joined in several strikes against Kurita's force.

Comdr. Dan Smith of the *Enterprise*'s Air Group 20 arrived to find Kurita's ships proceeding at 20 knots eastward despite the damage they had suffered. Kurita's guns opened up before they came within range, and Smith watched the colored bursts carefully. They trailed his formation so he stopped worrying about flak and ordered an attack against the *Yamato* and *Musashi*.

Air Group 13 now arrived from the *Franklin*. Smith called over the radio to the *Franklin*'s leader, "You take the *Yamato*. We'll take *Musashi*."

He winged over and his formation followed. Japanese guns stopped firing when they entered a cloud bank but opened up with renewed intensity once they emerged. Smith led his torpedo planes in; eight torpedoes seemed to score direct hits, three appeared to be near misses.

The *Musashi* lay still in the water, her entire forecastle awash. Kurita, noting the *Musashi*'s condition, ordered her to reverse course.

Kurita was almost in a state of shock. His attack force had undergone five air attacks in the last six hours. He was behind schedule, having intended to steam through San Bernardino Strait after sundown. The fierceness of the American attacks had increased each time, and he was completely without air support to counter them.

He decided to retire temporarily beyond the range of the relentless navy planes and to proceed with the attack later. This decision, of course, further upset the timetable to rendezvous with Nishimura's and Shima's forces coming up from the south.

Toyoda's carefully laid plans seemed to have failed because Kurita thought that Ozawa's carriers had not diverted Halsey from the invasion area. His central force had been savagely reduced, and Kurita felt that he was fighting the battle alone with nothing to show for his sacrifices. He retreated through the Sibuyan Sea while fliers from Davison's Task Group 38.4 made a final attack just before 6:00 P.M.

The *Musashi* had received nineteen torpedo and seventeen bomb hits. American navy fliers were astounded that she remained afloat.

They reported to Davison that they believed she would sink. He, in turn, passed the word to Mitscher and Halsey, who did not believe it.

They were wrong. The *Musashi* sank not long after the last attack when efforts to beach her on the north coast of Sibuyan Island failed. She capsized at twilight, taking 2,200 members of her crew with her to the bottom of the sea.

In Tokyo, when Toyoda learned that Kurita was in retreat, he was beside himself. He had told Kurita earlier that the assault on the Philippines had to be stopped even at the sacrifice of the entire Japanese fleet.

Kurita, who had planned only a temporary withdrawal, had already turned his force around and headed back toward San Bernardino Strait when he received a blunt message from his commander in chief: "With confidence in heavenly guidance, the entire force will attack!"

Adm. Soemu Toyoda.
Courtesy U.S. Navy

After attacking Japanese shipping in the China Sea during January 1945, an SB2–C returns to the *Hornet* and awaits landing instructions.
Courtesy U.S. Navy

American carrier rides heavy seas off Iwo Jima on February 19, 1945, in support of invasion forces. *Official U.S. Navy photograph*

The Sixth Fleet during the invasion of Iwo Jima on September 14, 1945. Mount Suribachi is at center. *Official U.S. Navy photograph*

D Day on Iwo Jima, as Fourth Division Marines land on the volcanic island.
Official U.S. Navy photograph

The *Yamato* maneuvers to avoid navy bombs and torpedoes on April 7, 1945.
Courtesy U.S. Navy

Finally, the *Yamato* goes down.
Courtesy U.S. Navy

The fleet assembles in Tokyo Bay. With Mount Fujiyama in the background, fleets of Allied nations anchor around the *Missouri* for the final Japanese surrender.
Courtesy U.S. Navy

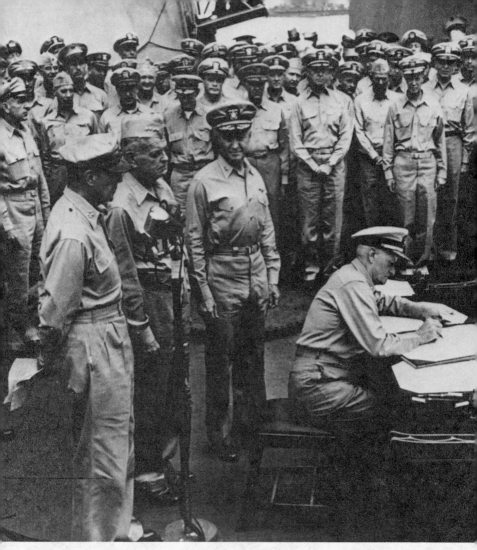

Admiral Nimitz signs the Japanese surrender document. Looking on, from left: Gen. Douglas MacArthur, Adm. William F. Halsey, and Rear Adm. Forrest P. Sherman, Nimitz's deputy chief of staff.
Courtesy U.S. Navy

16

"WHAT THE HELL'S THE MATTER WITH YOU?"

Kurita radioed messages to Toyoda and Admiral Nishimura, whose southern attack force was also en route to Leyte Gulf. "My four battleships, six cruisers, two light cruisers, and eleven destroyers will pass through the San Bernardino Strait at 1:00 A.M. tonight. Will proceed southward down east coast of Samar and arrive Leyte Gulf 11:00 A.M. October 25."

Halsey was still obsessed with the absence of any report on Japanese carriers. "It is unthinkable that the Japs would undertake a major operation without carrier support," he told his staff.

Admiral Mitscher, with Sherman's Task Group 38.3, remained under constant attack from bases in the Philippines. Rain squalls gave some respite from attackers, but pilots reported that many of the 150 planes they had shot down were carrier types. Mitscher's suspicions that carriers were in the vicinity were strengthened by these disclosures, and he dispatched scouts to patrol the northeast.

While Kurita's main striking force had been retiring at 4:40 P.M. on the afternoon of October 24, Mitscher's planes finally contacted an enemy force 200 miles off northern Luzon. At first they reported spotting three battleships, six carriers, and six destroyers. Ranging farther afield, the planes then reported three more carriers, three cruisers, and three destroyers, all on a westerly heading.

Kurita having reversed his course, orders came from Halsey after dark on October 24 to steam west at 25 knots. After steaming west for what seemed like an interminable time, the task group's chief of staff, James Russell, turned to Davison. "Admiral, at about twenty-two hundred hours we'll run aground on the island of Samar."

Davison smiled. "Well, Jerry Bogan will run aground first, won't he?"

Bogan's task group was farther to the west. Russell replied, "Sir, that's right."

That ended their conversation. Then, as suddenly as Halsey had given his preceding order, he issued a new one: "Steam north at 25 knots."

All ships made simultaneous 90-degree turns to the right.

A short time later, Captain Russell heard Halsey's watch officer come on the tactical radio net and using Halsey's voice call, ask Mitscher what he made of the situation. With no delay Mitscher's chief of staff, Commodore Arleigh Burke, came on and using Mitscher's voice call, said, "I recommend you form Leo." Leo was the voice call for Task Force Thirty-four. In voice communication, when a voice call is given as the originator of a message, the message bears the authority of the officer whose voice call is used whether the person speaking is the staff watch officer, chief of staff, or the officer himself.

There was a pause of several minutes, then Halsey ordered, "Form Leo."

The word was passed to the designated ships in Davison's task group to break away from the formation and report to Vice-Adm. Willis A. Lee to become part of his Task Force Thirty-four. In the process, Davison's Task Group 38.4 shrank to about two thirds of its normal size.

Unknown to Davison and Russell, Commodore Burke had prepared a number of messages in the last few hours for his boss, Admiral Mitscher, to send to Halsey. In effect, they all said, we should plug the straits. Get your battleships down there. We can polish off the carriers to the north.

Each time, Mitscher had glanced at the messages and shook his head. He was under the same impression as Davison that Halsey had information they did not. It was axiomatic that one never questioned a commander once a decision was made.

"No," Mitscher replied, "they have more intelligence than we do. But this doesn't look right to me."

Ever since Halsey had learned that Japanese carriers had been located north of Luzon, he had felt a sense of relief. The reports of a southern attack force apparently coming through Surigao Strait, had been confirmed by noon on October 24. He believed that at last the Japanese fleet was all accounted for.

Halsey paced the bridge of his flagship. The news called for a decisive move by his Third Fleet. It appeared that concerted action was planned by the Japanese for the following day, October 25.

Halsey finally decided. He would take Task Force Thirty-four under Vice-Adm. Willis A. Lee, Jr., with six new battleships and his fast carriers to attack the northern carrier force.

Halsey briefed Admiral Lee on his estimate of the situation and his decision to go after the carriers. Lee objected. He suspected that the Japanese might be trying to divert attention from a main striking force that could spell disaster for the invasion fleet off Leyte. "I don't trust the sons of bitches," he said forcefully.

Halsey was adamant. "Destruction of the enemy carrier force offers the best possibility of defending the invasion front."

"It will leave the San Bernardino Strait unguarded," Lee said.

"The center force has been struck severe blows," Halsey said. "They may inflict more damage, but any advantage the Japs may gain can be overcome by prompt action of the fast carriers." He added that if Kurita did return, Kinkaid's fleet of battleships could repulse him.

If Halsey had known that Ozawa's carriers were almost planeless, perhaps his decision would have been to remain guarding the Leyte Gulf invasion forces.

Toyoda's plan was finally working out as he had intended.

At 11:30 on the night of October 24, Sherman's Task Group 38.3 joined Halsey and the other two task groups for the run north. Mitscher was in command of the fast carrier task force under Halsey. Halsey's flagship the *New Jersey* was integrated tactically with Task Group 38.3 after Task Force Thirty-four—Leo—was formed. After dark on October 24, the *New Jersey*, Task Force Thirty-four, and the three task groups headed north to make contact with Ozawa's ships.

While Leo was being formed, Russell watched the radarscope as battleships and some of the cruisers moved like amoebas changing shape. It was fascinating to see the ships carefully threading their way through the huge formation and join up in the east in a traditional battle line, with battleships in the center and destroyers and cruisers in the van and in the rear.

Davison joined him, and they looked with amazement as the Leo formation continued to steam north with them.

They stared at the radarscope in astonishment. They could not believe that the Leo formation had not been ordered to head south to protect the San Bernardino Strait.

Davison turned to Russell, "Jim, we're playing a helluva dirty trick on the transports in Leyte Gulf."

"Do you wish to say anything to Admiral Mitscher?"

Davison signified that he did not, saying that Mitscher had more information than they had.

Earlier, at 7:25 P.M., Vice-Adm. Thomas C. Kinkaid, commander of the Seventh Fleet, had received an urgent message that an enemy force had been sighted off Sibuyan Island. Kinkaid had no doubt that the enemy's prime target was the transports in Leyte Gulf. At first, he was not unduly alarmed because he had received word from Halsey shortly after 3 P.M. that Task Force Thirty-four would be formed and assumed that its heavy ships would engage such a force and turn it back. Halsey had, however, failed to advise Kinkaid that he was taking it against the northern Japanese carrier force. The San Bernardino Strait, therefore, was completely undefended.

While Halsey's fleet steamed north, enemy ships were reported heading for Leyte from the south. Also, night scouts revealed that the shore beacons were lighted in the San Bernardino Strait and that a Japanese force was coming through the strait.

Halsey had told Kinkaid that he was taking three groups to attack the enemy carrier force at dawn on the 25th. The fourth, McCain's Task Group 38.1, was still far south but en route back north under Halsey's emergency orders. Kinkaid thought it was guarding the San Bernardino Strait.

He also believed that Halsey had promised him that Task Force Thirty-four would be available if Kurita returned, or at least he had assumed that he would. Halsey had had no such intention.

An antisubmarine plane assigned to the Seventh Air Force reported at 12:37 A.M. on October 25 that a large Japanese fleet was passing out of the eastern end of the San Bernardino Strait off the north coast of Samar. This was Kurita's fleet, headed toward Leyte Gulf. Later, Kinkaid received word that still another surface force was coming up from the south.

Rear Adm. Jesse B. Oldendorf, commanding the Leyte bombardment and fire support ships, was shocked to receive word to "prepare for a night engagement."

He in turn dashed off a message to his commanders, "Consider surface attack tonight via Surigao Strait imminent. Make all preparations."

Admiral Oldendorf planned to plug Surigao Strait. He flanked both sides with cruisers and destroyers and sent five torpedo boats and scouting destroyers deep into it.

Admiral Nishimura's seven warships now emerged from the Mindanao Sea through the Surigao Strait to rendezvous with Kurita, who was coming down from the north. They were attacked repeatedly by PT boats and destroyers, who reported that the Japanese warships were in two groups, one 40 miles behind the other. Admiral Nishimura was ahead with the battleships *Fuso* and *Yamashiro* and a heavy cruiser and four destroyers.

In the rear, a second force under Admiral Shima had two heavy cruisers, a light cruiser, and four destroyers. Shima had left Japan's Inland Sea under orders to assist Nishimura, but the latter had had no report of Shima's whereabouts. Even more incredible, the only word Admiral Kurita had received from Nishimura was that he had located the Americans.

Oldendorf had positioned his battleships across the entrance to Leyte Gulf and sent his PT boats in first. Five of his six battleships had been repaired after having been damaged at Pearl Harbor. He also had four heavy cruisers, including the Royal Australian Navy's *Shropshire*. His destroyers went against Nishimura's ship at 3 A.M., hitting several with torpedoes and sinking the destroyer *Yamagumo*.

Nishimura's fleet, with the battleships *Yamashiro* and *Fuso*, the cruiser *Mogami*, and the destroyer *Shigure*, proceeded north to continue the battle. They sailed into a well-laid trap. Moving in a single column, they allowed Oldendorf's older battleships to cross the "T" ahead of them, so that only the forward batteries of Nishimura's ships could be brought to bear in battle. It was an event of which admirals had long dreamed but few had ever seen as the massed firepower of Oldendorf's ships sent full broadsides into Nishimura's ships, making them exploding hells. Nishimura was one of the first to die, perishing at 4:19 A.M.

Admiral Shima, who took orders only from Admiral Toyoda in Japan, entered the Surigao Strait just as the holocaust ended. His ship blinked a challenge to a ship heading south.

"I am the *Shigure*," the ship replied. Then it sped on, the only survivor of Nishimura's fleet.

"I am the *Nachi*," Shima's ship answered.

Neither ship bothered to question the other further but went their separate ways.

Shima's flagship passed the burning cruiser *Mogami* and quickly recognized that ships ahead were not Japanese. He ordered a turn, which was executed in such haste that his flagship collided with the *Mogami*. Although his cruiser was badly damaged, he steamed south and escaped through Surigao Strait. The *Mogami* got underway later but planes from escort carriers found her. She was sunk along with the *Abukumo*, also of Shima's force.

Admiral Clifton Sprague's six escort carriers (called CVEs), supported by three destroyers and four destroyer escorts, were designed primarily to support amphibious operations. They were not intended to fight against heavy warships: They were thin-skinned, and their attack aircraft were TBM torpedo planes that could carry torpedoes and 500-pound bombs or depth charges. The CVEs were, as many bluejackets humorously said, combustible, vulnerable, and expendable.

The CVE's deck was only half the length of that of a standard carrier, and each carried a complement of eighteen to thirty-six planes composed of Avengers and an improved model of the old Wildcat. The landing area was built over a hull designed for a tanker or merchantman. Baby flattops were, therefore, used primarily for the air support of troops and for antisubmarine patrols. Now they faced some of the mightiest warships in the Japanese navy.

Sprague's group was one of three that had arrived on October 18 to support the invasion. As Kurita headed directly toward them, they were 50 miles off the southern coast of Samar. Rear Adm. Felix Stump headed another group 30 miles to the southeast, and Rear Adm. Thomas L. Sprague had a third group 120 miles away.

The two opposing forces spotted each other simultaneously. Kurita quickly changed course to the east and when 18 miles away, ordered the *Yamato* to open fire—the first time those big 18-inch guns had been used in anger.

It was a minute before 7:00 A.M. on October 25 when salvos started creeping toward the escort carriers. There had been no time to change the loading of the planes, and even the torpedo planes had only small general-purpose bombs normally used for troop support.

Sprague ordered the destroyers to attack first. "Lay a smoke screen between the Japs and our carriers."

Slow destroyer escorts formed a large circle, with the *St. Lô* to the north and the *Kalinin Bay, Gambier Bay, Kitkun Bay, White Plains*, and Sprague's flagship *Fanshaw Bay* completing the formation.

The *Gambier Bay* and *Kalinin Bay* received severe punishment as Japanese cruisers poured their fire into them. Thin-skinned destroyer escorts attacked the cruisers, each with only two 5-inch guns to challenge the cruisers' heavy batteries.

It was an unequal contest, but the escort carriers emitted heavy smoke for concealment and made wildly evasive turns at full speed, barely dodging most of the heavy shells from the cruisers. In spite of American air and torpedo attacks, Japanese cruisers closed in, and hits were scored on the *Fanshaw*, *Kalinin*, and *Gambier*.

An order from the flagship barked over the radio. "Small boys [U.S. destroyers] on the starboard quarter, intercept enemy cruiser coming down on the port quarter." Destroyers and destroyer escorts fought valiantly, but there was little they could do. Soon the destroyer *Hoel* sank after heavy fire, and the *Johnson* received mortal wounds.

Sprague's force was now completely out of torpedoes. It was pressed closer and closer to Samar, only 15 miles away, by Japanese battleship attacks from astern.

Halsey's strong force continued to steam north at maximum speed after a search plane from the *Lexington* had sighted Ozawa's fleet late in the afternoon of the previous day. After Ozawa was located, Mitscher's Task Force Thirty-eight proceeded to close the distance separating them. The previous night, Mitscher had recommended to Halsey that the strategy be changed. Halsey had agreed that Lee's Task Force Thirty-four, with its six new battleships, should precede the carriers by 10 miles.

During the early morning hours of October 25, while Kurita's attack force moved along the coast of Samar to engage Oldendorf's fleet near Leyte Gulf, Mitscher's planes had lost contact with Ozawa's fleet. Mitscher was worried that the Japanese would spot them and launch an attack so he ordered some planes into the air. Meanwhile, search planes roamed widely over the surrounding areas to locate the enemy carriers.

It was a cloudless morning as Mitscher's attack planes remained 50 miles in advance of the fleet with all eyes searching for telltale signs of Ozawa's presence.

While Kurita's ships were attacking Oldendorf's fleet near Leyte, Halsey received word from Kinkaid. "Is TF 34 guarding San Bernardino Strait?"

Halsey impatiently replied that Task Force Thirty-four was with him. A frantic wire came back immediately, reporting that Kurita's battleships were shelling escort carriers off Samar.

Mitscher's staff remained in steady conference, trying to anticipate Ozawa's next move. When the carriers failed to show up in their search sectors, Mitscher paid close attention to one member of his staff who said, "I think, sir, enemy carriers are farther east."

"You may be right. Send four planes from the *Essex* combat air patrol to search the northeast."

At 7:30 A.M., the search by scouts to the east bore fruit. A pilot spotted enemy carriers on a northeasterly course and reported their latitude and longitude. Once the coordinates were plotted, it was revealed that the Japanese carriers were 130 miles away.

Mitscher broke radio silence to call up his airborne planes. "Ninety-nine Rebel. Take charge of incoming strike and get the carriers."

This message was for target coordinator David McCampbell, who issued orders to his attack groups. "Follow me in," he called as he spotted the Japanese fleet steaming within a radius of five miles with four carriers, two or more battleships, and a number of smaller ships. His wingman, Lt. Wayne Morris, followed McCampbell in an attack on the Japanese fighters. McCampbell, who would end his operational tour with more victories than any other navy pilot, soon brought his score to thirty-four. There were twenty-seven aces in his group.

While Ozawa's fleet came under attack, "Ziggy" Sprague called in plain English from his flagship in Leyte Gulf, "I am being shelled by a Japanese battleship." This message was picked up by Seventh Fleet Commander Kinkaid aboard the *Wasatch* in Leyte Gulf.

Sprague's support fleet seemed doomed to annihilation as Kurita's ships steamed toward it. Admiral Lee's battleships, which everyone but the men in Halsey's command thought were guarding the San Bernardino Strait, were still heading toward Ozawa's fleet under Halsey's orders.

Meanwhile, with Ozawa's carriers in sight, McCampbell swung toward them and gave his plane full throttle to provide protection for the strike groups.

Commander Daniel Smith called his air group, "Pick one out, boys, and let him have it."

McCampbell spotted fifteen to eighteen Oscar single-engine fighters dead ahead, which were quickly eliminated. As his group approached the enemy fleet, not a single enemy airplane appeared, but the sky seemed carpeted by flak.

McCampbell signaled to attack as the Japanese ships "went every whichway." He watched the carrier turn out of formation as if preparing to launch airplanes. Bombers plummeted down on the hapless carrier, and McCampbell ordered torpedo planes to head for a battleship.

When Smith's group finished its attacks, every ship trailed oil and the carrier *Chitose*, smothered by bombs, sank. The largest carrier, the *Zuikaku*, was hit aft by a torpedo, and the light carriers *Zuiho* and *Choyoda* were bombed heavily. The *Choyoda* was hit so badly that it had to leave the protection of the formation. Surface ships also took a drubbing, and the destroyer *Akitsuki* blew up and sank, while the light cruiser *Tama* was slowed dramatically by torpedo hits.

While the first strike was underway, Halsey received another urgent dispatch from Kinkaid. "Jap battleships and cruisers are fifteen miles astern of my escort carriers off Samar."

Halsey was irritated by the message. This quiet, efficient officer, who had been in all major Pacific actions, had never panicked. Then Comdr. Malcolm T. Wordell reported that the *Zuiho*, the carrier that had sunk the old *Hornet*, was under attack.

Kinkaid continued to send frantic messages. At 8:02, he reported that enemy ships (the remnants of Nishimura's fleet) were retiring through the Surigao Strait. Halsey was relieved that the situation at Leyte Gulf seemed to be under control but then he was confused by another message from Kinkaid received at 8:22 A.M. "Enemy battleships and cruiser reported firing on TU-77.4.3." This task unit was Clifton Sprague's group of CVEs.

At 9:00 A.M. Kinkaid wired, "Our CVEs being attacked by four BBs, eight cruisers plus others. Request Lee cover Leyte and at top speed."

At 9:22, Kinkaid wired, "CTU 77.4.3 under attack by cruisers and BBs. Request immediate air strike. Also request support by heavy ships. My OBBs," a reference to his old battleships, "low on ammunition."

Halsey still refused to act, and Kinkaid was desperate by 10:00 A.M. His next message was sent in the clear, and it was picked up by Nimitz' radio monitors. The message, which was immediately referred to Nimitz, said, "Where is Lee? Send Lee."

Nimitz sent off a message that contained the usual nonsense wordage at beginning and end to confuse Japanese decoders: "Turkey trots to water GG, From Cincpac, Action Com Third Fleet, Info CTF 77, where is rpt where is Task Force Thirty-four RR the world wonders."

Before a message was delivered, all padding was supposed to be dropped. Despite the letters RR, the last three words seemed to make sense to Halsey's decoders, and they were kept in the message that went to Halsey. Halsey flushed as he read the message, assuming that he was being rebuked. His hands shook, and he snatched off his cap, hurled it to the deck, and swore.

Rear Adm. Robert B. Carney grabbed Halsey's arm. "Stop it! What the hell's the matter with you? Pull yourself together."

Halsey thrust the message at Carney and rushed off. He was bitter and for an hour angrily refused to give the order to Admiral Lee to return.

Admiral King in Washington had also been alerted. He was angry with Halsey, telling his chief of staff, "He has left the Strait of San Bernardino open for the Japanese to strike the transports at Leyte!"

At Leyte Gulf, Sprague was convinced that his force would be quickly destroyed by Kurita's ships, which moved in at 8:30 A.M. An order was issued over the TBS "talk between ships" system. "Small boys [destroyers] on the starboard quarter interpose with smoke between carriers and enemy cruisers."

Rolling clouds of smoke created momentary protection but the task group's torpedo planes, unable to rearm, were forced to make dummy runs on enemy ships.

While Kinkaid was sending frantic wires to Halsey, Sprague managed to move the carrier formation to a southwesterly direction by 9:10 A.M. so he could head for Leyte Gulf. He expected total destruction now that they were almost defenseless. Japanese cruisers bore down on them until they were only 10,000 yards away. This was point-blank range for their 8-inch guns, and Sprague resigned himself to the inevitable. He had lost the *Gambier Bay*, three destroyers were sunk or sinking, and other ships were badly hit.

Sprague, lost in thought, looked up as someone shouted, "They're turning back!"

He could hardly believe it. It was true! Just as his force faced annihilation, the Japanese abandoned the battle.

The two carrier groups to the south, in the enemy's rear, were now in position to launch attacks. Admiral Stump, in the center, had found time to equip his planes with torpedoes and semiarmor piercing bombs as well as rockets. He launched six attacks. A lone enemy kamikaze plane got through to the escort carrier *St. Lô* and sank it.

Kurita, after learning what had happened to Nishimura, beat a hasty retreat at 9:11 A.M. His force had been cut in half with the loss of one of his five battleships and half his ten cruisers. As he headed back for San Bernardino Strait, McCain's task group harassed him from the air while Thirteenth Air Force B–24s pounded him en route to Brunei.

The whole operation was an inept exhibition of Japanese sea power in that neither Kurita, Nishimura, or Shima coordinated their separate drives. After the war, Kurita explained his actions by saying that once the Americans knew he was coming, he did not believe that they would leave their transports in Leyte Gulf. He thus gave them credit for more sense than Halsey demonstrated at the time. He also believed Japanese reports that four Essex-class carriers, possibly six, had been sunk earlier. Of course, these reports were in error. When he encountered the CVEs, he did not know what to believe, thinking that they were fast carriers.

Kurita claimed that at first he went north intending to join the action against Halsey's forces, who were attacking Ozawa, but that action receded to the north so rapidly that the distance required more fuel than his destroyers had available. Therefore, he retired through the San Bernardino Strait.

Kurita had launched cruiser scout planes over Leyte Gulf, but they just disappeared, so he was operating blindly without any information about disposition of the American fleet. He assumed, in error, that there were no ships left in Leyte Gulf. Also, he believed that there were two active American airstrips on Leyte—which was not true—so he would have to face land-based airpower.

Halsey finally ordered Lee to return to the San Bernardino Strait at maximum speed, and his ships turned south. By now, of course, Kurita was in retreat and all danger to Kinkaid's fleet was past. Much to Bogan's dismay, Halsey ordered his carrier task group to provide air cover.

With the wind from the northeast, and Lee's battleships steaming at maximum speed, Bogan's ships were left farther and farther behind because they had to turn into the wind repeatedly to keep planes in the air.

Lee sent word over the voice tactical net through two linking destroyers that had been placed in position for line-of-sight transmission. "Close up on me," meaning don't lag behind.

Bogan was infuriated. "This is Bogan," he replied. "You are running away from me! Suggest you retire to the protection of the carriers' guns." Although Lee had the navy's most modern battleships, he of course had to have fighter cover when he came within range of shore-based Japanese bombers.

Bogan was angered because he had been denied a chance to continue his attacks on the Japanese carriers, leaving all the "pie and cake" up north because it was now apparent that Ozawa's almost planeless ships were sitting ducks with practically no aerial defenses.

After Task Force Thirty-four and Bogan's task group were sent south, the destruction of Ozawa's ships continued without letup. Halsey remained bitter, believing that he had been called off the biggest sea battle of the century and that a major part of his command had been forced to take part in an unnecessary battle at Leyte Gulf. At the time, he was not aware that that battle was all over, with Kurita in full retreat and that Task Force Thirty-four and Bogan's group would arrive too late to take part.

Mitscher, with the two remaining groups, carried on the attack against Ozawa, whose fleet was in a deplorable state after the second wave of American planes finished their bombing at 11:00 A.M. His flagship the *Zuikaku* proved difficult to steer so he transferred to the light cruiser *Oyoda*. He also decided to draw the American carriers farther north, but then a third wave of 150 planes appeared under the direction of Comdr. Richard L. Kibbe of the *Franklin*'s Air Group 13 and Comdr. Hugh Winters of the *Lexington*'s Air Group 19.

Mitscher had told them, "Stay over the target as long as your gas holds out."

Winters looked down at the Japanese fleet and counted three carriers, two battleships, and three cruisers. They lacked formation, and there were cripples among them. He called his group's attention to two carriers heading north and directed them to attack the *Zuikaku*. Their bombs covered the carrier's deck, then torpedoes hit and plumes of water shot high into the air. The *Zuikaku* caught fire but burned for two hours before she sank.

The *Zuiho* was tougher to hit. Smaller and extremely maneuverable at high speeds, she stoutly absorbed several strikes.

Winters wrote rapidly on his knee pad, not trusting his memory at the height of the air battle, that a cruiser and a destroyer were sneaking off to the northwest. He called the air group commander, "Follow that oil slick to the northwest. You'll find a big Jap cruiser."

Mitscher, apprised of the situation, sent his cruisers and destroyers forward to pick off the stragglers and cripples. The *Chiyoda* became the first victim.

Air group commanders, in the excitement of engaging in one at-

tack after another, failed to satisfy the curiosity of carrier commanders as to details of the action. The calls repeated over and over,
"Get the carriers!" Finally, in exasperation, Winters called back to
the *Lexington*. "They're all going under the water." He heard a
whoop on the radio, then silence. At last, an excited voice said,
"That's all we wanted to know."

Commander Malcolm T. Wordell of the *Langley*'s Air Group 44
coordinated the last two strikes of the day. His planes were equipped
with armor-piercing bombs that finally sank the stubborn *Zuiho* after
three hours of action.

Ozawa had fulfilled his mission as decoy and turned hastily toward Japan with the remnants of his fleet, including the battleship-
carriers *Ise* and *Hyuga*. He had lost four carriers, a light cruiser, two
destroyers, and all his aircraft.

Instead of limping northeast to his home port, Ozawa would have
been wiser to have fled south. Because the wind was from the northeast that day, the American carriers could launch planes without
changing course from the direction in which the Japanese ships were
fleeing, and it was easier to stay with them. If the Japanese ships
had gone toward the Philippines, the American carriers would have
had to turn away from them each time. It took seven minutes to
turn into the wind to launch or recover planes. Thus, some Japanese
carriers might have had time to escape.

Once Japanese ships were in home waters, however, they were
turned over to American submarine commanders, and other American ships were ordered not to follow them.

The Japanese were amazed that American carriers could remain
on station so long. That was possible because eight to twelve oilers
were stationed approximately 400 miles east of Leyte to refuel ships
on a specific schedule. The Japanese were led to believe that the
Americans had more ships than they actually had because available
ships were refueled so quickly in the combat zone.

Capt. William Rassieur guarded the oilers with two small carriers.
These were not converted ships, but rather a type that Kaiser Indus-
tries were producing at the rate of one a week expressly as escort
carriers. Rassieur's *Sargent Bay* had a 500-foot deck, and its planes
flew cover for oilers, which were also guarded by a huge destroyer
screen and other ships totaling twenty-eight in number. At times, as
many as ten carriers were under his protection as they came in on
the specified days and hours between their operations in order to be
refueled.

The small escort carriers were covered with only three-eighths of an inch of steel, which a shell could pass through as if through paper, but they provided the margin for victory at Leyte Gulf. Pilots disliked them because every foot of their flight decks was needed to get airborne, and the ships rolled badly in heavy seas. During an extremely bad storm, it was necessary to steam at two or three knots with the wind on the stern.

The first small carrier, the *Liscome Bay*, had gone down during the invasion of the Gilberts, breaking apart quickly after it was hit by a torpedo. Almost all her men were lost. It was a fact that captains of these carriers never forgot.

Kaiser also produced these escort carriers for the British. They were identical, except that the British had ordered bath tubs instead of shower stalls.

At 10:30 A.M., while the last of Ozawa's ships were being chased north, planes from the *Hancock, Hornet,* and *Wasp* left McCain's group, although they were 335 miles from the Japanese. They had to be lightly loaded because of the distance, but the carriers were closing fast and the return flight would not be so long. The planes located Kurita's ships along the coast of Samar at 1:10 P.M. and swooped down to attack the fleeing ships. A second strike of fifty-three planes went after the Japanese with bombs and rockets at 3:00 P.M.

Halsey kept alert eyes on the dispatches. By now, it was apparent that Kurita's center force was in full retreat, heading for the San Bernardino escape route. Halsey ordered Task Force Thirty-four to block the exit, but three hours before Lee's ships arrived Kurita sneaked through under cover of darkness at 9:30 P.M. with almost all his remaining ships. The large destroyer *Nowaki* failed to make it and was destroyed.

Carriers of Bogan's group, which came down to cover Task Force Thirty-four, joined McCain's group, launching at dawn the following morning and attacking the enemy in Tablas Strait along the east coast of Mindoro. The light cruiser *Noshiro* succumbed to their bombs. Fifth Air Force B–24s also made an attack on Kurita's remaining ships but only managed to straddle the *Yamato*. Kurita's First Diversion Attack Force at last reached the Sulu Sea beyond the range of Third Fleet carriers.

It had been a nerve-shattering experience for all participants, and Halsey warmly praised their handling of a tight situation. "For brilliance, courage, and tireless fighting heart the all-hands performance since early October will never be surpassed. It has been an honor to be your commander. Well done, Halsey."

Halsey could not say the same for his own decision making.

Under cover of the great sea battles, Japan managed to get two thousand men ashore at Ormoc with protection provided by the destroyer *Uranami* and the light cruiser *Kinu*. After Japanese troops were safely on the beaches, Stump's escort carriers sank the two warships and two of the transports.

One final action completed the historic battle. The *Shiranuhi*, one of Shima's destroyers, was caught off Panay Island by carrier planes and went to the bottom.

The Japanese almost succeeded in destroying the Leyte beachhead and its support ships, but without sufficient carrier aviation to provide decisive support, the land-based airplanes and Kamikaze Corps were unable to protect surface ships. Kurita could have done considerable damage if he had not broken off the action. He was, however, acting almost blindly, with neither air cover nor scouts ahead of his ships, and the confined waters of Leyte Gulf were no place to fight without airpower.

Kurita suffered from extremely poor communications with other forces. He never received three important messages from Ozawa. Also, in his last drive to the invasion area, he thought he faced a carrier group of five or six carriers and battleships instead of the escort carriers that had fought so valiantly. If he had known that Mitscher's carriers were attacking Ozawa on the morning of October 25, he would have continued into Leyte Gulf, knowing that he would encounter little opposition.

Kinkaid's Seventh Fleet, whose primary mission was to land troops and support them, had fought aggressively and with remarkable courage.

Total American losses were the light carrier *Princeton* and the escort carriers *Gambier Bay* and *St. Lô*, plus two destroyers and a destroyer escort.

The Japanese suffered a staggering blow. Their Combined Fleet in effect ceased to exist. They lost three battleships, the *Musashi*, *Yamashiro*, and *Fuso*; the large carrier *Zuikaku*; and the light carriers *Chitose*, *Chiyoda*, and *Zuiho*. Their other losses included six heavy cruisers, four light cruisers, and eleven destroyers.

After the invasion of the Marianas and the Allied triumph at the Battle of the Philippine Sea, the Imperial Japanese Navy found that it had lost 1,500 trained flying personnel. It was a setback from which it would never recover.

17

A LESSON
ABOUT AIRPOWER

Once four divisions of Lieutenant General Krueger's Sixth Army were put ashore by Kinkaid's Seventh Fleet, Admiral Halsey wired Nimitz at Guam and King in Washington. "In the course of protecting our Leyte landings, the back of the Japanese fleet has been broken."

Halsey wired MacArthur on October 26: "After seventeen days of steady fighting, the fast carrier force is virtually out of bombs, torpedoes, and provisions. Its pilots are exhausted. Unable to provide any intensive direct air support. When will your land-based air take over responsibility for direct support to the troops in Leyte–Samar area?" General Kenney responded that his Fifth Air Force would take over all targets in the Philippines and that the navy should confine itself to shipping.

Until now, carriers had methodically helped to clean out the remaining Japanese planes at their bases and provide direct support to ground troops. The *Enterprise*'s Dan Smith at this time fulfilled a long standing desire to explode a locomotive. On another day, flying so low that he could see under the trees, Smith spotted a number of parked aircraft. Circling above, he was astonished to see hundreds of airplanes concealed under palm trees, hidden from above by thick vegetation. He flashed the word to the *Enterprise* and organized an immediate attack. In the strike that followed, 120 Japanese planes were destroyed.

These were the kinds of strikes ground troops had grown accustomed to, and reduced Japanese air operations resulting from the destruction of planes in storage were soon evident.

After many difficulties, the army established airstrips for P–38 fighters, but defense of the area was beyond their limited capabilities. Army long-range B–24 bombers and P–38s found it impossible to stop the landing of the enemy's crack First Division despite strong attacks.

When Lt. Gen. Sosaku Zusuki, commander of the Thirty-fifth Imperial Army, landed on the same day, it was evident that Allied air had lost control of the air space above Leyte after most of the carrier planes had been withdrawn. During this difficult period, the Japanese increased their Leyte forces by 22,400 men because the main source of enemy air strength was on Luzon, out of reach of Army Air Force planes.

When units of the Third Fleet were ordered to Ulithi, Halsey had to leave two groups of seven carriers to aid the deteriorating air situation. Every ship in the fleet was stripped of ammunition for the carriers remaining behind.

On the morning of October 30, 1944, Task Force Fifty-eight arrived southeast of the island of Kyushu for strikes against airfields. It was given the mission of launching heavy neutralizing blows at airfields on Japan's main islands to form a barrier between invasion forces in the Philippines and Japan's principal airfields.

The Japanese had spotted Task Force Fifty-eight the day before. It was only 100 miles east of Kyushu's southern tip when fighters were launched at 5:45 A.M.

The Japanese retaliated, and the *Enterprise* and *Yorktown* suffered bomb hits while American fighters over Kyushu were bagging four hundred airplanes, mostly on the ground.

Spruance led the task force to the northeast, and it was an impressive sight. Hundreds of planes were launched toward Honshu, Japan's main island. Warships and docks at Kure and at the naval base at Kobe received well-timed attacks that left sixteen combat ships damaged. Despite heavy flak, the battleship *Yamato* and five carriers were severely damaged.

While Americans were over Honshu, Japanese bombers struck the fleet. The *Franklin* was launching her second strike on October 30 when Russell saw a sizable kamikaze attack begin. Combat air patrol knocked down all but six. He watched as those six got overhead and came down in long dives. Four kamikazes each picked out a carrier, and one hit Davison's flagship *Franklin*. The Japanese plane went through the flight deck and burst into flames in the aft elevator well, setting fire to the interior of the ship.

The *San Jacinto*, *Belleau Wood*, and *Enterprise* each got their kamikazes.

Two more Japanese planes plummeted, and one was quickly splashed. The other plane, having dropped a bomb on the *Franklin* that missed, flew across the formation of ships at low altitude and crashed into the stern of the *Belleau Wood* just below the level of the flight deck.

One Japanese pilot was shot down by combat air patrol and was picked up with a crease across the back of one hand where a 50-caliber bullet had wounded him slightly. The pilot was put on sulfa drugs to prevent infection. Later, he was sent to the flagship *New Jersey* for interrogation and then transferred to a carrier. Although he had been on the American fleet's flagship for more than a month, the doctors on the carrier found out that he had just broken out with a case of gonorrhea.

The carrier captain sent a message to the captain of the fleet's flagship, the *New Jersey*, saying, "What sort of brothel do you run on your ship? We understand the incubation period is nine days."

Sulfa drugs, which had been given to the Japanese pilot on the *New Jersey* to prevent infection in the wounded hand, had not been strong enough to cure the gonorrhea but had instead suppressed it for a time. When the sulfa was discontinued, the gonorrhea broke out anew.

Although carrier crews were exhausted after this sweep of bases in the home islands and hardly fit for further operations, they were ordered to continue supporting MacArthur's invasion forces by attacking targets on Leyte, Luzon, and the Visayans, a group of islands between Luzon and Mindanao. The situation on Leyte remained tense and insecure despite their renewed efforts, but Halsey called for retirement of the rest of his fleet to Ulithi, postponing with regret his plans to strike at the heart of Japan to test her strength.

Halsey's attack groups badly needed more recuperation at Ulithi, but Japanese aircraft from Luzon posed such a threat to Leyte's ground troops that they had to be liquidated. The situation became so serious that Halsey ordered his fast carriers back to the battle-front.

McCain replaced Mitscher in command of Task Force Thirty-eight as Task Group 38.1 was placed under the command of Rear Adm. Alfred E. Montgomery. Task Group 38.3 remained under Sherman as they sortied from Ulithi to meet Bogan's group halfway between Ulithi and Luzon. Davison's group returned to Ulithi as part of Halsey's alternative action and replenishment plan for continuous operations.

The fast carriers arrived before dawn on November 5, 160 miles from Manila and only 80 miles from the coast after a high-speed dash from the rendezvous. Montgomery's carriers were assigned the Clark Field complex on the central plains of Luzon, where six Japanese airfields and fourteen runways were in constant use. Bogan's carriers were given southern Luzon. The fields in the middle, plus shipping in the Manila area, were assigned to Sherman's group, which included the *Essex, Ticonderoga*, and *Lexington*.

Fighters swept the fields at dawn and caught the Japanese by surprise. Hellcats found good shooting, and fifty-eight Japanese planes succumbed to their attacks. They reported back to the flagship that hundreds of Japanese aircraft, many of which were obviously flown in from Japan and Formosa, were camouflaged on the ground.

Sherman's pilots pounded shipping in Manila Bay, sinking the heavy cruiser *Nachi* in shallow water as it attempted to escape. After Manila was captured, top secret war plans, detailing Japanese strategy and operational procedures, were recovered from the ship by divers.

Two kamikazes attacked the carriers but were destroyed before they could do any damage. A third, braving a tornado of fire from 20 and 40 mm guns and 5-inchers, slammed into the bridge of the *Lexington*. Capt. Ernest W. Litch winced as the blinding flash quickly turned into smoke and flames. Surgeons and hospital corpsmen immediately took care of the wounded, and the chaplains hurried to attend to their sad duties.

The *Ticonderoga*'s guns roared at four planes intent on crash dives from 3,000 feet and just managed to destroy them before they hit the ship. The day was past when a ship could feel safe if it destroyed most of an attacking force. Now, even one kamikaze could inflict serious damage.

On the following day, all three carrier groups went after shore targets. During the two-day assaults, nine ships were sunk, including the *Nachi* and two oilers. Damage was caused to other Japanese ships as well.

Men fighting the desperate battle on Leyte would now have four hundred fewer Japanese planes to contend with. Clearly, these strikes were worthwhile; Japanese air opposition declined quickly. The *Lexington* and *Reno* were damaged and twenty-five planes lost in the strikes. Eleven more planes were apparently lost to operational accidents.

The Third Fleet hoped to return to Luzon again, but a storm changed their plans. Refueling was necessary so the fleet returned to an area 400 miles west of Saipan. Halsey meanwhile recalled Bogan's group to Ulithi for a welcome respite, sending Davison's group to replace them.

• Sherman assumed tactical command of the fleet on his *Essex* flagship. After midnight on November 10, he was handed a dispatch from Halsey. "Cancel fueling. Reverse course and proceed at best speed toward Central Philippines to support our ground forces on Leyte Island." This sudden change of plans was brought about because Japanese heavy warships were reported heading for Balabac Strait, which separated the southwestern Philippine island of Palawan from Borneo.

The more Halsey learned of this new threat, the more concerned he became because the Japanese force included the huge *Yamato* with its 18-inch guns and three older battleships, the *Nagato, Kongo,* and *Haruna*, along with a cruiser and four destroyers. He was also advised that a reinforcing convoy could be expected to arrive at Ormoc Bay the following day. The Third Fleet was a thousand·miles away but it steamed up to 26 knots and headed back.

After a spectacular high-speed run, carriers arrived 200 miles off the San Bernardino Strait early on November 11. Search planes failed to find a single enemy·ship. At last, a convoy was located, but there was no trace of battleships. Four cargo ships, five destroyers, and a destroyer escort were heading south between Leyte and the northern tip of Cebu.

Sherman launched 347 planes and attacked the convoy as it rounded Apali Point at 11:00 A.M. Bombers from the *Essex, Ticonderoga,* and *Langley* destroyed the four transports in a matter of minutes.

Limited airfield facilities on Leyte and lack of strong air force concentrations of fighters and bombers forced MacArthur to insist on continued use of carriers for his Philippine operations. By agreement with MacArthur, Sherman launched his main strikes at Luzon, where shipping in the Subic Bay–Lingayen Gulf and in Manila Bay offered the greatest concentration of targets. In a closely timed operation, fighters swept Clark Field of enemy planes at dawn on November 13 while bombers attacked shipping.

It was a wise decision because little opposition was met over ship-crowded Manila Bay. During attacks, flak caused heavy losses to

American planes, twenty-five being shot down during the day. The following day, reconnaissance photographs revealed that the docks at Manila and Cavite naval yard had been hit hard. Japanese ships in the bay also suffered, with a light cruiser, four destroyers, three tankers, and three cargo ships resting on the bottom. All these losses were serious, but loss of the tankers began to have an especially adverse effect on all Japanese operations.

Task Force Thirty-eight now withdrew for refueling and replenishment of military supplies.

Army engineers struggled to build more airfields on Leyte, but heavy rains caused one delay after another. It was inevitable, therefore, that MacArthur should request of Nimitz that Halsey's fast carriers be brought back for the Mindoro operation scheduled for early December.

McCain's carriers made strikes against Luzon's airfields and shipping, but kamikaze attacks against his ships were a deadly menace that grew daily. Still, during November, fast carriers sank 134,000 tons of ships and destroyed more than 700 aircraft while losing only 117 planes and not one Allied ship.

Manila was no longer useful as a port for the Japanese because the bay was cluttered with sunken hulks. Most important, it ceased to become a troop and supply center to reinforce the Japanese forces on Leyte.

Halsey decided that his fast carrier forces must have a rest, and he called for their withdrawal.

In the southwest Pacific, a forgotten battlefront as far as headlines were concerned, men still died as attacks continued against Japan's isolated outposts. Submarines continued their relentless hunts, and the *Sealion* found big game when it sank the veteran battleship *Kongo*.

Then, on November 28, Comdr. Joseph F. Enright led his submarine the *Archerfish* in an attack against the largest aircraft carrier afloat. While the *Shinano*, a converted battleship, tried to reach the safety of Japan's Inland Sea, the *Archerfish* fired a spread of torpedoes at her. Enright thought he got a hit, but the *Shinano* steamed over the horizon at 28 knots. She was on builder's trials with a navy yard crew aboard. The *Archerfish*'s torpedoes had ruptured a gasoline tank, and raw fuel entered an elevator well. The crew opened up the ship to try to rid it of gasoline fumes. This brought the air/gas ratio to the explosion point and out of range of the *Archerfish's* vision, she exploded. The *Shinano* had never launched an airplane, was still not fully completed, and therefore was not watertight. As a result, she sank quickly.

MacArthur was finding the recapture of the Philippines more difficult than he had thought. Heavy rains made the jungles a quagmire, and advances were measured in yards instead of miles.

The Japanese air force, with a continual flow of replacement crews pouring in, made the job more difficult and, despite all efforts to prevent it, the Japanese army managed to continually reinforce its beleaguered troops.

The Third Fleet left Ulithi after a rest period to assist the Mindoro invasion. When it was temporarily canceled, Halsey ordered them to reverse course. Days later, they set out again for an assault on Luzon to prevent Japanese interference during the renewed Mindoro invasion. They had orders to maintain consistent action for the first three critical days before the invasion because air force fighter support from Leyte's airfields was out of the question.

McCain had seven large carriers and six light carriers at his disposal, but he also had at least a hundred airfields to cover. He and his staff devised a new technique that it was hoped would blanket Luzon's fields day and night. Aircraft had to be over the fields twenty-four hours a day. McCain assigned areas of responsibility to each of his three groups, and the airfields were divided equally among the carriers. First priority was given to the destruction of enemy aircraft. Fuel tanks, gas trucks, and storage facilities that might interfere with air operations were almost of equal importance. If planes found themselves temporarily out of assigned targets, they were told to attack enemy ships.

Carriers reached their launching points 200 miles northeast of Manila on December 14. Night and day, they stood guard over Japanese airfields, pouncing whenever a Japanese plane appeared. Kamikazes desperately tried to reach the carriers, but not one made it through combat patrol.

For the next three days, enemy aircraft failed to penetrate the invasion front as landings at Mindoro proceeded without aerial opposition. McCain's planes shot down sixty-four of the enemy and ripped apart another two hundred on the ground without losing a single plane to a Japanese attacker. Only antiaircraft fire posed a threat to American planes, its guns destroying fifty-four altogether.

Vice-Adm. Shigeru Fukudome, commander of the Japanese Second Air Fleet on Luzon, had taken a stinging defeat. He had been able to keep his air strength between six and seven hundred planes until the middle of December.

The carriers withdrew for refueling, informing MacArthur that they would return on the 19th if they were needed.

Strikes scheduled for that day were out of the question because the Third Fleet blundered into a killer typhoon that sank three destroyers and damaged many other ships. Loss of life was heavy, totaling 790 sailors. The typhoon accomplished what Japan's dwindling aviation could no longer do—it destroyed 150 carrier aircraft.

In Washington, Admiral King privately called for an investigation. Vice-Adm. John Hoover, who headed the inquiry, placed the blame on Halsey, who insisted that he had not been negligent and blamed the weather for the disaster. He was saved from further reprimand by a whitewash of the whole affair. Halsey's mistakes, the investigating committee reported, resulted from errors in judgment brought on by the war's stress. In a move that was inconsistent with their findings, the committee commended Halsey for his desire to keep hitting the Japanese even if he had to fight his way through a typhoon. (Halsey had actually told Nimitz and MacArthur the typhoon would delay his return to the battlefronts. He concluded his dispatch by saying, "Unable to strike Luzon before 21st at dawn.")

King privately agreed with Hoover but permitted Halsey to retain his command.

MacArthur's forces had landed on Mindoro on December 15. The island, slightly larger than Leyte, lies south of Luzon and is separated from it by a narrow channel. MacArthur needed this toehold to build airstrips for his coming Luzon invasion.

The invasion proceeded smoothly until Kinkaid received the shocking word on December 26 that Japanese surface forces were heading for Mindoro. Four cruisers and several destroyers were immediately dispatched to meet this threat. While Japanese warships headed for Mindoro Strait, army planes attacked, and then PT boats went into action and repulsed the threat. Ships off the beachhead were, however, lashed from the air by Japanese bombers.

After the first of the year, with the Mindoro operation proceeding according to plan, Admiral Kinkaid went to see General MacArthur about the invasion of Luzon.

"I believe a landing in the Manila area would be less costly," he said. "Convoys would be less exposed to kamikaze attacks."

MacArthur shook his head. "For army purposes, the plains of Luzon are needed as a place to maneuver."

They discussed plans for several minutes, then MacArthur said thoughtfully, "I believe the Japs are off balance. We should hit them quickly with a knockout punch—a great assault on Luzon."

After extensive arguments with his staff, MacArthur agreed to postpone the Lingayen Gulf operation until January 9, 1945, because he needed the close cooperation of the Third Fleet. Halsey meanwhile laid plans for his carriers to attack Japanese airpower on Formosa and at the tip of Luzon prior to and during the landing phases.

In coordination with southwest Pacific forces, Halsey divided Luzon with an imaginary line that crossed inland, north of the Lingayen Gulf. "All Jap airfields north of that line are fair game for us," Halsey told his commanders. "General Kenney's Fifth Air Force has all hunting rights south of it."

The Japanese now learned the lesson about airpower that Yamamoto had tried to emphasize earlier in the war. Lacking the industrial capacity of the United States, they never found it possible to match the airpower now unleashed upon them.

In early 1945, each large carrier had seventy-three aircraft. Thus, America's fifteen carriers could together launch a thousand aircraft on each strike compared with the six hundred formerly available for major operations. These aircraft were important in more ways than one. During kamikaze attacks, it was sometimes not enough even to kill the Japanese pilot. His plane had to be hit such a devastating blow that it would drop straight into the ocean and not come crashing on board a ship.

Early proponents of airpower—men like Towers, King, Halsey, and Mitscher—now felt vindicated. Properly applied airpower was now bringing immediate tactical and strategic gains that otherwise would have been impossible to achieve.

Meanwhile, bombers of the Fourteenth Air Force and the Twentieth Bomber Command in India and China continued to strike telling blows at Formosa, while Marianas-based B–29s of the Twenty-first Bomber Command laid the foundations for the eventual destruction of the homeland.

Despite almost daily attacks against the Japanese air force in the Luzon–Visaya area, by scraping the bottom of the barrel of their air reserves throughout the Far East, the Japanese were able to come up with 450 planes, 300 north of Manila in the complex of fields around Clark.

MacArthur's planners were as precise with details for their Lingayen Gulf landings as they had been for the Leyte landings. Ships from all over the western Pacific converged on Leyte after the start of the new year.

Kamikazes continued to make life miserable for the Allied fleets, and at times their actions were downright disastrous. On January 4, the escort carrier *Ommaney Bay* was sunk, and on the same day, the H.M.A.S. *Australia* was heavily damaged by two kamikaze crashes on board.

After leaving Ulithi on December 30, the Third Fleet arrived on the scene with two fighter squadrons of marines. Their gull-winged Corsairs were placed on the *Essex*, the first time that marine pilots had operated from fast carriers since a few days prior to Pearl Harbor when the *Saratoga* had delivered twelve marine fighters to Wake Island.

The Japanese hoarded their planes on Luzon but kept another four hundred in reserve on Formosa. This prompted Task Force Thirty-eight to pay another visit to the strategic island and despite bad weather, attacks destroyed planes on the ground and sank a number of ships. Formosa's northern fields were not effectively hit because they were fogged in.

After refueling on January 5, Halsey was all set to move into the China Sea, but word from MacArthur changed his plans. That day, Admiral Oldendorf's heavy ships and minesweepers preceded the invasion fleet into Lingayen Gulf, while eleven escort carriers stood by to protect them. Oldendorf sent spotter planes over land prior to starting ship-to-shore preinvasion bombardment. The first pilot circled the area and reported, "I can't see a single military installation. If there are any, they're camouflaged."

"Cancel the bombardment," Oldendorf ordered.

The minesweepers went to work. Not one mine was found. Oldendorf was astonished. He looked up as antiaircraft fire broke out throughout the fleet. Japanese army fighters swept down, and it was obvious that they were out for big game. The first blow was a suicide dive on the destroyer *Walker*. Japanese pilots, however, shifted quickly to battleships, and the *New Mexico* shuddered under the impact.

Oldendorf decided to withdraw his bombardment ships as the raids continued. He dictated an urgent message to Kinkaid.

Consider need of additional air power urgent and vital. Our CVEs entirely inadequate providing air cover. Japanese suicide bombers seem able to attack without much interference owing to radar difficulties.

Believe in addition all fields small as well as large near Lingayen must be continuously bombed and kept neutralized.

Kinkaid was upset by the message. The situation was far worse than he had thought. He looked again at the losses listed with the memorandum. Twenty-one ships had been hit in the last twenty-five hours.

He wired Halsey to return his fast carriers immediately to protect the invasion forces. The weather was foul, but Halsey sent his fliers back over Luzon. The men of the Seventh Fleet had to be protected at all costs. When the kamikaze attacks were reduced, Oldendorf sent his bombardment ships into the gulf to continue the work they had started.

Amphibious forces passed through Leyte Gulf on January 4, and the great mass of transport and cargo ships found no opposition from the air and only one torpedo attack. Cautiously, the great fleet moved toward Lingayen, occasionally beset by individual plane attacks that failed to damage any of the ships and by one Japanese destroyer, whose attack was unsuccessful. The next two days were without major mishap. When troops went ashore, the XIV Corps landed near the town of Lingayen and the I Corps at San Fabian.

Planes from escort carriers rushed to attack ahead of the advancing troops, lashing Japanese defenses with bombs and rockets. The enemy's greatest resistance developed in the section northeast of San Fabian so planes concentrated there.

When Sixth Army troops reported that Japanese airpower was sufficently neutralized on Luzon and Formosa, Halsey decided to undertake a pet project, which he called "Operation Gratitude." In other words, he had not forgotten his original intention of sweeping the South China Sea.

Halsey was particularly intrigued by a report that the battleship-carriers *Ise* and *Hyuga* were at Singapore. He learned that they had left on January 9, possibly to interfere with Lingayen supply routes, so that night he ordered the Third Fleet to head out into the China Sea through Luzon Strait.

Halsey anticipated that he would find the *Ise* and the *Hyuga* with their cruisers and destroyers near Camranh Bay on the Indochina coast. His hopes were in vain. American submarines had destroyed the Japanese tankers, forcing the big ships to return to Singapore. Halsey's fliers nevertheless swept airfields along the coast, destroying fourteen enemy planes in the air and another ninety-five on the ground. Four Japanese convoys, hugging the coast for protection, fell prey to the attackers, and the light cruiser *Kashii* also went down. In all, forty ships succumbed, totaling 127,000 tons.

On Luzon, Admiral Fukudome, commander of all naval aircraft in the archipelago, was ordered to Singapore with his remaining thirty flyable planes. His two air fleets had originally totaled almost seven hundred aircraft.

Nimitz remained in doubt about a possible attempt by the Japanese to hurl their remaining ships against the Lingayen Gulf invasion area. He ordered Halsey to position his Third Fleet in as strategic a position as possible in the northern portion of the South China Sea.

"Continue all efforts to locate enemy heavy ships," he wired. "If more important targets do not appear, strike Hong Kong at your discretion."

Despite miserable weather on January 15 and McCain's recommendation to call off a strike against Formosa, Halsey decided to attack. With slight air opposition, Halsey's fliers went in under the overcast and sank eight ships at Takao. Thirty-four Japanese planes were destroyed, half on the ground.

Bad weather continued unabated but despite the adverse effects on operations, Halsey ordered mainland attacks against Hong Kong and Canton. Returning from Canton, pilots described the flak in awed terms. For the first time in months, United States losses exceeded those of Japan. With forty-seven enemy down, the carriers lost sixty-one planes—thirty-one because of operational accidents.

"We have completed a 3,800-mile cruise in the China Sea and not one Japanese plane got within 20 miles of our ships," Halsey wired Nimitz. "That's gratitude."

Sir Bruce Fraser, who had taken command of the British Pacific Fleet from Admiral Somerville on November 22, 1944, had the necessary combat experience and flair for command of large forces to revitalize the fleet. For the first three years of the war, Fraser had been third sea lord and controller of the British Royal Navy. As commander of the British Home Fleet, he had led the successful attack on the German battlecruiser *Scharnhorst* in 1943.

Fraser established his headquarters in Sydney, Australia but met frequently with Admiral Nimitz, with whom he established cordial relations, To lead the British Pacific Fleet at sea, he chose Vice-Adm. Sir Bernard Rawlings, a tall Cornishman who had often proven his adeptness as a combat officer and was well liked for his keen sense of humor.

Rear Adm. Sir Philip Vian, a veteran destroyer combat officer, was appointed flag officer in command of the First Aircraft Carrier Squadron from his flagship the *Indomitable*. Vian was an aggressive officer who inspired his air groups.

Fraser's British fleet struck Palembang's oil refineries on January 24 and again on the 29th at the request of Admiral Nimitz. It was not an auspicious beginning. Forty-one aircraft were lost, including fourteen in operational accidents on deck. Production at the refineries was reduced by these raids, but they were not destroyed.

The British were not the only ones to lose heavily. The Japanese lost sixty-eight aircraft, more than half of which were lost on the ground.

These strikes demonstrated British inexperience in this type of operation, but they were learning fast.

In late February, Fraser ordered his fleet to move to Manus in the Admiralty Islands so that it would be closer to the war zone, and they arrived there on March 7. He had hoped that his British fleet could take part in the invasion of Okinawa, now scheduled for April 1, but Admiral King's authorization was withheld, and they remained in the hot, humid anchorage with nothing to do. Life on board the carriers was particularly uncomfortable because their armored steel flight decks absorbed more heat than did traditional wooden decks. It was literally possible to fry an egg on them.

Although Fraser was answerable to the British Admiralty in London, he reported to King and to Nimitz for fleet operations. This was a frustrating period for the British commander. Finally, on March 15 Admiral Fraser received word from Nimitz that Rawlings should report to him to engage in operations associated with the invasion of Okinawa.

Rawlings immediately wired Nimitz that his British fleet was reporting for duty and would be ready to sail from Manus on March 17. "It is with a feeling of great pride and pleasure that the British

Pacific Fleet joins the United States Naval Forces under your command."

In his reply the following day, Nimitz said, "The British Carrier Task Force and attached units will greatly increase our striking power and demonstrate our unity of purpose against Japan. The United States Pacific Fleet welcomes you."

The harbor at Ulithi was jammed with American warships when Task Force 113 arrived on March 20.

Rawlings readily agreed that his fleet would play a subsidiary role because crews on his carriers were not sufficiently experienced to operate closely with America's fast carriers. As a result, the British ships were placed to the left of the American Fifth Fleet's battle line off the islands of Sakishima Gunto, which were located to the southwest of Okinawa. Rawlings' fleet was charged with responsibility for neutralizing airfields on the islands of Miyake and Ishigaki, part of the Sakishima Islands that form a chain of stepping stones between Formosa and Okinawa. His fleet was designated Task Force Fifty-seven. Most of the fliers had been trained in American Hellcat and Corsair fighters and Avenger bombers, although there were some British two-seat fighter reconnaissance Fairey Fireflies and Super-marine Seafires which were carrier versions of the land-based Spit-fire fighter.

United States Navy officers, who had trained the British fliers in American aircraft, were impressed by the steel flight decks on British carriers, on which fires from crashes could be more quickly extinguished than on the wooden decks of American carriers.

MacArthur, recalling vividly how ticklish the stiuation had become when Japanese surface forces almost reached the beachhead at Leyte, still worried about a repeat performance in the Lingayen Gulf. Nimitz told him not to be concerned because four enemy battleships were definitely in Empire waters, and other powerful fleet units were in Singapore.

"Best naval protection for the Philippines is to proceed with offensive operations against Japan," he radioed.

While the Third Fleet was busy at sea, the fighting on Luzon continued despite serious organized resistance. Manila did not fall until February 23, and it was not until April 16 that the Philippines were officially liberated. Final resistance groups fought on for another three months.

Eighty thousand Japanese died, and the American army lost slightly more than 3,000 men. It had been the toughest fighting that

MacArthur's veterans had encountered since the start of the war.

General Tomoyuki Yamashita had wanted to fight only a delaying action on Leyte while he prepared for a defensive battle on Luzon. Because he was overruled, his army needlessly lost a large number of troops along with thousands of tons of vital supplies.

Japanese snipers were still active on Corregidor on March 21 when General MacArthur returned in a PT boat, the way he had left "the Rock" thirty-six months before. He strode up to the assault commander, Col. George M. Jones, as the men stood stiffly at attention and saluted smartly. With a new flag in his hand, MacArthur approached the color guard at the base of the battered flagpole. "Hoist the colors to its peak and let no enemy ever haul them down!"

MacArthur's Southwest Pacific Area was the most active battlefront during the first two years of the war. Later, as he advanced along the coast of New Guinea, his operations became less important and decisive. Actually, Nimitz's Central Pacific command occupied far more important bastions on the road back to the main islands than anything MacArthur's command had taken. Once the Philippines were liberated, MacArthur's future operations contributed little to the defeat of Japan.

Japanese-held Iwo Jima, a volcanic island between the Marianas and Japan, now stood almost alone in an American-controlled Central Pacific. With B–29 Superfortresses participating in strikes against Japan, its desirability as a haven for badly shot-up bombers grew acute. Iwo's occupation would permit fighter escorts for the big bombers. Search planes covering the southern coast of Japan and Japanese patrol vessels that flashed early warnings of B–29 raids to the homeland could be eliminated. The Japanese were aware of this, and planned to contest every foot of ground.

Taking Iwo Jima was a job ideally suited to the navy and marines and preparations had been underway for months.

Fifth Fleet Commander Spruance was put in charge of the assault against the island, which was only four and a half miles long. He was promised the fast carriers, which were only a small part of the nine hundred ships scheduled to participate in the invasion.

Rear Adm. Calvin T. Durgin's support carrier group of eleven escort carriers headed for Iwo on February 16. In a two-pronged offensive, fast carriers stood off Honshu to help isolate Iwo from reinforcements from Japan's main islands.

It was the largest carrier task force ever assembled. Task Force Fifty-eight, the advance units of the Fifth Fleet, had 11 carriers, 5 light carriers, 8 fast battleships, a battle cruiser, 5 heavy cruisers, 11 light cruisers, 81 destroyers, and over 1,200 aircraft. Such was the resurgence of American naval might since the disaster at Pearl Harbor that only four of these ships had been with the fleet on December 7, 1941.

These same ships, with different designations, had again exchanged top commanders. In other words, the Third Fleet now became the Fifth Fleet under Spruance and Mitscher instead of Halsey and McCain.

After they departed from Ulithi, it was obvious that something big was up. There was much speculation, but the truth did not come out until they were out of sight of land.

Officers reported to wardrooms on each ship to hear an identical message from the captain. "Gentlemen, it gives me great pleasure to announce you will strike Tokyo!"

Later, all hands were given the word. The bridge speaker reverberated with excitement. "This is the captain speaking. Our target is Tokyo. We will strike at dawn on the 16th."

The invasion of Iwo Jima, now set for February 19, would be difficult, and everyone knew it. It was agreed that while escort carriers neutralized defenses at Iwo Jima, the fast carriers could perform a more useful function if they struck hard at Tokyo and the Kobe–Nagoya area in advance of the invasion. "The fleet will be in a dangerous position off the coast of Japan," Spruance told his staff. "If we can't take it, it will be worse off at Okinawa later on."

The ever-present Japanese early-warning picket boats were eliminated by a large screen of destroyers ahead of the fleet.

Some 120 miles off the coast of Honshu, silent pilots soberly read Mitscher's final memo on their bulletin boards. "The coming raid on Tokyo will produce the greatest air victory of the war for carrier aviation, but only if every air group commander, squadron commander, combat team leader, section leader and individual pilot abides by the fundamental rules of air combat that have been taught since the war started. Those of us who can't get over the target will be doing all we can to get you back safely."

General quarters sounded in the predawn darkness. Planes were ready, wings folded tightly to their fuselages as fighter pilots hurried on deck from the final briefing.

The air officer's voice brought them to a standstill. "Time check. On the mark it will be zero six thirty-two . . . Mark!"

Pilots synchronized their watches, shivering as the cold wind penetrated their flight gear.

"Standby to start engines. Stand clear of propellers!" came the call. "Start engines!"

A rippling roar broke the stillness on each carrier's deck, and blue flames stabbed backward from the planes. Plane directors, identified by wands or special globes over hand-held flashlights, signaled their first planes to unfold wings.

Waving lights, intelligible to the pilots, brought each plane forward on the dark flight decks.

"All hands. Standby for a turn to starboard," the bullhorns announced.

Gracefully, the big carriers made wide turns.

"Launch aircraft!"

Bombers from the carriers waited over Tokyo until fighters finished their sweeps. The sky was so overcast that the bombers had to circle back to the coast without dropping bombs.

It was over Chiba that they ran into the stiffest opposition. *Hancock*'s Fighting Eighty downed seventy-one Japanese planes, surpassing the previous record by the *Lexington*'s group during the Marianas "Turkey Shoot."

Over Honshu, fighters bore the brunt of resistance while bombers from the *Lexington, Bunker Hill*, and *San Jacinto* attacked the Ota airframe plant. B–29s had struck it a week before, but the carrier planes caused extensive new damage.

In all, seven hundred intercepters rose from the Tokyo plain to resist the heavy attack. Twenty-four American planes fell to Japanese fighters but they, in turn, destroyed 281 Japanese planes in the air and another 200 on the ground.

That night, the *Saratoga* and *Enterprise* launched their night fighters for a sweep of Tokyo's airfields and ranged as far west as the city of Hamamatsu.

The following day, bad weather limited sorties but on the 17th, two hundred planes, half of them bombers, attacked airfields and aircraft and engine plants on the northwest outskirts of Tokyo. Enemy fighters met them at the coast, and they had a running fight to and from the targets.

Planes from the *Essex, Bunker Hill*, and *Cowpens* singled out an important plant for significant damage when they attacked the Tama–Musashino aircraft engine factory.

The weather grew progressively worse so by noon Spruance and Mitscher called off the operation and proceeded to Iwo Jima.

Although attack groups had found Japanese fighters alert and aggressive, losing to them thirty-four fighters and two torpedo bombers, not a single Japanese bomber penetrated to the carriers offshore.

The Japanese lost a total of 416 planes in the air and another 354 on the ground, planes they desperately needed.

In the dusky dawn of a Pacific morning two days later, blacked-out ships approached Iwo Jima. Landings were made, and the butchery on both sides soon rose to such heights that veteran combat officers were sickened by the slaughter. The smell of death was everywhere as Japanese soldiers perished in their foxholes, refusing to retreat. Yard-by-yard advances were made against a tough, resourceful foe who used the island's natural terrain to exact the maximum cost from its invaders. The Japanese had dug deep into the volcanic soil so they were protected from all but direct hits.

At twilight on February 21, kamikazes struck the ships.

Lt. Comdr. A. B. Metsger, outside the pilot house at his air control station on the *Saratoga*, had plotted an incoming flight of planes fewer than 100 miles from his ship. At first, they had been identified as friendly planes, even though the IFF (Identification of Friend and Foe) gave no such indication. At this stage of the war, however, the IFF was not fully reliable.

Fighters were sent aloft as a precautionary measure to intercept the incoming planes and positively identify them. They rode above the cloud deck at 2,000 feet at first and then investigated below it without spotting the planes. Metsger kept an eye on his radar scope and although the incoming planes and American fighters seemed to merge, there was no announcement of an intercept.

Metsger believed that the incoming flight would pass well clear of the *Saratoga* but when it was abreast, it suddenly turned directly toward his ship. Metsger watched the plot, and when the unidentified planes were a few miles distant, he walked to the starboard side of the bridge to see what they might be.

Several fighters broke through the clouds and headed straight for the *Saratoga*. To Metsger they appeared in their head-on view to be F6F Fighters. He was quickly disillusioned when puffs appeared at their wing tips; he knew that he was being fired upon. Then he recognized the pattern of their approach as that of suicide attackers. Several of these planes slammed into the *Saratoga*, killing and wounding a large number of the carrier's men but not causing sufficient damage to destroy the ship's watertight integrity.

More Japanese planes continued to crash into the *Saratoga*'s upper works, with one hitting below the waterline but causing only minor damage. Although six or seven Japanese pilots rammed the *Saratoga*, Metsger was relieved that none of them seemed to have caused sufficient damage to risk her loss.

He was grateful that the *Saratoga* had been built before design engineers tried to get the most out of every pound of steel. She was a tough ship, and the strength bulkhead on the forward part of Metsger's stateroom protected it from serious damage. One bomb exploded six feet from this bulkhead, and the only damage to Metsger's stateroom was a cracked washbasin.

After the first Japanese plane struck the *Saratoga*, gunners became trigger happy. The *Saratoga*'s last torpedo plane, launched prior to the attack, flew up the usual distance ahead and turned around to fly back on a reverse course. As the pilot came abreast of his ship, some of the ship's gunners cut loose at him. Metsger noted with relief that the tracers were not close. Once the pilot saw them, he turned away, apparently unharmed. Metsger continued to worry that the gunners might hit one of their own planes. After the battle, Metsger was reassured to hear that the pilot had survived the encounter.

Despite their troubles, Metsger occasionally caught glimpses of the light carrier *Bismarck Sea* after she was hit, and was appalled when she succumbed so quickly to the fiery onslaught.

After the *Saratoga* had left Hawaii to take part in the Iwo Jima operation, Lt. A. M. Buckley talked to Metsger about arranging a future request for transfer ashore because of his age. He was in his late 30s, one of the oldest officers on the ship, and too old to be a lieutenant and a catapult officer.

Metsger asked why he did not request a transfer now.

Buckley replied that he did not want to be transferred before the action, but he wanted his request made so it would not be viewed as a reaction to combat.

Metsger understood, and he was saddened when Buckley was one of the first to be killed.

Jobs performed by catapult crews were highly dangerous. One of the younger men in Buckley's crew was cited when the first wave of kamikaze planes attacked the ship. A Japanese pilot smashed into an American airplane on the catapult and set it on fire with its pilot, Ens. R. H. Powell, trapped inside. Seaman Harry W. Margerum climbed on the burning plane, cut Powell loose, and dragged him through flames over the plane's wing to the edge of the deck where both men collapsed.

Metsger was proud of these youngsters, whose ages ranged from 18 to 21 but who quickly matured as tough, responsible, and courageous men. Each met severe challenge, not only as individuals but as a group under Capt. L. A. "Fish" Moebus.

The forward part of the *Saratoga* suffered several more hits in late afternoon. As night fell, all hands fought to get the fires out. They were acutely aware that their sister ship, the *Lexington*, had been lost as a result of gasoline fires after suffering only minor damage. As the responsible officer, the *Saratoga*'s Lt. (jg.) H. H. Brewer managed to control the gasoline system despite great difficulties so it never contributed to their problems. Brewer worked his fueling crew to the point of total exhaustion to help save the ship. Even before the attack, the *Saratoga*'s fueling system had been none too efficient, especially when compared with Essex-class carriers. With around-the-clock operations, Brewer's crew served beyond the point of exhaustion, somehow managing to defuel airplanes when they were struck below and refuel them to ready them for flight.

When the *Saratoga* was first hit, the fuel crew was changing from the daytime flight-deck arrangement to the nighttime arrangement. In the course of working airplanes back and forth, several airplanes had to be left in the hangar deck with fuel in them, and these caused major troubles when the ship was hit.

Aircraft maintenance men suffered heavily because they were in the shop when the suiciders hit. The plane of one kamikaze, apparently shot down, glanced off the water just outboard of the ship and bounced into the ship's side abreast of the maintenance shop. The bomb went through outer and inner skins of the ship and exploded in the shop, killing all hands.

After nightfall, several airplanes circled the *Saratoga,* some from her own complement and some from other ships. Once it was determined that the *Saratoga*'s landing area and arresting gear were functioning properly, a communication's arrangement was jury-rigged, and these planes were brought on board. One plane had been circling for some time, waiting for the ship to recover him. Metsger had watched him off and on with growing concern as the ship's guns followed him as he circled. Metsger hoped that the pilot would not turn toward the ship until he was ordered to do so. If he did, Metsger was sure that some gunners would open fire. After dark, no one could tell who was friend or enemy.

Lt. Comdr. J. A. Bescos, the ship's flight deck officer, watched as a pilot from another ship landed on the *Saratoga*. After parking and switching off his engine, the pilot remained in his cockpit. Bescos thought he looked worried but relieved to be down.

He walked up to the plane. When the pilot remained seated, Bescos climbed on a wing to see if he was injured.

The pilot looked up. "Boy, am I glad to be aboard! I'm glad this isn't the *Saratoga*. You ought to see her!"

Mount Suribachi, highest point on Iwo Jima, was reached on February 23 by an assault team. Lt. Harold G. Shrier withdrew a small flag from his pack after he got to the summit and handed it to Platoon Sgt. Ernest I. Thomas, who raised it on an improvised staff.

Battalion Comdr. Col. Chandler W. Johnson decided that a larger flag, which could be seen by all, was needed. He sent a four-man patrol with a new flag, and the familiar picture was taken of this second flag-raising.

Seabees performed their usual miracles and extended Iwo Jima's runway to 4,000 feet by March 2. Two days later, they leaned on their tools and watched with satisfaction as a crippled B–29 made a safe landing. It had to be refueled by hand before it could proceed to Saipan.

By the time organized resistance at Iwo Jima ended on March 17, losses on both sides were enormous for the scale of the operation. Japanese losses were 21,300, and the total American casualties numbered 22,082, including almost 5,000 dead.

The invasion of Iwo Jima was the most savage and costly battle in the history of the United States Marine Corps. Admiral Nimitz described it best: "Uncommon valor was a common virtue."

High seas made operations difficult on February 25 as rolling carriers pitched violently, but four hundred fighters headed for the snow-covered airfields of Tokyo. To their surprise, pilots found them deserted. The Japanese had flown their planes to safer havens, fully expecting American planes to return after their previous strikes. The enemy flying in from airfields outside the area, contested the operation, losing fifty more fighters, while United States Navy losses were limited to three planes.

Further strikes by fighters proved impossible because of deteriorating weather over the island of Honshu. Two hundred radar-equipped B–29 Superfortresses from the Marianas, more capable of riding through bad weather over Japan, dropped hundreds of tons of bombs in the largest daylight raid of the war. Japanese radio broadcasts, which were monitored constantly, assailed the Americans for their "arrogance and lawlessness." Prime Minister Kuniaki Koiso said, "I have requested an audience with the Emperor to offer the apologies of myself and my cabinet for this unforgivable negligence."

For the rest of the war, Japan had to rely primarily on land-based airpower and kamikaze pilots. Her surface ships holed up in home ports, increasingly at the mercy of American aircraft.

18

OPEN SEASON

While preparations for the April 1 Okinawa invasion were underway, the Twenty-first Bomber Command in the Marianas was assigned to photograph the island while it continued its attacks on Honshu's principal cities. B–29s were also ordered to carry out diversionary attacks on southern Kyushu during the invasion's critical stages.

Spruance, who would direct the invasion, had broad responsibilities beyond the initial amphibious operation. No one doubted that the invasion would be difficult, and it was expected to take three months to secure the strategic island.

The assembly of ships was started seven months prior to D Day. Excluding personnel-landing craft, the total rose to 1,457 ships.

Mitscher's Task Force Fifty-eight had sixteen carriers, eight new battleships, two new battle cruisers, and fourteen heavy and light cruisers. It departed from Ulithi on March 14, and each task group of four carriers was assigned a senior pilot in command. Rear Adm. Joseph J. Clark had Task Group 58.1; Rear Adm. Ralph E. Davison, Task Group 58.2; Rear Adm. Frederick C. Sherman, Task Group 58.3; and Rear Adm. Arthur W. Radford, Task Group 58.4.

Ralph Davison, Task Group 58.2's commander, was a learned man and always considerate of his officers. He had one failing, if such it could be called. He loved whiskey but drank only when he was in port. For him, it was an outlet made necessary by the tremendous pressures of a combat command, and he was not alone among those who indulged.

His chief of staff, James Russell, had great respect for his boss, knowing that he was one of the navy's outstanding commanders. At sea, Davison was cool as a cucumber, but Russell saw another side when Davison reported on board at Ulithi prior to the Okinawa campaign.

As always, Russell had carefully prepared the orders for the new sortie. March 14, as Davison came aboard, Russell said, "Here's the operations' order, admiral."

In a euphoric haze, Davison smiled. "Where do I sign?"

"Admiral, this is going to be a very serious operation, and I would strongly recommend that you read at least part of the order before you sign it. At least the main part."

"Oh, what's a chief of staff for?" Davison quickly scrawled his name on it. Once they were at sea, however, he went over it carefully.

Russell advised Davison later that Rear Adm. Arleigh Burke, Mitscher's chief of staff, had stressed that his boss wanted no more aircraft carriers lost. The sinking of the *Princeton* had shocked him, and he wanted it to be the last carrier lost in his command in World War II.

At the time, Russell had explained to Burke, skippers should be counseled to put their carriers into a tight turn to starboard when it was on fire. He explained that Essex-class carriers listed outboard on turns and putting such a carrier into a tight turn to starboard sloped the decks to port away from ship controls on the island. He reminded Burke that conflagration control stations in the hangar and repair lockers on the flight deck were on the starboard side, while the main air intake for the machinery spaces below the island were also on the starboard side of the ship. Therefore, turning to starboard would carry flaming gasoline over the port side of the ship away from control stations and air downtakes.

It was standard procedure to pair two cruisers with each carrier, depending upon their positions in the task group formation. One would be alongside a carrier to assist it with fire hoses and repair parties. The other cruiser would take the cripple in tow if she lost power, and four destroyers would form an antisubmarine screen around the cripple and her two cruiser escorts. These destroyers were usually drawn from the circular screen of twenty-four destroyers. Meanwhile, the other destroyers provided not only antisubmarine protection but also deadly antiaircraft fire from their guns, which used shells with radar fuses. Destroyers equipped with underwater sonar were used primarily against submarines.

Once a cripple had been taken care of, the task group reformed to carry on the battle.

After Russell explained the proposed procedure to Burke, he replied, "This looks good to me, Jim. I think that's the best you can do." Burke had stressed again, Russell said, that Mitscher did not want to lose any more aircraft carriers.

Davison agreed with his chief of staff that high-test gasoline was a dangerous element on board carriers. The gasoline was stored in so-called saddle tanks. A central tank had two saddles around it. Using seawater under pressure, gasoline was displaced from the outer saddle first, then the inner saddle, and finally from the central tank. Thus, maximum protection from water blankets was obtained as the gasoline was drawn off. Seawater pressure forced the gasoline to refueling stations on hangar and flight deck. Fuel levels were never permitted to get below 5 percent; otherwise, there would be a mixture of gasoline and seawater. Gasoline was always carefully filtered at the outlets to prevent water from getting into a plane's tank because a pure supply of fuel was essential.

Davison loved to banter with his officers. Once in a while, his officers would be forced to turn to a dictionary to decipher a word or two in a personally drafted message. Capt. Oscar A. "Tex" Weller, skipper of the *Wasp,* was once accused of "meretricious conduct" when he tried to get an extra night fighter for his air group. Weller was even more confused when his dictionary gave one meaning of meretricious as "of or pertaining to prostitution."

In another case, Davison accused an officer of a retromingent act. The dictionary described such an act as "the ability to project excretion forward like a skunk."

While the *Franklin* was undergoing repairs at Bremerton, Washington, following the damage it sustained in a lone Val attack the previous October 30, Davison and his staff had been on the *Lexington.* The *Franklin* reported back to the fleet on March 12, 1945, and all agreed that she looked like new. Davison shifted his flag the next day. Six days later she suffered another kamikaze attack, and the *Pittsburgh* took her in tow according to the task group's operational plan, and they headed for Ulithi.

The *Franklin* cast off her towline on March 20 after she had got steam up in four boilers. Although the *Franklin* had power on only two of her four shafts, she was making 25 knots when she neared Ulithi.

For four days Mitscher's pilots swept Honshu almost unmolested, destroying 548 planes and damaging important military bases and seaports. They returned to Okinawa on March 23 to participate in the heavy bombardment of the island prior to its invasion. Japanese planes failed to put in an appearance for several days but on the morning of March 27, kamikazes came over by the hundreds, making the lives of thousands of navy personnel a living hell twenty-four hours a day.

Maj. Gen. Curtis E. LeMay's Twentieth Air Force blitz of Japan's major cities during March caused enormous destruction, and he saw in its continuation the best way to defeat Japan without an invasion. It was his firm belief, as he later told General Arnold, that the Japanese could be forced to surrender possibly as early as October 1, 1945, if his strategic bombers were used effectively. Therefore, when Admiral Nimitz exercised his right to call on the Twentieth for assistance in bombing Kyushu's airfields and installations to reduce the menace of kamikaze attacks on his ships, LeMay was unhappy. He believed that his command would be far more effective bombing industrial targets. Direct orders from General Arnold could not be ignored so he agreed to send his B–29s to Kyushu to help knock out the airfields from which the suicide aircraft were flying. He sent the first B–29s on March 27, while other Superfortresses were mining the Shimonoseki Strait between Honshu and Kyushu. They made a further strike on March 30. These raids did not really interfere with LeMay's plans for firebombing Japanese cities because his command was temporarily out of incendiary bombs following the massive early March raids.

Once preinvasion strikes were completed, LeMay went to see Admiral Nimitz at his Guam headquarters. "We've been lucky on the weather, admiral. I'm sure you've seen the photographs I've sent you. We've got everything flat on Kyushu. I believe we ought to get back to strategic bombing. All we can do now is put more holes in the fields, and we can't stop an occasional airplane from taking off that the Japs have hid down the road someplace. We've done all we can."

Nimitz respected LeMay, and the feeling was mutual. "You've done a fine job," Nimitz said, putting an arm around him. "Let's check with Sherman to see what he says."

Nimitz's chief of staff, Rear Adm Forrest P. Sherman, refused to release LeMay's command. LeMay persisted so Sherman sent a telegram to Admiral King in Washington, stating that the navy would be forced to pull off and leave the ground troops on shore if the Twentieth did not continue to bomb Kyushu's airfields. LeMay knew he had lost and although he realized that all services had to help during an amphibious operation, he believed that his command's operations were being wasted.

Sherman continued to call on LeMay for B–29 strikes at Kyushu's fields, and LeMay finally appealed to General Arnold. The air force chief of staff discussed the matter with King, who supported Sherman and Nimitz, and LeMay became resigned to continuing such attacks.

After the war, Japanese officials reported that these B–29 attacks were more effective than LeMay had thought at the time. They seriously disrupted kamikaze missions, particularly when long-delay bomb fuses were used.

Some 548,000 soldiers, sailors, and marines were poised for the invasion of Okinawa on Easter Sunday, April 1, 1945. They watched the tremendous bombardment by fire support ships and carrier planes as they headed inland to wipe out tactical targets.

The big moment arrived, and the first wave of 20,000 men landed at Hagushi's beaches. To their astonishment and relief, there was virtually no opposition.

The Fifth Fleet continued to fight off waves of suicide planes as the unopposed land forces moved inland during the first five days. Because of kamikaze attacks, Spruance spread his fleet east of Okinawa as much as 100 miles, and Mitscher's carriers confined activities to an area 60 miles square.

The newly arrived British Pacific Fleet, Task Force Fifty-seven, was positioned south of Okinawa with its four carriers. Task Group 52.1, with seventeen escort carriers, stood off to the southeast. Admiral Turner's amphibious forces of 1,200 ships almost encircled the island.

Attacks by suiciders were bad enough, especially on April 6 when 355 one-way attackers made a mass raid, but now remnants of the Japanese fleet decided on their own kamikaze mission. Two thirds of Japan's remaining ships sailed the same day from the Inland Sea.

Day after day fast carriers sent their fighters aloft to destroy the kamikazes before they could crash into ships. Fliers from the *Essex* broke the carrier record by shooting down sixty-five planes, while *Belleau Wood*'s Fighting Thirty destroyed forty-seven more. Yet the kamikazes came in seemingly endless waves from Kyushu's fields.

Crews and pilots reached the point of exhaustion, but humor relieved the grimness of the period. Capt. William G. Tomlinson of the *Belleau Wood* wired Mitscher, "Forty-seven bogies splashed. Does this exceed game limit?"

"Negative!" Mitscher replied. "This is open season. Well done."

Hundreds of attackers were downed and only two American planes were lost in the April 6 attempt to destroy the invasion fleet. Twenty-four Japanese pilots managed to hurl their planes and bombs onto ships; three destroyers were sunk, two ammunition ships blown up, and one tank landing ship (LST) was lost.

Attacks abated for two days, but on April 11 the Japanese again turned their full fury on the fleet.

"Abandon all close support operations," Mitscher advised his task force.

There were times when it seemed as if the Japanese would sacrifice every plane in their air arsenal. Throngs of suiciders were splashed flaming into the ocean, but the battleship *Missouri* still suffered damage, as did the carrier *Enterprise*.

Kamikazes ignored the carriers on the next day and concentrated on invasion ships. Carrier pilots lashed out at the deadly attackers, scoring 151, but kamikazes caused more destruction than on any previous mission.

Spruance alerted patrol submarines to keep an eye on Japanese surface ships, which had left the Island Sea on April 6. Submarines spotted them and wired him immediately. "At least one battleship, supporting destroyers, course one nine zero."

Vice-Adm. Seiichi Ito actually had nine ships. His flagship the *Yamato*, the light cruiser *Yahagi*, and seven destroyers were under his command as he left Tokuyama Harbor.

An *Essex* Hellcat reported their position precisely.

"Pilots, man your planes!" The strident cry echoed once more off the flattops while pilots rushed to their planes. Avengers were loaded with torpedoes, Helldivers with semi-armor piercing bombs, and fighters with 500-pound bombs slung underneath their fuselages.

Every task group contributed. Some 386 planes headed north while navy PBMs kept the enemy fleet under constant observation.

During the night, pilots found the waiting monotonous and lighted one cigarette after another to while away the hours until the enemy task force was close enough for them to attack.

"I've got them on radar," one pilot radioed excitedly after daybreak.

His comrades listened for further word, but their earphones remained silent.

Antiaircraft fire exploded dead ahead, bringing them to anxious readiness. They dropped through the clouds from 10,000 feet as rain pelted their windshields. Lt. Thaddeus T. Coleman broke through at 3,000 feet and saw the ships below maneuvering evasively on the ocean's surface as he began his dive.

Torpedo planes rushed to attack the mighty *Yamato*, scoring hits that promptly made her list. Planes dropped torpedoes from the other side, momentarily slamming the battleship back onto an even keel.

The first wave pulled away, noting that the *Yamato* and *Yahagi* were badly damaged and positive that two destroyers were going down.

Task Group 58.4 arrived with Hellcats, Helldivers, and Avengers and found the *Yamato* still able to fight but the *Yahagi* dead in the water. They concentrated on the *Yahagi*, and she succumbed to their fierce attacks.

Then Comdr. John J. Hyland of the *Intrepid*'s Air Group 10 led his planes against the *Yamato*. The big ship reeled with explosions from a torpedo and eight bombs.

Lt. Thomas H. Stetson, skipper of Torpedo Nine, led the attack as the battleship listed heavily to port. He could see the massive armor belt, now above the waterline on her starboard side, as he directed his group's torpedoes to her vulnerable underbelly.

"Lower your depth settings from 10 to 20 feet," Stetson called.

They made perfect runs, and not a shot was fired. Sweeping over the shattered hulk, Stetson saw the bottom rip out of the ship as she rolled on her beam ends and went down, taking Vice-Adm. Ito and most of the crew with her.

It had been a magnificently executed attack, and only four dive-bombers, three torpedo planes, and three fighters were lost. All but four pilots and eight crewmen were promptly rescued.

The *Hancock* was bombed shortly before noon, but fires were brought under control, and she landed her planes safely.

Japan had lost six more ships from her dwindling fleet.

Over objections from many in the War and Navy Departments, the Joint Chiefs decided on April 3 that in the active areas of the Pacific, MacArthur would retain his command of army ground and air forces except for the Twentieth Air Force, which would remain under Arnold's personal control. Certain units in inactive areas of the South Pacific were removed from MacArthur's jurisdiction. Nimitz remained in charge of all naval forces in the Pacific so there was functionally no change in the divided command; MacArthur and Nimitz were told to complete their current campaigns under the old command structure.

On April 13, word was flashed to the fleet that President Franklin D. Roosevelt was dead and had been succeeded by Harry S Truman. There was a feeling of personal loss among many of the Americans because the president had always loved the navy.

The Tenth Army had come against Lt. Gen. Mitsuru Ushijima's first defense line on April 11, and Okinawa's troops found it impossible to penetrate elaborately prepared positions. Ushijima had devised this strategy to lure the Americans out of reach of the protection provided by the Fifth Fleet's devastating guns.

The Pacific Fleet meanwhile suffered daily attacks climaxed by another major suicide raid on April 16 involving 165 planes. After that raid, attacks diminished. The Japanese boasted about the tremendous destruction they caused, but they claimed to have destroyed far more United States ships than were actually sunk. B–29s had proved helpful and with an improved picket-line defense, kamikazes found hunting less lucrative.

Lt. Gen. Simon B. Buckner's ground forces ran into more stubborn opposition as they fought inland. The Japanese contested every foot of ground, permitting gains literally only over their dead bodies.

American carriers provided close support every hour as ground forces fought for small advances. It was an exhausting task for the pilots, flying constantly into deadly ground fire while they sought pinpoint targets ahead of the troops.

The British had only one carrier squadron so, unlike the Americans, they could not rotate their carriers on and off the battle scene. After thirty-two days at sea, British airmen were so exhausted by their almost daily operations that on April 23 they were ordered to return to San Pedro Roads on Leyte for rest and replenishment. It had been a grueling operational tour, and British airmen were now experienced professionals, though at a cost of sixteen pilots and thirteen aircrew members killed or missing. They had, however, exacted a severe toll. They had destroyed forty-five Japanese planes in the air and on the ground. More importantly, British Task Force Fifty-Seven had denied Japan use of the Sakishima airfields.

An American liaison officer on board the British carrier *Indefatigable* was impressed by the lack of serious damage to the carrier after a kamikaze crashed on board. He told the captain, "When a kamikaze hits a United States carrier, it's six months repair at Pearl. In a Limey carrier it's a case of 'Sweepers, man your brooms.'" The British carriers had armored steel flight decks, as do all postwar United States carriers.

Admiral Rawlings strongly resisted a request by Admiral King that all or part of his British Pacific Fleet return to the southwest Pacific to support an assault on Tarakan in Borneo that was now scheduled for May 1. Rawlings received the word from the Seventh Fleet Commander Adm. Kinkaid. Nimitz and Spruance both voiced strong opposition, and the proposal was canceled on April 27.

In Australia, Sir Bruce Fraser voiced again his doubts about the divided command between Nimitz and MacArthur in the Pacific. He told his staff that indecision by the Americans was causing a nearly calamitous state of affairs for the British fleet and was a direct result of the lack of a supreme commander in the Pacific theater.

Task Force Fifty-seven returned to the area around Okinawa on May 1, and the carrier *Formidable* was hit by a Japanese bomb on its flight deck, destroying a Corsair and ten Avengers. The *Formidable*'s Capt. P. Ruck-Keene, boiling with rage, radioed his flagship the *Indomitable* that the man responsible was a "little yellow bastard."

Admiral Vian signaled, "Are you addressing me?"

The captain hastily signaled back that he was referring to the Japanese pilot.

The war in Europe ended officially on May 8 but around Okinawa the Japanese unleashed one of their worst kamikaze attacks. A Zeke fighter dropped a bomb on the carrier *Victorious*, while another Zeke crashed on its flight deck. Although the attacks were beaten off, a kamikaze started fires on the *Formidable* that took fifteen minutes to put out. All British carriers survived the attacks, but operations on board the *Victorious* were limited, and the *Formidable* was down to four serviceable Avengers and eleven Corsair fighters.

Rawlings and Vian received permission to withdraw from action until May 12, and the American Task Group 52.1 took its place. When the British task group returned, Nimitz advised Rawlings that his group need not cover Sakishima Gunto after May 25.

The strain on the British air and ground crews had been severe. They had been at sea for sixty-two days with only eight days for recuperation at Leyte between operations.

British ships had frequently fought off waves of Japanese planes but not once did they see a Japanese ship. The task group's five carriers had each been hit at least once by Japanese suicide planes; they had destroyed fifty-seven Japanese planes on the ground and in the air. On this second tour, they lost an additional six pilots and two aircrew members.

Rawlings' carriers had started with 218 aircraft, but they had needed 203 replacements to keep them at operational strength. Due to all causes, the British lost 98 airplanes.

Spruance and Nimitz were warm in their praise of the British effort and expressed their satisfaction to both Rawlings and to Sir Bruce Fraser in Australia.

On May 20, twelve Avengers from Sherman's group were set up for a special attack. Their pilots were briefed about a particularly stubborn ridge surmounting a natural amphitheater to the south.

"This small ridge," the briefing officer said, pointing to a map of the battlefield, "has held up our ground forces advancing towards Shuri for a week. Three hundred infantrymen have died trying to capture it. It must be pulverized."

Avenger pilots headed for the target, worried about having to drop bombs only 50 yards from their own troops but determined to destroy the Japanese stronghold. In pairs, they dove to within 200 feet of the ground and dropped their bombs, feeling the concussions slap back at them as they pulled away.

Artillery opened a barrage, and troops swarmed over the ridge, quickly capturing the gun positions from the stunned Japanese defenders and losing only two men in the well-coordinated ground and air attack. It opened up the whole Shuri defense line, and American troops charged forward, gaining thousands of feet where formerly they had been lucky to gain a yard.

Organized resistance ended in the latter part of June, but colossal mopping-up operations lay ahead. Amid its victories, the army was saddened by the loss of its ground forces commander, Lieutenant General Buckner, who was killed a week before.

Lt. Gen. Mitsuru Ushijima thrust a hara-kiri knife into his stomach three days later, and the rest of his generals followed suit. The Japanese lost 111,351 ground troops, while untold others were lost from their air force and navy.

Emperor Hirohito and his government officials desperately desired peace but army militarists refused to concede. Devastating

B–29 raids were now pulverizing Japan's cities, and both navy and civilian leaders realized that their nation had lost the war.

Okinawa had been a deadly battle in which 12,250 Americans were killed, with the navy losing the largest number, 4,907. Kamikaze attacks caused the heaviest casualties in dead and wounded, and the fleet lost thirty-six ships, though none larger than a destroyer.

Plane losses were also high: 269 destroyed in combat, 229 crashed on board their carriers, and 292 from all other causes. Air combat took the lives of 205 men.

Despite intelligence estimates that the Japanese had been short of airplanes, they lost 7,830 planes and probably 12,000 airmen.

McCain summarized his feelings to Nimitz about using fast carriers in such operations. "It is wasteful to use fast carriers in direct support of ground troops over a long period. It fails to exploit the assets of mobility, surprise, and concentration, and is undesirable. Such use invites danger to the carriers while diverting them from more worthwhile targets which only they can attack."

Halsey added his objections. "Fast carriers can support landing operations far better by going into offensive action. I recommend defense employment only when offensive action is impossible or when such defense use is the only means of preventing defeat of, or disastrous losses to, the invasion forces."

There was no doubt in anyone's mind that carriers were too vulnerable to suicide attacks so close to Japanese bases.

The British navy meanwhile disposed of the last ships that the Japanese navy had based at Singapore, including four heavy cruisers, minesweepers, and luggers.

The last stepping stones were in Allied hands by the spring of 1945. An important strategic decision was now needed for the next move.

After war in Europe came to an end on May 8—VE Day—the Joint Chiefs asked MacArthur and Nimitz for their views on how to bring the Pacific war to a close. Nimitz said that the home islands should be encircled and bombing stepped up to a great crescendo before Kyushu was invaded.

At a conference in early April, Nimitz had stressed that their next strategic move should be a siege of the home islands or a blockade.

Army representatives disagreed, claiming that the home islands would have to be invaded or the Japanese would never quit.

Nimitz was not convinced. "It is apparent," he said, "that both alternatives have their merits and demerits." He refused to specify which alternative he preferred.

Planners with the Joint Chiefs recommended an early invasion, saying that the Japanese would not otherwise surrender. The idea of an invasion was resisted by others, who believed that an invasion of the home islands would result in enormous casualties.

The arguments continued after VE Day, but all members of the Joint Chiefs finally agreed that an invasion should be considered as the basis for planning. After the war, some members of the Joint Chiefs claimed that they had reluctantly agreed to an invasion of Japan's home islands but that they preferred a blockade and bombing instead. This was true, but not one member of the Joint Chiefs voiced strong objections at the time.

MacArthur and Marshall, both of whom favored a direct assault on the main islands, now pressed for an invasion of Kyushu, Japan's southernmost island. The occupation of part of Kyushu, they argued, would permit the establishment of naval and air facilities to be used in a mass invasion of the Tokyo plain.

High surf precluded an invasion of Kyushu after November 1 so that date became the planning target. MacArthur favored a November invasion of Kyushu and said that he would get the men and supplies by cleaning out bases throughout the Pacific. Two plans finally reached the agreement stage; one for Kyushu and the other for the occupation of the Chusan Archipelago in the East China Sea.

Opposition to the invasion plans continued to develop because the desperate Japanese resistance on Okinawa foreshadowed an even more aggressive defense of Kyushu.

The Joint Chiefs, weighing all possibilities, decided on November 1 for the invasion of southern Kyushu but deferred the Chusan operation.

MacArthur planned the invasion as the biggest of any he had led in the Pacific. The navy offered two fleets for support. Halsey's Third Fleet, with the fast carrier groups, would be augmented by units of the British Pacific Fleet to provide support for landings through strong attacks against Honshu and Hokkaido. They would be based at Eniwetok and the Marianas. Spruance's Fifth Fleet would have amphibious support and covering ships.

Land, sea, and air forces would congregate in the Philippines, Okinawa, and the Marianas for the huge undertaking. Okinawa would be the staging area for half a million men, and 212 attack transports and 555 LSTs would transport them to the shores of Kyushu.

MacArthur planned for fourteen divisions, three of which would be marine, while holding three divisions in reserve to meet an expected Japanese defense force of ten divisions.

Every planner and commander knew that it would be a hazardous undertaking. They considered the expected 50,000 casualties in the first thirty days and sadly shook their heads, wondering if there was not a less costly way to bring about Japan's final surrender.

19

TOLERATING
THE INTOLERABLE

Halsey relieved Spruance of command of the Fifth Fleet, which then became the Third Fleet, off Okinawa on May 27 and led it for a second time into the path of a vicious typhoon. Extensive damage was caused to his ships, and there was a large loss of life.

Once again Admiral King told Vice-Admiral Hoover to conduct an investigation. He placed the blame squarely on Halsey and his carrier commander John McCain. Hoover told King that Halsey deserved to be court-martialed, saying that if he was not a war hero he would be tried.

King agreed privately with Hoover's assessment, but he did not want to take on such an explosive issue at this stage of the war. Secretary of Navy Forrestal reluctantly agreed.

Expressions of anger and distress were broadcast from radio stations in Japan as the air war was stepped up. The Far East Air Force, the Twentieth Air Force, and carrier planes dominated the skies over Japan's prostrate empire. While B–29 strikes continued to level her cities and factories, carrier planes sought to establish air supremacy in the skies over Kyushu in anticipation of the coming invasion.

One enigma remained. What would Russia do? Imperial General Headquarters in Tokyo expected American landings on their southern island of Kyushu if Russia did not join the war in the near future.

Russian intentions became clearer on April 5. She renounced her neutrality pact with Japan.

Japan's only hope of avoiding total annihilation lay in the use of her Kamikaze Corps. She did not, however, expect to rely solely on suicide planes because she had an equal number of planes for normal attack purposes. Even though suicide planes numbered 5,350, more than the determination of their pilots was needed to destroy the United States Pacific Fleet and its troop transports.

The Japanese on the Chinese mainland now consolidated their forces, and Lt. Gen. Albert C. Wedemeyer reported that they were withdrawing into Shanghai and Hong Kong, permitting a revitalized Chinese Nationalist Army to concentrate in the Canton–Hong Kong area.

The Japanese government was desperate, looking hopefully for a face-saving formula to get out of her present predicament. The devastating attacks at home and the loss of her bitterly won possessions in the south, had created a chaotic situation in the government that was not fully comprehended by the Allied powers.

While B–29s saturated Honshu, Kyushu, and Shikoku with firebombs and devastated her vital factories, the emperor initiated discussions to end the war. He received support from every group except the army. After Okinawa capitulated, Kuniakai Koiso's cabinet resigned.

Hirohito ignored his senior statesmen and appointed the reluctant seventy-nine-year-old Adm. Baron Kantaro Suzuki as prime minister. His appointment was viewed with great interest by officials of the American government because on April 13, the day Roosevelt died, he had said, "I must admit Roosevelt's leadership has been very effective. It has been responsible for the Americans' advantageous position today. I can understand the great loss his passing means to the American people, and my profound sympathy goes to them."

Suzuki, with the emperor's support, decided that Japan could not continue the war because of factory damage, ship losses, a deteriorating food situation, and the attitude of the Japanese people. He revealed his thoughts to the emperor, and they both agreed that steps should be taken immediately to establish peace. Suzuki started conversations with the Russian ambassador, whom he hoped to use as an intermediary, but army reaction was violent.

Hirohito personally called a meeting of the prime minister and five members of his cabinet on June 20. "I think it is necessary," he said, "to have a plan to end the war at once as well as to defend the islands."

Suzuki called his cabinet into session. "Today the emperor has said what everyone has wanted to say but yet was afraid to say. The war must be ended."

Task Force Thirty-eight returned to Leyte Gulf for provisioning on June 13 and after a long rest while ships were refueled, they headed north on July 1. Crews were wild with excitement when bullhorns announced, "We're headed again for Japan."

Many an eyebrow lifted in wonder when the Joint Chiefs of Staff sent a top secret message to MacArthur, Nimitz, and General LeMay on July 3. "The Japanese cities of Kukura, Niigata, Kyoto, and Hiroshima will not be attacked by elements under your command."

Halsey's Third Fleet operated on Japan's slim lifeline with surgical smoothness, halting all shipping from the Asiatic mainland to the home islands. Even shipping between the main islands came under attack.

Halsey received specific instructions from Nimitz, "Launch air attacks on northern Honshu and Hokkaido and bombard coastal cities."

Fliers from Halsey's carriers took off for Tokyo at 4:00 A.M. on July 10 after weathering a bad front. Fighters swept low, and then torpedo and dive-bombers plunged at their targets.

McCain's three carrier groups had ten large carriers and six light carriers with Adms. Thomas L. Sprague, Jerry Bogan, and Arthur Radford in charge. While attackers struck vicious blows, not one Japanese fighter rose to do battle. Even flak was of minor concern. It was evident that Japan had decided to hoard its airpower. Attackers found 109 planes on the ground to destroy, while damaging an additional 231.

It was a two-pronged offensive. The Fifth Air Force and the Tactical Air Force on Okinawa had devastated fields the day before. Army Air Forces Mustang fighters, based on Iwo Jima, added to the devastation by sweeping the Tokyo area following a massive 550-plane strike at industrial and refinery centers by the Twentieth's B–29s.

If Japanese defenders were confused by the variety of attacks, they had every reason to be. Marine Corsair fighters and carrier air groups with navy Avenger torpedo bombers struck Kyushu's fields on July 11 while carriers were off Tokyo Bay. As if these attacks were not enough, Rear Adm. John F. Shafroth, Jr., bombarded the steel-producing city of Kamaishi with surface gunfire in what must have been for top Japanese navy officers a humiliating attack.

Halsey moved north and on July 14 and 15 sent his carrier planes to bomb the ferry route between the northern tip of Honshu and southern Hokkaido. Railroad ferry boats, carrying coal for the industrial furnaces of Honshu, received a devastating blow. Five were sunk, one was left burning, and three others were damaged.

Navy fliers had a field day all over northern Japan. They were given no particular targets. "Choose a target of opportunity," they were told.

On July 14, the big guns of the warships created a hell on earth for the town of Muroran on the southern coast where the Nihon steel company, the Wanishi iron and steel manufacturing company, and a synthetic oil refinery were devastated. The Japanese refused to contest the action.

For all practical purposes, the Japanese navy had ceased to exist. There were only a few ships left that could pose even a limited threat to Allied forces. Nimitz wired Halsey, "Continued existence of remaining Japanese naval forces makes it necessary to use on defense missions larger naval forces than would otherwise be necessary. Remaining ships must be eliminated. This is the responsibility of the Pacific Fleet."

Halsey put his intelligence reports to work, and they located the hiding places of the remaining ships. Some were in coves of the Inland Sea near Kure, close to Hiroshima. They included the battleship *Haruna*; the carrier-battleships *Ise* and *Hyuga*; three carriers, including the *Amagi*, which had never been in combat; and the *Katsuragi* and *Ryuho*. Six cruisers, the heavy cruisers *Tone* and *Aoba* and the fast light cruisers *Iwate*, *Izuma*, *Settsu*, and *Oyoda* completed the list of capital ships in this area. The last was Admiral Ozawa's flagship.

Nimitz's deputy, Admiral John Towers, finally got his chance for a Pacific command when he was ordered to replace Spruance as head of the Fifth Fleet in the closing months of the war. King's animosity toward Towers had denied this brilliant airman a command role throughout the war although he was responsible more than any other man for the development of the fast carrier forces. Admiral John Hoover was brought in as Nimitz's deputy to replace Towers after Nimitz convinced King that Towers should have a fleet command before the end of the war.

Towers was a stickler for protocol, and the officers mess at Pearl Harbor had been well run. Staff officers appreciated the excellent food, and the fact the martinis were made with top quality gin. Hoover quickly changed the policy of buying the best gin, and not only the martinis declined in quality, but so did the food.

Shortly after Hoover was named Nimitz' deputy, Julius Ochs

Adler, publisher of *The New York Times*, stopped at Pearl Harbor en route to Nimitz' forward headquarters on Guam. Nimitz told Hoover to make sure that the famous publisher and philanthropist was well treated because his paper could be influential in maintaining the navy's postwar image.

Hoover's aide and flag lieutenant personally briefed all those who were to attend the dinner in Adler's honor, stressing that they should be judicious in what they said so that Adler would return home with a favorable impression of the navy. He particularly stressed that there should be no inappropriate remarks about Jews.

As the dinner neared its end, Hoover relaxed, pleased that all members of his staff had conducted themselves with decorum. The only argument that had developed was how the *Times* had survived without comic strips.

Now, to his shock, he heard one of his most senior officers ask, "Tell me, Mr. Adler, isn't it true that *The New York Times* is supported by a bunch of wealthy Jews?"

The staff were aghast and almost slid under the table. Nimitz was so incensed that he fired Hoover and brought back a former deputy, Adm. John H. Newton.

After intelligence data were completed about location of the remnants of the Japanese fleet, Halsey ordered a series of strikes. The battleship *Nagato*, Halsey noted, was tied up and camouflaged at the naval base at Yokosuka on Tokyo Bay. He glanced at the antiaircraft guns around the area and shuddered.

British Task Force Thirty-seven joined the Third Fleet on July 17 for two more strikes at Tokyo's airfields. Heavy cloud cover reduced the scope of operations, and only four planes were destroyed on the ground.

On this date, the cruiser *Indianapolis* started its utterly secret and fateful journey across the Pacific with the first atomic bomb. It delivered the bomb to the 509th Composite Group on Tinian and headed for the Philippines. Sailing alone, it was routed through an error at Guam over the known position of a Japanese submarine and was sunk on July 30. The torpedo explosion and rapid sinking prevented her from transmitting a distress signal, and her fate became known only after survivors were later sighted in the area.

As long as the 34,000-ton battleship *Nagato* remained in Yokosuka, it was a challenge to Halsey's pilots. Despite dozens of flak batteries, fighters armed with 1,000-pound armor-piercing bombs dove on the *Nagato* while torpedo planes executed a coordinated attack on antiaircraft positions. The *Nagato* was badly damaged but refused to sink although an adjacent destroyer went down.

All across the Tokyo plain, carrier planes struck again at airfields without opposition except the deadly antiaircraft fire. United States planes got thirty-nine planes, and the British got eleven, but American losses numbered twelve planes and twenty-two men.

July 24 dawned bright and clear. "A good day to strike Kure," Halsey said.

Words were translated into action and bombers headed for the naval base. Japanese ships could not be attacked there by torpedo planes because of the manner in which the ships were anchored, a lesson learned early in the attacks against the *Nagato*. Dive-bombers and fighters did score five hits on the *Ise*, and the *Hyuga* was struck such deadly blows that it settled to the bottom. The veteran *Haruna*, which had often been announced as sunk since the earliest days of the war, received only one hit. The *Amagi* received a hit on her flight deck, and the carrier *Ryuho* was so well camouflaged that pilots failed to find her. The flight deck of the carrier *Katsuragi* looked like a gabled roof, but her machinery was not badly damaged, and later she was used to repatriate troops. Ozawa's cruiser the *Oyoda* received four direct hits and some near misses while the older cruisers *Iwate* and *Settsu* were hit so severely that they settled into the mud.

The Japanese had taken enough punishment. They struck back, particularly when carrier planes approached Nagoya, Osaka, and Miho.

It had been a good two days for the Third Fleet, with over a quarter of a million tons of enemy warships either sunk or badly damaged. One hundred planes were destroyed on the ground and with the resurgence of enemy activity in the air, another thirty-one were shot down. This was not without its price. Thirty-two American planes were lost.

Halsey ordered his carriers to strike Kure again on July 28 because warships berthed there did not seem seriously damaged.

"Concentrate on the *Haruna*," he said.

Carrier pilots did as they were instructed, and finally the *Haruna* settled to the bottom. Far East Air Force B–24 bombers from Okinawa also attacked. They failed to score hits on the *Haruna* but they sank *Aoba*. The *Ise* also met her doom, and the carrier *Amagi* was ripped open after incessant attacks.

When the strike was over, the *Oyoda, Tone,* and *Izuma* were on the bottom, and the carrier *Katsuragi* was badly damaged, but again no one found the *Ryuho*.

Halsey was jubilant. He sent a personal message to all ships. "Mark well this day the 28th of July. To the Dumbos and life-guards, to combat air patrol and men of the surface team, to the valiant British force on the right flank. Well done. For the flying fighters who fought it out over Japan to a smashing victory, I have no words that can add to the record with their courage, their blood, and their lives."

Meanwhile, the industrial center of Hamamatsu suffered a night raid as fliers from the carrier *Bon Homme Richard* dealt a deadly blow.

The Third Fleet steamed back and forth across Japan's doorstep, dealing body blows that weakened and disheartened the distraught nation. Hirohito again personally intervened to end the slaughter of his people. On July 20, he appealed to the Soviet government to receive Prince Konoye as special ambassador in an endeavor to improve relations between the Japanese and the Russians. He also asked the Soviet Union to intercede with the United States to stop the war. Moscow bluntly declined his appeals because the Potsdam Conference was about to begin.

The Potsdam Conference met from July 17 to August 2, and afterward a declaration was issued. Hirohito and Prime Minister Suzuki read the Potsdam Declaration with dismay because it called for Japan's unconditional surrender. Despite their feelings, the cabinet wanted to accept the terms. It would do anything to call a halt to a war that threatened their survival as a race.

War Minister Gen. Korechiki Anami refused to concede, claiming that the army as yet was undefeated.

On July 16, the United States had tested the first atomic bomb in New Mexico. Scientists had been awed and speechless as the huge flash lightened the desert sky with a brilliance greater than the sun's. President Harry S Truman had ordered the bomb used to shorten the war, and the 509th Composite Group of the Twentieth Air Force's 313th Wing, which had been trained to drop the bomb, prepared for its first mission from Tinian in the Marianas.

Top commanders now realized why certain targets had been given sanctuary from B–29 and carrier attacks. These were reserved as the targets of an atomic attack. At first, Kyoto, Hiroshima, Kokura, and Niigata were listed as targets. Kyoto was removed from the list because it was a historic shrine city. Nagasaki was chosen instead.

On August 6, 1945, the world's first nuclear weapon was exploded above the city of Hiroshima, and the world was shocked by the destruction. Three days later, a second bomb destroyed most of Nagasaki.

The British Pacific Fleet, now designated Task Force Thirty-seven, had joined the Americans 300 miles east of Japan on July 16 after refitting at Sydney, Australia. Admiral Vian's First Aircraft Carrier Squadron was at full strength with 255 aircraft. The American Third Fleet had nine fleet carriers and six light carriers.

Nimitz had ordered the combined fleets to reduce Japan's tactical army and navy air forces during July and August by attacking strategic targets on the mainland. The British fleet saw its first action on July 17 when it used bombs and rockets to hit airfields northeast of Tokyo at Sendai, Masuda, and Matsushima.

The British had been eager to join the attacks against the remaining Japanese capital ships, but Admiral Halsey refused to permit them to take part in such raids. His excuse was that British aircraft did not have sufficient range. This was not correct, of course, because most of the aircraft on the British carriers were American types. Apparently this refusal was Halsey's own decision, one made so that the United States Navy could take its own revenge on the Imperial Navy for its attack on Pearl Harbor.

The British fleet continued its attacks on shipping and air bases throughout July and were then given a ten-day respite from operations.

On August 9, British air groups swung into action again, concentrating on Japanese airfields and shipping in bays and harbors.

Lt. Hampton "Hammy" Gray, a Royal Canadian Naval Reserve pilot, was senior pilot of the *Formidable*'s 1841 Squadron. He had taken part in the bombing of the German battleship *Tirpitz* in August 1944, in the Atlantic, and since coming to the Pacific had earned new honors for operations off Okinawa.

The blond, boyish-looking pilot sauntered to his Corsair, his plump body rolling with the *Formidable*'s deck. He climbed into the cockpit and prepared to take off. With a casual wave to deck hands who had come to admire this modest young man, Gray headed toward Japan.

He led his flight to the island of Honshu. Then, Gray methodically searched for a target. He spotted five warships in Onagawa Wan on the shores of Japan's main island. He dropped lower, and the others in his section followed him just above the water as he prepared to make his attack. Shore batteries concentrated on the lead plane, and Gray's Corsair was quickly riddled and caught fire, but he held his fighter true until his bomb was released. His plane, now a flaming torch, crashed into the water while the bombs from the formation he had led exploded on the destroyer and sank it. His valor was recognized posthumously when the British government awarded him a Victoria Cross. He was the only member of the British Pacific Fleet to be so honored.

Despite the destruction of Hiroshima and Nagasaki by atomic bombs, Japan's war minister and his chiefs of staff still refused to accept the terms of the Potsdam agreement, holding out for a negotiated peace. Emperor Hirohito took decisive action. "To stop the war on this occasion is the only way to save the nation from destruction," he told an Imperial Conference. "I decide this war shall be stopped!" He had no constitutional authority to make such a decision, but while his cabinet ministers broke down and cried at their nation's humiliation, word was relayed to Switzerland that the Japanese wished to end the war.

At a meeting on August 14, War Minister Anami, Army Chief of Staff Gen. Yoshijiro Umezu, and Navy Chief of Staff Toyoda begged for one final battle on the home islands to defend the nation's honor. The emperor refused and made arrangements to record an imperial message for broadcast the following day.

That day, the Japanese people heard their emperor for the first time, and most people prostrated themselves. His high-pitched voice almost breaking with emotion, the emperor said, "To our good and loyal subjects. After pondering deeply the general trends of the Empire today, We have decided to effect a settlement of the present situation by resorting to an extraordinary measure.

"We, the Emperor, have ordered the Imperial Government to notify the Governments of the United States, Great Britain, China and the Soviet Union that We accept their Joint Declaration."

The military situation could not be reversed, he told them, and with the employment of a new and inhuman bomb, a continuation of the war would not only "lead to the annihilation of our Nation, but to the destruction of human civilization as well."

He spoke of his regrets for Japan's Asian allies and for those who died in four long years of savagery which "pains Our heart night and day."

In conclusion, he said that he was resolved to pave the way for a "grand" peace for all generations to come by enduring the unendurable and tolerating the intolerable. This last comment referred to the coming occupation of Japan.

Some were still not convinced and sought to thwart their emperor's wishes, but they were in the minority. The majority went into national mourning and obeyed the wishes of their sovereign.

The Japanese government accepted surrender terms on August 10, with one exception: The emperor should not be deprived of his throne. Swedish and Swiss emissaries transmitted the agreement through diplomatic channels to Washington.

After serious discussion, the Allies agreed that Japan could keep her emperor but stipulated that he must take orders from them. They put their thoughts in words, "From the moment of surrender, authority of the Emperor and the Japanese government to rule the state shall be subject to the Supreme Commander of Allied Powers who will take such steps as he deems proper to effectuate the surrender terms.

"The ultimate form of government for Japan shall, in accordance with the Potsdam Declaration, be established by the freely expressed will of the Japanese people."

Halsey, when advised of what was going on, said, "Have we got enough fuel to turn around and hit the bastards once more before they quit?"

While governments considered their next move, a raging typhoon stopped further carrier attacks against Japan.

No final determination for ending the war was received by August 12 so McCain sent word to his carrier commanders, "The fact that we are ordered to strike indicates the enemy may have thrown an unacceptable joker into surrender terms. This war could last months longer. We cannot afford to relax. Now is the time to pour it on."

Fast carrier task force planes struck Tokyo on August 15 and were met by forty-five enemy fighters, twenty-six of whom were downed.

While the second strike headed for the target, pilots heard, "Cease fire. Cease fire. The war's over. Cease fire!"

They jubilantly jettisoned their bombs and headed back to their carriers.

President Truman had announced the end of the war in Washington, and King had immediately wired Nimitz, "Suspend all offensive hostile action. Remain alert."

McCain issued sharp orders to his pilots after they returned. "I want wartime vigilance maintained until we're sure the Japanese plan no further attacks."

McCain queried Halsey what his ships should do if attacked.

"All snoopers shall be investigated and shot down," Halsey replied, "not vindictively but in a friendly sort of way."

Their alertness paid off: Thirty-eight Japanese planes were shot down on VJ Day.

In anticipation of surrender, on or about August 15, the Imperial High Command ordered all commanders to destroy their war records. This was a general order, and it was religiously obeyed, much to the distress of later historians.

Although the dropping of the world's first two atomic bombs was given credit for ending the war, Japan had already been defeated. The sea-air blockade of the Japanese home islands and the direct bombing attacks on industrial and urban targets had brought about this defeat by the end of July. The production of civilian goods was down so low that the nation faced economic collapse, and munitions output had been reduced so severely by the destruction of factories that military operations could no longer be sustained.

The urban incendiary attacks by the Twentieth Air Force had profound repercussions on civilian morale, weakening Japan's will to remain in the war. Sixty-six cities, virtually all those of economic significance, were subjected to bombing raids and suffered destruction ranging from 25 to 90 percent.

After the war, following months of conducting a thorough survey, officials of the Strategic Bombing Survey reached the conclusion that Japan would have surrendered prior to December 31, 1945, and in all probability by November 1 even if the atomic bombs had not been dropped and even if no invasion had been planned or contemplated.

Although few acknowledged it at the time, Japan was defeated by the effective use of airpower, and the men of the Pacific Fleet had contributed more than their share toward her defeat. Airpower was the primary but not, however, the sole reason for Japan's surrender. Certainly the long and costly drive across the Central Pacific to secure the Marianas as air-base sites was a prerequisite for the final strategic air offensive against Japan. Japan's capability of sustaining her armed forces, particularly those outside her home islands, was undermined by the war at sea. As an island empire, Japan was entirely dependent upon sea transportation, and was particularly susceptible to sea power. When Nimitz's Pacific Fleet cut off Japan's ocean commerce, it marked the beginning of the end. By a large margin his submarines sank more ships than the entire air effort. More men were killed in action in submarines than were lost in naval air actions.

Allied fleet units entered the coastal waters of Japan on August 27 while hundreds of planes rode above. Landings were made at Yokosuka, Yokohama, and along selected points of Sagami and Tokyo bays. Major occupation forces did not land until August 30.

General MacArthur flew to Atsugi airfield on August 29, and Admiral Nimitz arrived the same day. Admiral King, the man most responsible for the navy's victory in the Pacific, remained in Washington; Nimitz, whose genius as an organizer forged a mighty retaliatory fleet and led it to victory, took his place.

The September 2 surrender ceremony was scheduled to take place aboard the battleship *Missouri*, anchored off Yokohama.

Admiral Towers was assigned as a spectator. Although he had never been given the personal recognition his efforts deserve as the architect of naval victory in the Pacific, the war's sudden end, brought about through the effective use of airpower, is ample justification for his long support of aviation. While serving under Nimitz, Towers had with quiet efficiency made the recommendations that resulted in the successful development of the fast carrier forces. His personality conflict with Admiral King was so serious that he was forced to work behind the scenes. Nimitz, who appreciated Towers' background in naval aviation, had wholeheartedly supported his recommendations.

The fact that Nimitz received credit for organizing the Pacific Fleet and leading it to victory in the Pacific certainly must have been upsetting to Towers. Nevertheless, his admiration for Nimitz remained strong even though he considered his boss to be part of the "old navy" governed by surface officers. He had long fought them but in the final analysis, he won the conclusive victory over them in his own, quiet way.

In Tokyo Bay, with Mount Fujiyama barely visible because of the leaden skies, 258 ships, representing nations that had fought Japan, rode at anchor while preparations were completed for the surrender ceremony. The big carriers remained outside to launch a ceremonial armada of planes at the appropriate moment.

Admiral Halsey had ordered major units of his Third Fleet to anchor in Sagami Wan, an inlet southwest of Tokyo Bay. The units included his flagship the *Missouri* and the H.M.S. *Duke of York*, which bore the flag of Admiral Sir Bruce Fraser, along with other elements of the British Pacific Fleet.

Fleet Admiral Nimitz came aboard the *Missouri* on September 2 at 8:05 A.M. and his five-starred flag was broken at the main truck while General of the Army Douglas MacArthur's flag was placed next to it. For the occasion, Halsey had shifted his four-starred flag to the *Iowa*.

When Halsey saw Lt. Gen. Jonathan M. Wainwright, the man who had surrendered American forces in the Philippines to the Japanese in the war's early months, he was appalled by his sunken eyes, pitted cheeks, and snow-white hair. Wainwright's long prison confinement had taken a terrible toll, and Halsey's voice was hoarse when he called, "Hi, skinny." Their hands touched briefly as each fought to hold back the tears.

At 8:56, the Japanese delegation was brought from Yokohama by the American destroyer *Lansdowne*. It was headed by Foreign Minister Mamoru Shigemitsu and Gen. Yoshijiro Umezu, chief of the army general staff, who had been ordered by Emperor Hirohito to sign on behalf of the Imperial General Headquarters despite his bitter protests. He and Navy Chief of Staff Toyoda had argued unsuccessfully for one final battle to preserve the nation's honor. The eleven-man delegation included representatives from the Japanese army, navy, and the Foreign Office.

The atmosphere was frigid as the Japanese were piped on board. Shigemitsu, who had lost a leg to a terrorist's bomb in China, was in pain as he limped across the deck because the wooden stump that replaced his leg fit poorly. Shigemitsu's helplessness seemed to symbolize his nation's dire straits. He was dressed formally in top hat, cutaway coat, and striped trousers. In contrast, Umezu strode on board with a blank stare, dressed in the olive drab of a general officer with cavalry boots and a sword.

The Japanese were arranged in three rows on the *Missouri*'s deck facing a table covered with a green cloth. Military men from all nations at war with Japan stood across from it. The Americans wore khaki "suntan" uniforms without ties, in contrast to the others in more formal attire. The British delegation wore shorts and white knee stockings, while the Russians wore red-epauletted uniforms. Representatives from Australia, Canada, France, New Zealand, and the Netherlands were in more traditional uniforms.

While everyone waited for MacArthur to appear, the Japanese retained their dignity, but it was obvious that they were uncomfortable.

At 9 A.M., a small door opened and MacArthur, followed by Nimitz and Halsey, strode to the table facing the Japanese. MacArthur picked up a piece of paper. In an emotional voice, he said, "We are gathered here, representatives of the major warring powers, to conclude a solemn agreement whereby peace may be restored. The issues, involving divergent ideals and ideologies, have been determined on the battlefields of the world and hence are not for our discussion or debate."

Nimitz listened without expression. Secretary of the Navy James Forrestal had tried to convince President Truman that Nimitz should sign as the representative for all powers, but he had been overruled. MacArthur was appointed supreme commander for the occasion.

Lt. Gen. Sir Arthur E. Percival, the British officer who had been forced to surrender Singapore at the start of the war, stared stonily at Colonel Ichiji Sugita, who had been the Japanese interpreter for his country when its officials had dictated the terms of the British surrender. Their eyes locked without expression for a brief moment.

MacArthur's emotion made his hands shake as he continued to read from his prepared text. "The terms and conditions upon which the surrender of the Japanese Imperial Force is here to be given and accepted are contained in the instrument of surrender now before you.

"As Supreme Commander of the Allied Powers, it is my firm purpose, in the tradition of the countries I represent, to proceed in the discharge of my responsibilities with justice and tolerance, while taking all necessary dispositions to insure that the terms of the surrender are fully, promptly, and faithfully complied with."

He stepped back and motioned for the Japanese to sign. Shigemitsu stumbled forward, his wooden leg almost tripping him while the wind whipped at his hat. He sat down, placed his silk hat on the table, and with trembling hands, removed his yellow gloves and placed them on top of his hat. He picked up a pen but it remained poised uncertainly above the document.

MacArthur's voice was sharp. "Sutherland! Show him where to sign." The chief of staff walked up quickly, showed the embarrassed foreign minister where to sign, and then stepped back. Shigemitsu signed at 9:04 A.M.

General Umezu followed him to the table and scrawled his name under that of Shigemitsu. Blank-faced, the general marched stiffly back to his delegation, some of whom had tears in their eyes.

MacArthur stepped forward. "Will Generals Wainwright and Percival join me as I sign?"

They moved up behind him. They had recently been released from Japanese internment in Manchuria. Both were haggard and distraught after more than three years in Japanese prison camps.

MacArthur sat down to sign the surrender documents on behalf of all Allied powers. He used six pens, signing his name in segments using a different pen for each. He gave the first pen to Wainwright. The second went to Percival. The third pen he later gave to West Point where he had once been commandant. The fourth was destined for the American archives, and the fifth was given to his aide, Gen. Courtney Whitney. He finished his signature with a red-barreled pen that he placed in his shirt pocket to give later to his wife Jean and their son Arthur in Manila.

Admiral Chester Nimitz signed for the United States, and Sir Bruce Fraser for Great Britain. Representatives of the other Allied nations completed the process with their signatures.

MacArthur went before the microphones for the last time. "It is my earnest hope—indeed the hope of all mankind—that from this solemn occasion a better world shall emerge out of the blood and carnage of the past; a world founded upon faith and understanding, a world dedicated to the dignity of man and the fulfillment of his most cherished wish for freedom, tolerance and justice."

For the first time that morning the sun broke through as General MacArthur said, "Let us pray that peace be now restored to the world, and that God will preserve it always. These proceedings are closed."

Overhead, 450 carrier planes and a large fleet of land-based bombers swept majestically over the *Missouri* in a triumphant climax to the end of hostilities. Lt. Robert T. "Rudder" Kieling, from the *Bon Homme Richard*, led a four-plane division of night-fighter squadron VFN–91. Throughout the war, massed formations had been avoided because of the danger of midair collisions, so Kieling's overriding consideration was the danger posed by hundreds of aircraft flying a prescribed course without room to deviate. The necessity of maintaining a precise formation among hundreds of similar formations took all the skill he had acquired since joining the Pacific Fleet. He was awed by the sight of so many aircraft in a confined airspace, passing in an unbroken line that stretched for miles.

Kieling glanced below, marveling at the number of Allied warships anchored in Tokyo Bay. He had never seen so many, even at Ulithi, and could only imagine how overwhelming the sight must have appeared to the Japanese officials as they accepted defeat. He, like the thousands of other fliers who had fought to bring about Japan's collapse, had seen the war only in bits and pieces. Now, as the aerial armada swept over Tokyo, Kieling looked down at the devastation wrought by airpower on this once-thriving city of millions. No vehicles were visible, and only a few people could be seen threading their way through vast wastelands where homes and factories had once stood.

As the air groups turned back toward the coast of Japan, Kieling knew that the scenes he had just witnessed would remain forever in his memory. He could not help but wonder if Japan might not have chosen a different course had its leaders realized before the war the futility of pitting themselves against the vast industrial and military power of the Allied nations. As the coastline receded behind him, Kieling thought with a touch of sadness that if the Japanese had known more of the truth, this tragic war might never have been fought.

What Kieling did not know, and which was revealed only after the war, was that Admiral Yamamoto had known the extent of the Allied economic potential and had used his influence in vain to prevent or delay the war. He had been a frequent visitor to the United States and Great Britain and he had argued with Japanese government and military officials that it would be folly to fight these nations. A few men in the Imperial Japanese Navy agreed with him, but they were powerless against the rising tide of nationalism in the Japanese army.

In retrospect, it is now apparent that the war was started by those who did not understand sea power, and was lost by those who did not understand airpower.

When Yamamoto realized that war was inevitable, he had told government officials that he could only be successful against the United States and Great Britain in the first six months to a year of war. "I will show you an uninterrupted succession of victories, but I must also tell you that if the war be prolonged for two or three years I have no confidence in our ultimate victory."

His prophecy came true with startling accuracy.

SELECTED BIBLIOGRAPHY

Agawa, Hiroyuki. *The Reluctant Admiral: Yamamoto and the Imperial Navy.* Translated by John Bester. Tokyo, New York, and San Francisco: Kodansha International, Ltd., 1979.

Buell, Thomas B. *Master of Sea Power: A Biography of Fleet Admiral Ernest J. King.* Boston: Little, Brown & Company, 1980.

Hough, Richard. *Death of the Battleship: The Tragic Close of the Era of Sea Power.* New York: Macmillan, Inc., 1963.

Jablonski, Edward. *Airwar.* Garden City, New York: Doubleday & Company, Inc., 1971.

Merrill, James M. *A Sailor's Admiral: A Biography of William F. Halsey.* New York: Thomas Y. Crowell Co., Publishers, 1976.

Millot, Bernard. *The Battle of the Coral Sea.* Annapolis, Maryland: Naval Institute Press, 1974.

Morison, Samuel Eliot. *The Two-Ocean War: A Short History of the United States Navy in the Second World War.* Boston: Atlantic Monthly Press, 1963.

Morrison, Wilbur H. *Wings over the Seven Seas: United States Naval Aviation's Fight for Survival.* Cranbury, New Jersey: A. S. Barnes & Co., Inc., 1974.

————, *Point of No Return: The Story of the Twentieth Air Force.* New York: Times Books, 1979.

Potter, E. B. *Nimitz.* Annapolis, Maryland: Naval Institute Press, 1976.

Reynolds, Clark G. *The Fast Carriers: The Forging of an Air Navy.* New York: McGraw-Hill, Inc., 1968.

Winton, John. *The Forgotten Fleet: The British Navy in the Pacific.* New York: Coward, McCann and Geoghegan, Inc., 1970.

Index

Aircraft *(cont.)*
 105, 113, 115, 126, 130, 131,
 133, 135–138, 141, 142,
 147–149, 157, 177, 187, 188,
 198, 201, 202, 204, 208–210
 SB2C Helldiver, 187, 203, 204,
 208–210, 273, 274
 SB2U Vindicator, 6, 93, 95
 Supermarine Seafire, 259
 TBD Devastator, 60, 76, 77, 81,
 98–101
 TBF Avenger, 93, 94, 130, 137,
 142, 144, 147, 157, 172, 175,
 180, 187, 193, 195, 201–203,
 236, 259, 273, 274, 276, 277,
 283
 Val, 7, 10, 129, 138, 143, 144,
 159, 160, 166, 270
 Zeke, 10, 138, 159–161, 166, 168,
 175, 197, 198, 204–206
 Zero, 1, 19, 21, 76, 78, 81, 85, 86,
 93–95, 98–101, 103, 104,
 110–112, 114, 123, 126–129,
 135, 137, 140, 142, 147, 148,
 152, 157, 158, 173, 178, 180,
 198, 205, 206
Air Forces
 Fifth Air Force (American), 133,
 182, 244, 246, 254, 283
 Seventh Air Force (American),
 92, 174, 181, 211, 217, 234
 Eleventh Air Force (American),
 161
 Thirteenth Air Force (American),
 133, 241
 Fourteenth Air Force (American), 254
 Twentieth Air Force (American),
 175, 271, 274, 281, 283, 287,
 291
Aiso, Comdr. Kunizo, 107, 115
Akutan, 110, 111
Aleutian Islands, 66, 89, 91, 106,
 108, 109, 111, 116, 117, 161
ABDA (American-British-Dutch-
 Australian Command), 49, 50
Anami, Gen. Korechiki, 287, 289

Andrews, Adm. Adolphus, 25
Aoki, Capt. Taijiro, 103, 105
Arcadia Conference, 41
 Wavell named supreme com-
 mander in Far East at, 41
 Combined Chiefs of Staff formed
 at, 42
 Defeat of Germany first re-
 affirmed at, 41
Armies
 Fourth Air Army (Japanese), 219
 Sixth Army (American), 190,
 221, 246, 256
 Tenth Army (American), 275
 Seventeenth Army (Japanese), 134
 Thirty-fifth Imperial Army (Jap-
 anese), 247
Armistead, Capt. Kirk, 93
Arnold, Gen. H. H., 42, 120, 121,
 157, 163, 170, 181, 186, 271,
 272, 274
Arnold, Comdr. Jackson D., 216
Aslito Field, 195, 211
Attu, 91, 111, 161
Auchinleck, Sir Claude John Eyre,
 87
Ault, Comdr. William B., 59, 60,
 75, 76, 81

Babcock, Ellis C., 203
Babcock, Capt. John V., 23
Baldinus, Lt. Lawrence, 131
Ballale, 159, 160
Bangs, Lt. Lou, 204–206, 208, 209
Bataan, surrender of, 62
Bauer, Lt. Col. Harold W., 138
Bean, Comdr. Lawrence L., 143
Bell, Maj. Gordon A., 135, 136
Bellinger, Rear Adm. P.N.L., 11
Bescos, Lt. Comdr. J. A., 266
Bismarck Archipelago, 51, 57, 124,
 135, 181, 182
Bismarck Sea, 65, 190
Blakely, Rear Adm. Charles A., 26
Blanchard, Comdr. J. W., 196
Blitch, Comdr. Jack, 216
Bogan, Rear Adm. Gerald F., 217,

224, 228, 231, 232, 241, 244, 249, 250, 283
Bonin Islands, 195, 214
Borneo, 250, 276
Bougainville, 57, 69, 70, 71, 128, 132, 140, 152, 159, 165, 171–173, 175, 183
Boyington, Maj. Gregory, 168
Brannon, Capt. Dale, 126
Brett, Lt. Comdr. James, 81
Brewer, Lt. (jg) H. H., 265
Brockman, Jr., Lt. Comdr. William H., 106
Brooke, Field Marshal Alan, 42
Brooks, Ens. G. W., 129
Brooks, Capt. N. C., 85
Brown, Capt. C. R., 169
Brown, Lt. (jg) George B., 202, 203
Brown, Jr., Ens. H. S., 76
Brown, Vice-Adm. Wilson, 56–59, 67, 87
Browning, Capt. Miles, 96
Brunei Bay, 222, 241
Buckmaster, Capt. Elliott, 67, 82, 103, 104, 113
Buckley, Lt. A. M., 264
Buckner, Lt. Gen. Simon B., 275, 277
Bungo Strait, 13, 223
Buracker, Comdr. William H., 5, 6
Capt. William H., 224, 225
Burch, Lt. Comdr. W. O., 47, 48, 76, 81, 82
Bureau of Aeronautics (U.S.), 18, 24, 153
Bureau of Navigation, 23, 25, 42
Burke, Comdr. Arleigh, 232
Rear Adm., 269, 270

Caldwell, Lt. Turner, 128, 130
Callaghan, Rear Adm. Daniel J., 146, 147
Campbell, Comdr. Grafton B., 216
Campbell, Lt. Lucius D., 109, 110, 114, 115
Carl, Capt. Marion, 128, 133, 138, 159

Carmody, Lt. Doan, 148
Carney, Rear Adm. Robert B., 240
Caroline Islands, 66, 157, 167, 178, 179, 184–186, 188, 192, 193, 211, 214, 216
Cartwright, Lt. Comdr. F. J., 37
Casablanca Conference, 155
    division of resources between Europe and Pacific agreed to at, 155
    invasion of Sicily approved at, 156
    cross-channel 1943 invasion of Europe rejected at, 156
    agreement to continue Pacific operations at same level agreed to at, 156
Cavite Naval Yard, 31, 251
Cawley, Aviation Radioman D. J., 201, 204, 205
Chappell, Jr., Maj. C. J., 6
Chase, Lt. William, 93
Chayashi, Capt. Sueo, 142
Chiang Kai-shek, Generalissimo, 62
Churchill, Prime Minister Winston, 38, 41, 42, 52, 53, 155–57, 175, 214
Clark Field, 217, 249, 250
Clark, Rear Adm. Joseph J., 268
Clement, Lt. Col. William, 29
Cole, Lt. Shelby O., 114
Coleman, Lt. Thaddeus T., 274
Colley, Chief Aviation Radioman Wayne C., 210
Collins, Capt. James F., 94
Combined Chiefs of Staff, 42, 51, 67, 155, 180, 215
Coral Sea, 65–68, 70, 71, 73, 75, 81
    Battle of, 84, 85, 87–91, 96, 104, 115, 117, 195
Corregidor, 260
Crace, Rear Adm. John g., 68, 69, 73–75, 78, 80
Cram, Maj. Jack, 136, 137
Crenshaw, Lt. James R., 202
Crommelin, Capt. John, 208, 209, 220

Johnson, Col. Chandler W., 266
Johnson, Ens. John P., 59
Johnson, Lt. W. E., 148
Joint Chiefs of Staff, 51–54, 56, 57,
    118–121, 137, 155, 161, 162,
    165–167, 170, 179, 183, 186,
    214, 215, 274, 278, 279, 283
Jomard Passage, 70–75
Jones, Col. George M., 260
Jorgenson, Ens. J. H., 82

Kahili, 152, 158, 168
Kai-shek, Generalissimo Chiang,
    175
Kaka, Capt. Tomeo, 105–107
Kakuta, Rear Adm. Kakuji, 91,
    144, 188, 193
Kamikaze Corps, 219, 245, 252,
    255, 256, 263, 264, 270–273,
    275, 276, 278, 281
Kane, Comdr. William, 194, 201,
    204, 206
Kaneohe, 10, 11, 13, 115
Kanno, Chief Petty Officer Kenzo,
    80
Kavieng, 124, 182, 183, 211
Keller, Lt. A. G., 30
Kelly, Col. Laurence B., 217
Kenney, Lt. Gen. George, 122, 133,
    180, 246, 254
Kibbe, Comdr. Richard L., 242
Kieling, Lt. Robert T., 295, 296
Kimmel, Adm. Husband E., 5, 13,
    15, 16
    relief of, 27
King, Adm. Ernest J., 5, 22–28,
    41–43, 51–54, 57, 67, 68, 84,
    87–91, 117–121, 125, 134, 137,
    138, 145, 150, 153–155, 157,
    161–164, 167, 169, 170, 173,
    175, 176, 178–183, 186, 187,
    191, 192, 211–214, 216, 221,
    222, 240, 246, 253, 254, 258,
    271, 272, 276, 281, 284, 290,
    292
Kinkaid, Rear Adm. Thomas C.,

139, 141, 142, 145–147, 190,
    219, 220, 222, 233, 234,
    237–241, 245, 246, 253, 256,
    276
Kiska, 91, 111, 161
Knox, Secretary of Navy Frank, 16,
    27, 53, 87, 88, 155, 192
Kobe, 247, 261
Koboyashi, Lt. Michio, 103
Kodiak, 108, 110
Koga, Adm. Mineichi, 161, 173,
    174, 186, 188
Koiso, Prime Minister Kuniaki, 267
Kolombangara, 152, 157, 158, 165
Komatsu, Warrant Officer Sakio,
    196
Kondo, Rear Adm. Nobutake, 32
    Vice-Adm., 106, 140, 144, 146,
    148, 149
Konoye, Prince, 21, 287
Kossler, Comdr. H. J., 196
Krueger, Lt. Gen. Walter, 190, 221,
    246
Kure, 247, 284, 286
Kurile Islands, 1, 4, 161
Kurita, Rear Adm. Takeo, 113
    Vice-Adm., 31, 172–174, 188,
    189, 222–225, 227–231, 233,
    235, 236–238, 240–242, 244,
    245
Kuroda, Lt. Gen. Shiganori, 217
Kurusu, Saburo, 21, 22
Kusaka, Chief of Staff Ryunosuke,
    102
Kwajalein Atoll, 44–46, 177, 181,
    182, 184
Kyoto, 283, 289
Kyushu, 193, 247, 268, 271, 272,
    278, 279, 281–283

Lae, 55, 58
Lanphier, Jr., Capt. Thomas G.,
    160
Larsen, Lt. Harold, 130
Leach, Capt. John C., 37

305

Leahy, Adm. William D., 26, 42, 120, 212
Leary, Vice-Adm. Herbert F., 57
Lee, Lt. Comdr. James R., 148, 244
Lee, Jr., Rear Adm. Willis A., 149
    Vice-Adm., 233, 237–241
LeMay, Maj. Gen. Curtis E., 271, 272, 283
Leslie, Lt. Comdr. Maxwell, 102
Leyte, 213, 215, 219, 222, 224, 233, 237, 240, 243, 245–255, 259, 260, 275, 276
Leyte Gulf, 220, 223, 227, 228, 231, 234, 235, 238, 239, 241, 242, 244, 256
Lindley, Tech. Sgt. John D., 126
Lindsey, Lt. Comdr. Eugene E., 98, 100
Lingayen Gulf, 254–257, 259
Litch, Capt. Ernest W., 249
Lohnishi, Vice-Adm. Takajiro, 219
Luedemann, Lt. Carl F., 202
Louisiade Archipelago, 65, 70, 71, 73
Luzon, 179, 186, 212, 213, 216–218, 220, 225, 228, 231, 247–250, 252–256, 259, 260

McCain, Capt. John S., 25
    Rear Adm., 133, 154, 209
    Vice-Adm., 215, 221, 222, 224, 234, 241, 244, 248, 251, 252, 257, 261, 278, 281, 283, 290, 291
McCampbell, Comdr. David, 197, 198, 225–227, 238, 239
McCluskey, Lt. Comdr. Clarence W., 96, 102
McConnell, Comdr. Robert, 49
MacArthur, Gen. Douglas, 21, 29, 51, 53–56, 67, 68, 70, 71, 74, 77, 80, 87–89, 117–121, 148, 151, 163, 166–168, 173, 175, 178, 180–183, 186, 189–192, 212–214, 219, 222, 246, 248, 250–255, 259, 260, 274–276,
278–280, 283, 292, 295
Majuro, 181, 192
Makin, 47, 163, 174
Malaita Island, 69, 128, 130
Mandai, Ens. Hisao, 105–107
Mangrum, Maj. Richard D., 126, 131, 135
Manila, 39, 213, 217, 221, 224–226, 251, 252, 254, 259
Manila Bay, 212, 249, 250
Manus, 190, 258
Marcus Island, 49, 174, 191
Margerum, Seaman Harry W., 265
Mariana Islands, 162, 164, 167, 175, 179–186, 188, 191–193, 195, 196, 200, 210–212, 215, 245, 254, 260, 262, 267, 268, 279, 280, 287, 291
Marshall, Gen. George C., 15, 16, 41, 42, 51, 52, 54, 87, 88, 118–121, 155–157, 162, 163, 175, 179, 180, 214, 279
Marshall Islands, 43, 46, 48, 56, 163, 164, 167, 174, 176–178, 181–185
Marushige, Rear Adm. Kuninori, 69, 70, 74
Maruyama, Lt. Gen. Masao, 140
Mason, Capt. Charles P., 143
Massey, Lt. Comdr. Lance E., 46, 101
Matsunaga, Rear Adm. Sadaichi, 33, 35
Medal of Honor, 10, 40, 58, 113, 135, 138, 140, 158, 160, 161, 168, 172, 175, 180, 183, 197, 227
Mester, Lt. Cecil, 205
Metsger, Lt. Comdr. A. B., 263–266
Midway, 13, 14, 39, 40, 66, 85, 89, 91–97, 106–107, 111–114, 116
    Battle of, 117, 125, 127, 128, 164, 187–189
Mikawa, Rear Adm. Gunichi, 2, 124, 125

Vice-Adm., 146
Miller, Lt. Henry L., 60–62
Mindanao, 179, 186, 195, 215, 248
Mindoro, 213, 224, 228, 244,
    251–253
Misimi Island, 72, 74, 75
Mitchell, Ens. Albert, 112
Mitchell, Maj. John W., 160
Mitscher, Capt. Marc A., 61
    Rear Adm., 154, 160, 184, 185
    Vice-Adm., 187–199, 200, 201,
    206–211, 214, 216–218, 221,
    224, 230–234, 237, 238, 242,
    245, 248, 254, 261, 263,
    268–270, 272, 273
Moebus, Capt. L. A., 265
Moffett, Rear Adm. William A.,
    22–24
Montgomery, Rear Adm. Alfred
    E., 173, 248, 249
Morotai, 214, 215
Morris, Lt. Wayne, 238
Mountbatten, Vice-Adm. Lord
    Louis, 167
Murata, Lt. Comdr. Shigeharu, 7
Murphy, Jr., Lt. Comdr. John W.,
    112, 113
Murray, Rear Adm. George D.,
    139
Munda, 165, 166, 168

Nagano, Adm. Osami, 151, 173,
    211
Nagasaki, atomic bombing of, 288,
    289
Nagoya, 261, 286
Nagumo, Vice-Adm. Chuichi, 1, 2,
    4, 6, 8, 12, 13, 15, 39, 64,
    91–97, 101–103, 105, 106, 127,
    129, 140–142, 144, 159, 193
    death of, 211
Neale, Lt. Comdr. E. T., 30
Nelson, Lt. Charles W., 202
Nelson, Lt. R. S., 200
New Britain Island, 57, 117, 134,
    180, 183

New Caledonia, 65, 123
New Georgia Island, 124, 152, 165
New Guinea, 67, 72, 84, 117, 119,
    151, 163, 166–168, 173, 174,
    177, 184, 186, 190, 192, 193,
    260
New Hebrides, 51, 65, 68, 89, 120,
    137, 139, 141
New Ireland Island, 57, 124, 182
Newton, Rear Adm. John H., 6, 13,
    285
Niigata, 283, 287
Nimitz, Adm. Chester W., 42, 51,
    54–56, 67–70, 83, 84, 87–92,
    115–120, 130, 133, 135,
    137–139, 151, 153, 157,
    162–165, 168–171, 173, 175,
    178–183, 186, 190, 192,
    211–217, 222, 239, 246, 251,
    253, 257–259, 266, 271,
    274–279, 283–285, 288, 290,
    292–295
Nishimura, Vice-Adm. Shoji, 223,
    237, 229, 231, 235, 239–241
Nomura, Amb. Kichisaburo, 21, 22
Norris, Maj. Benjamin W., 93, 95
Nouméa, 67, 84, 123
Noyes, Rear Adm. Leigh, 121

Obayashi, Rear Adm. Sueo, 189
Octagon Conference, 214
    Churchill offers British navy to
    the Pacific at, 214, 215
Ofstie, Capt. Ralph A., 169
O'Hare, Lt. Edward H., 58, 86, 175
Okinawa, 212, 216, 218, 220, 258,
    261, 268–70, 272, 275, 276,
    278–280, 282, 283, 286, 288
Okuma, Count Shigenobu, 14
Okumiya, Masatake, 110
Oldendorf, Rear Adm. Jesse B.,
    234, 235, 237, 255, 256
Omark, Lt. Warren R., 202, 203
Omori, Vice-Adm. Sentaro, 2
Owen, Acting Capt. George, 11
Ozawa, Vice-Adm. Jisaburo, 159,